Abergavenny

Historic Market Town

Chris Barber

Chris Barber (signature)

Blorenge Books

First Published 2011

ISBN 978-1-872730-43-1

Printed by Gomer Press Limited
Llandysul Enterprise Park, Llandysul, Credigion SA44 4JL

Tel: 01559 363758

Front Cover: View across the river Usk towards Sugar Loaf and Abergavenny Castle

Back Cover: View across Castle Meadows with Ysgryd Fawr in the background

To my wife Anne Marie with grateful thanks
for her support and encouragement

Brecon 20
A40

through traffic

CONTENTS

ERRATA

Due to the unauthorized use of the photograph and omission of credits on page 87, I am happy to provide the following:

The picture of The Abergavenny Millennium Tapestry (Founder Sheila Bevan) is a scanned version of a bookmark which was created from an original specialist high resolution photograph which is the copyright of Mr Richard Kenward of Artisan Digital Services 01873 890456. The designer and copyright holder of the tapestry is Susie Martin and the stitching was supervised by Sarah Windrum.

'The situation of Abergavenny is most delightful; it stands at the extremity of a pass where the mountains abruptly terminate, and the vales of Usk begins to take a greater expansion. The name is derived from its situation at the mouth of the Gavenny, which flows by the outskirts of the town, and falls into the Usk, to the south-west of the castle.'

William Coxe 1801

FOREWORD

It is a great privilege to write a foreword to *Abergavenny, Historic Market Town*. My memories of Abergavenny go back a long time. I was born in 1942 to a railway family (both my father and grandfather worked on the LNWR) and my house in St Helen's Road was very close to the large (and noisy) locomotive sheds. I am an Honorary Burgess of Abergavenny and I am very proud to be a citizen of this unique historic town where I have lived and worked for most of my life.

Over the years, through articles in the *Abergavenny Chronicle* and in the many books that he has written, Chris Barber has delighted and enlightened us with his in-depth insight into our history and heritage, whether it be in Abergavenny and district or further afield in the Brecon Beacons, Torfaen and elsewhere in South-East Wales. The bibliography and list of his own publications at the back of the book bear testimony to his passion for this region, his knowledge and respect for its history and his love of our beautiful countryside.

Many other excellent books have been published about aspects of Abergavenny at various times in its history and they are rightly acknowledged in the bibliography at the end of the book. It is very fitting that Chris should pay tribute to a good friend Albert Lyons, who faithfully recorded in his photographs so much of the life and buildings in the town. His records provide an invaluable chronicle of Abergavenny.

This book, *Abergavenny, Historic Market Town*, is special in that it brings together all the different threads to offer the reader a comprehensive and detailed history of Abergavenny through the ages. On reading it, one feels a sense of awe, joy, amazement and, at times, horror about what happened in the past as facts perhaps only partly known previously are brought to one's attention. From Abergavenny's beginnings in the mists of prehistory to its present day, Chris Barber gives us fascinating details of the town's long and chequered history, a story of the state of the rich and the poor, of war and peace, of treachery and bravery, but also a story at times full of happiness, sadness, pride, nostalgia and many moving personal memories.

This book is enhanced by many memorable photographs that show views now obscured or changed. The outstanding illustrations by Michael Blackmore give us a fascinating and revealing insight into our past. The beautiful poem by Anne Marie Barber on page 22 is a wonderfully evocative picture of the town past and present.

We owe a great debt of gratitude to Chris Barber for his years of dedication, passion and sheer hard work in researching the material for this book. I fully endorse his wish that 'this labour of love during the last three decades will prove interesting and informative to both residents and visitors'. His reward will be your enjoyment when you read the story of *Abergavenny Historic Market Town*.

Alan Breeze

Honorary Burgess of Abergavenny
Mayor of Abergavenny
1980 -81, 1985-86 and 2002-2003

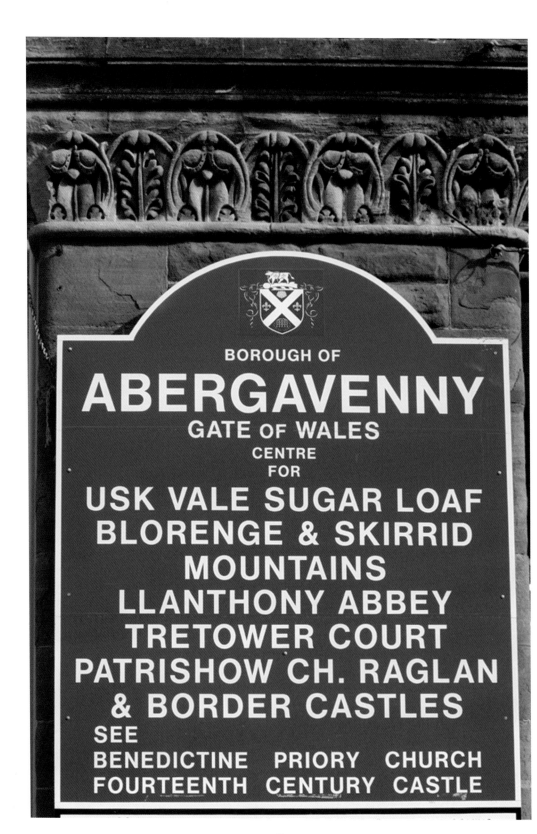

INTRODUCTION

Abergavenny and the places in its neighbourhood, demand the attention of the antiquary, the artists, and the poet, as much as any spot in the kingdom.

John White 1877

My earliest memory of Abergavenny is probably when at the age of seven I first visited the town with my parents. We had travelled the twenty miles from our home in Newport because my father wished to visit St Mary's Priory Church. He was a keen photographer and was taking pictures for a book that he was writing, entitled 'West of the Wye'. His purpose was to photograph all the monuments and effigies in St Mary's which he told us were so important that this church was known as the 'Westminster of South Wales'.

I was particularly fascinated by the sleeping knights clad in armour with dogs and lions at their feet and my father, who had been researching the history of the church for his book, was able to tell us their names and some of the details of their lives.

On another occasion, we visited Abergavenny Castle, where I listened in awe to my father's friend, the well known Gwent historian, Fred Hando who related the gruesome story of how the wicked Lord of Abergavenny, William de Braose invited a band of Welshmen to a great banquet at the castle on Christmas Day in 1175 and massacred them all. My introduction to local history certainly began here in Abergavenny and I have continued to be fascinated ever since.

It was in 1979, that I came to live in the neighbouring village of Llanfoist and it is my love and fascination for this area, which has led to my writing so much about it during the last thirty years. Abergavenny is beautifully situated for it is almost encircled by hills and there are few towns set in a more delectable location, and with roads heading off in all directions the historic Marches and borderlands of Wales are also easily accessible.

One can even enjoy shopping in Abergavenny and this is evident from the large number of people who regularly come here from places such as Newport, Cardiff and the Valley towns of North Monmouthshire. The main attraction of course is the Tuesday market, but most of our visitors just enjoy being in the town, surrounded by the shapely hills. Yes, one can certainly feel at peace here and if you are a keen walker then there are a great variety of walks available, which can be enjoyed by people of all abilities.

The story of Abergavenny must surely start in the days of prehistory, for it is a reasonable conjecture that there was a settlement here long before the Romans invaders crossed the Severn to commence their long battles with the Silures of south-east Wales. As a gateway to the valley of the Usk this location would have been considered of strategic importance.

Abergavenny takes its name from the river Gavenny which enters the Usk on its south side and is formed of Cefn-wy (ridge water). The Normans who did not understand the meaning of the word changed it to Bergavenny, berg signifying town. In 1602 it was called Burgavenny which was sometimes written as Bergavenni and Abergevenye. It is of interest that the name Bergavenny once featured on the first milestone on the Monmouth road.

Y Fenni, the current Welsh name for the town is a corruption of Efenni, the mutated form of Gefenni, the old name for the river Gavenny which in turn has previously been known as Gebenni and Geuenni (in the ancient Charters of Llandaff).

The modern name of Abergavenny relates to the meeting of the waters of the Gavenny with the Usk and examples of similar names are: Abercarn, Aberdare, Abertillery and Aberystwyth which all indicate the point at which a smaller stream joins the main river.

The geographical position of a town influences its character and history and this fact is especially true of Abergavenny. Its riverside location has long been a place of strategic importance and as one that needed to be defended the Romans and Normans have certainly left evidence of their occupation. It was Antonius, the Roman historian-cartographer who called the place GOBANNIUM and named it so in his Itinerary. This is confirmed by the accuracy of his calculated distance between the forts of ISCA (Caerleon), BURRIUM (USK) and MAGNA CASTRA (Kenchester), near Hereford.

After the Battle of Hastings William the Conqueror soon subdued south-east Britain, and then set his 'dogs of war' to roam the Welsh border and carve out separate domains. He was obviously a shrewd man, for this freed him from the incessant demands of his barons for exalted positions and greater shares in the spoils of war.

William FitzOsbern, builder of the first Norman stone castle in Wales at Chepstow, was sent to occupy the Southern Marches and make plans for the conquest of South Wales. He set up motte and bailey defences in Gwent and Hereford but died in 1071.

Much of North Gwent was conquered by Hameline de Ballon, who by 1090 had hurriedly erected a wooden palisade on a motte overlooking the river Usk, where it is joined by the river Gavenny. In due course it was replaced by a stone keep and around this hated symbol of Norman power the town, as we know it today, began to grow.

The Marcher Lords, who were unconcerned about the cruel deeds they committed during their lifetime, invariably, and hypocritically, took steps to ensure their salvation after death. To do so Hamelin de Ballon sent his masons to build a priory for Benedictine monks and the existing church of St Mary which is in a far better state of preservation than the castle contains some of the finest monumental tombs in Britain.

Abergavenny certainly suffered the ravages of border warfare, particularly from the time of the Welsh uprising of 1400 led by Owain Glyndwr who reached Abergavenny in 1404 and reduced the town to a smoking ruin, but was unable to take the castle which was held by Colonel James Proger.

Gradually the town recovered, but two hundred years later the peaceful existence of its inhabitants was shattered by the Civil War. The castle was garrisoned for King Charles I who twice passed through the town on his way to Raglan Castle and other loyal homes of refuge in South Wales. When Oliver Cromwell's army chased the royalist forces out of town his soldiers damaged many of its finest buildings. The ancient priory church was used as a stable and the insensitive Roundhead troops vandalised the building, using the furnishings and antique woodwork as firewood.

The town then took no further part in the struggle but remained strongly Jacobite and lost its charter and market for rioting at William III's accession in 1688. It is of interest that Abergavenny Castle was once famous for a half-mile of Scots fir which were planted as a way of showing sympathy for the Stuart cause.

As times improved, the town became wealthy and was even described as 'the best in the countie.' However, it became less prosperous and less respected when the misplaced cunning of the flannel traders caused the town to lose its principal source of trade. This happened when the purchasers discovered that the innermost folds of the flannel they bought was very much inferior to the outer ends of rolls which they had been able to inspect.

Trade in Abergavenny improved when it became famous for making wigs, which due to a secret method of bleaching had a whiteness which could not be equalled elsewhere. When wigs became unfashionable the town became known for the excellence of its shoes. As Abergavenny is a market town it is perhaps right and proper that a dairy product was next to bring some modest gain to the local people and the town. The owners of farms amid the surrounding hills were pleased when it was widely advertised that Abergavenny was an ideal place in which to stay for the cure of tuberculosis, but only if the stay was coupled with a diet of goat's whey. So apart from selling the more usual farm products in the town market, further profit was made in selling goat's milk. The whey it was claimed, had greater curative powers than the bitter spa waters of Bath, Builth or Llandrindod Wells.

In the nineteenth century there was a revival of Welsh culture in the town when an enthusiastic literary society was formed, which was strongly supported by Sir Benjamin and Augusta Hall (who later became Lord and Lady Llanover). An annual eisteddfod was held in the town for nearly thirty years, drawing writers, poets and musicians from all over Wales to Abergavenny.

During the latter part of the nineteenth century Abergavenny became an important railway centre with three passenger stations and a large locomotive shed which could accommodate one hundred engines. Over a thousand railway workers were employed in the Abergavenny area during that exciting period, which is now remembered with much nostalgia.

Today, Abergavenny is still a bustling market town and a popular holiday centre with many attractions: fishing in the river Usk, walks in the surrounding hills, the Brecon Beacons National Park and the Blaenavon Industrial Landscape World Heritage Site. Many tourists who come here must be inspired by the attractive metal panel on the wall near the entrance to the Market. It proudly claims that Abergavenny is a Gateway to Wales and lists some of the places of historic interest within easy reach of the town.

I have endeavoured to make this book as comprehensive as possible, but at the same time I am conscious of the buildings and events that have not been included and no doubt these omissions will be drawn to my attention when the book is published.

The people who live in Abergavenny are rightly proud of their town's long history and its beautiful situation in the Usk Valley and I hope that this book, which has been a labour of love during the last three decades, will prove interesting and informative to both residents and visitors.

Chris Barber MBE FRGS
Llanfoist 2011

Cross Street, Abergavenny c.1900

Chapter One
IN PRAISE OF ABERGAVENNY

This landscape gives the keynote of the neighbourhood of Abergavenny; but there is not within the four corners of Great Britain a district so wonderful for the varied character of its Beauty.

John White 1877

Most writers who have described Abergavenny are of the opinion that it is situated in a well chosen location. The earliest mention of it as a place of importance must surely be the one provided by the Roman historian Tacitus, who tells us that GOBANNIUM was a military station mid-way between ISCA (Caerleon) and Y GAER (Brecon) on the road north to DEVA (Chester).

John Leland the 16th century antiquarian found the country around Abergavenny, 'somewhat mountayneous.' He also described the place as a 'faire walled town, neatly inhabited.' Another visitor writing in 1602 was even more convinced of Abergavenny's attributes for he remarked that it 'was a fine town, wealthy and thriving and the very best in the Shire.'

John Wesley, the founder of the Methodist Movement, first visited Abergavenny in 1739 and recorded in his journal that he returned on 'Saturday 3rd October, 1741. We had a plain useful sermon on the Pharisee and the publican praying in the Temple which I explained at large in the evening to the best-dressed congregation I have ever yet seen in Wales.'

William Coxe came here during his tour of Monmouthshire in 1799 and was obviously very impressed with the town and its location:

'The situation of Abergavenny is most delightful; it stands at the extremity of a pass where the mountains abruptly terminate, and the vales of Usk begins to take a greater expansion. The name is derived from its situation at the mouth of the Gavenny, which flows by the outskirts of the town, and falls into the Usk, to the south-west of the castle.

Abergavenny stretches at the feet of hills and mountains, which gradually swelling from the vale, unite the extremes of wildness and fertility, and are interesting from the contrast of their shape and appearance.

To the west rises the Blorenge, magnificent from its height and continuity; it forms the northern extremity of the chain, which reaches from Pontypool, and terminates near the confines of the county. The highest part towers above the Usk and the town of Abergavenny; its sides are concave; the summit is covered with russet herbage, without a single bush; the midland parts are chequered with underwood, intermixed with fertile meadows, and the base is clothed with timber trees. At the northern extremity, the rich knoll of Upper Llanfoist presents a wood of fine oak, ash and elm, forming an extensive mantle of thick and dark foliage.

To the north are the Pen y Vale hills, which sweep from the extremity of the town, and rise into four undulating eminences; they appear at a little distance to be separate, but are connected together, and intersected by narrow glens, which are watered by lively murmuring streams that rise on their sides, and swell the Usk with their tributary waters.

Mynyd Pen y Fal otherwise known as the Sugar Loaf

The Blorenge towering above the river Usk

These four eminences are known by distinct appellations. The Derry, the most easterly, is of convex shape, and derives its name from a grove of small oaks which clothes its sides and summit; the next is the Rholben; the third is the Graig Llanwenarth; and the fourth is the hill Llanwenarth; both so called from their situation in the parish, and above the church of Llanwenarth.

These four hills support, on their broad and extensive base, the Pen y Vale, called the Sugar Loaf, from its shape. The undulating outline of this elegant summit is embossed in the middle with the cone, which assumes different appearances.

It looks like a piked ridge from the opposite side of the Usk; sometimes appears in a globular shape, but at a distance, and particularly at the south-eastern side of the Skyrrid, assumes the form of a pyramid, and resembles the crater of a volcano. The cone is the highest object in the vicinity, has nothing rugged or craggy, and is characterised by smoothness and beauty.

The most singular and interesting mountain in the neighbourhood is the Great Skyrrid, or St Michael's Mount, which stretches from north to south, or more accurately from north-east to south-west: it is an insulated mount, rising abruptly from the plain; the north-eastern side appears a steep ridge of a brown hue; towards the south and south-east, it slopes gradually into cultivation. The summit is covered with heath, or russet herbage, and its feet are clothed with wood, or enriched with corn and pasture.

In one point of view, particularly from the Little Skyrrid, it assumes the appearance of an enormous barrow or tumulus, piled up by the hands of giants. To the north it terminates in a bold craggy precipice, divided into two points; this double summit is occasioned by a fissure or rent, from which the name of Skyrrid is supposed to be derived. At a small distance from Llanfihangel, on the Herefordshire road, this precipitous rock seems like two detached mountains, of a conical shape, and as I observed some clouds resting on the highest summit, its stupendous crag appeared like the rugged crater of a volcano, vomiting volumes of smoke.'

Ysgyryd Fawr is also known as the 'Holy Mountain'

Looking up the river Usk towards the 'Sugar Loaf'

J.T. Barber, who came here in 1803 and was particularly impressed by the surrounding hills:-

'On approaching Abergavenny, the tourist's attention is involuntarily arrested by the singular beauty and variety of interest which the spot embraces, particularly by its encircling hills. The road skirting the Little Skyridd, a well formed hill richly laid out in wood and pasture, opens to a fine display of the Vale of Usk beneath; on the opposite side of which the continuous ridge of the wild Pontypool hills, which form the western boundary of the county, terminate in the healthy high-swelling Blorenge; a tract of wood sweeps along its base, and mixes with the sylvan knoll of Llanfoist, decorating its northern extremity. Further to the right, the elegant smooth cone of the Sugar Loaf, the highest of the Monmouthshire mountains presents itself, issuing from among the four tributary eminences of the Pen-y-Val hills. Eastward of the mountain is the Great Skyrrid, an object of considerable interest; its bipartite and truly Alpine summit, without being a forced opposition, strikingly contrasts with the general undulating line of the neighbouring hills, and rears a distinct and noble character to the scene. The views from this mountain are scarcely inferior to those from the Sugar Loaf; while its craggy form, its asperitous summit, jagged into an immense fissure, and shelving to ridge apex of fearful narrowness, impress a mixed emotion of awe and admiration on the adventurous climber of the height, that more than compensates for a small inferiority of altitude.

Ysgyryd Fach - the 'Little Skirrid'

The expansive bases of these mountains nearly approximately, descend to a finely-wooded fertile valley, through which the River Usk, rushing from a majestic portal of wood, winds in a bright translucid stream, with all th impetuosity of its mountain character. At the foot of one of the confederated hills, sustaining the lowering cone of the Sugar-Loaf, which gently inclines to the river, Abergavenny is situated; a straggling irregular town, pleasantly-interspersed with trees, but deriving its highest attraction from the charm of its position.'

A bird's eye view of Abergavenny from the north escarpment of the Blorenge

Henry Skrine visited the town in 1812 and commented:

'A more beautiful position than this town occupies can hardly be imagined... but the town itself disappointed me, being, when I first saw it, irregularly built, ill-paved, and the passage through the principal street being shamefully obstructed by a heavy old market house. Modern improvements have removed the last two inconveniences, but much more is required to be done, to make the internal accommodation of Abergavenny equal to the beauty of its exterior...'

The well known topographer of the period, Samuel Lewis, confirmed Skrine's opinion, when in 1831, he observed that: 'The streets are narrow and the houses irregularly built but improvements have been made by the enlargement of the market place.'

John White, who wrote a guidebook to the town and its neighbourhood in 1877 sums up the situation of Abergavenny in a very convincing manner:-

'The Usk is seen winding its silvery course between banks lined with tall and luxuriant trees. Behind all this, the eye discovers an immense mass of mountains darkening the horizon. Immediately westwards is seen the broad breasted Blorenge (Blawreng) scowling upon the plain beneath and towering magnificently and proudly. To the right we find the Little Scyrryd which presents a humble contrast to the grand character of the rest of the landscape. If this glorious assemblage of nature's charms does not rivit the eye of the traveller as it bursts upon his view, he may be put down as devoid of all feeling for the beautiful and sublime.'

Sunset over the river Usk near Abergavenny

The same writer also provides a convincing answer to the question of whether Monmouthshire was in England or Wales:-

'Monmouthshire was by an act of Henry VIII nominally added to the English counties to be included in the circuits of the English judges, nevertheless it virtually remained as much a part of Wales as before, and continued to be included as such in most of the tourists' accounts and Histories of the Principality. The Welsh in speaking of the extent of the Principality always said "Y Tair Sir arddeg o Cymry," - the thirteen counties of Wales'.

Wirt Sikes, the United Consul to Wales in 1879, added:

'The special charm of Abergavenny town is its situation at the base of and surrounded by mountains, and shadowed in the near distance by the russet peak called Mynydd Pen-y-Fal, about 2,000 feet high.

A clean, quaint collection of stone houses is Abergavenny, with half a dozen comely churches and chapels, and a ruined castle. Modern map-makers have had the effrontery to tell us that Abergavenny is not in Wales, but in England - a statement which would be disproved, one would suppose, by the Welsh name of the town, its Welsh customs, Welsh history, and Welsh people; but if any obstinate person should side with the aforesaid map-makers in spite of these, let him be crushed by an invitation to a concert at the Cymmreigyddion Hall, in Tudor Street, Abergavenny. It must be a bold spirit which would call Cymreigyddion Hall an English place of entertainment...although Monmouthshire is included in the English judge's circuit, we are certainly in Wales, by the testimony of all our senses, as well as by the evidence of history. Monmouthshire is a Welsh county, and will so remain, in spite of map-makers...'

It is fascinating to read the varying impressions that people have of a place which they have often gained from just one or two brief visits and when the weather is perhaps a little unusual. In 1905 Charles Harper observed that:-

'When it is a period of sunshine, Abergavenny bathes in a mellow heat; when the mists gather and disperse in those times of rains and vapours, the townsmen, if they have souls for such things are free of a beautiful effect; and when storms of thunder and lightning break over those lovely summits and go reverberating from end to end of the vale, like the tatoo of some infernal drummer, then the town commands a spectacle of theatrical grandeur.'

The prolific travel writer, A.G. Bradley observed that Abergavenny:-

'...like most border towns that sprung from a Norman castle, and for obvious reasons, its streets are on a slope. It is now an English and not a Welsh town both in habit and appearance, boasting a mayor and corporation, ten thousand people, golf links, cricket ground, and a famous salmon river. It is on the main line for Bristol, London or the north, has a marquis close at hand and a select and wealthy neighbourhood, so it should be happy. It manufactures nothing notable, I believe, but has a railroad which climbs the mountains across the Usk and taps the mining country which lies for the most part so mercifully hidden behind them and should bring trade and traffic. In short, Abergavenny is in itself a pleasant average country town, neither remarkable nor the reverse in its construction.'

Edward J. Burrow in 1903 summed up in one sentence the feelings that many local people still have for Abergavenny as a place of importance in their own particular lives:-

'When the country folk come in to do their week's shopping, all is different; there is a long row of vehicles all up the main street, and the pavement is thronged with farmers and their women folk, to each of whom Abergavenny is the hub of the world.'

Sir Owen M. Edwards writing in 1890 commented:

'Abergavenny has just claims to be considered the most beautiful place, as far as situation is concerned, in the thirteen shires of Wales. Those who will not admit these claims must at least confess that, as a centre for rambles, it has few places to surpass it. It stands between the picturesque mountains of the east of Breconshire and the pleasant plains of the north east of Monmouth, - in the heart of the country where Vaughan the Silurist discovered the first traces of the wild beauty of nature.'

Abergavenny Town Hall and the Sugar Loaf

Abergavenny

Flowing through you dawn to dusk
The mighty river of the Usk
With Castle Meadows green and wide
That sits along its river side.
The people of the town take pride
To walk along the meadow's side
To see its ever changing scene
As yellow flowers form a screen.

Or water floods onto the grass
So people can no longer pass,
As winter hits the watery plain
And all the Usk is filled with rain.
When morning sun gleams on the grass
To light the meadow and its path
You see the town above you rise
With castle walls and their demise.

For French invaders came to stay
And built the castle in their day
A Norman Lord ruled over all
And kept the grandest banqueting hall.
And to the hall Welsh leaders came
To banquet there, but they were slain
Their swords were handed to their hosts
But soon the room was filled with ghosts.

But history has come full sway
As I stand here this summer's day
And turn around full circle wide
To see four hills adorn your sides,
Sugar Loaf with octopus arms
Skirrid Fawr and all its charms
Skirrid Fach so small and round
And Blorenge's close and looming mound.

Then as I look to town I see
A handsome dome of copper green
Which marks the top of market hall
Where many traders have their stall.
And to the hall great hordes have come
The heartbeat there beats like a drum
For people are what fire the towns
As time moves on through ups and downs.

Anne Marie Barber 2011

Chapter Two
THE ROMAN FORT OF GOBANNIUM

Coins and other relics which have been unearthed are evidence of the town's occupation by the Romans, who called it Gobannium.

Arthur Mee 1951

In 1848 the site of a Roman cemetery consisting of numerous burials both by cremation and inhumation was discovered to the west of Bailey Park. Also found was a Roman burial urn which can be seen on display in the National Museum of Wales at Cardiff.

The first information of any value about Roman Abergavenny was written by Haverfield in the transactions of the Honourable Society of Cymmrodorian in 1898.

'Here in a broad valley beside the river is a natural site for a Roman fort, and there is evidence, scanty but sufficient to show that a fort existed. Horsley in the 18th century, knew of bricks found on the south side of the town, some of which had Leg.II AVG stamped on them and also Roman coins. He was also told of a Roman balneum or sudatory, not very long before, to be seen at the castle, but since filled up, though of this he was not entirely satisfied. More recently an amphora neck and stylus (used for writing on wax) has been recorded from the same spot.

In another part of the town, or rather in its northern outskirts in Saunders' Nurseries, burials had been noted in and before 1848, and in particular a cist of rude stones containing as grave furniture a Samian saucer stamped IVLLIN, and other pottery. A hoard of silver coins are stated to have been met with near these graves.'

'While trenching the nursery ground, Anderson, a gardener, came upon what is called a 'cistvaen'. On the west side of the cistvaen he also came upon a hard concrete bottom, part of a roadway leading in the direction of the Sugar Loaf mountain from the Priory.

The late Rev T. Price, of Cwmdu, after examining the spot, thought that this must be a Roman road; and that it was customary with the Roman armies to bury their dead on each side of their military roads.

In the cistvaen, were found five vases, each resting in a patera, and arranged in the order of the five points on dice. The centre vase, which is larger than the others, contained something like a dark paste, supposed by Mr Price to consist of the ashes of a human heart. The vase was fastened to the patera as if by clay. Immediately surrounding the patera charred bones were discovered to the depth of about two inches.

Three of the smaller vases and paterae when exposed to the air soon crumbled away or fell to pieces. Mr Price came to the conclusion that the cistvaen contained the remains of a Roman general.

The patera which contained the larger vase is of Samian ware, highly glazed. In the centre of the upper side are stamped the letters I V L L I N, the potter's mark, and supposed by some to be a contraction for Julius of Lincoln.'

Gobannium was founded in the first century AD as an auxiliary fort that was part of a network established in order to subdue the fierce Silures the tribe that the Romans found most difficult to subdue. The name Gobannium is most likely derived from the Welsh word gobann, meaning 'ironsmith'. Alternatively Gobannium may be seen as a latinised form of Gavenny, the local river name.

Tacitus writing in the 1st century, gave Gobannium a mention placing it firmly on the Roman map as a military station half way between Isca (Caerleon) headquarters of the Second Augustan Legion, and Y Gaer (Brecon) on the road north to Deva (Chester). Antoninus, another Roman historian also listed GOBANNIUM in his Itinerary and placed it between ISCA SILURUM (Caerleon) and MAGNA CASTRA (Kenchester).

Evidence that occupation existed from 50AD to 200AD has been provided by inscriptions on Roman pottery, coins and bricks stamped with the name of the Second Augustan Legion, have also been found near the castle and were probably part of a bath house built outside the fort.

Further evidence confirming the presence of a Roman fort in Abergavenny was uncovered by the Abergavenny Archaeological Society in a series of excavations. In 1964-5 they undertook an excavation in Flannel Street, prior to the construction of the new Post Office and Telephone Exchange. They discovered a ditch and the site of the north-west gateway. The ditch, about 25 ft wide and some 4 ft deep, ran roughly along the line of the western end of Flannel Street. A quantity of Roman pottery mostly dating from the 1st century was found, but no structures, although what might have been a cobbled roadway came to light.

In 1967-8 members of the Society dug trenches along the northern edge of Tudor Street in advance of the re-development scheme. Further excavations were undertaken during the summer of 1972 on the site of an orchard behind Nos 31 to 39 Cross Street. A section of the south-west turf and timber rampart was revealed and also the timber slots of a granary building. Among the many finds were a Sestertius of Nero, a bronze coin, a facet-cut glass beaker and early imported drinking vessels. A well preserved road, running across the site was uncovered and also several structures associated with a kiln or furnace which seemed to be of the second century.

This excavation was funded by the Department of the Environment, the Board of Celtic Studies, the Cambrian Archaeological Association, the Haverfield Trust and the Welsh Archaeology Fund.

It is thought that Gobannium was established as part of a chain of forts linked by roads in order to conquer the fierce Silures either by Ostorius (Governor AD 47-52) or Didius Gallus (AD 52-57). An interesting display of finds from the excavations can be seen in Abergavenny Museum and they include brooches, pottery, coins, horse harnesses and fragments of legionary armour.

Display of Roman artifacts and examples of legionary armour in Abergavenny Museum
Copyright Monmouthshire County Council, Abergavenny Museum

The auxilary fort of Gobannium lies buried beneath modern streets and buildings, and the main part is under the Castle Street car park. It was planned on the same lines as a legionary fortress, though on a much smaller and simpler scale, and probably comprised not more than five acres. Instead of being garrisoned by a legion (or division) of first-line troops, it was held by a smaller regiment, 1,000 or 500 strong, infantry or cavalry of second-line auxillary troops.

In about 100 AD, Gobannium was rebuilt by troops of the Second Augustan Legion and in about 250 AD the fort's defences were improved. On the south-west the defences followed the scarp above the river meadows, and on the north-west probably along the line of the ditch under Flannel Street. The defences on the north-east side lay somewhere on the slope leading down from the Castle Street area to Cross Street. The south-eastern side may have been near the line of the north-west curtain wall of the castle.

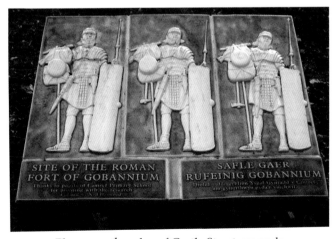

Plaque on the edge of Castle Street car park
marking the site of the auxilary fort of Gobannium

The Leopard Cup

The Abergavenny Leopard Cup was discovered by Gary Mapps, while metal detecting near Abergavenny in 2003. He reported the find to the Portable Antiquities Scheme and the area was investigated by the Glamorgan Gwent Archaeological Trust.

An excavation revealed that the Bronze cup had been placed upside down in a small pit containing a cremation and this was thought to be part of a cemetery beside a Roman road.

The cup displays craftsmanship of a high standard and was most likely made in Italy during the first century AD. Similar vessels have been found at the city of Pompeii, which was destroyed, then buried by the eruption of Vesuvius in 79AD.

It is the decorative handle, carved into the shape of a leopard with silver spots, which gives the cup its name. In Roman mythology the leopard is the companion of Bacchus, the god of wine. His worship involved feasting, drinking, music and dancing. Leopards, captured in both Africa and Asia were also popular with the Romans for display and fighting in the amphitheatre arena.

Such a beautiful cup was an expensive item and probably belonged to a person of status who cherished it so much that he wanted it to be buried with him. It has been described as one of the finest Roman vessels to be found in Wales and is kept at the National Museum in Cardiff.

The Leopard Cup - drawing by Michael Blackmore

Chapter Three
ABERGAVENNY CASTLE

Abergavenny was a place of great importance during most stormy and troublesome times. It was one of a chain of fortresses, the defenders of which were continually kept on the alert, and it is well known that, within its precincts, many an interesting event took place.

Edward J. Burrow 1903

The first castle at Abergavenny was established by Hamelin de Ballon (sometimes spelt Balun and Baladun), the son of Dru de Ballon, a nobleman who took his name from the family seat, Ballon, a small town in Maine, on the river Orne, which flows into the Sarthe and through it into the Loire. Dru de Ballon had come over with William the Conqueror and received large grants in Cornwall. His sons who settled in England were Hamelin of Abergavenny, Wyoned and Wynebald. The latter was doubtless engaged in the Conquest of Gwent, for he had some property at Caerleon, but his chief estates lay in Cornwall.

Both Dru and Hamelin de Ballon took part in the Battle of Hastings (1066) in which King Harold was killed. William rewarded the knights by giving them permission to penetrate deeper and deeper towards the Welsh border. In due course Hamelin de Ballon arrived in Gwent and as there is no account of any battle having taken place between the Normans and the Welsh it is probable that the invaders achieved their purpose with little resistance.

In about 1087, recognising the strategic importance of this location, Hamelin de Ballon obtained a grant from King William and took possession. He consolidated his position near the old Roman fort by ordering his men to dig a circular ditch and heap up a large mound within it to form a motte and bailey castle. The mound and ditch is shown in an engraving dated 1776 and they were certainly seen by William Coxe in 1799. A timber stockade was built around the mound and a timber tower erected on top of the artificial mound. An outer enclosure, also surrounded by a stockade was accessed by a bridge built across the ditch. Hamelin also built St John's Church and a vicarage adjoining the church.

It was William the Conqueror's son William Rufus who gave Hamelin the title Lord of Abergavenny. After residing here for nearly twenty years this Norman knight died in 1091, leaving a daughter Emelina, who married Reginald the grandson of William FitzOsbern, Hamelin's old commander. This is proved by two documents, first the charter of Reginald FitzRoger to Godstow nunnery and secondly the confirmation of his father's gift to his son Reginald de Baelun.

Hamelin de Ballon was buried in St Mary's Priory which he had founded as a cell to the Abbey of St Vincent near Le Mans. The lordship of Monmouth was left to his nephew Withenock, son of his brother William, and the lordship of Abergavenny to his nephew Brian de Wallingford, the illegitimate son of Count Alan of Brittany. This lordship did not pass to Hamelin's daughter for she may have not been legitimate and it was certainly not advisable to have a border fortress in the hands of a woman, especially as the Norman conquest of Breconshire was far from complete, so it is probable that King Henry acted accordingly. It is supposed that the lordship of Abergavenny stretched from halfway to Crickhowell down to Mamhilad in one direction and from some unknown boundary over the Blaenavon hills to Whitecastle in the other.

An impression of Abergavenny motte and bailey castle c.1100 by Michael Blackmore

Engraving of Abergavenny Castle (1776) showing Hamelin's de Ballon's mound and ditch

Brian de Wallingford, who was also known as Fitzcount is notorious for his sacrilegious plundering of Llandaff Cathedral. Later to atone for his wrong doings he became a Crusader and travelled to the Holy Land, where it may be assumed he died. He is supposed to have had two leper sons, whom he placed in the priory, before going to the Holy Land, and granted large endowments to the priory on behalf of his unfortunate youngsters.

His sons did not succeed to the lordship of Abergavenny, being lepers, so the castle and its lands passed to Milo, Constable of England and Earl of Hereford. Milo was killed by a chance arrow whilst hunting in the Forest of Dean on Christmas Day 1143 and he was buried at the second Llanthony established at Gloucester, close to St Peter's abbey.

When Milo, Lord of Abergavenny, died he left five sons and three daughters. It was the fate of each son to meet with an untimely death and each of them died childless. Roger, the eldest, married, but, following his grandfather's example (Walter Fitzwalter, who became a monk at Llanthony Priory), he took the cowl and later died in the Abbey of Gloucester in 1154.

Roger, the Earl of Hereford died in 1155 and his brother Walter succeeded to the estate, but not to the earldom. He had neither the earldom of Hereford nor the castle of Gloucester, but he was lord of Abergavenny, of Grosmont, Skenfrith and Whitecastle as well as of Brecon and a greater part of Breconshire.

Lord Walter died without issue and probably unmarried, as no wife is mentioned. He was succeeded by Lord Henry de Hereford, the third son of Milo and fourth lord of Abergavenny. In what year Walter died and Henry became lord is not known, but Henry did not hold the lordship for long. In fact very little is known of him at all - scarcely more than a brief notice of his death. One or two grants to Gloucester occur in his name as 'Henry de Hereford', in which he mentions his grandfather, Walter de Gloucester and that is all. Henry de Hereford was killed at Arnold's Castle in Upper Gwent by Sitsyllt ap Dyfnwal of Llanover and his brother Mahel, the last of the sons of Milo, succeeded as fifth lord of Abergavenny and Brecon. Mahel was lord of Abergavenny for just one year when he was accidently killed in 1175 by a stone falling from the keep of Bronllys Castle.

William de Braose, a nephew of Henry de Hereford became the next Lord of Abergavenny and on taking up his inheritance he established himself in the castle with his wife Maud St Valerie. She is sometimes referred to as Maud Wallbee and is reputed to have been as powerful and grasping as her evil husband. Her dowry included Brecknock and Hay and it was not long before the Lordship of Abergavenny became the most powerful in Wales.

The de Braose's took their name from Briouze, near Falaise in Normandy and the first of the line in England was a previous William de Braose (born c.1049) who was granted the barony of Bramber (Sussex) at the time of the Conquest. He was succeeded by his son Philip (c.1096), who conquered the lordships of Radnor and Builth. Shortly after 1130, his possessions passed to his eldest son William de Braose II (born c. 1100 in Bramber, Sussex), the third baron, who in c.1155 also inherited one-half of the honour of Barnstaple, agreeing to pay a fee of 1,000 marks. He married Bertha de Gloucester, daughter of Milo, the Earl of Hereford and hereditary Constable of England.

Following Mahel's death, Brecknockshire, Overwent and Gower passed to William de Braose through his mother Bertha the second daughter of Milo Fitzwalter, Earl of Herford. She had inherited the vast Welsh possessions of her grandfather Bernard Neufmarché.

Through his marriage to Maud de S. Valerie, by whom he had three sons, William de Braose came into possession of a large part of the area around Hay-on-Wye which had been seized by her father. During the time he ruled the lordship of Brecknock he held the castles of Brecon, Pengelli, Blaenllynfi, Abergavenny, Whitecastle, Skenfrith, Grosmont, Hay, Bronllys, Painscastle and Radnor.

For thirty years William was a leading Lord of the Marches of South Wales, a kinglet in his own kingdom, with power of life and death in his hands, free to do as he pleased with the people under his control.

His long suffering wife was Matilduis de Sancto Walerico who is, generally referred to as Maud or Matilda. It would seem that the family of Saint Walery or Valery derived their name from a sea-port in France, so called from Valeries, a disciple of St Columba. It was from this sea port that William, Duke of Normandy, set sail on his England expedition.

The Christmas Day Massacre

The most famous story concerning Abergavenny Castle tells of the terrible massacre that took place there in 1175. A party of seventy Welshmen were invited by William de Braose to attend a banquet in the castle on Christmas Day. Their leader was Sitsyllt ap Dyfnawl, the local Welsh Prince, ruler of the area around Abergavenny which was called Gwent Uwchcoed (the lower reaches of the Usk and Wye were known as Gwent Iscoed). Not suspecting the baron's motives, the Welshmen came willingly and on their arrival were treated with warm hospitality.

Sitsyllt was no stranger to this castle, for early one morning in 1172, he and his men had managed to force their way inside, just as the guard was being withdrawn. They captured the constable, his family and most of the soldiers. During the attack, Henry Fitz-Milo, 4th Lord of Abergavenny, was killed. He was the uncle of William de Braose and the last of the Hamelin line. The castle then remained in Sitsyllt's possession until he was persuaded by his brother-in-law, Rhys ap Gruffyd, a staunch ally of King Henry II, to surrender it to the Norman Lordship. Soon afterwards Sitsyllt was summoned by the king to attend his court at Gloucester. It was a royal gathering of Welsh princes and even included those who had committed violent acts against the Normans. Undoubtedly this was a day of goodwill, when crimes were forgotten and bonds of trust and friendship were forged. Sitsyllt was one of the many Welshmen to be granted the king's pardon that day, in return for his voluntary withdrawal from Abergavenny Castle.

Sitsyllt had been strongly opposed to the Norman invasion in spite of the fact that his father Dyfnwal had been allowed to retain all of his possessions after Hamelin had conquered Gwent. He was still the lord of the manors of Castell Arnault, Parc Lettice and Llangattock Coed-Morgan. So when Sitsyllt inherited these possessions, he was the last of the Welsh rulers to have any control or authority in this area. This situation was due to the fact that his father had married Hamelin's illegitimate daughter, thus uniting the Normans with the Welsh .

Sitsyllt was married to Gladys the sister of Prince Rhys ap Gruffyd. His name is recorded as a witness to a grant to Lord Baderon de Monmouth as 'Seisello fil Dun alli'. This was in about 1150 in the time of Prior Robert of Monmouth. One of Sitsyllt's daughters was the wife of Cynfyn ap Cynyllyn, the son of the founder of Partishow Church in the Black Mountains.

It was soon after their visit to Gloucester that Sitsyllt and other local Welsh noblemen received the invitation from William de Braose, the new Lord of Abergavenny to gather at his castle for a celebration of the reconciliation at a grand banquet.

When the band of Welshmen led by Sitsyllt ap Dyfnawl arrived for the banquet, they were politely asked to leave their weapons in the gatehouse and they duly complied. They then made their way into the Great Hall and sat down at the long tables loaded with food. William de Braose rose to his feet and welcomed them all to Abergavenny Castle. But after the goblets of mead had been passed around, he changed the tone of his voice and announced that henceforth all the Welshmen of his domain should be deprived of the right to carry arms, and that all those who were present should swear to abandon that right. His guests were deeply shocked by his words and no doubt stared at him in astonishment, for they had come here that night in good faith and had not expected such a demand.

William de Braose then gave a pre-arranged signal and soldiers led by Ranulph Poer, the Sheriff of Hereford, rushed into the hall with gleaming swords in their hands. The Welshmen now rose to their feet in horror. Without weapons they were unable to defend themselves and were savagely cut to pieces. Their blood mingled with the wine they had been drinking and one by one they fell to the stone floor until the massacre was complete. It is reputed however, that Prince Iorwerth of Caerleon managed to escape. It is said that he managed to procure a Norman's sword and hewing his way to the door, he escaped into the blackness of the December night.

Not satisfied with this bloodshed, the next morning William de Braose, ordered his men to saddle their horses and they rode down the Usk Valley to Sitsyllt's home at Castell Arnallt. The Welshman's widow, Angharad, was forced to stand helpless as her seven-year old son Cadwaladr was slain before her very eyes.

This famous event is described as follows in the Welsh *Chronicle of the Princes*:

> '... Seisyll ap Dyfnwal was slain through treachery in the castle of Abergavenny by the lord of Brycheiniog. And along with him Geoffrey, his son, and the best men of Gwent were slain. And the French made for Seisyll's court; and after seizing Gwladus, his wife, they slew Cadwaladr, his son. And on that day there befell a pitiful massacre in Gwent. And from that time forth, after that treachery, none dared place trust in the French.'

It was not until the young sons of the massacred Welshmen reached fighting age that an act of reprisal was undertaken. In 1182, led by Iorwerth of Caerleon, they attacked Abergavenny Castle. Using scaling ladders, they stormed the castle walls and killed or took prisoner the entire garrison. They partially destroyed the castle but to their disappointment William de Braose and his wife Maud, were not in residence at the time.

Gerald of Wales describes the capture of the castle by the Welsh in 1182 as follows:

> 'Burning with revenge, they concealed themselves in the overgrown ditches of Abergavenny Castle, which they had occupied while the castellan was away. The previous day one of their number, a man called Seisyll the son of Eudas, had said to the constable, as if he were warning him, but apparently more for a joke and a laugh than seriously: "that is where we shall climb in tonight".

As he spoke he pointed to one of the corners of the wall, where it seemed to be lower than elsewhere...

The constable and his household stayed on guard all night, refusing to take off their armour and remaining on the alert until first light. In the end, tired out by their vigil and feeling safe now that day had dawned, they all retired to bed. Thereupon their enemies dragged the scaling-ladders which they had prepared to the precise corner of the walls which Seisyll had pointed out. The constable and his wife were captured and so were most of his men. A few escaped, finding refuge in the master tower. The Welsh occupied the castle and burned the whole place down.'

After their attack on Abergavenny Castle the band of Welshmen then went to Llandingat (Dingestow), where Ranulph le Poer, Sheriff of Herefordshire, was erecting a castle. The avengers stormed the half-finished walls and killed Ranulph le Poer plus nine of his soldiers. William de Braose who was also there at the time was dragged from a deep trench into which he had fallen, but a rush of his own men saved his life.

The descendants of Sitsyllt continued to live in the neighbourhood of Abergavenny and from Aeddan, his eldest son came the families of Arnold of Llanfihangel Crucorney, Probert of Pant Glas, Reynolds of Llantrisant and Morgan of Llanwenarth. One of Sitsyllt's uncles was Garwyn and descended from him were the Prices of Llanfoist. The name Sitsylly has undergone various alterations including Sytsylt, Sissillt or Seisel and ultimately Cecil. The most famous member of this family was Robert Cecil who became a highly regarded counsellor to Queen Elizabeth I.

This is the site of the Great Hall which was used as a meeting place, a court room and also for dining. Stone corbels can be seen in the walls which once supported the timber roof. It was in the Great Hall that the famous massacre of 1175 took place.

Castell Arnallt

All that remains of Castell Arnallt is a large oblong grass covered mound of earth and rubble near the River Usk about four miles south east of Abergavenny, (SO 320100). It was once a base of the Welsh princes of Over Gwent (Gwent Uwch-Coed) and would have been a timber construction.

The site was scheduled in 1947 and a topographical survey carried out by Neil Phillips in 2000 showed that the site appears to have 'contained a large number of buildings and may well have had multivallate defences that evolved over the times in which they were used.' It is known that this was once the fortified home of Seisyllt ap Dyfnwal. He had been created Lord of Over Gwent in return for releasing a hostage, Hugh de Beauchamp. Seisyll and his eldest son Geoffrey were murdered at Abergavenny Castle in 1175 and Castell Arnallt was destroyed shortly afterwards.

There is a record that in 1349 Castell Arnallt was in the possession of John Wallis, who was also known as Gallis. He paid rent for the land to Lawrence Hastings, the 13th Lord of Abergavenny, but it is most unlikely that an inhabited residence stood here after 1175, so Wallis probably used the estate purely for agricultural purposes.

The site of Castell Arnallt, once the fortified home of Seisyllt ap Dyfnwal

Giraldus Cambrensis visits Abergavenny

The 12th century chronicler, Giraldus Cambrensis, who was a cousin, once removed of the wife of Sitsyllt Dyfnawl visited Abergavenny during his tour of Wales with Archbishop Baldwin in 1188, and stated in his Itinerary that this was 'a castle dishonoured by treachery more often than any other in Wales.' It was now thirteen years after the massacre in the Great Hall and Geoffrey in mentioning the incident remarked that, 'William de Braose proposed this ordinance to be received of them with corporall oath. That no traveller by the waie amongst them should bear any bow or other lawful weapon, which oath they refused to take, because they would not stand to that ordinance, he condemned them all to death.'

He passed no judgement on his host, William de Braose, but went on to remark:

> 'We leave to others the relation of those frequent and cruel excesses which in our times have arisen among the inhabitants of these parts against the governors of castles and the vindictive relations of the governors against the natives.'

He preferred to think that it was the work of the dead Henry II rather than that of the living William de Braose and abstains from describing the slaughter, lest bad men should think that crime succeeds.

It would appear that Giraldus had a sneaking regard for William de Braose and liked him for his custom of putting, 'the name of the Lord before many of his sentences saying, 'Let this be done in the name of the Lord: Let that be done by God's will.'

Giraldus Cambrensis in St David's Cathedral

Giraldus extolls the feats of the Welsh archers, though they had acquired nothing like the efficiency that distinguished them a century later under Edward I. The long bow had not yet been developed, but the men of Gwent at that time were using short bows of elm which had considerable penetration powers.

A fascinating description is also given by Giraldus of the wounding of one of De Braose's horsemen during the Welsh attack on the castle. The rider was struck by an arrow which passed through his armour, his thigh and his saddle, mortally wounding the horse. As the poor animal spun around the man received another arrow through his other thigh and in agony he was fixed firmly to his horse.

Giraldus also noted that the oak door frame in the castle was 'four fingers thick' and had been pierced by several arrows. He went on to say that the 'bows used by these people are not made of horn, ivory or yew, but of wild elm, unpolished, rude and uncouth, but stout; not calculated to shoot an arrow to a great distance, but to inflict very severe wounds in a close fight.'

It was from this short bow that the Welsh archers developed the long bow which became a powerful weapon in the wars against the Scots, and, later, the French campaigns.

Archbishop Baldwin accompanied by the faithful Giraldus preached the Crusade at Abergavenny in 1188 with the aim of persuading local knights and their men to go to Palestine to help fight in the Holy War. Many local men were persuaded to take the Cross but those who could afford it usually bought the privilege of not joining up, by contributing a pound or two to the war chest.

William de Braose was a typical Norman, being a compound of ferocity, piety, valor and meaness, cunning and superstition. His career gives a very clear picture of the times in which he lived and the facts of his rapid rise to power and his headlong fall is a fascinating yet tragic story.

In 1191, William, in order to defray the cost of King Richard's crusade to the Holy Land, gave him 1,000 marks to have the wardship of Gilbert, Lord of Monmouth. Ten years later, another payment to the Crown gave him authority to add to his demesne any lands he could capture from the Welsh. He seized Elfael and in 1196 acquired full rights in Barnstaple by agreement with the co-heir. In 1200 he received the Honour of Limerick on payment of 5,000 marks by instalments of 500 marks a year.

From 1192-99 he was Sheriff of Herefordshire, and in 1196, Justice Itinerant for Staffordshire. He accompanied Richard I to Normandy in 1195 but also supported Prince John's claim to the throne, witnessing various royal grants, and he was in attendance on John in Normandy at the time of Prince Arthur's death in 1203. He also served in the French war of 1204 and was obviously high in King John's favour.

However, in 1207 William fell out with King John over money matters and was ordered to contribute a large sum for the king's expedition to North Wales. The money did not appear on the appointed day and King John decided that William de Braose was not to be trusted.

Not only had he not paid the dues for the lands which he had received, but also because he was suspected of intrigue with the king's enemies in Ireland and Wales. Why he did not pay the money due to the Crown is difficult to understand, for he seems to have had ample means, being then at the zenith of his power and prosperity. Perhaps he hoped that John's own difficulties with his troublesome barons might shortly set himself free of debt. At the end of six years, after the grant of Limerick, de Braose had only paid 700 marks in total, instead of 500 a year.

In 1209, King John, was so suspicious of William's fidelity that he demanded to have his sons given up as hostages, but Maud de Braose told the messengers that she would not trust a man who had murdered his own nephew (Prince Arthur). Consequently, William's estates were confiscated. Prince Arthur was the true heir to the English crown and was thus a threat to John's sovereignty. He had just disappeared and rumour said that John had stabbed him with a dagger and dropped the body from a boat in a river three miles from where the prince was imprisoned. How much de Braose knew of these events is not recorded, but there is a suggestion that the gift of Limerick in the same year, 1203, was to ensure his silence. Matthew Paris, a monastic historian, writing in 1210, explains the reason for King John's displeasure against William de Braose:

'When the Pope had excommunicated the realm of England, the king took pledges of such of his nobles as he thought were disaffected to him: amongst others, he sent messengers to William de Braose to demand his sons as pledges, to whom Maud his wife, being the readier speaker, answered (though what she said was no less her husband's sentiment than her own), "That the king who had proved so base a guardian to his nephew

Prince Arthur, whom instead of setting in, he deprived of, his right, should have none of her children." The king was so highly displeased with this message, that he ordered some soldiers to be sent to seize this lord; but he, having timely intelligence of this order, fled into Ireland with his wife and children...'

So William and his family put to sea, but there were fierce storms raging. For three days and three nights their ship was tossed about violently until it finally reached the coast of Ireland. It had been de Braose's intention to seek shelter with Lord Walter de Lacy who had married his daughter Margaret, but the mountainous waves drove the ship to Wicklow, where William Marshall, Earl of Pembroke and Striguil was then staying. He gave the de Braose family a warm welcome and they stayed under his roof for twenty days.

When John de Grey, Bishop of Norwich, who was Justicar in Ireland, heard that the Earl had sheltered de Braose, he asked him why he had given help to a traitor to the king and ordered him to give de Braose up at once.

Earl Marshall answered:

'I have no traitor here, but I have sheltered my Lord William as I ought to do, especially as I did not know that the king had any cause of complaint against him. And since I have harboured him I should be guilty of an act of treachery if I gave him into your hands. I will conduct him in safety until he is out of my hands. The bishop ought not to ask me to do something which would be a cause of reproach to me.'

Having answered the bishop's message, courteously, wisely and loyally, the Earl conducted William and his family in safety to Walter de Lacy. This elder brother of Hugh de Lacy, Earl of Ulster, was the sixth Baron Lacy and second Lord of Meath. The two brothers had made war in Ireland on Meiler FitzHenry and in April 1207 he was summoned to England to answer for his misdeeds. He managed to make peace with the king and returned to Ireland in June 1208. He and most of his family helped de Braose against King John and as a result were driven out of Ireland.

King John

King John assembled a large army at Pembroke in 1210 and sailed for Ireland. His force took several of the fortresses of his enemies and Walter de Lacy fled with several others who were afraid of falling into the king's hands.

Maud and her son William fled to Scotland, where they were taken prisoner in Galloway by Duncan of Garrick, and brought to King John at Carrickfergus. From there they were taken to England. William de Braose met them at Bristol on 20 September, 1210, and finally agreed to pay a sum of 40,000 marks. But he still failed to pay up and was declared an outlaw. He sailed from the port of Shoreham in disguise to France where he died in August 1211 at Corbeil and was buried by a fellow exile, Stephen Langton, the Archbishop of Canterbury, in the abbey church of Saint Victor, Paris. Maud and her son William were imprisoned in Windsor Castle by King John and starved to death.

It was William's second son, Giles de Braose who became the sixth Lord of Abergavenny. However, having been banished to France, he was unable to take up residence. He had been made bishop of Hereford in 1200, but had left the country on account of King John's animosity towards his family.

From what is known of him, Giles de Braose seems to have been an administrator, a builder and an intriguer. In fact anything but a religious ecclesiasta. When his father William had become rebellious and King John had starved his mother Maud and his brother William to death, Giles no doubt became a thorn in the king's side. He was incessantly involved in intrigues and his personal allies were the princes of Wales.

In 1213 Giles returned from exile in France, and paid a fine of 9,000 marks for his father's lands on 21 October, 1215. The de Braose estates were restored to him, but he died at Gloucester in that same year and was buried in Hereford Cathedral. Among the monuments in the north choir aisle in Hereford Cathedral is the effigy of a bishop in full canonicals, holding in his hand the model of a tower. It is believed to represent Giles de Braose, who was responsible for causing the erection of the central tower.

Giles de Braose depicted in a window in Brecon Cathedral

Giles was succeeded by his brother Reginald, who became the seventh Lord of Abergavenny. He had married as his second wife, Gwladys Ddu (dark Gladys), the daughter of Prince Llywelyn by Joan, an illegitimate daughter of King John. For some time Reginald and his father-in-law, Llywelyn, fought against King John. However, it was the year of 'Magna Carta' and Reginald de Braose on obtaining full possession of his estates now adhered to the throne and refused further support to the Welsh prince.

In 1216, King John spent three days plundering and burning Hay Castle as an act of revenge against the de Braose family. He died ten weeks later and a chronicler of the time commented, 'Hell itself was the blacker and fouler by his death.'

The last lord of this family was another William de Braose, Reginald's son, who as a loyal suppporter of Henry II, opposed Prince Llywelyn. The Prince, angry at the loss of support from the de Braose family attacked Abergavenny Castle and took William away as his prisoner. Some time later he was freed on the payment of 3,000 marks. He also promised his daughter Isabel to Llywelyn's son Dafydd with Builth Castle as her dowry, and signed an agreement not to oppose Llywelyn again.

In 1230, William was a guest of Llywelyn at his castle in Aber, North Wales and foolishly started an affair with Llywelyn's wife Joan. When the Welsh prince discovered the intrigue, he reacted by hanging William from a tree within sight of one of the castle windows. Joan suffered a less cruel fate than that of William's grandmother, Maud de Braose, for when she died she was buried at Llanfaes Priory in Anglesey. A coffin lid which is said to bear her image can be seen in the porch of Beaumaris Church.

With the death of this last William de Braose, the male line, of this main branch of the family ceased and the estates of the lordship were divided between William's daughters who had all married into important families. Isabel the eldest, married Dafydd, the son of Llywelyn; the youngest Maud married Roger Mortimer, Earl of Wigmore, which meant that two of the most powerful families in the Welsh Marches became related. It was Eva, the third daughter, who received the lordship and the Abergavenny estates and she married William de Cantelupe, who was the son of the powerful Baron of Aston Cantelupe. Eva had been a ward of this baron, and upon her marriage she conferred the lordship of Abergavenny to her husband who thus became the ninth lord. The de Braose family are represented in stone at St Mary's Priory Church, only by Eva de Braose (d.1246), the daughter of William Marshall, Earl of Pembroke , and wife of William de Braose, grandson of the notorious Lord of Abergavenny of the same name.

The Cantelupe Family

William de Cantelupe died in 1254 when his son and successor, George was a minor and a ward of Prince Edward (afterwards King Edward I), who drew a good annual income from Abergavenny for twenty years.

George de Cantelupe died in 1272 and was the last of the Cantelupe lords. He was buried in St Marys Priory Church and his effigy carved in wood is a beautiful example of a rare kind. Joan, the sister of George de Cantelupe, married Henry, Lord Hastings, and as a result a fourth family came into possession of the lordship.

The Hastings Family

John Hastings was the 12th Lord of Abergavenny and when he died in 1325, his son Lawrence at five years of age, became entitled to Abergavenny Castle and large estates in the locality. These estates were managed by the Crown until he attained his majority and on October 13, 1339, Lawrence Hastings was created Earl of Pembroke and he went with King Edward II to fight in Flanders. In 1344 he led 60 men at arms, two bannerets, 12 knights, 45 esquires and 100 archers on horseback from Gwent for the King of Brittany. He was a great favourite of Edward II and according to one source, he was summoned to Parliament in 1338 and made a Knight of Edward's Round Table in 1345. In 1347 he served in Gascony under Henry Duke of Lancaster and with the Earl of Northampton he defeated the fleet near Crotoy.

Lawrence Hasting married Agnes, the daughter of the famous Roger Mortimer, Earl of March but died soon afterwards in 1348 from the Black Death. He was the last lord of Abergavenny to be buried here.   There were two more Lords de Hastings, both Lords of Abergavenny and Earls of Pembroke, and when the last one died in 1389 in a tournament at Woodstock, his widow married into the Beauchamp family.

The Beauchamp Family

The first lord of this family was William who in 1403 proved very unpopular and was accused of cruelty. Some of the town's people were charged with felony and the Constable of the castle, with the permission of Lord William, set up a gallows to put three men to death. There was a riot and the townsmen surged to the castle gates, in front of which the execution was to have taken place. This was one of the biggest riots that have ever taken place in Abergavenny and they forced the Lord of Abergavenny to give up the execution.

William Beauchamp died in 1411, and was succeeded by his son Richard, who was also created Earl of Worcester in 1421 by his marriage with Isabel Despencer. When he succeeded to the lordship of Glamorgan and held his court at Cardiff Castle. On his death during the wars in France in 1431, he was buried in Tewkesbury Abbey. His widow then married, by special dispensation from the Pope, his relative, Richard Beauchamp, Earl of Warwick, one of the most distinguished knights of the age.

The Nevill Family

The associations of the Nevill family with Abergavenny date back to the early part of the 15th century when Richard Beauchamp, the 18th Lord of Abergavenny was killed in France in 1417. He left an only daughter, Elizabeth, who married Sir William Nevill. An effort was made to prevent Sir William from acquiring the lordship, but he succeeded after a long struggle, and it was as Baron Bergavenny that he took his place in Edward IV's Parliament in 1450.

Jasper Tudor depicted in a window at Cardiff Castle

In 1486 the Nevill tenure was interrupted when Jasper Tudor, Duke of Bedford and Earl of Pembroke was granted the lordship by his nephew Henry VII. He was also lord of Newport, Caldicot and Magor; and steward of the duchy lordships of Monmouth and constable of the three castles of Grosmont, Skenfrith and Whitecastle. On his death in 1495 without issue the lordship reverted to the Crown but in the reign of Henry VIII was restored to George, grandson of Sir Edward Nevill.

When Henry, the son of George Nevill died in 1586, the castle descended to his brother, Sir Edward Nevill. He was followed by his son Henry who died in 1649 and then his son John, who died in 1660.

Then followed George Nevill (died 1666), George Nevill (died 1694), George Nevill (died 1720), George Nevill (died 1723), Edward Nevill (died 1724), and William Nevill (died 1744) George Neville, the next baron, was, in 1784, created Viscount Neville and Earl of Abergavenny. He was followed by Henry Nevill (died 1843), John Nevill (died 1845) and William Nevill (died 1868). The next in line was William Nevill, who was created Marquess of Abergavenny in 1876.

In the old days the castle had always been the residence of the Lords of Abergavenny, but after it fell into decay, the Nevill family, for many years had no official residence in or near the town. It was in October 1898 that the Marquess purchased a mansion called 'The Brooks' for £10,000 and it was renamed 'Nevill Hall'. The meadows between the house and the river had already belonged to the Nevills being part of the old demesne land of the castle and lordship which had been in that family since the fifteenth century.

In 1891 William Nevill, KG., First Marquess of Abergavenny (who was created a peer of United Kingdom in 1876), was Patron of 21 livings which included Aberystwyth Rectory, Bryngwyn Rectory, Goytre Rectory, Llangattock-nigh-Usk Rectory and Llanwenarth Citra Rectory, all in Monmouthshire. Whenever a rector of any of these parish churches left his rectory or died, he was in a position to appoint a new Rector.

In 1898 the Marquess's eldest son, Reginald William Bransby, on the application of his father was pronounced 'a person of unsound mind' by the Master in Lunacy. His 'custody and regulation' was granted to the Marquess's second son Lord Henry Nevill.

According to Lady Cicely Nevill, Duchess of York in 1907, descended from the Nevills are seven kings of England, three Queens. four Princes of Wales, four Kings of Scotland, two Queens of Scotland, one Queen of Spain and one Queen of Bohemnia.

In 1911 the Marquess of Abergavenny was described in the *Abergavenny Chronicle* as:

> 'An aristocrat of the old school, who is one of our oldest living peers - he is in his 85th year - and he has a claim to prominence for several things. He owns property in about seven counties; he is a founder of the famous Constitutional Club; he is a Nevill and a descendant of Warwick - the king-maker and he holds the patronage of twenty-four church livings.'

On Tuesday 11th September 1913, the 87th birthday of the Marquess was celebrated by the staff at Nevill Hall who were treated to supper and a dance. The workmen of the estate also had an excellent dinner provided for them at the Greyhound Hotel, where Eridge, venison, rabbit pie and Christmas pudding featured on the menu.

William Nevill, 1st Marquess of Abergavenny, died on 12th December 1915 and his title and estate passed to his eldest son. The second son, Lord Henry Nevill, then applied for the authority from the Lord Justice in Lunacy, to sell by private auction on private contract the entire estate.

In January 1917, Nevill Hall and 2,825 acres, by direction of the Marquess, was advertised for £20,000. The Mansion House and an estate of 191 acres was subsequently purchased by Thomas Parry JP of the Croft, Caerleon for £13,000 in November 1917. He sold the property with certain lands, in July of the following year to Sir James Herbert Cory, MP for £6,500. Two years later Sir James Cory sold the Mansion House and estate to James Pitman and others as trustees of the Blaina & District Hospital for £11,000.

In July 1924 a claim to be the rightful Marquess of Abergavenny was put forward by Vincent St John Nevill, a white-haired distinguished-looking man, who was sentenced to twelve months' hard labour at Hastings Quarter Sessions for false pretences.

He maintained that he was connected with the Nevills of Eridge Castle, Tunbridge Wells and later said he had come into the estate and there was £350,000 due to him. He claimed to be the legitimate son of the first Marquess of Abergavenny and as a youngster had been placed for education with the Rev Mr Verrall of Hayward's Heath, Sussex. When seventeen he decided to travel and visited France and Brazil, finally settling down in the United States, where he remained for 35 years earning his living by his pen.

He arrived in England in 1819 with his daughter with a view to establishing his claim to the Marquisate of Abergavenny. The court did not believe his story and he was sentenced to six months for fraud.

In August 1920, the death occurred at Hove of Lord George (Montacute) Nevill J.P. D.L., third son of the first Marquess of Abergavenny. Born in 1856, Lord George was the third of five sons of the first Marquess. The title originated in 1876 and the present Marquess was Reginald William Bransby Nevill J.P. of Eaton Square, London and Tunbridge Wells. The heir presumptive was Lord Henry Gilbert Ralph Nevill, second son of the first Marquess.

In January 1938, Henry Gilbert Ralph Nevill, 3rd Marquess of Abergavenny was killed while hunting at Groombridge, East Sussex. He was the second son of the first Marquess (the fifth Earl of Abergavenny) upon whom the marquisate was conferred in 1876. He succeeded his brother, known as 'The Bachelor Marquis' in 1927. He resided at Eridge Castle, near Tunbridge Wells in Sussex, which is one of the stately homes of England. It was founded by Gilbert de Nevill, a companion-in-arms of William the Conqueror and the family owned a great deal of land. In 1573 Queen Elizabeth I spent six days at the castle as a guest of Lord Burgeny. It was said that the Nevills could once drive from Eridge to Brighton, a distance of over twenty miles, without leaving their estate. It has been held by the Nevills for nearly 700 years and was rebuilt about two centuries ago.

The fatal accident occurred while he was taking part in a children's meet at the Eridge Hunt of which he was formerly master. At the age of 83 he was still an expert horseman but his horse caught a hoof in a wire and he was thrown heavily on his head, breaking his neck. He died in the arms of Mr B.W. Poile of Southborough, Kent, in about five minutes. The body was taken to Eridge Castle.

Although the Marquess was married three times, he had no son and the titles passed to his nephew, Major John Henry Guy Temple Montacute Lanarch-Nevill, the elder son of a younger brother who served in the Great War.

John Henry Guy Nevill, the only remaining peer of the Nevill family, the 5th Marquis of Abergavenny died in 1999 at the age of 85. He was born on November 8th, 1914, the elder son of Lieutenant Colonel Guy Lanarch-Nevill who had assumed the extra surname in honour of his wife's family. Known as John Abergavenny, the last Nevill peer lived at Ickfield House, Sussex. He married Patricia Harrison in 1938 and they had four daughters and a son, Lord Lewes, who died of cancer at the age of 17 in 1965.

Christopher Nevill, born in 1955, the son of the 5th Marquis's younger brother Lord Rupert Nevill, a former private secretary to the Duke of Edinburgh, has inherited the peerage. The Nevill Estate company still owns the castle and grounds, which are leased to Monmouthshire County Council.

View of the ruins from Castle Meadows

The South West Tower was built in about 1300 and provided
living quarters for the lord of Abergavenny and his family

Abergavenny Castle during the Civil War

During the Civil War, the Castle was held for the king by a garrison commanded by Colonel Proger. Sir Trevor Williams of Llangibby with four other prominent men of the county on the Parliament side were arrested for disloyalty and confined in the castle. But Charles I, after the battle of Naseby, during one of his three visits to Abergavenny, moved, it is said by their tears and entreaties, ordered their release. This act of leniency caused the aged Marquis of Worcester (his most loyal and devoted Welsh supporter) the remark: 'Sire, you may chance to gain the Kingdom of Heaven by such acts as these, but if ever you get the kingdom of England by such ways, I will be your bondman.'

By the end of 1645 Abergavenny was held by the Parliamentary party, who had a small force here. An attack was made by Lord Charles Somerset on the 24th of January 1646 with some Royalist troops from Raglan, but they were driven back and fifty of their men taken prisoners.

In 1646 the town and castle were sacked by Fairfax's troops and the castle after being 'slighted' was never restored and remained uninhabited. It then became a quarry for stone and over the years many local buildings were constructed from its materials.

The Ruins of Abergavenny Castle

The only remains of Hamelin de Ballon's castle of 1087 are the motte and a section of the bank under the east tower which was part of the east rampart of a bailey to the north of the motte. If we were able to travel back in time we would find Abergavenny Castle in its finest condition during the 13th and 14th centuries, when it belonged to the Hastings family. Lawrence de Hastings was killed whilst jousting at the castle in 1389 and he became the last lord of Abergavenny to be buried in St Mary's. Since the early 15th century no lords of Abergavenny have lived at the castle, for after that time the castle was held for the lord by a castellan, or constable, with a small garrison.

During the passing centuries the castle, just like many others, was robbed of large amounts of stone which was used to construct other local buildings. Today, all that remains of the 12th century fortress are the masonry of two towers and the connecting outer walls to the foundations of the keep which stood on a mound which had been formed on a terminal moraine. The original wooden keep was rebuilt in stone between 1150 and 1182. It was the strongest of the defences and a final refuge for the garrison when the outer walls had been stormed. The bridge which led to it over a ditch is mentioned by Giraldus Cambrensis as being used when the castle was captured in 1182.

It is of interest that the River Usk has changed its course, for it once flowed closer to the motte. The lodge at the entrance to the castle was built in Victorian times and it stands near the site of a defensive ditch and drawbridge.

The sham keep which stands on top of the old Norman motte was built in 1818 by the Marquess of Abergavenny, whose main home at that time was Eridge Castle in Kent. His Abergavenny estate steward supervised the construction of this building, which took two years to complete and was known as 'The Court House'.

After making use of it for a few years the Neville family then leased it as a private house. In 1881 the Abergavenny Improvements Commissioners leased the castle and its grounds as a facility for the people of the town and as an attraction for visitors. The new 'keep' became known as 'Castle House' and refreshments were provided there.

The gatehouse was built during the early years of the 15th century and may have been as a result of the threat of the Glyndwr uprising. It replaced William de Braose's simpler entrance through the curtain wall

This sham keep standing on top of the old Norman motte was built as a hunting lodge in 1818 by the Marquess of Abergavenny whose main home at that time was Eridge Castle in Kent. The building of the keep, which became known as 'The Court House' took two years to be completed and the work was supervised by Baker-Gabb the Marquess's Abergavenny steward. It was used by the Nevile family for a few years and then leased as a private house.

The Marquess of Abergavenny let the castle to the Abergavenny Improvements Commissioners at a nominal rent and also spent about £100 in extending the boundary wall. The precincts of the castle were laid out with walks, flower beds and tennis courts and provided with seats. Along the side wall of the western aspect of the old baronial banqueting hall a rustic gallery of trellis was erected. During the summer months the grounds were opened until 10 p.m. and a band was engaged for the season. Gas lamps were fixed to the trees to light up the place at night time. An entrance fee of 2d was charged and season tickets were available for a family at 7s 6d per annum. Special trains were laid on every Bank Holiday to bring large numbers of people to Abergavenny, where they spent an enjoyable day at the castle.

In the early years of the 20th century garden parties were often held in the castle grounds and on the day of the investiture of Edward VII as Prince of Wales, dinners and teas were provided for no less than 4,288 people. This was a banquet on a massive scale served in three marquees and in a temporary dining hall erected on the site of the Great Hall where the historic massacre of 1175 took place.

The cost of laying out the castle grounds was about £650, of which £431 was given by Crawshay Bailey the ironmaster and £100 by the Marquess of Abergavenny, who let the castle to the Abergavenny Improvement Commissioners at a nominal rent. He also spent about £100 on extending the boundary wall. The work was all done under the direction of the Board, prominent among whom was the chairman, Mr Edwin Tucker.

At the official opening it was stated by Mr Conway that:

> 'The grounds were opened with the object of providing a benefit to the people of the hills, who could come down from their smoky regions to ruminate over the ruins and enjoy the fresh air of the beautiful vales around: and thus by benefiting them the people of Abergavenny hoped to be able to realise a good sum of money from their visits.'

About 7,000 people were present at the opening ceremony, performed by Edwin Tucker, and among them was 'a good sprinkling of the gentry'. The prices for admission on this first day was 1s for adults and 6d for children. Upwards of £200 were taken at the gates, whilst the turnstile registered between 8,000 and 9,000 persons, including those who entered the grounds by means of passes.

In those days at the beginning of the twentieth century, the first Monday in the month was called 'Mabon's Monday' and the miners were given a holiday. This holiday was due to the efforts of the Welsh MP Mr W. Abrahams, who was known as 'Mabon', and it was an occasion for school and club outings. At Abergavenny Castle they were assured of excellent dinners and teas 'at very reasonable prices'.

Huge parties came by train from the mining towns to Brecon Road Station. There they would form a procession and parade through the town to the castle, singing songs and hymns as only Welsh people can.

On each summer bank holiday the party finished up with a huge firework display, after which the crowds made their way back to Brecon Road and the frequent trains which took them home. The coming of the motor car put an end to these parties.

Abergavenny had a memorable day on Whit Monday June 6th 1881, when there was a grand fete and demonstration on the occasion of the opening of the castle and grounds as a place of public recreation. The London & North Western Railway brought between

There used to be a rustic hall on the site of the massacre of Welsh nobles, with a staircase leading to the top of the western wall of the castle, along which a platform was constructed to enable visitors to traverse the wall throughout the whole of its available length to a second similar wooden staircase leading down into a space bounded on the south and west by the remains of the round and pentagonal towers.

2,000 and 3,000 visitors to the town for the celebrations. The total number of people admitted to the castle on that day was 4,035. The motto 'Ne Vile Velis' was worked in fire to celebrate the opening and it literally translates 'Do not wish a mean thing'.

Friendly Societies, schools from the valley-head towns etc used to come to the castle for their annual outings and have their dinners and teas in the rustic banqueting hall and in the dining rooms of the Castle House. Both the tennis court and the banqueting hall were frequently used for dancing.

The Great Hall was just inside William de Braose's Curtain wall and occupied the whole width from the polygonal tower to the gatehouse. The stone corbels from which the roof timbers sprang can be seen high on the wall. The actual hall was on the first floor with large store chambers underneath. It was entered through a doorway at the top of an outside stairway. The two garderobes (toilets) which can be seen in the west wall would have drained into the castle ditch.

The South West Tower was built about 1300 and it is here that the Lord of Abergavenny and his family would have resided.

The South West Tower

Reconstruction of the old round keep - Michael Blackmore

Proposed Demolition of the Sham Keep

In November 1960 there was a proposal by Abergavenny Borough Council to demolish the sham keep for it was considered to be in an 'advanced state of disrepair.' A surveyor had reported that the walls were spreading, the foundations giving and the property was in a very dangerous state. The Inspector of Ancient Monuments expressed the view that it was not worth spending between £2,000 and £3,000 on making the building safe, especially as it was 'lacking in historical and archaeological interest.' There was no help likely to be available from the Marquess of Abergavenny for he had intimated that he was not willing to make any financial contribution, but he had no objection to the keep being demolished. Fortunately the proposed demolition did not take place and in later years the sham keep was restored and is now an important part of the museum.

The Victorian Keep has been restored and contains part of the museum

THE LORDS OF ABERGAVENNY

1st   Hamelin de Ballon, Conqueror of Over Gwent

2nd   Brian de Wallingford

3rd   Walter, the son of Miles, Earl of Hereford

4th   Henry de Hereford - slain by Sitsyllyt ap Dyfnwal who took the castle in 1172

5th   William de Braose - died in France 1212

6th   Giles de Braose - died at Gloucester in 1215 and buried in Hereford Cathedral

7th   Reginald de Braose - died 1228 and buried in Priory Church of Brecon

8th   William de Braose - hanged by Prince Llewelyn in 1229

9th   William de Cantelupe - died 1256

10th   George de Cantelupe -1273) and buried in St Marys Priory Church

11th   John Hastings (d.1313)

12th   John Hastings - died 1325

13th   Lawrence Hastings - died 1348 - buried in St Mary's Priory Church

14th   John Hastings died at Calais in 1773 - buried at Hereford

15th   John Hastings - accidently killed in 1389 in a tournament at Woodstock

16th   Reginald, Lord Grey de Rhuthyn - sold the lordship to William Beauchamp

17th   William Beauchamp - died in 1411

18th   Richard Beauchamp - killed in France - buried in the choir of Tewkesbury Abbey

19th   Sir Edward Nevill - 3rd Baron Bergavenny - died 1476

20th   Sir George Nevill - 4th Baron Bergavenny - died 1492

21st   Sir George Nevill - 5th Baron Bergavenny - died 1535

22nd   Henry Nevill - 6th Baron Bergavenny - died 1587

23rd	Edward Nevill - 7th Baron Bergavenny - died 1589
24th	Edward Nevill - 8th Baron Bergavenny - died 1622
25th	Henry Nevill - 9th Baron Bergavenny - died 1641
26th	John Nevill - 10th Baron Bergavenny - died 1662
27th	George Nevill - 11th Baron Bergavenny - died 1666
28th	George Nevill - 12th Baron Bergavenny - died 1695
29th	George Nevill - 13th Baron Bergavenny - died 1721
30th	George Nevill - 14th Baron Bergavenny - died 1723
31st	Edward Nevill - 15th Baron Bergavenny - died 1724
32nd	William Nevill - 16th Baron Bergavenny - died 1744
33rd	George Nevill - 1st Earl of Abergavenny (17th Baron) - died 1785
34th	Henry Nevill - 2nd Earl of Abergavenny (18th Baron) -died 1843
35th	John Nevill - 3rd Earl of Abergavenny (19th Baron) - died 1845
36th	William Nevill - 4th Earl of Abergavenny (20th Baron) - died 1868
37th	William Nevill 1st Marquess of Abergavenny (21st Baron) - died 1915
38th	Reginald Nevill - 2nd Marquess of Abergavenny (22nd Baron) - died 1927
39th	Henry Gilbert Nevil - 3rd Marquess of Abergavenny (23rd Baron) - died 1938
40th	Guy Temple Montacute Lanarch-Nevil - 4th Marquess of Abergavenny (24th Baron) - died 1954
41st	John Henry Nevill - 5th Marquess of Abergavenny (25th Baron) - died 1999
42nd	Christopher Nevill - 6th Marquess of Abergavenny (title of Baron dropped)

The Marquess's Monmouthshire estates were administered from Abergavenny until about 1910 when the office was closed and transferred to Sussex and the family mainly resided at Eridge Castle in Kent. In 1792 the Second Earl of Abergavenny converted the old Eridge Park hunting lodge into a Gothic Castle which was named Eridge Castle and it became the Nevill family's main residence. It was demolished in 1938 and replaced by a modern house known as Eridge Park.

The Museum in Abergavenny Castle

There was talk of starting a museum in Abergavenny as early as 1902 and a collection of items of historic interest was begun, but nothing was done about it until 1957 when Alfred Jackson obtained approval for a museum to be established within the precincts of Abergavenny Castle. After many years of campaigning the Abergavenny & District Museum Society was formed under the Presidency of Lord Raglan, the vice-president being Dr Dilwyn John C.B.E., Director of the National Museum of Wales. Alfred Jackson became the founder chairman of the society's management committee while his brother E.G. Jackson was the honorary secretary. It was the latter who led a voluntary working party which carried out almost all the decoration and conversion work at the museum. The first honorary curator was Mr D.M. Thacker, who was also curator of White Castle at Llantilio Crossenny. Considerable help was also given by the Abergavenny Rotary Club.

The museum was housed in an annexe to what was known as Baker's Keep, which was erected in 1800 on a mound, where the first castle, a wooden structure, was built by Hamelin de Ballon in about 1090. Baker's Keep is well situated, occupying a commanding view of the surrounding countryside.

Lord Raglan performed the opening ceremony in July 1959 and congratulated members of the Museum Society on a wonderful achievement. He pointed out that a museum should have two purposes: 'It should preserve from destruction objects of historical and scientific interest. It should also be a place of instruction and interest for all visitors. At the same time, a museum must always be a cheerful and pleasing place to be in. This museum is such a place at present and I hope it will remain so.'

The collection includes various archaeological finds from the surrounding area, domestic items, prints, maps, paintings and photographs. The permanent displays include a Welsh Farmhouse kitchen c.1900, a Saddler's shop and the old shop of Basil Jones which closed in 1989 following the death of Jerry Jones, the last of Basil Jones's children. Members of the Jones family ran the small shop at 58 Cross Street for more than 80 years and the interior of the shop has been reconstructed in the museum complete with the same yellowed and cracked ceiling and walls.

The collection of items from the shop spans a period of nearly one hundred years and includes familiar items from a bygone age: Minerva Soap, Camp Coffee, Palethorpe's Sausages, Rowntrees Toffees and Chivers Jellies. There are tins and boxes dating from the late 1940s and early 1950s.

One of the oldest objects on display in the museum is a bronze axe-head which dates back to 500-1000 BC and was discovered on the slopes of the Blorenge by two schoolboys. Numerous Roman coins can be seen as well as two replicas of gold coins minted in the reign of Claudius AD 53 that were found in a field at Llanelen in 1962.

The collection also includes a triple-string harp which was made in Llanover and left in the will of Mrs Elizabeth Lilian Rosser of Brecon Road, Abergavenny. It had been in her family for 100 years and had been played before Queen Victoria at the Royal Albert Hall by her father John Elias Evans of Llandysul, Cardiganshire. Mrs Rosser was born at Llanover School House, where her mother was headmistress. She herself played the harp, violin, piano and organ and was organist at Llanover Church for many years.

The Welsh Border kitchen has been furnished to represent a North Monmouthshire or Breconshire farmhouse kitchen as it might have appeared in the 19th century. This reconstruction owes its existence to the acquisition of a massive stone fireplace and an oak 'stud and panel' partition, both Elizabethan and typical of the locality. They were rescued from two buildings in Tudor Street which were demolished under the Council's slum clearance scheme. The 'Farmhouse Kitchen' is immediately below the back room of the museum and it is of interest that the north-east wall is medieval being part of the outer bailey wall of the castle. The other walls and the stone flagged floor date from the early part of the 19th century.

The fireplace is filled by a cast-iron range and on the hobs stand a pair of iron grate ornaments in the form of Scottish Shepherds, a circular iron bakestone and a brass-handled kettle. At the side is a pot-crane or sway to which is hooked a griddle frying-pan. Above the mantleshelf, fixed to the chimney breast, is an oak rack which originally accommodated two meat spits.

The mantleshelf has a display of brass candlesticks, candlesnuffers, a horn lantern, a coffee grinder, an iron-stand, sheep shears and nippers for cutting up sugar 'loaves'. There are also three laundering irons - a common flat iron, a box iron and an Italian iron. From the mantleshelf brackets hang a spring balance, a steelyard, flesh and toasting forks, bellows and a copper warming pan.

Reconstruction of a Welsh Border Kitchen
Copyright Monmouthshire County Council, Abergavenny Museum

The handsome Welsh dresser came from Chapel Farm, Llanvapley and its shelves are filled with 'Willow Pattern' dishes and plates from some of the numerous factories which once produced this popular earthenware. Flowered copper-lustre and other jugs hang from the cup hooks and the dresser supports a large harvest jug, two 'Britannia metal' tea pots, a cheese dish and a mahogany tea caddy with compartments for India and China tea.

Until 1971 when it was taken over by Abergavenny Borough Council, the museum was run entirely by volunteers under the guidance of the Honorary Curator, Mr D. Thacker. Today it is operated by Monmouthshire County Council.

Charles I riding along Mill Street when he visited Abergavenny in 1645
Painting by Michael Blackmore

'Abergavenny did not play a very important part in the civil wars, though Charles I paid three visits to the town. The first occasion was on the 1st July 1645, when he came from Hereford to meet the commissioners of array of the Welsh counties. During his stay he was the guest of Mr James Gunter at the Priory, where he slept two nights.'

Sir Joseph Bradney
1906

Chapter Four
ST MARY'S PRIORY CHURCH

The Priory Church of St Mary is a magnificent old building, and the monuments have delighted many generations of antiquaries. This is the Westminster of South Wales, for the great ones of all ages are buried here: Norman, Plantaganet, Tudor, and Stuart, with carved wood, or marble, or freestone above them.

The Nationalist - a Victorian Publication

This large cruciform building with its central battlemented tower, was formerly a chapel to the old Benedictine Priory which stood outside the town, by the East Gate. The chancel formed the monastic church while the nave served as the parish church. The Priory was founded by Hamelin de Ballon in about 1087 and he endowed it to support a prior and twelve monks. It was dedicated to the Virgin Mary and attached as a cell to the abbey of St Vincent, just outside Le Mans in the French province of Maine. The foundation charter dates from the reign of William Rufus (1087-1100) and the first prior was Durand.

William de Braose, in the reign of King John, 'gave the tithes of his castle, i.e., of bread, wine, beer, cyder, all manner of flesh, fish, salt, honey, wax, tallow, and in general whatsoever should be brought thither and spent there, upon condition that the abbot and convent of St Vincent's in Mans should daily pray for the soul of King Henry the First, as also for the soul of him the said William, and the soul of Maud his wife.'

In 1300 Lord John Hastings became concerned about the evil conduct of the Prior, Fulk Gaston, and his four associates. He reported the matter to the Pope who ordered the Bishop of the Diocese to institute an inquiry; the result of which was that the Prior was dismissed and a monk, Richard of Bromwich was sent to the Priory to restore order. He was here for five years and was then recalled to Worcester.

When the monks decided to enlarge the priory church, they opened a large and lofty arch into the tower, but comparatively soon after they seem to have required further enlargement and built transepts, to which they cut the present archways. As they ornamented these with Ball and Flower they gave us accurate evidence of their 14th century date.

Well over 100 years later a further enlargement was required, and they built a double nave west of the Bell Tower, almost cutting away its only remaining wall in order to make an arch of similar size to that leading from the older church, and they took the very unusual course of departing from their own architectural style, and for appearance sake made this arch like its eastern forerunner.

It was very courageous to cut away all four walls of a tower of this immense weight, leaving it standing on four legs like an office stool. Certainly the monks did it successfully, for after many centuries their work stands in perfect condition. But of course they much weakened the Tower, so if the bells are to be rung they must be perfectly hung and all their fittings kept in perfect order.

In 1404 the priory was badly damaged when Owain Glyndwr sacked Abergavenny and at the time of its dissolution in 1543 there were only four monks and a prior (William Marley) living there, while its revenues amounted to a mere £59 4s per annum. At that time the priory possessed the manors of Hardwick and Llwynu with their demesne land

St Mary's Priory Church in 1905 with a horse and carriage waiting at the cab stand.
The wide porch and twin gabled west front were part of the 1881-82 restoration.

Present day view of the front entrance to St Mary's Priory Church

and chapels. The property also included the deer park on the Rholben and Sugar Loaf, together with the farms Porth y Parc (Gateway to the Park) and the Lodge Farm. From that time the priory church became the parish church of St Mary and today there are very few signs of the Benedictine priory that once stood here.

A Victorian writer once described St Mary's as the 'Westminster Abbey of South Wales', so impressed was he with its fine monuments, tombs and mural tablets. The church is indeed quite famous for its fascinating collection of monumental effigies of Marcher barons and memorials to some of the important families who once lived in this part of Gwent. These monuments are in fact older than the existing church for it was mainly rebuilt in the 14th century.

The chancel was the monastic church while the nave was the parish church and together they extend to a length of about 172 feet. The width of the nave and the north aisle is 45 feet, and of the choir and two side aisles 67 feet. Five arches separate the nave from the north aisle and they appear light and graceful when compared to the solid masonry of the tower arches, which are adorned with ballflower ornament and sculptured heads. The East End of the Nave inclines to one side and this is frequently the case in early Cruciform Churches, being said to be symbolical of Christ on the Cross.

The 14th century choir stalls

The **choir stalls** are a rare legacy from medieval times and were once separated from the nave by a rood screen. There are twelve on each side, carved in oak, dating from about 1380. They end with the stalls of the prior and sub-prior set under lofty pinnacles decorated with fine open tracery on their four sides. One stall is elavated and bears the name of 'Wynchester' (William of Winchester), a prior in 1493 and this is the place where he once sat. The misericords (hinged seats), which were raised to give some support to the monks as they stood through long services are plain. But little figures with shields are carved below the arms, and on the sloping tops of the tracery-panelled bench ends

57

are two carved dragons, a dog, and a lion. Poppy-heads adorn the other bench-ends. It is of interest that the choir stalls bear some 18th century graffiti carved during the time when they were used by the boys of Abergavenny grammar school for their weekly Welsh language service.

The seat of William of Wichester, who was prior of St Mary's in 1493

Carving of a dog on a bench end

Up until the end of the 18th century St Mary's consisted of a nave and north aisle and a chancel, the nave being separated from the north aisle by three Gothic arches. In 1828 the nave and its north aisle were made into one by the destruction of the ancient arches and columns. The Chancel was stripped of its leaded roof, lowered several feet, and slated. Unfortunately these alterations destroyed the Clerestory windows, traces of which can be seen from the garden. A lath and plaster ceiling was added, the East Window was made smaller than the original and a three decker pulpit was placed at the west end.

While these extensive renovations were being carried out at St Mary's Church, divine services were held at the old church (St John's) in the Free Grammar School. St Mary's was later re-opened by Bishop Copplestone.

In 1874 when the Reverend Canon Capel was vicar, a report on the condition of the church was requested from Sir Gilbert Scott RA. It stated:

'The church is one of much interest, dating for the most part from the second half of the 18th century; it has been altered at various times, the most conspicuous feature of a later date beeing the central tower; this rests on four arches of the original design, which possess much beauty. Externally though very plain, the tower is one of some dignity and is not by any means without architectural character. Few churches have suffered more from decay and injudicious repair than this. The whole of the west front (with the exception of the window is modern, and of the meanest design; the front of the north transept is only one degree better and the north aisle of the nave has lost its original buttresses and the other features it may have possessed, the windows only excepted. The whole of the eastern portion of the church has been left untouched by the restorer(!), but it is hard to say whether the contemplation of its almost ruinous condition, or the modern restorations of the remainder, is the more painful, The most outrageous treatment has, however, been reserved for the interior of the nave. It is doubtful whether any ancient church in the kingdom has been altered in so ruthless a manner and it is needless to say that the very first step towards restoration must be to bring it back to its original form.'

A committee was formed under the direction of the vicar and a large sum of money was obtained by subscriptions, bazaars and other means and the work of restoration was energetically taken in hand at a cost of £6,000. By 1882 the nave and north aisle had been completely restored to their original form, the eastern portion had been put into a state of repair and the opening services were held on the 14th December in that year.

The *Abergavenny Chronicle* (December 15, 1882) gave an account of the work carried out as follows:

St Mary's Restoration

'A great deal of work has been undertaken in the restoration of the nave and north aisle. It was commented that previously "The grand old edifice has been barbourosly treated, - stripped of its architectural beauties, and its interior fittings arranged in a manner revolting to the feelings of churchmen."

The noble pillars and arches had been destroyed, the nave and north aisle being thrown into one and an ungainly circular gallery was built around this portion, cutting across the arch of the tower between the nave and the transepts and chancel completely excluding the latter from participation in any service that was being carried on in the other portion of the church.

The seats or pews were of the horse-box fashion, much in favour with lounging christians who like to do service completely at their ease. All these objectionable features have been swept away and St Mary's Church once more has the appearance of belonging to the establishment.

The approach to the western entrance is also very much improved, the ground being lowered and cleared away, so as to bring the church more clearly into view.

Fortunately for the work of the restoration, the architect found in the eastern portion namely, the tower, transepts, choir, chancel, and side chapels, sufficiently distinct features to enable him to form an idea of the original style of the building; and on clearing away the stone flooring of the nave and aisle it became evident that these had at one time been separated by a handsome arcade; and so now, on entering the outer porch, we find it contains a central arch and two lateral porches, the central one having a wide and lofty moulded archway, with handsome wrought iron gates, and the side porches extensive and internal doorways, fitted with oak paneled doors, and three-light tracery headed windows. This is in place of the old porch with the staircase leading up to the gallery and organ loft.

Passing into the church, we find complete metamorphosis. There are two lofty roofs of handsome open constructions, one 48 feet and the other 54 feet up to the ridge. These are separated by a noble arcade of moulded pillars and arches. Corresponding in style with the other portions of the interior, rising to the height of 26 feet and finishing with labels, terminating at the extremities with carved heads. The roofs have a very elegant appearance.

The work of clearing away the old brick archway into the transept, brought to light the disused spiral stairs in the interior of the north-west pillar of the tower, leading up to the belfry and battlements of the tower.

The nave viewed from the west end to the chancel beyond

In place of the cold stone floor there is a neatly laid flooring of Gregory's burnettized wooded blocks; the alleys are laid with Godwin's encaustic tiles, and amongst these running the whole length of the nave and aisle, are handsome iron gratings masking the hot water pipes, by means of which the church is heated.

The pulpit is of beautiful Painswick stone, elegantly carved from the design of the architect, and is placed at the south-eastern end of the nave, at the steps leading up to the temporary chancel (in the space under the tower); while at the north-eastern corner of the chancel steps, is a handsome eagle lectern in brass.

The grand old Norman font, quite a curiosity in itself, is mounted at the western end of the collonade.'

In 1896, when F.W.G Whitfield was Vicar, the large chancel, which had been closed for many years, was restored, the choir and side chapels were opened for worship at a cost of £600.

The Windows

The window made by Frederick W. Cole in the north transept which was installed in 1954 as a memorial to Colonel Williams depicts a nativity scene with shepherds and kings. A modern window in the Nave sheds light on the stone pulpit and it illustrates the Acts of the Apostles. There are scenes of St Paul's Conversion and six full-length figures of other saints.

Window in north transept

This window in the Nave
illustrates the Acts of the Apostles

The east window of the Sanctuary was installed as a memorial
to Brigadier General Barnett-Barker, DSO of the Royal Welsh Fusiliers

The east window of the Sanctuary was extended to the original Norman arch after the First World War, when the arch was restored as a War Memorial. It is particularly fine and worth more than a casual glance. In the centre can be seen the Madonna sitting in a throne with the infant Jesus standing on her lap. On one side is St Christopher, walking out of a stream with young Jesus on his shoulder. St Michael stands with his scales on the other side and portrayed in the outer lights are the saints Luke and Mark. Below is a Crucifixion scene, with the cross formed from the foliage of a lily and small figures of angels, saints and martyrs can be seen in the tracery. This window was donated by Mrs Randle Barker as a memorial to her husband Brigadier General Barnett-Barker, DSO of the Royal Welsh Fusiliers, who fell at the second battle of the Somme in March 1918.

Local solicitor John G. Williams described this window in great detail in 1964 and he explains its symbolic features as follows:-

'The beautiful stained glass window above the altar is divided into 22 sections and these are set out in such a way as to be full of various numerical symbols. In the centre of the semi-circle at the top part of the arch is the prominent figure in red and gold of the Risen Christ which forms a triangle with the two lesser figures below to the left and to the right and which are enclosed with the same complex design in the stonework.

The equilateral triangle being the simplest and most perfect form of a geometrical figure is used throughout the world to signify the Divinity and in this case, it can be said to symbolise God the Father, God the Son and God the Holy Christ.

The whole window is divided into three main sections with two tall arches on either side of and separated by a tall section which widens out at the top into the shape of a flower bud, and contains the central figure of the Risen Christ.

These remind us of the number three which occurs so often in the New Testament as in the three wise men with their three symbolic gifts, three years of the ministry of Jesus and the three days he spent in the tomb.

Below the celestial figure depicted in the upper part of the window are five equal sections reminding us that the number five alludes to man with his five senses and the five digits on each of his limbs. Around the central figure in red and gold are six angels making a total of the mystic seven which recall the seven stages of creation, seven days of the week, seven angels, seven golden candlesticks and the seven stories that are mentioned in the Bible, and these seven sections are all contained in the top part of the centre of the three main sections.

The seven sections of the upper part of the centre main section when combined with the five lower sections mentioned above, make the complete number of 12, which can be compared with the 12 tribes of Israel, 12 Disciples, 12 jewels on the priest's breast-plate corresponding to the 12 zoadical constellations and the 12 gates of the New Jerusalem and its measurements in twelve or its multiples as described in the Book of Revelations.

When to the above 12 are added the remaining 10, to total 22, we have the number of letters in the mysterious Hebrew alphabet which is said to comprise of three mother letters, seven double letters and 12 simple letters.'

The Font

It is likely that this font was previously in St John's Church before it became a grammar school in 1542. The bowl is Norman and has a very fine specimen of early rope carving around its base. This style can be found in the work of the Herefordshire school of stone carvers. Fine examples of their work can be seen at Kilpeck just off the A465 on the way to Hereford.

The bowl is carved from a large piece of stone and of such a size to allow a baby to be totally immersed during baptism, which was once the custom. Also of interest is evidence on the rim of padlocks which once secured a lid and prevented the blessed water from being stolen for inappropriate purposes.

During the Commonwealth, when Oliver Cromwell was Protector of England, a Baptist minister named Abbot was placed in charge of St Mary's. He did not approve of infant baptism and had the font buried in the churchyard. In his favour he was the first man to keep registers of the church and these included births but not baptisms!

The font lay in the ground for two centuries until it was discovered in 1897 and restored to its proper place and use. A brass at the Victorian base bears the inscription, 'To the Glory of God and in Memory of a fondly loved Mother, this Font was restored Aug. 12th, 1897.'

The Royal Coat of Arms

On the right hand wall of the nave just inside the church can be seen the large and brightly coloured Royal Arms of Queen Anne, dated 1709. It was during the time of Henry VIII that Royal Arms were first displayed as a symbol of his supremacy over the Church of England after the Reformation.

The Organ

The organ is thought to be about 300 years old and the earliest known records of it date from 1734 when it was purchased for the Lord Mayor's Chapel in Bristol. It was acquired for St Mary's in 1830.

In 1998 the sudden collapse of the floor in the Lewis Chapel caused movement to the large organ which was then dismantled. During a thorough archeological investigation it was discovered that a medieval chamber had caused the floor to collapse. Even though it had been filled in, several bodies had to be reburied.

It was decided to reconstruct the organ and move it to the South Transept where it would be closer to the congregation. The project was supervised by the noted organ historian, Stephen Bicknell who also designed the new organ case and gallery. The building work was undertaken by William Drake of Buckfastleigh in Devon and Ian Ceney from Solihull was the consulting engineer.

Memorial Stones, Tablets and Brasses

There are many memorials in the church commemorating local people who have lived in or near Abergavenny during the passing centuries and the following are just a few examples.

A memorial stone in the floor at the end of the left side of the choir stalls bears the inscription 'To the memory of R. Gunter, died 4th March 1700'. The Gunters who are of French descent came over with William the Conqueror in 1066 and remained in this country. A branch of the family settled in Abergavenny and kept up the tradition of being associated with the king.

According to Camden's *Britannica* (1696) there was in the Herbert Chapel, between the monuments of Sir William ap Thomas and Sir Richard Herbert, of Coldbrook, a large flat sone set in the floor bearing the following inscription:

> 'Underneath this flat stone lieth the body of William Herbert of Coldbrook, Esquire, son and heir of Rees Herbert, Esquire, son and heirs of Sir William Herbert, Knight, son and heirs of Richard Herbert, Knight, which William Herbert had three wives, viz: Denise, Jane and Anne; by the first he had a son and daughter; by the second six sons and five daughters, which William departed out of this world, Anno Domini 1579.'

On this stone there was a brass plate with an engraving of William with the first wife on the right-hand and portraits of two children under her while on his left hand were his other two wives and under the first of them portraits of her eleven children.

Octavius Morgan in *Some of the Ancient Monuments in the Priory Church* (1872), comments that this stone was no longer to be found and he considered that its position was occupied by the gravestone of Sir James Herbert, of Coldbrook, who died on 6th June, 1709.

This flat sepulchral stone bears a defaced inscription commemorating the last male survivor of the Coldbrook branch of the Herbert family:

Here lieth the body of Sir James
Herbert, of Coldbrook, Knt.
Who departed this life ye 6th
Day of June, 1709 in the 65th year
of his age; having in his
Lifetime enjoyed in his native
Country all the chief honours
Due to his birth and quallity as a member
of Parliament, etc., as they were enjoyed
By his ancestors ever since the reign
of King Henry the first, he being the
nineteenth in descent from Herbert
Lord Chamberlain to the said King
and the ninth from Sir Richard Herbert
of Coldbrook, interred under the tomb
on his left side, who with his brother
William, first Earl of Pembroke of that
Name, was (valiantly fighting......
King Edward the Fourth, in that
Great quarrel between the Houses of York
and Lancaster) taken prisoner......
Banbury, and beheaded at Northampton
In the year 1469; both the said brothers
being sons of Sir William Thomas and
Gladice de Gam, who are interred under
the middle tomb; ye said Sir James
Herbert leveing behind him Lady Judith
Herbert, who deceased the 12th day
of November the same year. They
left behind them one daughter, his
sole heir, named Judith, married
To Sir Thomas Powell, of Broadway
In ye county of Carmarthen, Baronet,
To whom she hath born several sons
and daughters. Here also lyeth the body
of Sir James Powell, fifth son of ye said Sir Thos
Powell, grandson of ye said Sir James
Herbert, who died an infant ye 11th
Day of April, 1709.

A mural tablet on the south wall of the Nave commemorates a popular local surgeon who once lived in the town:

In memory of William Steel, for 55 years
a resident in this town, Died Nov. 11th,1861.
'A Surgeon, kind, skillful and courageous.'

Other members of this family who were also doctors and surgeons are buried in the churchyard at Llanfoist.

A brass on the chancel floor depicts Maurice Hughes, who was vicar from 1599 to 1631 and also Headmaster of King Henry VIII Grammar School. The Latin inscription reads:

> Under this stone lies buried the body of
> Morris Hughes, formerly a student of
> the University of Oxford, Vicar of
> Abergavenny and Headmaster of the free
> school of the same town, who died
> the 16th day of January in the year
> 1631, leaving behind him his wife
> Joan (the daughter of Rice Harbert,
> of Coldbrook, Esquire, son of Sir
> Richard Herbert, Knight), and one son,
> namely Robert Hughes, Clerk, and one
> daughter, namely Catherine Hughes.

A brass tablet in the floor of the choir is in memory of John Stephens, grocer, who died in 1662, and his son John Stephens, who died in 1672, The inscription reads:

HERE LYETH THE BODY OF IOHN STEPHENS
LATE OF THIS TOWN GROCER WHO DEPAR
TED THIS LIFE THE XVI DAY OF MARCH
1662
HERE LYETH ALSO THE BODY OF IOHN
STEPHENS OF THIS TOWN GROCER
SON OF THE FORESAID IOHN STEPHENS
WHO DEPARTED THIS LIFE THE XXIII TH
DAY OF MAY 1672
HERE LYETH ONE OF ABELS RACE
WHOM CAIN DID HVNT FROM PLACE TO PLACE
YET NOT DISMAID ABOVT HE WENT
WORKING VNTILL HIS DAIES WERE SPENT
NOW HAVING DONE HE TAKES A NAP
HERE IN OVR COMON MOTHERS LAP
WAITING TO HEARE TH BRIDEGROOM SAY
ARISE MY DEARE AND COME AWAY
Obiit Hen. Maurice xxx Die July 1652

The Tombs and Effigies

Discounting Westminster Abbey and the great cathedrals of the land, it is the parish church of All Saints, Harewood, Yorkshire which contains the largest collection of Medieval effigies in Britain with twelve dating from about 1419 to 1510. St Mary's Priory Church, Abergavenny comes a close second with ten figures which cover a much wider period, extending from the middle of the thirteenth century to about 1510. The collection not only includes effigies in alabaster but also in wood and free stone. This wealth of monuments was created because the great families who held the lordships of Abergavenny in the 13th and 14th centuries chose to be buried in the town's Priory Church.

The monumental effigies were first mentioned by Thomas Churchyard, following his tour of Wales in 1586. His poem on *The Worthiness of Wales* (published in 1587 and reprinted in 1776) was dedicated to 'Her Most Excellent Majesty Queen Elizabeth'. It gives a long description of the effigies, when they were in perfect condition, and when the church windows contained the arms, in coloured glass, of the families and Lords of Abergavenny.

Richard Symonds, who accompanied Charles I on a visit to Abergavenny, in 1645, comments in his *Diary of the Marchings of the Royal Army* (printed by the Camden Society in 1859) that the monuments were in good order and that he had seen in the Church a 'fair gilt Rood-screen and Old Organs.'

Gough in his edition of *Camden*, shows that they remained in the same condition the following year 1646, but from this date there is no authentic record, either as to when they were mutilated, or when they were repaired. It is probable that they were mutilated during the Civil War and restored in Charles II's reign. A parish list of charities dated 1690 records that Thomas Herbert of Usk bequeathed money for the repair of the Herbert Chapel monuments.

The Herbert Chapel was originally known as the South Aisle

In September 1974 the restoration of the Herbert Chapel was completed at a cost of £12,000 and the chapel re-dedicated in a service conducted by the Bishop of Monmouth, the very Reverend Derek Childs. The work carried out included replastering and redecorating. All the windows received new mullions and one which had been blocked up for at least one hundred years was completely replaced.

Undoubtedly, the greatest treasure of St Mary's can be seen in the north transept and is carved from a single piece of oak. It is a massive figure which is ten feet long with a large beard and dishevelled hair. At the bottom of the beard, where the curls part, is a small cavity, which may have once contained an ornamental relic.

This 10 ft recumbent figure representing Jesse asleep is the finest in existence

At one time this carving was believed to represent St Christopher, carrying, according to legend, the child Jesus across a river. However, it was later realised that it is in fact the remains of a Jesse tree and probably the finest in existence. It depicts Jesse asleep, reclining on his left side; his head covered with a cap. He reposes on a cushion supported by an angel. From the left side of his body grows the stem of a tree which is held or supported by the left hand of the figure, just above the tree which has been sawn off. It is a representation of the genealogy of Christ, from David, formed by a tree growing out of the body of Jesse, the father of David. Originally the tree would have been complete with branches where statuettes would have been positioned among the foliage to represent the various persons from whom he was descended. The highest statue of all would have been a representation of the Saviour. It was probably lying under the window of the Lewis Chapel when the poet Churchyard came here in 1587. He described it as 'a most famous worke in manner of a genealogy of kings, called the Roote of Jesse, which work is defaced and pulled down in pieces'.

It is such a remarkable relic that it has been valued at about £8m. At one time it would have been embellished with colourful paint and gilding to probably form the reredos to the High Altar, being part of the long dismantled screen between the Choir and the Lady Chapel, which occupied the present Chancel.

These Jesse figures are usually represented in windows, but they were occasionally made to form the Reredos of an Altar and this one is particularly interesting for it is possibly the only Jesse figure carved in wood in the world. It was probably pulled down at the time of the Reformation and the bulk of it used for firewood, The culprits were probably Colonel Fairfax and his Roundheads who tore down and burned most of the furnishings and antique woodwork in this church.

Another very fine wooden figure which is rated one of the finest in Britain depicts a young man of slender proportions and was originally beautifully coloured. For many years it was incorrectly identified as representing George de Cantelupe, the 10th lord of Abergavenny. but research undertaken by experts in recent times, has indicated that the person depicted is really **Sir John de Hasting**s, the 12th Lord of Abergavenny, who was responsible for the 14th century rebuilding of the church, including the tower. It interesting to trace his family background and the story of his descendants who also bore the title Lord of Abergavenny.

A wooden effigy depicting Sir John de Hastings, 12th Lord of Abergavenny

When the de Cantelupe line ended in 1273 with the death of George de Cantelupe, the lordship went to his sister Joan. She was married to Henry, Lord Hastings, and their son John succeeded as eleventh Lord. On coming of age in 1295 John Hastings was summoned to Parliament as Baron de Bergavenny, and appears to have distinguished himself as a faithful soldier in King Edward's wars in France, Scotland and Wales. He married Joanne the daughter of George de Cantelupe, but died in 1313 and was followed by his son John as twelfth lord of Abergavenny. On receiving a knighthood he became Sir John de Hastings who died in 1324 and was buried here in St Mary's Priory Church. His tomb would have originally stood in the centre of the choir.

He is depicted clad in a hauberk and hoods of chain mail covered with a long surcoat, his hands clasped in prayer and his left leg crossed over the right while his head rests on cushions and his feet on an animal which is deprived of the head, but which from the claws is known to be a lion. There are few wooden effigies in existence and being lighter than those carved in stone they were usually carried in the funeral procession.

A tomb slab which was found in the churchyard when it was being cleared and levelled in 1961 now lies on the floor of the Herbert Chapel. It bears dedication to Richard de Hastings and Sir John Hastings and was part of a 14th century tomb.

On the north side of the chancel are two reconstructed tombs, bearing effigies which have been identified as follows. The one bearing a shield on her breast is believed to represent **Eva de Braose** (the wife of William de Cantelupe) who died in 1246 It depicts her lying on a stone slab with her head resting on an oblong cushion and with a dog at her feet. Covering the body is a large shield bearing the arms of the Cantelupe family. This is unusual for generally only knights were carved with their shields.

Unknown Hastings lady

Nearby is the effigy of an unknown **Hasting lady** who is thought to have lived from 1350 to 1390 as suggested by her gown and hairstyle. A chain dangling from one hand and leading into her pocket suggests that she may have had a pet animal, stated by William Coxe to be a squirrel.

A popular story recalls how one day she was walking in the grounds of Abergavenny Castle when the squirrel ran from her. She followed it to the top of a wall, overbalanced and fell to her death.

Flanking the sanctuary are two aisles which have acquired the names of Lewis Chapel and Herbert Chapel and they contain some fascinating treasures. On the north side is the **Lewis Chapel** which takes its name from the 16th century monument of Dr David Lewis, the first Principal of Jesus College, Oxford and Judge of the High Court of Admiralty in the reign of Elizabeth I. He was born in Abergavenny and was the eldest son of Sir Lewis ap John (alias Wallis), Vicar of Abergavenny and Llantilio Pertholey. He took his father's Christian name 'Lewis' as his permanent surname, as was the practice at that time.

He was elected a Fellow of All Souls, Oxford, in 1541, and became the Member of Parliament for the county of Monmouthshire in 1554. In 1571 he became the first Principal of Jesus College, Oxford, and in 1575 was appointed a Commissioner of the High Court of Admiralty, which post he held till the time of his death. His many interesting law cases included the examination of Martin Frobisher - suspected of piracy in 1576, and three years later the trial of John Hawkins accused of slave trading.

Dr David Lewis, the first Principal of Jesus College, Oxford died in 1584

In 1573 he purchased the mansion and manor of Llandewi Rhydderch which continued in the possession of his descendants till the middle of the 18th century, when it was sold to the trustees of the will of Charles Williams of Caerleon and united to the Coldbrook estate. It is now known as Llandewi Court.

Dr David Lewis died unmarried on Monday April 27, 1584, at the College of Doctors of Commons, London at the age of 64. His body was brought back to Abergavenny to be buried here. Anthony Wood, in his *Athenae Oxoniensis*, written in 1691, says 'His body was brought down to be buried in the great church at his native place and now lies under a very fair monument, having thereon the ensigns of the Admiralty curiously carved but without inscription. This monument was built by him in his lifetime.'

It seems very probable that the monument was constructed by the Herefordshire sculptor, John Gildon, during Dr Lewis's lifetime as all the curious details have obviously been very carefully considered and no ordinary sculptor would have been likely to know them without his special instruction. The front of the tomb is ornamented with an arcade of three arches. In the centre arch is the anchor (the badge and ensign of the Admiralty) the ring, crossbar and flukes have, however, been broken away. The spaces around the anchor are filled with oak leaves, which no doubt refer to the oak, of which our ships were then built. This arch has been disfigured (probably by the actual builder of the tomb) with the words 'John Glydon made this tombe.' In the arch on the left side are three clasped books, two standing upright, with the third resting upon them and in front of them is a skull, now partly broken away. Around the whole is a wreath or scroll with the legend EN GLORIA MVNMDI, while the right panel bears a figure of the Serjeant of the Court of Admiralty carrying the official silver oar of the Court. At the head of the tomb are the arms of Wallis.

The effigy of Dr David Lewis shows him dressed in the habit of a High Court of Admiralty judge, complete with ruff and three chains. On his head is a round flat cap, encircled with an ornamental band indicating his Doctorate of Civil Law at Oxford. His head rests on a small clasped book, which in turn rests on a larger book and beneath that is a cushion. The hands are raised in prayer and his feet rest upon what appears to be the hull of a ship.

The tomb of **Sir Andrew Powell** (1565-1631) bears the effigies of himself and his wife Margaret. Born at Trostrey, near Usk, he became in 1607, one of the two judges of the Brecon circuit, for the counties of Glamorgan, Breconshire and Radnor. The recumbent figures are habited in the costume of the latter part of the reign of James I and the beginning of that of Charles I. Sir Andrew is wearing a ruff, a slashed doublet, breeches and a long gown. Judge Powell's wife, in her will, styles herself 'Margaret Powell, late of

Sir Andrew Powell and his wife Margaret

Dawkins, in the Parish of Bergavenny,' and instructs that '20s issuing out of her lands called y Spite, should be paid yearly towards the reparacion of the Chapel in St Mary's Church, Bergavenny, called the Herbert's Chapel, where a tomb then prepared for her was situate.' Margaret Powell is also commemorated by a tablet at Llangattock-nigh-Usk.

Over the tomb is a brass with a Latin inscription, part of which reads: 'Lately I was a judge, now waiting before the tribunal of a judge I am in fear. It is now that I am being judged.'

The **Herbert Chapel** on the south side of the sanctuary was thus named (in 1645) after members of the Herbert family who are buried here and it contains some of the finest monumental tombs in Britain and they reflect the long history of this historic town. Knights and their ladies who once rode with heads held high through the streets of Abergavenny lie here in effigy, crosslegged, with hands pressed together in prayer, while beneath the men's helmets their vacant eyes gaze towards the roof of the church.

Sir Richard Herbert the second son of William ap Thomas lies here beside his wife Margaret, a daughter of Thomas ap Gruffydd. Her brother was Sir Rhys ap Thomas who helped to place Henry VII on the throne. Represented in a full suit of Mail, Sir Richard Herbert was the son of Sir William ap Thomas (Sir Richard changed his name to Herbert) and Gwladys, daughter and heiress of Sir Dafydd Gam.

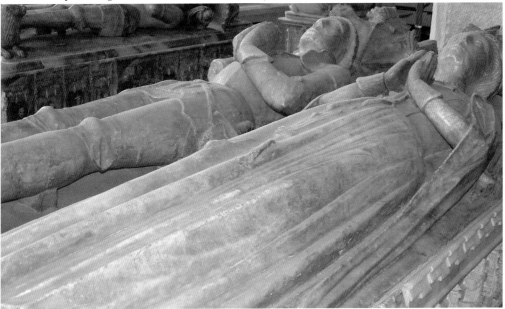

Sir Richard Herbert and his wife Margaret

On account of his stature, Sir Richard Herbert was known as Richard Hir (the tall) and he is depicted here with his feet resting on a lion, which is significant for he was renowned for his feats of strength. During the Wars of the Roses he fought under the emblem of the White Rose and the heroism that he displayed at the Battle of Edgecote (1469) was vividly described by his great-great-grandson, Lord Herbert of Chirbury in his autobiography: 'With his pole-axe he passed and re-passed twice through the enemy's army and killed with his own hand 140 men.'

Unfortunately when Sir Richard's soldiers were on the point of gaining an important victory, they mistook a small corps of the army for the advanced guard of the Lancastrian side, under the Earl of Warwick. They panicked and fled on all sides while Sir Richard Herbert and his brother Sir William, the first Earl of Pembroke bravely remained on the field of battle.

They were captured and taken in triumph to Banbury where they were sentenced to death the following day. Sir William begged that Richard, his younger brother be spared, saying, 'Let me dye, for I am olde, but save my brother, who is yonge, lusty and hardye, mete and apt to serve the greatest prince of Christendom.'

But, on the order of George, Duke of Clarence and Nevill, Earl of Warwick the two brothers were beheaded. Sir William was subsequently buried in Tintern Abbey and the headless body of Sir Richard was brought back to his home at Coldbrook Park for burial in St Mary's Priory Church. During the Battle of Edgecote there were no less than 400 men from Breconshire and Monmouthshire killed.

Sir Richard's wife Margaret is depicted in a long robe; her head rests on a cushion supported by two angels which unfortunately have been mutilated, and at her feet lie two dogs. The sculptor has made her effigy an impressive size, for at 6 feet 4 inches, she has been given the same bulk and length as her husband!

The effigies of **Sir William ap Thomas and his second wife Gwladys** are thought to have been carved in about 1460 and the armour depicted on Sir William is certainly of that date. He was the fifth son of Thomas the son of Gwilym (of Perth-hir in the parish of Rockfield) and Gwenllian, daughter of Howell Fychan of Llanvetherine, master sergeant of Usk Castle. In the tiny church at Llansantffraed, a few miles outside Abergavenny, can be seen a large stone inscribed with the names of many of William ap Thomas's family, beginning with Thomas ap Gwilym ap Jenkin who had married Maud the daughter of Sir John Morley of Llansantffraed. This stone was erected in 1624 by a descendant and the long link with the family is continued today through the Herberts.

Sir William ap Thomas and his wife Gwladys

All the Herberts trace their descent from this man who was twelfth in descent from Herbert Camerarius, one of William the Conqueror's companions, who held some Hampshire manors from the king.

The first wife of William ap Thomas was Elizabeth Bloet, heiress of Raglan, a sub-division of Usk, created by Richard Strongbow in 1174 for her father Sir Walter Bloet in return for help given in his Irish expedition. Through marriage, Elizabeth became Lady Berkeley and in 1399 Henry IV had conferred on the Berkeleys, the town and castle of Raglan. Sir James Berkely died in 1405 and it was shortly afterwards that his widow married William ap Thomas.

In 1415 William ap Thomas took a band of Gwent bowmen to the Battle of Agincourt and fought courageously beside Henry V. He must have looked quite outstanding in his suit of blue armour for he was referred to by his countrymen as 'Y Marchog glas o Went' - the blue knight of Gwent.

Five years after William's return to Raglan his wife died and he then married Gwladys the daughter of Dafydd Gam. She was a beautiful lady with raven hair and was known as Gwladys Ddu (Dark Gwladys). Both her father and her first husband Roger Vaughan of Bredwardine, were killed during the Battle of Agincourt, whilst bravely saving the life of Henry V. They were knighted as they lay dying on the battlefield.

Gwladys had just one son named Roger from her marriage with Sir Roger Vaughan but seven children were born as a result of her marriage with Sir William ap Thomas, who was knighted at Leicester on Whitsunday in 1426 by Henry VI. This young monarch must have had great difficulty holding the sword to perform the ceremony, being just 4 years of age!

In 1431 Sir William ap Thomas was made Steward to Lady Beauchamp, owner of the lordship of Abergavenny, to whom his wife was related by marriage. In 1432 he became the owner of the Manor of Raglan, after acquiring it from his stepson James who subsequently became Lord Berkeley.

During the next thirteen years Sir William constructed the earliest surviving part of Raglan Castle, a detached hexagonal keep of great strength. It is five storeys high, with walls 10 feet thick and is surrounded by its own moat. The yellow lichened surface of the stonework has resulted in it being known as the 'Yellow Tower of Gwent'. He also established a Red Deer Park at Llantilio Crossenny.

When Sir William ap Thomas died in London in April 1446, his body was brought back to Abergavenny for burial in the Herbert Chapel of St Mary's Priory Church and his effigy shows him dressed in armour with his feet resting on a lion, a symbol of courage and strength.

Soon afterwards, Gwladys left Raglan Castle and went to live with her eldest son, Sir Roger Vaughan at Tretower Court, where the addition of the western range of apartments, a hall and solar had no doubt been constructed with her comfort in mind.

Gwladys died in 1454 and an indication of her popularity was demonstrated by the procession of 3,000 knights, noblemen and peasants who followed her funeral from Coldbrook House (home of her son Sir Richard Herbert) to St Mary's Church. In her funeral elegy written by the celebrated Welsh poet, Lewis Glyn Cothi, she was termed 'Seren-y-Fenni' (The Star of Abergavenny).

Her effigy depicts her in a close garment covered with a loose robe, and her head rests on a cushion supported by two small figures; at her feet are the figures of two dogs, who hold the ends of her mantle.

William ap William the eldest son of William and Gwladys succeeded to the estates and became Ist Earl of Pembroke. He was commanded by the King to discontinue the Welsh custom of changing the surname at every descent and to assume the name of Herbert, in honour of his ancestor Herbert Fitz-Henry, Chamberlain to Henry I.

On the south side of the chapel in a canopied recess is an effigy of **Sir Richard Herbert of Ewyas** who died in 1510. He was a natural son of Sir William Herbert, the first Earl of Pembroke and this monument is possibly the finest in the church. It was his descendants who generously gave him the title of knight and the lordship of Ewyas, although he did not have the right or claim to either.

Sir Richard Herbert of Ewyas

His recumbent effigy, with clasped and uplifted hands, lies on the top of an alabaster tomb. He wears plate armour, his bare head rests on a helmet and his feet on a lion. On the front of the tomb are nine canopied niches, all but the centre one containing a seated shield-bearer.

Above are displayed the Herbert and Cradock arms. Sir Richard's wife was Margaret, the daughter of Sir Matthew Craddock, Knight of Swansea, Glamorganshire. At the back of the recess is an alabaster carving of the Assumption of the Virgin and on either side is a sculptured group, three men in armour and a woman who is represented ascending to heaven. She is supported by the remains of an angel under her feet and there are several others hovering about her.

A man in armour and a woman are represented kneeling below, in adoration of the central figure. These are probably Sir Richard Herbert and his wife while on either side are their three sons in armour and a daughter kneeling. Originally there was a long narrow piece of brass bearing an inscription, fixed on the edge of the monument.

It is of interest that Sir Richard Herbert on July 22, 1509, having served as a gentleman usher to Henry VII, was appointed Constable of 'Bergavenny Castle' by Henry VIII, who then held the lordship and castle of Abergavenny in his own hands. The appointment was made even though the castle was not inhabited at this time.

During restoration work the figure of Sir Richard was removed and a figure (known as a beadsman) of a black cloaked Benedictine monk, holding rosary beads and praying for Richard Herbert's soul was revealed. A replica of this remarkable find can now be seen exhibited alongside the monument.

Replica of the beadsman

At the centre of the west end of the chapel is the tomb and effigy of **Sir Lawrence de Hastings**, 13th Lord of Abergavenny, who died in 1348. He is shown as a reclining figure in mail with a short sheathed sword at his left side. Beneath his feet is a representation of a bull (without horns) which is thought to signify that he was a strong and brave man. Also it is relevant that a bull's head was the crest of the Hastings family.

Sir Lawrence de Hastings, 13th Lord of Abergavenny

Born in Abergavenny Castle in 1320, Lawrence was just six years of age when he inherited the lordship and consequently the castle and estates were in the hands of the Crown during his minority. He was a great favourite of King Edward III and according to one source he was summoned to Parliament in 1338. He came of age the following year, and on the 13th of October was created Earl of Pembroke. Following his grandfather's example in his devotion to the Crown he participated in the wars of the day. In 1339 he was in the train of Edward III in the abortive expedition into Flanders, and five years later he took to Brittany a retinue of 12 knights, 45 squires, 2 bannerets, 60 men-at-arms, and 100 mounted bowmen, most of whom were Welshmen from Gwent.

He afterwards served in Gascony under Henry Duke of Lancaster and Lord of Monmouth, from 1344-47. At the triumphant siege of Calais in 1347 he captured the entire French fleet near Cretoy, returning home a hero, but fell victim to the Black Death and died the following year, becoming the last Lord of Abergavenny to be buried in St Mary's Priory Church.

John, the son and heir of Sir Lawrence de Hastings was only one year old when his father died and it was Lawrence's widow, Agnes who then held the lordship for twenty years. John became the fourteenth Lord of Abergavenny when he came of age in 1369. He served in Aquitaine under the Black Prince, and in 1372 was appointed Lieutenant of Aquitaine. Whilst in command of the English fleet he was defeated off La Rochelle by France's Spanish allies. He was kept a prisoner till 1373 and then ransomed, but died at Calais on his way home.

His castles and lordships of Abergavenny and Chepstow were then seized by the Crown, his son John, being only two years of age. He was initially buried in the Church of the Friar Preachers at Hereford, but his body was afterwards removed to the Grey Friars at Newgate in London.

His son and heir, also named John, at the age of five, bore a sword at the coronation of Richard II, but twelve years later, just before gaining his inheritance, he was tragically killed at a tournament at Woodstock, by his best friend, Lord St John. The title of Lord of Abergavenny died with him.

His widow Phillipa, daughter of Edmund Mortimer, Earl of March subsequently remarried and the barony of Abergavenny remained in the hands of her family, until the beginning of the 15th century when an heiress of the Beauchamp family married Sir Edward Nevill, youngest son of Ralph, Earl of Westmoreland, which commenced the long descent of the Nevill lords of Abergavenny.

In the window recess to the south of Sir Lawrence's tomb is one presumed to be that of his illegitimate brother, **Sir William de Hastings**, who died a bachelor in 1349. His legs are crossed and his feet are shown resting on a greyhound.

The tomb of William Baker and his wife Johanna

In the north aisle of the Herbert Chapel, behind the choir stalls, is a magnificent 17th century monument to **William Baker**, steward of Lord Abergavenny, and his wife Johanna, sister of Dr David Lewis. They are carved in relief, kneeling at a double desk in a recess flanked by black Corinthian columns. The Latin inscription reads:

HIC IN CHRISTO QVIESCENS GVLIEMUS BAKERUS, AR.,
IRENARCHIA IUSTITLAE VINDEX, ILLIBATAE INTEGRITATIC, Etc.;
OB. 30 Oct., 1648.

Restoration of the St Mary's Church Monuments

A small committee was set up on 30 November, 1991 to examine ways of restoring the unique set of monuments in this church. A detailed survey of the tombs and effigies revealed that an urgent programme of restoration would have to be undertaken if they were to survive far into the next century. All the monuments would have to be dismantled and protected against rising damp It was estimated that the cost of this work was likely to be in excess of £300,000.

The St Mary's Church Monuments Restoration fund was set up and registered as a charity and in the first year £12,000 was raised. Cadw, the historic monuments group then offered to match pound for pound all funds raised for the project. Initially a target of £125,000 was set, but unforeseen problems such as the need to lower the floor in the Herbert Chapel and put in steps meant that the target had to be raised to £330,000. Further money came from the European Commission, the National Heritage Memorial Fund, and the Foundation for Sport and the Arts.

Restoration of the monuments commenced in January 1994 with conservator Michael Eastham working on the stone and alabaster monuments in the Herbert Chapel while Carol Galviv started on the Jesse tree and the wooden effigy of Sir John Hastings. It was an enormous task to restore all of the monuments so in due course the number of conservators in the team was increased and extra specialists brought in when needed.

Tremendous support was given to the project by local people, businesses and societies, local authorities, some corporate bodies and institutions and visitors to the Priory Church. The Fund also received grants of £5,000 from the Charities Aid Foundation Grants Council, £5,000 from the Pilgrims Trust, £24,000 (including a tax refund of £8,400) from the Foundation for Sport and the Arts. A substantial amount of money was also provided by the National Heritage Memorial Fund.

The Tower and its Peal of Eight Bells

The embattled tower is mainly in the Decorated and Perpendicular styles. It contains a peal of ten bells and their sound is particularly fine when heard on a still summer evening. They have an interesting history which commences at the dissolution of the monasteries in 1536-39, when the parishoners bought four bells. The heaviest one (the Tenor) was recast in 1603, the third recast in 1666 and the treble recast in 1706. A fifth bell was added in 1835 and a sixth in 1845. Two more were hung to commemorate Queen Victoria's Golden Jubilee in 1887. In April of that year it was reported in the *Abergavenny Chronicle* that:

> 'The rehanging of the bells, together with the additional bells has now been completed, and on wednesday next they will be rung by a team of bell-ringers who are coming over from Bristol for the purpose. They will ring a flourish in the morning and after lunch a peal of changes. There were originally six bells in the tower, the tenor was very poor and thin, though a pre-Reformation bell. The whole peal has been re-hung and re-fitted. Two treble bells have been added, and a bell from St John's Church, which was fortunately in the same key, has been added in place of the old second. With the exception of the two new bells, all the bells in the tower appear to have been cast at different times.'

In 1946 the peal of bells and its supports was replaced at a cost of £2,700 in thanksgiving for the end of the Second World War. Several of the bells were recast at Loughborough Foundry and the peal was increased to ten. The old sixth, a pre-Reformation bell dating from 1308 was kept back as being of antique value and it can now be seen inside the church.

The bells of St Mary's were taken down for recasting in 1947

The central tower was strengthened and in the summer of 1948 the bells were rehung by Tom Dexter and Jack Humphreys. Tom had previously rehung the Great Peter bell, weighing 10 3/4 tons at York Minster in 1926.

In 1958 a brass tablet commemorating the restoration of the bells was erected by the bell-ringers and their friends. It can be seen inside the church on the right hand side of the doorway to the stone stairs.

The 50th anniversary of the recasting of the service of the dedication of the bells by the Bishop of Monmouth, Bishop Morris was marked in August 1998 with the ringing of a full peal of the bells, one of six allowed each year.

Such is the fame of the bells of St Mary's that campanologists from all over the world visit the church to ring the bells which are said to be a 'perfect ten', as a result of their ideal weight and draft (length of rope).

Bell ringers of St Mary's preparing for action

The Garden of Ease

The last burial in St Mary's churchyard took place in 1855 and for many years the church had received no income for its upkeep so it was not possible to maintain the ground properly. It was decided in 1960 that it should be converted into a garden for enjoyment by the people of Abergavenny and in July of the following year it was officially opened as a Garden of Ease.

Abergavenny Rotary Club presented the Council with several seats for use in the garden which was described in the *Abergavenny Chronicle* as 'a masterpiece of horticultural achievement that would be appreciated by all who visit Abergavenny.'

St Mary's Churchyard was converted into a Garden of Ease in 1960

The large block of stone was once the base of a preaching cross. It probably stood at 'The High Cross' at the top end of Cross Street where four streets meet outside the Town Hall. The stone is also reputed to have been a tethering point for bull baiting, once a popular sport in the town.

The Old Priory

Founded in about 1090 by Hamelin de Balon for monks of the Benedictine Order, known as the Black Monks, St Mary's Priory stood beside the river Gavenny from which the town takes its name. The monastery and its manor was known as Monktown or Monkswick, which probably explains the name of nearby Monk Street and it lay just outside the east gate of the medieval town wall.

The Priory revenue of about £129 5s 8d per annum was obtained from a wood named Coed y Prior under the Blorenge, from Chapel Farm at the foot of the Deri, and lands on the Deri, Rholben and Sugar Loaf as well as some around and adjoining the Priory called the Priory Meads and Monks' field. The Priory also owned the tithes of the rectories of Llanfihangel Crucorney, Llandewi Rhydderch, Llanelen, Llandewi Skirrid and Bryngwyn, and part of the tithes of Llanwenarth.

St Mary's and the Priory House in the 1960s

During the last century of its existence there was a steady decline in the fortunes of the Priory. In 1534 the Prior, three monks and 50 inmates of the Priory gave their signatures to the Declaration of Royal supremacy in spirituals as well as temporals and that was previous to the Dissolution. When the Act came into effect there were only four monks and the Prior William Marley.

In the 1542 Charter it is stated that the Priory passed to the Crown on 4th February 1536. The Priory fishponds were sold by the King in 1536, subject to a rent of three groats per annum to be paid to the Lord of Abergavenny. These ponds were subsequently drained and several tenements and gardens were made on the area, separating the road to the mill. All of the Priory's possessions, amounting to £80 per annum were granted to James Gunter of Breconshire in 1546 with the following qualification:

> 'All and each of the premises are let to William Herbert of the household of the Lord most serene majesty, the present Lord King Henry VIII, esquire, by Indenture given under seal of the same lord king in the Court of Augmentations of the Revenues of the Crown on the 16 May in the 29th year of his reign (1537). To have to the same William and his assigns for the term of 21 years.'

The Priory and certain fields were only a small part of the total grant to Gunter, and the whole appears to have consisted of property in occupation. In addition to the portion leased to William Herbert were 'the rent and farm of the Manors of Hardwick, Llyon dee, Villa Monachorum and Llanelen, including various lands, tenements, meadows, feedings and pastures, fishponds and fisheries in the tenure of various persons both by the bounty of the Court and at will, and by indentures for a term of life or of years, by payment on the feasts usual there in equal parts, rendering therof per annum.'

Also mentioned were 'a certain grain mill, called Prior's Mill with its appertanances, let to Phillips, Miller by indenture for a term of years paying per annum £13 13s 4d' and 'two other mills, in the parish of Abergavenny, of which one is for grain, now or lately in the tenure of Watkyn Draper at a rental of 5/- per annum and the other for fulling, with garden, now or lately in the tenure of John David at 20/- per annum.'

It would appear that the entire landed estate of the Priory passed to James Gunter in the nature of an investment, and that he occupied the Priory when he could get possession from William Herbert, the lessee. If he did not get possession before the end of William Herbert's lease, then he would not have enjoyed his occupation of the Priory for long. The lease expired on 16th May, 1558 and James Gunter died on the 15th August that year.

King Charles I stayed in the house for two nights as the guest of the Gunters, when he came to Abergavenny on 1st July, 1645, from Hereford. This journey would have been via Grosmont, for the road via Pandy was not made until the 19th century. When he reached Campston, then the seat of James Prichard, he was entertained to dinner, and while there he knighted Sir Henry Lingen, the commander of the Royalist forces in Herefordshire. Continuing his journey, he passed through Llanvihangel Crucorney, but did not stop there, and reached the Priory House, in the evening.

An enquiry was held in the hall of Priory House, concerning those who were styled the chief hinderes of the 'Royal Cause in Monmouthshire'. Specially named as being opposed to the King were Sir Trevor Williams of Llangibby, Thomas Morgan of Machen and Tredegar and Colonel Henry Herbert of Coldbrook. These were described as being 'creatures of the Earl of Pembroke'. Colonel Herbert of Coldbrook was a determined parliamentarian, and did well out of it, for when Raglan Castle was surrendered, he was given the furniture and other spoils in the castle.

Sir Trevor William's fears and entreaties so prevailed upon the King that he and his comrades were not convicted of high treason, but were confined for a while within the walls of Abergavenny Castle. Charles in due course forgave them and the story goes that the Marquis of Worcester, with whom the King was staying at Raglan Castle, told his majesty bluntly that his great clemency might win him a crown in heaven, but that was no way to secure the crown of England.

It was a Gunter in the late 17th century who virtually rebuilt the building which was once the living quarters of the Benedictine monks. The Priory House was built from the materials of the monastic buildings and in the back part of the house, against the south wall of the church were portions of arches and ancient walling. From this it could be ascertained that there was once a south transept to the church.

The family of Gunter was a very ancient one in this county and in Breconshire. The first of them was Sir Peter de Gunter, a Norman, one of the companions of Bernard de Newmarche in his conquest of Brycheiniog. The name really is Gaunt d'orla (golden gauntlet), the arms being sable, a chevron between three gauntlets, which can still be seen in the Gunter memorials of the Priory Church. The seat of the Gunters in Breconshire was called after them Tregunter.

The first James Gunter, the grantee of the Priory, was the grandson of a William Gunter who had settled in Abergavenny as tenant of Porth-y-parc, whose father Lewis was the second son of William Gunter of Gilstone in Breconshire, the head of the family. James Gunter no doubt resided in the quarters occupied by the monks, as did his successors till the late part of the seventeenth century when a storey was added making the building higher than the nave and it concealed a great part of the church when viewed from the south side. He was a Member of Parliament for Monmouthshire, as were some of his his descendants.

Six generations of the family resided at Priory House till James Gunter, MP., who died suddenly in the House of Commons in 1712. His only child was a daughter who married George Milbourne of Wonastow, near Monmouth and brought the Priory to her husband. Their son Charles married Lady Martha Harley, daughter of the Earl of Oxford. Mary the only child of the marriage, became the wife of Thomas Swinnerton of Butterton in Staffordshire; their daughter and co-heir married Charles Kemeys Tynte and to this family (of Cefn Mably, Glamorgan), the Priory and the great tithes of the Parish passed.

It was in the latter part of the 18th century that the house was converted into a building with a frontage of 17 windows. It contained a fine staircase, oak panelling and valuable tapestries. Both Charles I and Charles II are said to have stayed there and one room was known as the King's Bedroom. On the staircase landing on the second floor was an ancient bed-frame which was said to have been the bed on which they had slept.

In the 18th century the house was occupied at times by the Milbornes and Thomas Swinnerton occasionally came there until he died in 1795. It was then put to a variety of purposes. In 1822-23 it became a school for young ladies run by Mary Peach and from about 1830 to 1872 it was a classical school conducted by Ralph Rutherford at which many of the inhabitants of Abergavenny received their education. Mr Rutherford was the father of J. T. Rutherford who became a repected clerk to the Abergavenny Urban District Council in 1899. The building was later used as a private residence and a boarding house.

By 1925 the Priory was empty and it was then purchased by the Parish from Lord Wharton who sold the property with the condition that the house should be used only for Church purposes. The architect W.D. Caroe advised that only the ground floor should be used, as the staircase and first floor was not fit for use.

The ground floor rooms were thus used for Church purposes from 1925 to 1940, but during those years a large sum of money had to be spent on the building because of its dilapidated condition. In 1936 tie-rods had to be put in the top floor because the walls were getting out of the perpendicular.

In 1940 the military authorities requisitioned the building for billeting American troops and after war ended the deterioration had become so great that only one room could be used for Church purposes. Such was the fate of many fine buildings used to accommodate soldiers.

The building was now in an abandoned state and a cow had even been seen looking out of one of the ground floor windows, while another was meandering through the open front door. It was tragic to see the fine 17th century panelling smashed in by the horns of the cattle, and the magnificent staircase half collapsed from dry rot.

It was unfortunate that some use could not have been found for this historic building and it could possibly have been an ideal location to accommodate the often discussed local museum. The conversion of the building into flats or its reversion to a former use as a hotel or guest house would at least have been better than demolition.

The Parochial Church Council wanted a church hall but the Priory which was of great length, yet only 20 feet wide, had been found difficult to adapt for church purposes. The Parochial Church Council had discussed the question of its use for years, and it was thought that the Priory could be widened by ten feet so as to make a hall which would hold about 300 people. But this would cost between £11,000 and £13,000, so it was considered cheaper to pull the building down and build a new hall altogether. It was decided to restore the transept which connects the Priory with the church and pull down the house, but leaving a wall over 7 feet high which would form a courtyard.

In February 1952 it was announced that the historic priory of Abergavenny which had been founded soon after the Norman Conquest for monks of the Benedictine Order was to be demolished at a cost of £150, because of its state of disrepair and no funds were available because over £5000 was needed for repairs to the parish church of St Marys.

The Mayor, Councillor J. S. Bousfield felt that it was a drastic step to pull the whole of the Priory down. Would it not be possible, he asked, to remove the top half of the building, and use the bottom half for church purposes, or alternatively rent it out and thus bring in some form of income for the Church and possibly the medieval part could be preserved.

Mr George Goodwin was of the opinion, however that it would be a good thing if the Priory was 'got out of the way' for the estimated demolition cost of £150. Dr N. R. Phillips (People's Warden) commented, 'It might be said it is a sacrilege to pull the Priory down, but if we don't pull it down it will probably fall down.'

When the mansion was finally demolished in 1953, the cost of the work was paid from the money granted by the government at the end of the war as compensation for damage caused by troops bilelted in the building.

The Priory Centre

Adjoining the Priory Church is the Priory Centre which was opened by HRH The Prince of Wales in 2000. It is proving to be an excellent amenity for the Church and Community and provides Conference Facilities, Exhibition space and Recreational areas. There is also a Licensed bar available for functions and reception.

The Tithe Barn

Close to the west side of St Mary's Priory Church is a large tithe barn in which was stored the tithes, or tenths, of the annual produce from monastic properties. The original barn was burnt by Owain Glyndwr's troops in 1404. Scorch marks from this fire were discovered during excavations of the site, prior to restoration work starting, by archaeologist George Nash.

The barn was later rebuilt with a pitched thatched roof and three large openings for waggon access. In the 17th century the building became a stable block for the Manor House which was built on the site of the Priory.

It is about 120 feet long, with great beams in its original gabled roof, narrow lancet windows in the lower walls, and roughly fashioned round windows in the gables. Of interest high up on the wall facing the church car park can be seen stone ledges and nesting holes for pigeons kept by the monks. Similar holes are also to be seen on the west wall of the south transept of the church. The birds were kept to supply eggs and provide a valuable source of meat in the winter when few cattle were kept due to the shortage of feed. Another source of food was in the fishponds which were situated in the area of the present day bus station. There appears to have been a date-stone in the east wall, but erosion by the weather rendered it undecipherable and it is impossible to say exactly when the barn was erected.

The Tithe Barn before restoration

The restored Tithe Barn was officially opened by HRH Prince Charles in October 2008

In about 1645 the old tithe barn became a theatre which was visited by the best companies of the day. Many of the names of the travelling players could at one time be seen crayoned on the oak beams.

In the 1770s Roger Kemble (father of the renowned actress Sarah Siddons), the head of a company of strolling players often played at any available theatre between Brecon, Monmouth and Bath and afterwards their tours were extended to Cheltenham and  Leamington. The Barn Theatre in Abergavenny was often used by this touring company and as much as £50 a night would be taken when 'Macbeth' or 'Hamlet' was produced. This theatre was the scene of many of Sarah Siddon's successes before she brought the world to her feet at Drury Lane in London. It closed as a theatre in about 1820 and became a timber warehouse.

The tithe barn has had a multitude of owners and uses through the centuries yet the name has remained the same. It has been a theatre, a merchant's store, a bark store for the tanners of the town, a discotheque, a boutique, a computer workshop, a furniture showroom and a carpet warehouse.

Sarah Siddons

In September 2001 the St Mary's Priory Development Trust under the chairmanship of Sir Trefor Morris, launched an appeal to raise £237,000 to restore the tithe barn and local architects Morgan and Horowskyj who designed the nearby Priory Centre drew up plans for the barn to be converted into a visitors' centre and a community arts/music facility. On 24th October 2008 Prince Charles the Patron of St Mary's Priory Development Trust paid a visit to Abergavenny to officially open the Tithe Barn which had been transformed at a cost of £1.9m into a centre for exhibitions, educational projects and hospitality. It was his second visit to St Mary's as Patron of the Trust and around 360 people packed into the church for an hour long Service of Thanksgiving which included a reading by the Bishop of Monmouth, Right Reverend Dominic Walker. The Prince was then given a tour of the Barn, before unveiling a plaque commemorating his visit.

On the ground floor is a reception/ sales area, a restaurant and toilets, while upstairs is an interpretation room containing a database on the history of the barn, the priory and the town of Abergavenny. There is also another room which is used for educational purposes.

A special feature in the exhibition room is a massive tapestry depicting one thousand years of Abergavenny's history. It is 24 feet long and 6 feet tall and fifty or more volunteers took turns to embroider the tapestry over a period of 5 years. No less that 400 to 500 different shades of wool were used to depict the landscape and various historical events shown on the tapestry which took four years to complete. All the work was carried out in the Lewis Chapel at St Mary's Priory Church where visitors took delight in watching the work in progress.

The Abergavenny Tapestry

The Priors of St Mary's

1130	Durand
1190	Henry
1291	Giles de Limines of Le Mans
1310	Fulk Gaston
1320	Richard of Bromwich
1400	Wm. Payham
1417	Robert Eton
1430	John Harton
1493	William de Winchester
1520	John de Lichfield
1529	William Mowtlow
1533	William Marley
1543	Priory Dissolved

Vicars of St Mary's Parish

1547	Lewis ap John
1560	Griffith Johns
	John ap James ap Howell Gwilym Jenkin
1589	William Prichard, M.A.
1599	Morris Hughes, M.A.
1632	Charles Herbert, M.A. (Dispossessed)
1660	Charles Herbert, M.A. (Reinstated)
1662	John Greenhaugh, B.A.
1691	Martin Baxter
1692	Anthony Seymour, B.A.
1699	Edward James, M.A.
1719	Evan Eustance, M.A.
1803	William Powell, B.D.
1863	Bury Capel, M.A.
1895	Frederick William Garfield Whitefield, M.A.
1904	Morgan Gilbert, M.A.
1912	Harold Henry Matthew, M.A.
1917	Morgan Evan Davies, M.A.
1962	Henry Rees Sproule-Jones
1977	Morgan Clement
1988	Colin Sykes
1993	Jeremy Winston
2012	Mark Soady

Chapter Five
THE TOWN WALL

That Abergavenny was once strongly fortified, there does not exist a doubt. The site of the walls may yet be traced, and some portions still remain; and if we may form a judgement from traditionary evidence, the fortifications were extensive.

Edward J. Burrow 1903

Abergavenny was originally defended by an earthen bank, sections of which have been detected in Castle Street. In 1251 the town received its first murage grant and further grants made in 1259-64 enabled the ditch and bank enclosure to be reinforced. Grants made in 1314-19 resulted in the old wooden walls being replaced by walls built in stone. The initial Norman town probably formed a rectangle centred on Castle Street and extending north-east to Cross Street. At a later date when the stone wall was built the town was oval in shape for the line of its walls is known from a plan made by Morrice for William Coxe in 1800. At this time the route of the town walls was evident for almost their entire length, although the section between the Priory and the Castle had vanished.

The wall, which would have been about 1.8 metres wide and 5 metres high only enclosed the higher portions of the town and inside this space lived the Norman garrison, together with numerous farriers, armourers, saddlers and other craftsmen necessary to the life of the Normans. There was no High Street and Cross Street ran at a lower level than it is now and terminated at a flight of steps leading into St John's Churchyard.

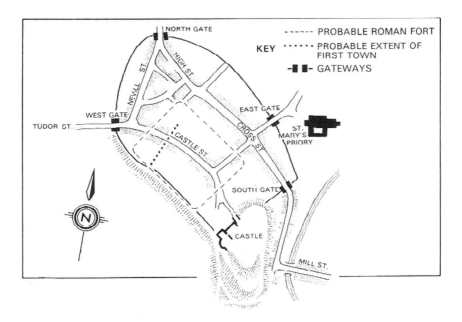

Map drawn by Michael Blackmore, showing the medieval Town Wall. A kink in the wall overlooking the river meadows marks the western end of the bank and ditch which defended the town on that side.

Within the walls of Bergavenny, as the town was then called, only Normans or Englishmen were allowed to own land, which was divided into a grid system with long strips called burgage plots, fronting the main streets. The plots were let at a standard rate of about one shilling a year. In return the burgesses (men of wealth and status) had certain obligations and duties to perform, including the defence of the town.

With the castle at its apex the wall ran along the top of the bank at the rear of Castle Street Car Park to the Tudor or West Gate which stood just above the point where Bibbeth Lane (later called Byefield Lane) and Tudor Street meet. It was named Tudor Gate after Jasper Tudor the uncle of Henry VII who was made Constable of Abergavenny.

This gate must have seen some stirring sights. For example not long after its completion, the ill-fated Richard de Clare, passed through it with his party on their way to West Wales, but were ambushed and slain by a band of Welshmen in Coed Gronwy (in the Black Mountains) after travelling just six miles.

No doubt many of the local Welsh chieftains who accepted the invitation of William de Braose to a banquet passed through the gate on Christmas Day 1175 on their way to the Castle, where they were all massacred by the baron's soldiers.

Another historic day was in March 1262, when Baron Peter de Montfort led his men through the gate to do battle with a Welsh force under Prince Llywellyn, beneath the Blorenge at Llanfoist.

1775 drawing of the arch of the Tudor Gate

Plaque marking site of the Tudor Gate

William Coxe

When William Coxe came here in 1800, Tudor Gate was still intact and considered to be the greatest curiosity in the town. He described the Tudor Gate as 'a strong gothic portal, defended by a portcullis of which the groove is visible.' It was the last survivor of the town's four gates and was pulled down in the early 19th century by the Abergavenny Improvement Commissioners. A basement doorway of this gatehouse was discovered in the 1960s and rebuilt at the rear of the Castle Museum.

From just outside the Tudor Gate a fine view of the adjoining countryside could be obtained. Coxe observed: 'A more pleasing assemblage of picturesque objects never entered into the composition of a landscape; the whole harmonises together, and produces an effect, which neither the pen nor pencil can adequately delineate.'

View from near the Tudor Street Gate in 1793

This 14th century basement doorway from the basement of Tudor Gate was revealed during demolition work in the 1960s and subsequently rebuilt at the rear of the Castle Museum.

Remnant of a later boundary wall, standing on the foundations of the original medieval wall near the Tudor Gate Surgery in Tudor Street

In Tudor Street beside the modern Health Practice building can be seen a remnant of a comparatively modern boundary wall, built on the massive foundations of the original wall. It stretches along the rear of the houses on the west side of Nevill Street and the North Gate was where the HSBC Bank in Frogmore Street stands. The wall then carried on round to the right and a section can be seen where it meets Market Street and then on to Monk Street, where it now forms the boundary wall of a cottage garden. Here stood the East Gate or Monks' Gate. In this gateway used to be a lock up for prisoners and beneath the building flowed the Cybi Brook. A sensation was caused in the nineteenth century by a prisoner who one night raised a few paving stones and gained his liberty by crawling out along the bed of the brook.

This lock up had a massive oak door studded with large nails and a substantial lock and keyhole. A century or more ago a local character well known for a drinking problem, was regularly incarcerated there. His sympathetic friends used to quench his thirst in an amusing way. They obtained a jug of beer from a neighbouring pub, put the stem of a big church warden pipe through the keyhole and poured the beer down the pipe. With such good friends to make him feel at home, a night in the clink no doubt had its attractions for this fellow.

From this gate the wall headed south-east to the Sun Inn (now the Coach and Horses), where the South Gate was situated. It was demolished by the Abergavenny Improvement Commissioners in 1795. From this gate the wall passed across Cross Street and headed up to the east side of the castle.

The Coach and Horses Inn, Cross Street stands on the site
of the South Gate which was demolished in 1795

The only sections of medieval masonry that have survived are to the rear of the properties on the north side of Nevill Street, a fragment at the foot of the rear wall of the market building, a length of wall to the rear of Laburnam Cottage in Monk Street and a sizeable portion to the rear of 23 and 24 Cross Street.

Abergavenny, in ancient times consisted of the streets which are now known as Cross Street, Castle Street, High Street, Nevill Street, St John's Street, Flannel Street and a small portion of Monk Street. At one time a curfew bell in St John's Church was rung to announce the closing of the town gates which meant that no one was then allowed to enter or leave the town.

Chaper Six
ROYAL CHARTERS

Abergavenny, although but a small town as regards population, is manifestly enterprising. It possesses that coveted distinction, a Mayor and Corporation.

Edward J. Burrow 1903

In 1542 Abergavenny received its first Royal Charter, when King Henry VIII incorporated the town under the style of Bailiffs and Commonalty, and granted the tithes of certain parishes, expropriated from the dissolved monasteries of Abergavenny and Usk for the purpose of endowing the King Henry VIII Grammar School.

Charles I in 1638, granted a new charter by which the town was to be governed by a chief steward, a deputy steward, a bailiff, ten capital burgesses, and fifteen inferior burgesses. The charter was granted on the petition of Henry, Lord of Abergavenny, Sir Basil Brooke, and the Lady Frances his wife, who had previously been the wife of Sir Thomas Nevill, eldest son and heir of Henry, Lord Abergavenny. The Charter gave wide powers for governing the town, including markets, fairs and the wollen trade. Courts of Record and Quarter Sessions were established, and numerous officials such as the Town Clerk, Supervisors of the Bridge, Steward and Sergeants at Mace, who had charge of the town prison were appointed.

On November 13th, 1656, the inhabitants of Abergavenny petitioned for the renewal of their Charter of Incorporation and it was submitted to a Committee of the Privy Council. The two people who took the matter in hand were Mr Shepherd and Mr Gabriel Best. In January 1657, they made their report to the Committee. The outcome was a new Charter. in which Abergavenny was to be incorporated as a borough under a Mayor, two Bailiffs and a Recorder.

There was to be a Court of Record called every fortnight. A Town Clerk was to be appointed and the Mayor was to be Clerk of the Market for surveyment of weights and measures. The Mayor and Bailiffs were to appoint an Alnager for the regulation of cloth in the town, and there were to be two surveyors of the bridges. Two sergeants were to be appointed to keep the town prison and execute the processes of Law. The gatehouse in Monk Street was to be the town prison and the Corporation were to have the use of the Market House or Town Hall for the keeping of their courts. There were to be two weekly markets and the three yearly fairs were to be continued as before.

The Mayor, Bailffs and Recorder were to see that all grain was brought into the market and not sold privately, forestalling the market. The Corporation were to have toll on the grain and on all that had been accustomed to pay toll.

The first Mayor and Burgesses were to continue in office until the 29th September 1658. This assumption was that the Charter came into operation on 29th September, 1657, but before the year came round, Oliver Cromwell the Lord Protector was dead.

These Charters lapsed in 1689 as a result of the revolution of 1688 which apparently caused riots in the town on the election of a bailiff. Also, in the following year on the accession of William III and Mary after the dethronement of James II, the inhabitants, by not showing sufficient enthusiasm for the Orange dynasty, or refusing to take the oath of allegiance, were deprived of their charter rights, and the Corporation of Burgavenny was dissolved.

William III and Queen Mary
from paintings by Sir Godfrey Kneller

From 1689, when the Charter was forfeited, until 1794 the town seems to have had no authority for its governance except the Parish Vestry and the Great Court Baron of the Lordship, the latter becoming each year more obsolete. An Act of Parliament in 1760 vested some of the tithes granted in 1542 to Jesus College, Oxford, and placed the remainder in the hands of Trustees for the care of the school, and for relieving the poor of the town, and building a workhouse.

How and by whom the town was governed during the greater part of the 18th century it is difficult to say, for apparently neither Charter nor Commissioners existed, and the town transactions during that period were not recorded, or if recorded, the record has been lost.

In 1720 a petition signed by 75 principal inhabitants was presented to George Nevill, 12th Lord Abergavenny, to use his influence to obtain a new Charter, but with no result.

In 1794 an Act of Parliament was obtained for paving and otherwise improving the streets of Abergavenny, the preamble being:-

'Whereas the streets and other public passages and places within the town of Abergavenny are not properly paved, cleansed, lighted or watched, and are subject to various encroachments, nuisances, and annoyances; and the present Market House is inconveniently situated and is fallen into decay; and the pipes for supplying the inhabitants with water are greatly out of repair. And whereas it would be of great benefit and convenience to the inhabitants and to persons resorting to and travelling through the same if the said streets and other public passages and places were properly paved, cleansed, lighted and kept free from encroachment nuisances and annoyances, and if the narrow parts thereof were widened and rendered commodious, and proper communications made between some of the said streets and other passages and places, and if some provision was made for watching the said town and if the said Market House was taken down and a proper market place provided in a convenient situation and power given to erect a new market house and other conveniences thereon, and if the pipes for supplying the inhabitants with water were amended, relaid and put in good repair.'

By the Act, a body of Commissioners was formed for carrying out these works and amongst those first nominated were Christopher Chambre, of Ty Mawr (Great House), Llanfoist; William Dinwoody, who owned and occupied Tydu (Tredillion); James Gabb, of 'Bailey Baker'; Charles Herbert, the father of Miss Rachel Herbert, who built and endowed Trinity Church and Almshouses; John Jones of Llanarth; Richard Lee, the father-in-law of John Jones; Thomas Swinnerton of the Priory, whose daughter Charles Kemeys Tynte had married; Benjamin Waddington of Llanover and John Hanbury Williams of Coldbrook. The first meeting of the Abergavenny Improvement Commissioners was held in the Greyhound Inn with John Hanbury Williams as chairman. In 1817 the meetings of the Improvement Commissioners were held at the Kings Head Inn and the magisterial business was transacted at the 'London Apprentice'. In later years when the building of the Town Hall was completed, the business of these two bodies was removed there.

An act of vandalism carried out by the Commissioners was the demolition of the old Tudor Gate, having decided that it obstructed Tudor Street. They improved the town's water supply by constructing an open reservoir in Pen-y-pound, from which water was conveyed to the town in wooden pipes. The old Market House was taken down and a new but somewhat inadequate one erected on part of the site now occupied by the present Town Hall.

In 1854, when an Improvement Act was obtained, the body of Commissioners thereby created, and fully justified, was under the successive leadership of Elmes Yelverton Steele, Isaac Isaacs, Edwin Tucker and Joseph Bishop, their title being 'Improvement Commissioners'.

The qualifications of a Commissioner were as follows:

> 'He must be of full age, and either rated for the relief of the poor of the parish in the annual sum of twenty pounds or upwards, or be possessed, either of a freehold estate, or a leasehold estate originally granted for a term of twenty-one years, each of the clear yearly value of not less than twenty pounds. Each Commissioner is elected for three years, and four have to retire annually by rotation, but are eligible for re-election.'

In 1870 the second Market Hall and Market were demolished and the present Town Hall and Market were built on their site. Cattle, sheep and other markets were constructed on the field adjoining Lion Street which up to that time had been used as the Town Cricket Field. This had the effect of doing away with the serious inconvenience that was caused by the sale of cattle and sheep in the public streets.

An excellent water supply was provided with the construction of a new reservoir at Llwyndu, fed by St Teilo's Well. Other springs were subsequently discovered, yielding a large amount of additional water and these were diverted into the reservoir. The water was conveyed by pipes directly to the town, thus preventing contamination by surface drainage. The site of the old reservoir in Pen-y-pound was sold. The town was resewered and relit throughout as a result of the gas works which had been erected on the Merthyr Road, near the Usk Bridge, by the private enterprise of Thomas Davies in 1821. This was purchased for £7,000. Pavements in most of the streets were relaid and widened. Several streets were also widened and greatly improved in appearance. Land in Baker Street was purchased from the Gabb family for the erection of a Police Court and Constabulary.

In 1871 great improvements were made in the sanitary conditions of the town. An Inspector of Nuisances was appointed and public conveniences were provided for the first time.

In 1880, a Provisional Order was obtained from Parliament for the purpose of extending the boundaries of the town. The Long Barn and Cantref districts especially, on which a large number of streets and houses had sprung up, were thus included within the rating area of the Town Government. By this step funds were raised to meet the costs of drainage, paving, lighting etc. in these new districts, without unfairly increasing the burden of taxation on the older districts.

The Local Government Act 1888 set up the county councils who initially were concerned with roads and bridges and diseases of animals. But they soon began to acquire additional powers under various statutes. With the passing of the Local Government Act of 1894, the century-long rule of the Improvement Commissioners came to an end and their functions passed to the Abergavenny Urban District Council.

A public meeting was held on April 24th 1897, to consider a proposed public petition to Her Majesty for the restoration of the ancient Charter which was granted to the town by King Henry VIII, and of which it had been deprived in the reign of King William III.

An application for the restoration of the town's Charter had been made in the Jubilee year (1887), but it was refused on the grounds that the population of the town did not exceed 10,000. The Charter which was eventually granted was a much more modern one than the old one. In the ten years that had elapsed great improvements had taken place. There had been a great deal of building going on and the population had increased. There were now 1,800 houses and taking an average of five individuals to a house, which in the case of Abergavenny was a moderate computation, it showed a population of 9,000.

In 1899 a new Charter of Incorporation was granted by Queen Victoria on 2nd August, and it came into force on November 1st of that year. The town had regained borough status after a lapse of two centuries. This municipal borough was divided into four wards (Castle Ward, Priory Ward, Cantreff Ward and Grofield Ward) and governed by a Corporation consisting of a mayor, four aldermen and twelve councillors.

The First Mayor of Abergavenny

Joseph Bishop

Joseph Bishop, the able and enterprising District Manager of the London and North Western Railway was appointed the first Mayor of Abergavenny under the restored Charter on 9th November 1899. Upon the creation of Abergavenny into a borough, he was unanimously requested by the council to accept the position of mayor.

He was a railway man who began his distinguished career in 1856 on the old Shrewsbury and Hereford line. In 1864 he was appointed manager of the London & North Western Railway in the Abergavenny District. He was appointed in 1868 to supervise the through working of the North Western Company's traffic to and from the North & West of England. By the end of his working life he had risen to the position of Distric Traffic Superintendant of the London & North Western Railway at Abergavenny.

In 1868 he had been elected a member of the Board of Improvement Commissioners and became chairman in 1883. He was elected to the Urban District Council in 1894 and appointed chairman the following year,

The last meeting of the Town Council that he attended was that of 18th April, 1900. He was prevented by illness from participating in any further municipal work and died in London at the age of 67 years, having given 25 years of service to the town. His funeral took place in Abergavenny on Thursday 12th June, 1902. Practically the whole of Abergavenny was said to be in mourning that day. Drawn blinds and shutters to shop fronts throughout the line of the funeral route testified to the honour in which Joseph Bishop was held by the residents of the town.

The First Working-Man Mayor of Abergavenny

In November 1921, Alderman J. R. Beckwith had the distinction of being the first working-man to become Mayor of Abergavenny. This honour was the reward of ten years continuous service on the Town Council. As a foreman fitter at the London & North Western Railway loco sheds he represented primarily the railway interests but was really an independent member. He had come to Abergavenny from Crewe thirty two years earlier.

Abergavenny Borough Council c.1910

Local Government Reorganisation

The borough council remained in place until 1974 when local government reorganisation saw the setting up of Monmouth District Council by the amalgamation of Abergavenny Borough and Rural Councils, Chepstow Urban and Rural Councils, Monmouth Borough and Rural Councils, Usk Urban Council and part of Pontypool Rural Council. At the same time Abergavenny Town Council was established with limited finance and limited powers and responsibilities. The district council became Monmouth Borough Council and was responsible for the running of Abergavenny's affairs in tandem with Gwent County Council until April 1996.

The Charter was mislaid following the 1974 local government re-organisation but found in 1977 in the safe-keeping of Monmouth District Council offices at Mamhilad. It is a seven page document with a paper, rather than a wax seal and sets out the composition and constitution of the authority and details of the areas of the wards. It details the areas of three of them and then states; 'Ward no 4, otherwise "Grofield Ward", shall comprise the remainder of the Urban District not included in the above wards.'

Gwent County Council then disappeared in a further reorganisation in 1996 and Monmouthshire County Council came to power as a unitary authority responsible for all the functions previously carried out by Gwent County Council and Monmouth Borough Council. These include education, social services, planning, housing, environmental health, leisure, highways, transport, libraries and finance.

Abergavenny Town Council now consists of fifteen members who are elected every four years and their function is to present the views of the residents of the town to the Welsh Office or Monmouthshire County Council and make recommendations to ensure that the Town remains an attractive shopping and tourist centre.

A Town Mayor is appointed annually and a list of all Mayors appointed since the Restoration of the Charter is recorded within the Town Hall. The Installation of the Mayor takes place in May and the ceremony is an impressive event with Councillors, Mace-Bearer and Clerk in full regalia, and the outgoing Mayor handing to his successor his special robes and the Mayoral chain.

The chains worn by the mayor and mayoress of Abergavenny date back to the restoration of the town's charter in 1901 when much of the civic regalia was donated to the newly formed council by the Marquess of Abergavenny. Made of gold it is composed of a portcullis in the centre with Nevill roses attached with chains to octagon shields bearing the letter 'A'. There are 12 roses, 6 enamelled in ruby and 6 in white. The badge, which is oval, bears the Nevill motto 'Ne Vile Velis' and has an enamelled raised centre with the Nevill Arms raised in bright silver. On the reverse of the badge is 'Presented by William, Marquess of Abergavenny, 1900'.

The silver gilt mace was subscribed for by certain of the Burgesses of the Borough and others and presented to the Town Council at its meeting held on the 9th of November, 1900. The names of the subscribers are engraved on the mace.

James Straker,
Mayor of Abergavenny in 1912

Installation of Mayor Peter Coleman
by the outgoing mayor Alan Breeze in 1981

Mayors of Abergavenny
Since Restoration of the Charter

1899	Joseph Bishop		1964	Stanley Clark
1900	William Williams		1965	Martin John Reeves
1902	Edwin Foster		1966	George Henry Tranter
1903	James Straker		1967	David Eric Thomas
1904	William Williams		1968	Ronald Popple Brown
1905	James Charles Gwatkin		1969	Jack Thornhill Jonathan
1906	William Davies Woodward		1970	John Malcolm Lewis
1907	Samuel Deverall		1971	Trevor Llewellyn Morgan
1908	William Williams		1972	William Leslie Fletcher
1909-11	John Owen Marsh		1973	Gethyn Jones
1912	James Straker		1974	Victor Pugsley
1913	John Henry Gilbert Harris		1975	Peter Williams
1914-18	Zachariah Wheatley		1976	Laurie Parry
1919-20	Joseph George Bishop		1977	Leslie Biggs
1921	John Rutland Beckwith		1978	Richard Smith
1922	Alfred Cromwell Graham		1979	Mrs Rosa Norris
1923	John Reginald Jacob		1980	Alan Breeze
1924	Peter Telford		1981	Peter Coleman
1925	Frederick Sadler		1982	Victor Barrett
1926	William Rosser		1983	Raymond Hill
1927	Arthur Phillip Thomas		1984	Richard Dodd
1928	Joseph George Bishop		1985	Alan Breeze
1929	William Horsington		1986	Peter Coleman
1930	William Devereux		1987	Mrs Rosa Norris
1931	Albert Ernest Tillman		1988	Raymond Hill
1932-34	Max Louis Beveridge		1989	Raymond Hill
1937	Edwin James Shapley		1990	Derek E. Bowen
1938-41	William Rosser		1991	Gilbert Fury
1942	William Horsington		1992	Douglas L. Edwards
1943	George Henry Tranter		1993	Chris J. Belcham
1944	Frederick Thomas Rosser		1994	Ken Webb
1945	Max Louis Beveridge		1995	Gilbert Fury
1946	Bertram R. Griffiths		1996	Norman G. Williams
1947-48	Ernest Rees		1997	Graham Preece
1949	Peter Telford		1998	Raymond Hill
1950	Sidney David Stanley James		1999	Gilbert Fury
1951	John Southwell Bousfield		2000	John Harvey
1952	Harold Augustus Poole		2001	Tony O'Donovan
1953	John Alick Morgan		2002	Alan Breeze
1954	Edward Harvey		2003	Victor Barrett
1955	Victor Reuben Pugsley		2004	Chris Woodhouse
1956	Reginald Silverthorne		2005	Raymond Hill
1957	Albert George Wycherley		2006	Tony O'Donovan
1958	William Horsington		2007	Martin Hickman
1959	Clifford James Jones		2008	John L. Prosser
1960	Frederick Ormond Pugh		2009	Douglas Edwards
1961	Arthur Pardoe James		2010	Norma Watkins
1962	Reginald Silverthorne		2011	Jane Foulser
1963	John Frederick Thurston			

The Abergavenny Coat of Arms

The Coat of Arms for Abergavenny as featured on the mural is derived from that of the Norman de Hastings family, with their distinctive bull on the helm, and that of the Nevill family who have long been associated with Abergavenny and who are Lords of Abergavenny to this day.

The Latin motto 'HOSTES NUNC AMICI' translates as 'ENEMIES ARE NOW FRIENDS" and possibly relates to rival factions dating back to the Civil War.

Twinning Arrangements

In 1968 a Twinning Agreement was made between Abergavenny and Ostringen, which is situated in the administrative County of Karlsruhe which is in the State of Baden-Wurtenburg. Wine production forms a considerable part of the town's economy. The official twinning was finalised on the 8th August 1968 in Abergavenny and in Oestringen on the 12th October 1968. The Abergavenny Town Mayor was Councillor R.P. Brown and the Burgermeister in Oestringen was H. Kimling. In 1974 the Abergavenny - Oestringen Association was formed to assist in the development of the twinning links and to encourage visits between interested groups.

Another twinning arrangement was made in 1988 between Abergavenny and Beaupréau in France to encourage links between the two towns. Beaupréau is situated in the middle of a triangle formed by the cities of Nantes, Angers and Cholet, and is just south of the Loire. It is a small town of about 5000 inhabitants and is surrounded by countryside similar to Abergavenny but without the hills. The main industry in the town is the manufacture of shoes.

The Official Twinning of Abergavenny with Sarno in Italy was approved by Abergavenny Town Council in November 1996. Sarno is about 25 miles from Naples and has a fine view of Mount Vesuvius. The town has a population of about 29,000 people and employment is provided by both agriculture and industry.

Chaper Seven
ABERGAVENNY MARKET AND TOWN HALL

On Tuesday when the country folk come in to do their week's shopping... there is a long row of vehicles all up the main street, and the pavement is thronged with farmers and their women-folk to each of whom Abergavenny is the hub of the world.

Edward J. Burrow 1903

The first reference to a market and fair being held in Abergavenny first appears in the Lordship of Abergavenny's Accounts for the year 1256-7. The next reference was in the town's Charter granted by Charles I in 1638. By this Charter three yearly fairs were established and vested in the bailiff and commalty and were held in May, Trinity and September. They were combined under the Abergavenny Improvement Act, 1854, incorporating the Markets and Fair Clauses Act of 1847. Most of the early fairs were held on the Christian Feast days, and the annual fair which used to be held on the third Tuesday in March, was probably associated with the Feast of the Annunciation of the Virgin Mary. The fairs were formerly carried out in the streets of the town and the ancient Fairfield which today, normally serves as one of the town's central car parks, has been the venue for the May and September fairs for about one hundred years.

It was on the site of the present day Town Hall that the first market was built from money left by Philip Jones of Hendre Obaith (where Llanarth Court now stands). In his will dated 1602 he left 200 marks 'to build a market house in Abergavenny after the fashion of the market house in Monmouth, also erected by Philip Jones.' This building apparently used to project into the street and caused much inconvenience to the horse and cart traffic. It stood in the middle of Cross Street (in front of the 1793 Market place), having a narrow thoroughfare on each side, scarcely wide enough for a waggon to pass between it and the penthouse opposite. This stately pile was built on pillars, forming a handsome collonade. At the north end was a broad flight of stone stairs ascending to the entrance into the hall, at the far end of which was a large apartment forming a convenient court of justice in which Quarter Sessions were held and the Grand Assize occasionally.

The tolls of this Market House were divided into three branches - between the parish clerk and sexton of St Mary's Church, in the following manner: the butchers' shambles and standings were let by the overseers of the parish, likewise the hall in which sessions were held, which was occasionally let by them to the strolling players. The proceeds were apportionated to the following purposes: £5 to the clerk and £2 to the sexton as a yearly salary, the remainder for the repairs of houses and the general purposes of the parish. The clerk and sexton received and collected the tolls upon wheat, cheese and butter sold in the Market-house which were divided equally between them.

Reference to the town's market is made in the Charter granted by King Charles I in 1638, which also mentioned the holding of two markets a week, on Tuesdays and Fridays and this has continued to the present day.

At a meeting on December 19th, 1792, it was unanimously resolved that 'the Market House is in a very ruinous and decayed state and its situation very inconvenient, as well to the inhabitants as to travellers passing through the town, and that it will be of the greatest convenience and advantage to the said inhabitants and parishioners and also of public utility to take down the same and build another on some more eligible and more convenient spot, and also to pave, light, cleanse and improve the said town.'

Abergavenny Town Hall was built in 1870

It was further resolved at the next meeting 'that Mr Nash, architect, should be sent to take a view of the old Market House, to hear the different opinions of the sixteen persons appointed, two from each ward, in regard to the different situations, estimates and expenses for erecting the Market House, to value the old materials and to point out what will be the probable expense for paving, lighting and cleansing the town.'

The Abergavenny Improvement Act of 1794 gave the Abergavenny Improvement Commissioners the power to erect a new Market House and to demolish the old one in order to widen Cross Street. Two pubs known as the 'Dog and Bull' and 'Plume of Feathers' and four shops were demolished to allow the street to be widened and make space for a new Market Hall and Wool Room designed by John Nash. It would seem that this famous architect was in the area at the time working on improvements to Kentchurch Court, near Grosmont. For his design of the new Market Hall, it is recorded that Nash received the sum of £52 10s and it was built in 1794 by John Knight at a cost of £810. It was built in the form of an open courtyard surrounded by market stalls. A total of thirty-nine stalls were let at a monthly rent of £1 11s 6d.

This new market was opened on 19th April 1796 and it was advertised in the *Hereford Journal* one week before. It was to be open at six in the morning, and closed at nine in the evening between Ladyday and Michaelmas, and seven in the morning and eight in the evening between Michaelmas and Ladyday.

Regulations were made prohibiting horses and carts from remaining in the market longer than was necessary to unload or reload goods and the butchers were forbidden to bring horses into the Meat Market for any purpose. The first Clerk of the Market was John Powell and he was instructed to keep out beggars and ballad singers.

It was constructed in the form of a parallelogram, part of which was built on the site of the old town wall. Under the house and branching both sides towards the front were the butchers' shambles. In front was a handsome iron railing with a double gate in the centre, and one on each side opening to two passages, where the corn was exposed for sale. The ground for the new Market Hall was purchased by the Commissioners for £1,312 10s. The materials and building cost £1,039 2s and the materials of the demolished Market-house and houses were sold in lots for £135.

The Commissioners decided that the collection of the market tolls by the clerk and sexton was a degredation of their offices and agreed to grant them a salary of £9 each per annum forever, to be charged upon the tolls of the Market-house in lieu of the former tolls granted to their predecessors by the bailiffs and burgesses of the town, who built the former Market-house in 1602.

In those days Markets and Fairs for cattle, sheep and horses were held in the streets all over the town, but in 1810 James Ashe Gabb was given permission to erect sheep pens on a site in Castle Street, which at that time was occupied as a coal yard, and upon which an Infants School was later built.

Records show that early in the 19th century there existed a Wheat Market, Barley Market, Wool Market, Butchers' Market, Fish Market and a Butter Market. These markets were held twice weekly on Tuesday and Saturday until 1826 when the Minutes of the Town Commissioners record that 'owing to the Saturday market interfering with the numerous markets held at different Ironworks in the neighbourhood, that Friday be fixed as the day for the second weekly market.'

The tolls of the market in 1823 realised under auction the sum of £420 for the year. Of interest is that it was ordered at this time that £1 1s 0d be paid to the landlord of the King's Head Inn for punch to be given to the takers of the market.

The Produce Market, below the Town Hall is a typical Victorian market hall, spacious and lofty with graceful iron pillars and lattice girders. The main Market day is on a Tuesday when Abergavenny is alive with people who come from far and wide to look for bargains and generally have an enjoyable day in the town. A 'Flea Market' is held on a Wednesday and other markets on Friday and Saturday.

The Cattle Market was established in 1863 and at the time of writing is leased and run by Abergavenny Market Auctioneers Ltd. There is currently a proposal to sell the site to a developer for the erection of a supermarket and a new library. A replacement cattle market will be established, possibly at Raglan.

In 1870 the Commissioners embarked upon a large scheme of reconstruction involving the re-building of the Market and Town Hall at a cost of £8,000. The new market which is still in use, measures 140 feet by 160 feet and has entrances in Cross Street and Market Street.

The Town Hall was designed by Wilson & Wilcox of Bath and built by Messrs S. J. Moreland & Sons of Gloucester in 1870. During the period of construction a fatal accident occurred when Thomas Watkins, a 26 year old labourer whilst working on the tower overbalanced and fell to his death.

The building provided a general market, assembly room, municipal offices, corn exchange and poor law offices. It was officially opened within a few days of May 4th 1871 and to mark the occasion the Abergavenny Choral Society gave an entertainment under the direction of a Mr Groves.

In November 1958 the town Mayor, Alderman William Horsington made a claim to be the only man in the borough, 50 years previously to have put his hand on the weather vane at the top of the Town Hall spire. Steeple jacks were covering the spire with copper and he went up with them to make sure that they were making a good job of it!

The Town Hall Clock

Something that many people in Abergavenny probably take for granted is the clock which was presented to the town by the famous ironmaster Crawshay Bailey at a cost of £512 12s 6d. It bears a plaque recording the fact that he gave it to the town in 1872. He in fact died just before the clock was installed and there was a public meeting in the Town Hall to discuss what should be done in recognition of his generosity. The meeting decided to invite his son (also called Crawshay Bailey) to a dinner, but the son declined, saying that the gift was not his, but that of his father, and that he was merely carrying out his father's wish to pay for the clock.

However, soon afterwards a memorial window to the late Crawshay Bailey was installed in Llanfoist Parish Church and in consideration of his generosity to the town, the Improvement Commissioners subscribed ten guineas towards its cost.

On May 25th 1872 the *Abergavenny Chronicle* reported that 'the new clock is now being fixed in the tower of the Town Hall and in a short time its chimes will be heard in the town.' Five days later at 10.00 am, the granddaughter of the late Crawshay Bailey set the clock in motion.

Observant people may notice that the north face of the clock, which can be seen from Market Street is painted black. This was to commemorate Queen Victoria's consort, Prince Albert who died in 1861.

The clock was manufactured by Messrs Gillett and Bland of Croydon, once a well-known firm of clockmakers. To keep the clock ticking requires 500 turns on a large crank handle and this is done once  a week. It runs for 8 days and strikes the hours upon a 14cwt bell and chimes the quarters on two other bells in due proportion. The clock shows the time on four dials, each six feet in diameter, three of which are illuminated, the fourth being of copper, with gilt figures and minutes on a black background. There used to be a similar clock at Maindiff Court and Llandewi Court.

Only the weather upsets the accuracy of the clock, for when there is glorious sunshine there is a tendency for the clock to gain. Pigeons were also known to cause trouble when the clock used to be illuminated by gas, the birds would flutter around and put out the light.

In November 1963 the clock then 92 years old was flooded when water poured through the wooden roof above it and washed grit into the centre of the works. It was put out of action for six days and its centre section had to be taken completely apart before it would operate again.

In 1890 a well known athlete tried to run from the Town Hall to the Swan Hotel before the clock could finish striking twelve. He apparently failed by one strike. This story sounds like a scene out of the film 'Chariots of Fire'. The athlete, Fred Cooper was born in Monk Street and the town was proud of the fact that this Abergavenny man was the first runner in the world to accomplish the 100 yard sprint in 10 seconds. In 1898 he became the 100 yards champion of Great Britain (10 seconds) and the 100 yards champion of Wales in 1899 (10 seconds). So Fred Cooper was no mean athlete and if he couldn't beat the Town Hall clock then the run to the Swan was perhaps impossible in such a time.

Nearly seventy years later Fred Cooper's race against the clock was revived in the form of a novelty event organised by the Abergavenny Holiday Week Committee. It was decided that a race to beat the Town Hall Clock would be held at midnight on 27th June 1959. The distance to the Swan was measured by Mr W. J. Hurst, the Borough Engineer and found to be 810 feet or 270 yards. An accurate measurement of the time that it took the clock to strike twelve was also made and found to be exactly 27.5 seconds. Any runner who succeeded in beating the clock would receive a voucher worth five guineas.

Abergavenny waited with considerable excitement for the day of the race to arrive. It was a Saturday night and by 20 minutes to midnight there were some two thousand people lining Cross Street on both sides of the road to watch a dozen athletes participate in this unusual event. The spectators heard the clock strike a quarter to twelve and the excitement grew but the twelve o' clock strike failed to happen. The hand ceased to move at 11.47 precisely and cries of 'The clock has stopped!' rang through the night air, whilst others saw the funny side of the situation and laughed until they cried.

The race against Crawshay Bailey's clock had to be abandoned, but the perplexed organisers persuaded the bewildered competitors to race down to the Swan Hotel so that there could at least be a winner for the crowd to cheer to victory.

Everyone was of course asking the same questions. 'Had the faithful old clock stopped of its own accord or was there dirty work afoot?' The last time that the clock had stopped was in 1912, when it was struck by lightning.

On the Monday morning, Mr Wells, manager of Messrs Rowe and Sons, the firm responsible for the maintenance of the clock, climbed the Town Hall stairs and went into the back of the balcony to investigate. He discovered that some joker had tied the pendulum to the door of the cupboard.

A group of men had waited at the back of the balcony until the clock struck a quarter to twelve. Then with a few of them steadying a wooden ladder, which had been lying handy on the floor, the intrepid hoaxer climbed it until he was in a position to open a wooden cupboard containing the pendulum.

He used a black shoelace to tie the pendulum to the door of the cupboard. By five to twelve 'Operation Tick Tock' had been completed and the young men were well away from the scene of their 'crime'.

Chapter Eight
STREETS IN ABERGAVENNY

Its main thoroughfare, known at various points of its length as Frogmore Street, Cross Street and High Street, is lined with well-equipped business houses which cater for every taste.

Edward J. Burrow 1903

In ancient times the streets in Abergavenny used to be very narrow, with the exception of Cross Street which was used by the Castle garrison for drilling purposes. It was not until about 1794 that the first attempts at pitching, paving and improving the streets took place, although in a very small way. At that time, according to the records, the inhabitants were ordered to remove and carry away 'all dung hills, muck, dirt and rubbish lying in the streets, or be liable to be prosecuted.' Prior to that time pigs were also allowed to stray about and even bull baiting was carried on in the streets. The last bull baiting recorded took place on 27th September 1784 when John Vaughan was caught by Thomas Leonard and John Price, chasing a bull belonging to them in the town at nightime. Vaughan was convicted and fined £5.

Cross Street is dominated by the green-capped Gothic tower of the Town Hall, which is a bold landmark, particularly when seen from the surrounding hills. Most of the buildings date back to the nineteenth century and during the last century the general appearance of Cross Street has changed very little.

No 1 Cross Street was once the vicarage of St John's Church. In 1938 during alterations an unsafe wall of the vicarage had to be removed and an old date-stone with sculptured edges and Tudor roses bearing the date 1513 was taken out and cleaned. It is now in Abergavenny Museum.

When this building ceased to be used as a vicarage it became a flannel factory and the little street adjoining the building was named Flannel Street. Later on the building became a bank owned by one of the Jones family who lived at Treowen Manor, near Dingestow. It later came into the possession of Sir Charles Salisbury and was known as 'Bank House'. When Alfred Jackson bought the building in 1938 he found one of the wooden supports of the old loom still in position.

The first Post Office in Abergavenny was opened at the shop of Mrs Price, ironmonger in Cross Street. Abutting onto the street was a small window with a shutter and the postal business was transacted there. Some years later the Post Office was removed to the shop of Mr E. S. Davies, Stationer, a few doors lower down the street. It was known as the Stamp Office. The shop was purchased in 1908 by Fred Sadler who operated it as a newsagent and stationery business. He passed it on to his son Frederick Vivian and it then went to his sons Frederick Thomas (Tom) and Vivian Devonald (Viv) who ran it for many years until it was finally sold and is now an Art Shop.

On 27th May 1857, Mr J. W. Bigglestone, on the recommendation of Sir Benjamin Hall, was appointed Postmaster by the Postmaster General, the Duke of Argyll. The business was carried on at the Stamp Office from 1857 to 1861, when Mr Bigglestone removed to a new premises which he occupied as a confectioner's shop. There was no recognised postal counter and persons desiring to transact business had to pass along a passage and knock at a shutter in the partition which divided the passage from the shop.

Cross Street in the days of horse drawn traffic

The same view when motor vehicles first started to make an appearance

There was no appointed staff, the postmaster being assisted by his brother and Mrs Bigglestone. But there were two town letter carriers and six rural postmen. On the death of her husband in 1878, Mrs Bigglestone was appointed Postmistress and Miss E. H. Bigglestone was appointed to the office on the death of her mother in 1884. She had acted as assistant in the office since December 1868. At the time she was appointed there were nine postmen (three town and six rural), four clerks and two sub-offices with three deliveries a day and despatches.

In 1912 there were 25 postmen (11 town and 14 rural), three sub-offices with four deliveries a day and ten despatches and an indoor staff of 14. The following year a new premises was erected in Frogmore Street.

View of High Street in 1913, from the corner of Nevill Street

High Street ran from the north gate to the crossing of Flannel Street and Market Street. On the upper walls of a building at the corner of High Street and St John Street is a large mural which was painted by local artist Frances Baines to celebrate the Millennium. The work was commissioned by Abergavenny Town Council and when completed in July 2000, was officially unveiled by Abergavenny mayor, councillor John Harvey and the leader of Monmouthshire County Council, councillor Colin White.

Four windows into the past give historical views of the town. These panels show Abergavenny scenes from the years 1100, 1665, 1865 and 1936. The first window is a view into 1100, when the castle had just been built by Hamelin de Ballon; in 1665 with a view of the Tudor West Gate; the Kings Arms pub and Nevill Street which was once the town's Market Square. A large stage wagon can be seen pulling into the wagon yard which stood on the site of the present day Post Office.

A third window depicts Abergavenny in about 1856 and shows one of the last horse-drawn trams on the old Llanfihangel Tramroad bridge which used to stand beside the roadbridge spanning the river Usk. The fourth window depicts Abergavenny Railway Station in 1936 which was a time when Abergavenny was an important railway centre for it had three stations.

' **Red Square'** in High Street is a nick name given to the location where during the late 1970's, three High Street buildings (No's 25, 25a and 26) were found to be in danger of collapse. The tenants were required to hastily to vacate the ground floor shops and the buildings were shored up with a maze of scaffolding which completely blocked the road, while the Monmouth District Council made up its mind what to do.

'Red Square' in High Street

There were indications that there were likely to be long delays before any action was taken on the site and traders were soon calling for immediate demolition and the re-opening of High Street. An action committee was set up with the town Mayor, Les Biggs as one of its members and there was talk of calling in the Ombudsman. Some 2,000 people signed a petition supporting the Chamber of Trade who were leading the fight.

In the New Year 1979 the weather took a hand. Gale force winds made the chimney stacks of the shored up buildings unsafe and a 90ft crane had to be hired from Birmingham to remove them. Calls for immediate demolition were renewed and in due course this was agreed by the Council and carried out.

In June massive red girders were erected to contain the Flannel Street and St John Street end shops at an estimated cost of £58,000. It was not until September 1979 that High Street was reopened to traffic, having been closed for more than two years.

The saga lasted for five years and in due course a shop front was constructed on the open space created by the demolition of the High Street buildings. It was designed by Monmouth District Council architect, Hugh Williamson and included a mixture of brickwork and rendering to tone with the present adjacent buildings.

The scheme costing about £110,000 has provided the town with a tourist information point. The windows are leased to the Abergavenny & District Tourist Association who arrange frequently changing and attractive displays.

The Old Bank in High Street was founded in 1837 by Joseph Bailey, Crawshay Bailey, William Morgan, Thomas Grantrex and William Williams. They traded as the Monmouthshire Agricultural and Commercial Bank. The Baileys were primarily industrialists while the other three directors were primarily bankers. William Morgan and William Williams were the two leading bankers in Abergavenny and Thomas Gratex at first concentrated his business at Monmouth and was later associated with Newport.

In 1867 Crawshay Bailey, then the senior partner, expressed a wish to curtail his business engagement because of his age. Negotiations were opened with the National Provincial Bank of England, and as from January 15th, 1868, the banking houses at Newport, Abergavenny and Monmouth were purchased for the sum of £20,000.

Crawshay Bailey and his former partner Thomas Grantrex were appointed local directors. The bank continued to play an important part in the life of the town.

In the late 1960s the National Provincial Bank of England joined with the Westminster Bank and today, because of its architectural significance the 'Old Bank' is a Grade two listed building that is now a branch of the National Westminster Bank. This historic building has a neo-classical Victorian facade and its appearance is unchanged except for the new wooden door. But inside, gone now are the elaborately moulded ceiling, portices and overmantle, the heavy counter and brass railings. In their place is a spacious office separated from the customer by a full length counter with eight cashier and enquiry points.

Burtons, the tailors covering the site of three early 19th century shops was opened on Friday 12th November 1937. It was described in the *Abergavenny Chronicle* as follows:

'A magnificent structure, noble in conception, graceful in design and occupying a prominent position in the centre of the town. Impressive in appearance and commanding the admiration of the general public, this triumph of the building profession should form an enduring monument to the vision and enterprise of Montague Burton, whose ever-increasing chain of tailoring establishments throughout Great Britain and Ireland forms one of the most interesting romances of trade.

The building and its two lofty storeys, with stately columns rising to the top, and crowned with a massive pediment, bearing the firm's name, which at night is illuminated, suggests solidity of construction enhance by artistic ensemble. There is also a dignity in its form and it makes a welcome addition to the town.

The new premises, which are faced with Empre stone, are fireproof throughout, the floors being of reinforced concrete covered with wood-block flooring.

Montague Burton's fine establishment is a substantial contribution to the local trading facilities of the future. It is interesting to note that every yard of cloth and trimmings used in the making of Montague Burton's garments is manufactured in Great Britain.

It is to be hoped that the Montague Burton example will be emulated by the enterprising tradesmen in the town, and thus add to the civic pride of Abergavenny. It is an accepted maxim that an attractive establishment not only helps to retain local trade, but also attracts trade from the surrounding towns.'

Above the shop-front of 22, High Street, is a small metal plaque which is known as a fire mark. It depicts a man standing alongside what is perhaps an old fire engine and underneath is the word 'Birmingham,' which was the name of the insurance company which insured the building against fire risks.

This fire mark was erected in the days when there was no organised method of fire-fighting, and each of the fire insurance companies had their own fire brigades.

It is sometimes said that when a Fire Insurance Company's fire brigade arrived at the scene of the fire and discovered that the building was marked by a competitor they would return to their station, but records of the old Fire Insurance Companies show that many payments were made to other companies as their share of extinguishing the flames.

Replica Fire Mark

Before 1800 these fire marks were made of lead, and often showed a number which indicated the policy number. They were later replaced by thin metal plates of tin, copper or iron and continued in use until about 1825.

Market Street is the oldest trading area in Abergavenny and at one time it was several feet lower than it is today. The row of quaint buildings with their distinctive colonnades date back to the 16th century. The iron columns have replaced the original woodenposts and the raised footway is an interesting feature.

These small shops were once all butchers' premises and in the early 19th century were known as 'The Shambles'. Each building has its cellar in which slaughtering operations were carried out. An elderly Abergavenny man once related in 1880 how he remembered 'the blood draining out onto the road and no decent person dared pass that way after nightfall!'

Market Street - drawing by Michael Blackmore

No 11 Market Street was previously the Market Tavern public house and the Straker and Chadwick premises was built in 1872 as an Estate Office for the ironmaster, Crawshay Bailey.

It was in 1872 that James Straker opened his first office in Abergavenny and William Chadwick's career began in 1898. He went into partnership with James Straker and his son Charles in 1912 to create the firm of J. Straker, Son and Chadwick. Charles Straker was killed a few years later during the First World War. Following the Second Worl War, William Chadwick was joined by his two sons Reginald and Peter Chadwick. In 1970 the third generation Chadwick (William) joined the family firm which has had a long association with Abergavenny's agricultural heritage.

At one time this street was known as 'Traitor's Lane', in memory of the time in about 1404 when Owain Glyndwr's forces besieged the walled town. A woman who sympathised with his cause opened a small gate (known as a sally port) and admitted the large band of Welshmen who immediately set about sacking and burning the timber buildings.

The town was practically destroyed and lost all its military importance. For nearly a century it lay derelict, but then gradually the buildings were reconstructed and the town had a peaceful existence until Oliver Cromwell paid a visit to crush a revolt of Royalist sympathisers.

When a new Cattle Market opened in 1868 the lane linked it with the Butter Market and by 1881 it was known as Market Street. At the end of the side wall of the market a steep flight of sixteen stone steps used to lead down to a number of houses which became the biggest slum in Abergavenny. When they were demolished and the present general market laid out the ground was made up to its present level.

In December 1873 a brewery was opened by Mr Facey on part of the site of the old slum buildings. He commemorated the event by inviting to dinner a number of his friends and the builders, engineers and workmen who had been engaged on the works.

When Facey's Brewery in Market Street was built in 1872 the Cybi brook was diverted to provide extra land for the premises. In 1892 the firm moved its retail trade from here to Cross Street. The brewery building was demolished many years ago.

Flannel Street is so-called because Welsh flannel, for which the town was once famous used to be produced there. The surrounding hills were ideal for sheep breeding to produce a fine species of wool. However, at the end of the eighteenth century the industry went into decline and moved to Newtown in Montgomeryshire where 'Abergavenny flannel' continued to be produced for some years.

'Flannel Street' appears on Wood's town plan of 1834, when a number of woollen merchants and drapers were in business, obtaining their cloth from farmhouse and cottage weavers and water-operated mills in the nearby hills. Coxe's plan of 1800 shows a 'tender field' where the fulled cloth was dried and stretched on 'tender-hooks' and this was where the present bus station is situated on the east side of the town.

In 1880 the street was called Butchers' Row for at that time there were five butchers' shops and a slaughter house there. The cellar of the present butcher's shop (Edwards) is lined with gravestones from the old St John's Church graveyard, which covered quite a large area. Records show that this street, Castle Street, and Lower Castle Street were in the now defunct Butchers' Ward.

Between 1842 and 1937 no less than twenty four businesses are recorded to have operated in this street. The only survivor is H.J. Edwards and Son, which has been trading as a buthchers since the early years of the twentieth century. Previously, the shop was run from 1884 by Mrs Anne Morgan and in about 1901 it was taken over by her

grandson John Edwards. He was joined by his son Harry, who upon his death in 1953 left the business to Eddie and Bill Jones, two of his employees. The shop was sold in 1972 to the present owner Neil Powell.

At one time Flannel Street was twice as long as it is today. Sadly many houses here and in other streets in his part of the town were condemned and demolished during the Borough Council's slum clearance scheme during the late 1950's and early 1960's.

One of the mysteries of Flannel Street was the discovery by workmen, in one of the buildings being demolished, of a large tombstone which had been lying face down on the ground floor. Its inscription recorded the burial of William Jenkins who died

Flannel Street

in 1782, his daughter Rachel (d.1778) and son James 'of this Town Breeches maker' (d.1812) and of Mr Zacharius Laurentius Appelt, 'Late Qr. Master in the 58th Regt. who died the 6th August 1795 aged 34 years.'

St John's Lane used to be called Bake-house lane because there was once a bakery there. It was the last cobbled street in the town, being resurfaced in 1979. There was also a bake house in Monk Street where most of the baking for the lower part of the town and Monk Street was done.

St John's Square before the modern Post Office was built, consisted of two co-joined triangular spaces and ran from the Masonic Hall (Old St John's Church) to Castle Street, where it was met at the south end by Nevill Street.

Over a century ago there were three licensed houses here: the Six Bells, the Quarrymen's Arms (patronised by the stone workers of the Deri Quarry) and the Bull Inn. Adjoining the Bull Inn were two early Victorian shops, one having a charming flat-

fronted window of 24 glass panes. The other shop, on the corner of Castle Street was the town carrier's office in the 1830's.

St John's Square

This view from St John's Square
to the King's Arms is rather different today

Chicken Street was removed completely in the 1960s to make way for the extensive buildings of the new Post Office. A picturesque corner of Abergavenny destroyed in the process was the six-foot wide covered passage which led from the north-west end of the street to St John's Square, between the Vine Tree Inn (now Grasshoppers) and No 3 Chicken Street. The latter building, erected in the early 17th century was of timber-framed construction and contained a fine ceiling of massive oak beams with enriched mouldings and a corbelled stone fireplace which suggests it was originally a wealthy merchant's home.

A butcher's shop at the corner of Chicken Street was built on the site of a wooden structure which had in front a remarkable and grotesque representation of St Crispin, the patron saint of the Cordwainers.

Nevill Street street is named after the Nevill family who were here as early as 1573, and are ancestors of the present Marquess of Abergavenny. Before that it seems to have been called Cow Street because cows were sold in the street. Cow Street perhaps seemed too common, so an era of respectability renamed it Rother Street and No.11 is still known as Rother House. The word Rother means 'horned cattle' but this breed of large pale brown cows is now extinct. At one time a cattle market used to be held in this street. The cattle driven by drovers from West Wales were put to graze on Castle Meadows for a few days to gain some weight while they waited for the weekly market. They were then driven up Byfield Lane to Rother Street to be sold.

The Old Cow Inn was once the town house of the Vaughan family of Tretower Court

An interesting building in Nevill Street is the old Cow Inn (now the Trading Post Restaurant), which had one entrance in Nevill Street and another in St John's Square. It was built in about 1600 as the town house of the Vaughan Family of Tretower Court and their arms which can be seen on the window mouldings consist of a chevron with three childs' heads with necks encircled by serpents. It is said that triplets of this family were once born with the umbilical cord wrapped around their necks, yet they survived. Also of interest are the red rose of Lancaster and the white rose of York, recalling the time when members of the Vaughan family fought in the Wars of the Roses (on each side!).

The Vaughan family were descendants of Ynyr, King of Gwent in the sixth century. Two members of this illustrious family were Sir Roger Vaughan who was knighted by King Henry V on the battlefield at Agincourt and Henry Vaughan, one of the early headmasters of King Henry VIII Grammar School in 1654.

The building became the Cow Inn in 1780 and this name is confirmed by a row of six brightly coloured bovine heads under the projecting soffit of the roof. Here the drovers came to take refreshment and to strike a bargain with purchasers of their cattle.

The stage waggons from London used to put up at the Bull Inn and where the adjoining shops stood at the corner turning into Castle Street were two gates opening into a large yard. This yard used to be the scene of most of the cock fighting in Abergavenny, which in days gone by occurred frequently.

In 1792 the town's first bank was established in Nevill Street. It was set up by the Blaenavon ironmasters Thomas Hill and Samuel Hopkins in partnership with Lewis Osborne and by 1810 it was known as the Abergavenny Bank.

The British Legion Club building (which closed in 2008) was once the Dragon's Head Inn. During renovation in 1961 a crude painting of an heraldic lion rampant was discovered on a plastered wattle and daub wall, now covered over. At the same time the 17th century oak door frame of the original entrance was removed and presented to the Museum.

Fortunately Nevill Street escaped the hands of the county planners and development companies and retains much of its past elegance, with a variety of styles dating from Elizabeth to Victoria. Its origin, is however much earlier, perhaps as far back as the 13th century when it formed a way connecting the west and north gates of the medieval town walls, part of which ran at the rear of the gardens on the west side of the street.

Rother House in Nevill Street has Tudor foundations but an Adam style front

Tudor Street as the name suggests mainly consisted of buildings erected in Tudor times and it was a thoroughfare of closely packed buildings with a time span of more than 400 years. The name over the years has been spelt in many ways, from Tider, Tyder and Tydder in the 17th century to Tidder and Tudor in the 18th century.

It was one of the main entrances to the town leading through the West Gate which stood opposite the Kings Arms and divided Castle Street from Tudor Street. Records show that there were once many public houses in the street, the earliest mentioned being the Bell, the Bush, the Coopers' Arms and the Cross Keys, which existed as far back as 1834. Later came the Beaufort Arms, the Albion Inn, the Foresters' Arms and the Milkmans' Arms.

The old Mission Hall which stood well back from the street and near the Bell Inn and had an iron crucifix over the entrance gateway. This was placed there by the Misses Ewens (nieces of Father Ignatius of Llanthony Monastery, Capel-y-ffin) who were in charge of the mission.

On the opposite side of the street stood the Wesleyan Methodists' meeting house of 17th century date. The Wesleyans had purchased and adapted this house in 1805 and made use of it until 1829 when the Castle Street chapel was opened. At the rear of the building was the Cymreigyddion Hall which opened in 1845 under the presidency of Sir Benjamin Hall of Llanover and was the centre for activities connected with local eisteddfodau. It was claimed at the time to be the largest public building in Monmouthshire. In 1854 the building was taken over by Captain Hill and the Volunteer Corps as a drill hall and from then onwards it became known as the Volunteers' Hall.

In 1862 the 'Popular Readings' took place there, having moved from the Grammar School (then still at old St John's Church), where they had commenced the year before with an audience of about sixty persons. This accommodation had proved quite inadequate and it was fortunate that the Volunteers' Hall was available, for the audiences at these functions expanded to some 600 - 700 people.

The object of this 'High Moral and Intellectual' entertainment was to allow the public to enjoy spoken extracts from the works of well-known writers and poets, interspersed with performances on the harp, pianaforte, woodwind and bass, a time limit of a quarter of an hour being imposed on each item on the programme. These were great days of dramatic verse and the audience listened with rapt attention to Tennyson's 'Charge of the Light Brigade', Longfellow's 'Wreck of the Hesperus' and Browning's 'A Night Ride from Ghent to Aix'. The public paid a penny on admitance and sixpence for a reserved seat. After deducting expenses such as the hire of the hall, lobby and piano, printing and advertising, the balance was distributed to selected local charities.

Leading off the main part of Tudor Street were courts reached by dark and narrow archways. Each side of the courts was lined with the walls of houses, many of them of great antiquity, dating back as far as 1550.

Tudor Street began to deteriorate between the two World Wars and by the time of the borough slum clearance this once respectable street had become an assemblage of neglected, vermin-infested slum properties. Because of their age the Borough Council were anxious to see these buildings demolished and the inhabitants rehoused elsewhere.

The plans for slum clearance in Abergavenny were announced on February 4th 1955. This vast demolition scheme which was carried out between 1957 and 1973 involved the re-housing of dozens of local families. The Town Council were told by their Public Health Committee that they considered three areas in the town consisting of 188 dwellings (some already derelict) could be cleared as slums and 177 displaced families could be rehoused within the next five years.

Councillor G. H. Tranter, Chairman of the Committee, stated that there were 1,470 dwellings in the town which were erected before 1875 and which were considered to have outlived their normal life. 'It is considered that 398 of them should be cleared within the next 20 years,' he stated. The three areas to be cleared were as follows:

Area 1 - Byfield Lane and Tudor Street
Area 2 - Part of Flannel Street, Chicken Street, part of St John's
Street, St John's Square, part of Nevill Street and part of Castle Street.
Area 3 - Part of Mill Street, Castle Terrace, Wilson's Lane, Malthouse Yard.

Three Storey houses in Tudor Street demolished in 1957

Tudor Street looking westward.
The Magistrates Court and Police Station are now on the right.

The Cardiff Architect, Sir Percy Thomas, a town planning expert commented that he considered that these buildings had 'nothing of historical or architectural interest'. It was indeed a sad time for the town. The Newport historian Fred Hando, writing in 1960 aptly commented:

'Standing in the archway of Old Court, with the scarlet creeper painting the tower of St John's across the open square, I wondered what lay ahead, how this challenging area would be developed. The *new look* demanded in so many of our towns today would be out-of-scale, out-of-taste, devastating, ulcer producing in Abergavenny.'

The ugly Post Office building in St John's Square is an example of what was considered forward thinking at that time. How ironic, that in later years Abergavenny town centre was designated a conservation area!

Now all that remains of old Tudor Street are a few houses built between 1910 and 1915, bearing the insgnia of the marquess of Abergavenny and Linda Vista which is a large Victorian house set in the beautiful well kept public gardens of the same name (see page 180).

Byefield lane before final demolition

Byefield Lane was the old route to Llanfoist and prior to the building of the Tudor Bridge, it led down a short steep decline to a ford across the river which used to flow much closer to the town and castle than it does now. This route which leads down to Castle Meadows was known as Pye Field Lane in the 18th century has now virtually disappeared. The meadows were held in the seventeenth century by the Baker family by long leases from the Lords of Abergavenny. Byfield Lane is now the entrance to a car park but the lane itself has now virtually disappeared.

Spanning the river Usk is a picturesque stone bridge which is known as **Tudor Bridge** because it was constructed on the orders of Jasper Tudor, one-time Lord of Abergavenny and uncle of Henry VII. Jasper had stood by his half-brother, Henry VI, throughout the Wars of the Roses, and for his support received the position of Chief Justicar, among other honours.

Tudor Bridge links Abergavenny with Llanfoist

When the Wars of the Roses ended, Jasper Tudor was in charge of Abergavenny and his nephew became Henry VII in 1509. Jasper issued an edict commanding the burgesses to rebuild the town which had been in virtual ruins for over one hundred years.

Before Tudor Bridge was constructed there would have been a ford at this point and the local inhabitants must have been much relieved when it was replaced by a bridge.

Originally the Tudor Bridge had sixteen arches, but when it was rebuilt at a later date the number of arches was reduced to eight. The bridge also used to be half its present width and admitted the passage of just one vehicle at a time. If a foot passenger happened to meet a cart or conveyance on the bridge he had to take refuge in one of the angular recesses until the vehicle had passed.

Drawing of the old Tudor Bridge by Joshua Gosselin (1739-1813)

It is recorded that, in 1645 Rees ap Rees bequeathed ten shillings 'towards the repairacon of the stone bridge lyinge over the river of Uske and servinge to the said towne of Bergavenny.'

On 17 December 1828, the mail coach which left the Royal Hotel at 3 o' clock attempted to cross the bridge in flood conditions and was washed over. The poor horses drowned but fortunately no human lives were lost. The mail bags were subsequently found in various parts of the Castle Meadow.

Castle Street is the oldest street in Abergavenny and in March 1825 it became the site of a sheep market which replaced a timber yard. People were then prohibited from exposing sheep for sale in any other part of the town. This street was largely destroyed by demolition between 1962 and 1964. Of remaining interest are the 17th century cottages just before the castle.

17th century cottages in Castle Street

Lower Castle Street was known in the 18th century as Castle Lane and on the north side used to stand the old stables of the Angel Hotel.

Frogmore Street was built outside the old town wall, for the gate on this side used to be situated at the south-west end of the street. It has been suggested that Frogmoor Street took its name from the fact that it originally passed through a marshy area inhabited by a large number of frogs! When in 1878, foundations were being laid for the Frogmore Street Baptist Church, a row of stepping stones was uncovered, confirming that this was indeed a very wet area.

Barclays Bank was formerly the Bennington & District County Bank and before that a mansion stood on the site. Its land at the rear extended from Lewis's Lane to Baker Street and it was the residence of Robert Morgan Kinsey, a wealthy sporting attorney who was sheriff in 1798 and died in 1805. It was later occupied by his brother General William Kinsey of the Madras Army, who died in 1837, grandfather of Elmes Yelverton Steel, the surgeon, who with his son, of the same name and profession were two of the town's much respected inhabitants.

Approached by a passage at the upper end of the street is the premises occupied by Dovers the printers. This building was erected during the early 19th century as the Catholic chapel of St Michael, replacing two earlier chapels - the first dating from the 17th century. The land and its buildings were given to the Franciscans by Peter Gunter, the Catholic recusant of Cross Street. Aftr his death his wife returned the property to the order. The chapel ceased to function after 1860 when the church of Our Lady and St Michael was opened in Pen-y-pound.

Frogmore Street was built outside the old town wall

November 1966 saw the closing of the Printing and Stationery business of M. Morgan and Company of Frogmore Street, which was founded in 1860 by Edwin Morgan and was later carried on by his grandson and great grandson. It was incorporated as a private company in 1920, all the shareholders being descended from the founder. Later it became a commercial printing works and also published the *Abergavenny Chronicle* until June 1965.

The Farmer's Arms in **Lion Street** stands on the site of the original Bethany Baptist Chapel which was demolished in about 1834. The first recorded licensee of this inn was William Watkins in 1865. **Tiverton Place** at the west end of Lion Street was once the site of a pottery which was destroyed by fire in 1817. Near here, the open Cybi brook crossed the street and pedestrians passed over it by means of stepping stones. It now runs through a culvert.

Pen-y-pound at one time was in a very dilapidated state, being almost always flooded in wet weather, and for the accommodation of pedestrians there was a footpath through the fields, running parallel with the road from the corner where the old Hereford road joins that road, right up to 'The Great Hill'. On the opposite side of Penypound Road was the Pound head or reservoir, from which a part of the town was supplied with water. In this reservoir, a donkey came to an untimely end. When the town's people discovered the remains of the animal in the reservoir they took a great dislike to the Pound water. Pipes were then laid to the spring at Llwyndu.

Pen-y-Pound House was once occupied by Dr Samuel Hopkins Steel and the name was later changed to Dyne House after Dyne Steel. The family originally came from the Forest of Dean and for half a century were the chief medical men in the town. Numerous members of this family are buried in Llanfoist churchyard.

The Grofield on the northern side of the town, immediately outside the Town Wall which bounded 'Rother Street', was a considerable tract of pasture land. The name means 'Big Field' (Gro' or Gros being Norman-French for big or great), and it is probable that in Norman times it was used by the town for grazing cattle. This land became the property of the Baker family and until 1830 it was open fields, with an ancient farmhouse.

After the demolition of the wall and consequent extension of the town, the 'Grofield' became available for building purposes, and it is now represented by Baker Street, Trinity Street, Victoria Street, Princes Street, Regent Street, Pant Lane and parts of the Merthyr and Brecon Roads.

The first building lease was granted by Mr Baker-Gabb on the 24th June, 1830. Numerous leases were granted in 1832 and by 1835 a large part of the estate had been leased. Since that time it has been completely built over to form part of the town.

To make sure that the railway employees could live near their jobs, the authorities built houses for them in nearby streets. The present Cantref Inn was the first building to be erected , just before Brecon Road Station was built. Then came the houses in Stanhope Street, North Street and St Helen's Road. A bell was installed at the rail-yard to signal to these employees when it was time for them to make their way to work and it was also rung to mark the end of their working day.

Monk Street is said to be so-called because St Mary's Priory and its manor used to be known as Monktown or Monkswick. However it has also been suggested that the street was named after General George Monck who was largely responsible for the restoration of Charles II. An Indian Restaurant now stands on part of the gatehouse site and a stone doorway in the rear yard probably belongs to the original structure. The gatehouse was once a lock up for prisoners, one of whom prised up a flagstone in his cell and escaped by crawling along the Cybi Brook which runs below on its way to join the Gavenny and the Usk.

There used to be a very fine timber-framed Tudor black and white mansion called Hope Hall in Monk Street. It was at one time the home of Lady Greenlys and when French prisoners were incarcerated in Abergavenny in 1813-14, after Napoleon's defeat, it was placed at the disposal of the officers as their headquarters. Being on parole, they were not allowed to go further than one mile from this house. In total there were 80 officers and some 200 soldiers and sailors held in Abergavenny.

In the 1820s Hope Hall was Evans and Rutherford's Academy for boys where a yearly charge of 36 guineas was made for board and instruction. It was demolished in 1909 and the building erected on the site subsequently became the headquarters of Abergavenny Rural District Council.

Between the churchyard and the Lower Monk Street turning there was once a row of picturesque thatched buildings. One of them, where the Pavillion Cinema was built, was the Nags Head Inn, the other being the London Apprentice, later re-named the London Inn. In 1885 it became a teetotal establishment being advertised in White's Guide for that year as The London Temperance Hotel and Coffee Tavern; the proprietor being Samuel Davies, Warden of Abergavenny Castle.

Lower Monk Street was once the main turnpike road into the town from the Monmouth direction. It used to be the location of a pub called the Omar Pasha, which was kept by a Mr Roberts who was a well known local character and his pub became the headquarters of a branch of the Ancient Order of Foresters of which he was a prominent member. A popular event during the year was the annual parade of the Foresters in colurful uniforms, representing Robin Hood and his merry men. Roberts always took the part of Robin Hood, but he was blind in one eye and wore a black patch. Local people always laughed and said that he looked more like a buccaneer than the famous hero of Sherwood Forest!

Demolished cottages in Lower Monk Street, once known as Ireland Street

Lower Monk Street extends from the Ross Road to Holywell Road and at its lowest level it crosses the Gavenny by a small bridge, which was built to replace one swept away by floods in May 1931. In the more distant past there was probably a ford here.

Below the bridge is a weir which channeled water required for the former corn mill at the foot of the castle in Mill Street. The area between the dried up mill race and the river was at one time called Priory Land and it is now occupied by the bus station and car park.

In 1973 the former police headquarters in Lower Monk Street was converted into a National Park Information Centre providing lecture room facilities, warden's office and a permanent exhibition on the work of the Brecon Beacons National Park. The Information centre was later moved to the Abergavenny Bus Station.

Former County Police Headquarters at the top of Lower Monk Street

Mill Street was the main thoroughfare into the town by which the London coach came into town until 1930 when a new road was constructed from the Swan Hotel to a new bridge over the Gavenny. The street takes its name from a mill which stood there in 1679. It was a grist mill which had a pair of grind stones meshed to an outer pit wheel. By 1854 the mill was owned by the Earl of Abergavenny who rented it to William Tucker. Later records show that the tennant was a Mr Hardwick and in 1879 it was in the possession of Ann Ackland. The overflow from the mill pond ran into the Gavenny brook and often caused flooding in the cellars of the nearby Unicorn Inn.

Mill Street before demolition

The last waterwheel in Mill Street was demolished in the 1960's and the existing waterwheel was erected as a feature by Ray Jones in memory of the tradespeople who once worked in Mill Street. A plaque informs the passer by, that on this site once stood Rees's Mill driven by water from the Cibi Brook and that it was demolished in 1972.

Near a stone bridge in Mill Street in the early years of the nineteenth century there was a ducking pool in which faithless wives and women of loose character were immersed. The custom was to parade the unfortunate woman in a cart round the town before the ceremony of ducking. On arrival at the pool, she was greeted by the hooting and jeering of the people gathered to witness the proceedings.

Despite her struggles and screams she was roughly lifted out of the cart and thrown into the pool, out of which she scrambled as best as she could.

One woman of loose character was known after her many duckings as 'Poll the Duck'. She was immersed on one occasion because she had given information to the military authorities as to the whereabouts of her husband who had deserted from the Army. In consequence of which he was arrested and subjected to the vigorous punishment awarded to deserters in those days.

Ducking stools were intended for shrews, scolds and immoral women. This stool, or chair, was fixed to the end of a long pole, arranged so as to be easily moved up and down over a mill pond, or preferably a pool of stagnant and noxious water. The woman was seated in the chair, and bound securely with cords, and then the men, taking hold of the long pole, dipped or ducked the culprit in the water. There, according to an old writer, 'the scold, shrew, or immoral woman is placed; bare-headed and shoeless, to abide the derision of those that passed by.' In Wales, as late as 1845, shrews were 'dipped' in mill ponds.

Turn Pike Trusts and Toll Houses

In the 1800's an Act was passed by the Government which allowed land-owners to erect houses on the town boundary in order to collect a toll. These were a form of taxation to pay for the upkeep of the roads. In due course it became impossible to enter or leave Abergavenny without paying a toll for there were similar toll houses and gates situated at the junction of Merthyr Road and Tudor Street, at the junction of Brecon Road and Chapel Road, at the junction of Monmouth Road and Station Road, at the corner of Holywell Road where it meets Lower Monk Street and at the corner of Hereford Road and Croesonnen Road.

The old Pen-y-Pound toll house was built in 1831 when the Turnpike Trust was given permission to improve the old Hereford road out of the town. At one time it was a sweet shop kept by Mrs Hibbett. This historic building has been enlarged and restored in recent years.

Emma King, who once kept a toll house in Monk Street

Near the Baptist Church in Frogmore Street there was a turnpike toll house with three gates, one opening on the road up Pen-y-pound, the other shutting off communication between Pen y pound Road and Brecon Road, and the third extending across to the Butcher's Arms. It was a small two-storeyed building. Afterwards the toll house and gates were removed, and a gate was fixed at the 'Round House', which was a one storeyed building at the junction of Frogmore Street with Merthyr Road. The entrance to the town from Brecon Road was behind the Round House and through the gardens behind the Brecon Road Brewery, and as far as the Station Hotel.

At the bottom of Chapel Road, where that road joins the Brecon Road stood what was called 'The Little Turnpike', which was a toll gate to catch any vehicles, horses and cattle that might be brought that way into town. The Turnpike Trust was dissolved in 1885 and The Highways Board took over the roads, to be replaced in turn by the County Council as Highway Authority.

In 1938 the Government created a system of trunk roads which were routes of national importance, and thereafter placed under the jurisdiction of the Ministry of Transport. A section of one of these national roads ran through Abergavenny and was known as the Newport - Abergavenny - Hereford - Shrewsbury trunk road. It is recorded that during that year this road was carrying 1,687 tons of traffic a day, the Brecon road 2,627 tons, Raglan road, 2,117 tons; Merthyr road, 2967 tons; Ross road, 632 tons and the Old Monmouth road, 1,132 tons per day.

All this traffic, whichever way it passed had to negotiate the narrow congested streets of the town centre. Even the important trunk road had to negotiate a right-angle turn at the junction of Cross Street and Monk Street as well as the narrow nature of the latter street. Pedestrians walked in constant danger upon the narrow pavements of the town's main streets.

In early August, 1962 the first stage of the Heads of the Valleys Road (A465) was opened from the Monmouth Road roundabout at Hardwick to the Aberbaiden roundabout at a cost of £70,000. Included in the cost was the concrete bridge which crossed the river Usk. Its central span stretched for 120 feet with two side-spans of 40 feet.

In the 1980s a useful link road was constructed from the Merthyr Road, along the old Abergavenny - Merthyr railway to join the Brecon Road with roundabouts at each end. A slip road from it into the western section of Union Road provides access to and exit from the ambulance station and Nevill Hall Hospital.

The Plaques History Trail

The Abergavenny History Society has done sterling work in marking some of the particularly interesting buildings in the town with circular blue plaques in order to help people learn more about Abergavenny and its history. Initially, nine were installed in 1981, then in 2003, fourteen more were added, and in 2010 these were supplemented by six brightly coloured children's plaques. Local schools were involved in carrying out the research which provided the inspiration for the Abergavenny scultor Jane Turner and the ceramic artist Ned Heywood of Chepstow to design the plaques. The schools involved in the project were: Our Lady & St Michael's RC Primary School, Gilwern Primary School, Govilon Primary School, Deri View Primary School, Cantref Primary School and Llanfihangel Crucorney Primary School. Plaques are to be found at the following sites:

Tan House (Mill St.), The Gunter Mansion (Cross St.), the medieval South Gate (Cross St.), the medieval Gate to St Mary's Priory (Monk St.), the medieval North Gate (Frogmore St.), St John's Church/King Henry VIII Grammar School, The Cow Inn (Nevill St.), medieval West Gate (Castle St./ Tudor St.), the Bull Inn (Nevill St.), 18th century Welsh Flannel Mill, Building where white periwigs were once made by hair bleacher, James Jones (Nevill St.), Georgian facade c.1750 (Nevill St.), Bailey Park which was initially leased by Crawshay Bailey in 1883 and later purchased for the town for £5,000 (Hereford Rd.), St Mary's Priory Tithe Barn (Monk St.), Abergavenny Town Hall, which was built in 1870 to replace John Nash's Market Hall (Cross St.), Angel Hotel - old coaching inn (Cross St.), the Kings Arms, one of the town's oldest inns (Nevill St.), High Cross (junction of High St. and Cross St.), Jettied Row of Shops originally built in the 16th century (Market St.), Sheep Market (Castle St.), boot and shoe industry (Cross St.), Roman barracks and granary (Castle St. Car Park), Birthplace of author Ethel Lina White (Frogmore St.). The children's plaques mark the following sites: King Henry VIII School (1542-1898), Abergavenny's medieval market place (St John's Square), where a hair bleacher lived c.1740 (Nevill St.), medieval West Gate (Tudor St.), Gobannium (Castle St. car park), 18th century flannel mill (Flannel St.).

Plaque on a building in Nevill Street where white periwigs were once made by hair bleacher, James Jones.

Plaque in St John's Square marking site of the medieval market place

Plaque marking the site of an 18th century flannel mill in Flannel Street

Plaque on the Town Hall, which was built on the site of John Nash's Market Hall

Chapter Nine
INDUSTRY AND BUSINESSES IN THE TOWN

Soon after the town had been deprived of its first Charter, Abergavenny began to decline as a place of importance; though it was once considerably enriched by the sale of its far-famed Welsh white flannels, of which large quantities were formerly sent to India.

Edward J. Burrow 1903

Abergavenny from early times has been an agricultural Market Town being a natural outlet for cattle and sheep from the Welsh mountains rearing grounds, as proved by existing records giving the sums realised by markets and fair tolls. Between 1500 and 1700 the road from Abergavenny to Brecon was the only way into Wales from London and this caused a great increase in the number of hostelries for people to stay the night and by 1760, an economic revival in the fortunes of the town was definitely taking place. A period of temporary prosperity resulted from the manufacture of full-bottomed, flaxen wigs which became fashionable in the late eighteenth century. This success was attributed to the local discovery of a technique for bleaching hair.

William Coxe in 1805 mentions that:

'During the preposterous fashion formerly prevalent among the beaux, of decorating their heads with flaxen periwigs of an enormous size, which were valued in proportion to their whiteness, and not infrequently sold at the price of forty or fifty guineas, a method was discovered and supposed to be invented in this neighbourhood, of bleaching hair; an employment which supported many persons, and was productive of considerable profit, until the fashion changed.'

The Reverend John Evans, writing in 1810, stated that this technique had given Abergavenny a leading role in wig making and that the industry employed many persons. In John White's Guide to the Town and Neighbourhood of Abergavenny, published in 1845, the author recalls that, on occasions, forty guineas had been paid for wigs manufactured in the town.

A method of bleaching periwigs had been invented in the town and in about 1740 a much respected hair bleacher was James Jones who had his home and business in Nevill Street. The building later became the Green Dragon Inn and in more recent years was owned by the British Legion, but is currently being redeveloped.

Fashions are ever changing and within a short time the demand for periwigs declined, and a petition was even sent to George III in 1765 emphasising the distress that the wig-makers were now in, for the nobility and people of high class were now wearing their own hair instead of wigs made from the hair of Welsh goats. This was followed by a humorous petition to the king from the 'Body of Carpenters' who implored him to have one of his legs amputated so that he might popularise the fashion of wearing a wooden leg and encourage the manufacture of such items!

However, before too long the Industrial Revolution arrived and mines and ironworks were rapidly established just over the other side of the Blorenge and in the Clydach Gorge, bringing new prosperity to the town.

The town became noted for the weaving of a very fine flannel, which was widely distributed and even exported to India. It was woven at No 1 Cross Street, which on ceasing to be the vicarage of St John's, became the flannel factory. It was from this business that Flannel Street took it name.

Another important business in the town was the manufacture of candles, before wax and composite candles were invented and prior to paraffin lamps coming into general use. These candles were taken to the hill towns of Blaenavon, Tredegar, Ebbw Vale and elsewhere to be sold in great quantities to the works and mines proprietors as well as to grocers. Deliveries were made three or four times a week.

There was a candle factory of considerable size at No 44 Mill Street, called then, the Sugar Loaf House, and where a representation of a loaf of sugar, shaped like a huge cone was suspended over the entrance door. This business was kept by a William Price, nicknamed 'Billy Farthing' because when farthings were first minted, he introduced them to Abergavenny.

Corn growing must have taken place on every available piece of land and there were once twelve water wheel powered grist mills on local streams which is an indication of the amount of corn grown and ground. The milling of corn was a prosperous trade during the late 19th century and water mills were erected on the course of the Cybi brook in Mill Street (Castle Mills), at Llwyndu (Chapel Mill), while on the course of the Kenfi were to be found Philpott's Mill, the Priory Mill, Little Mill, Llantilio Mill, and the Pontisgob Mill. Then later, after the introduction of steam power, Tucker Bros' Mills, in Lion Street were of great importance. Built in two stages, first the flour mill and then the corn mill, they were driven by steam power from the coal-fired boiler house in the rear where there were two boilers and from where steam was piped across Lion Street to a bakery. Tucker Brothers went bankrupt in 1905, and the Horsington Brothers bought the mill two years later for £750.

There was a Priory Mill in Ross road but it was almost completely washed away by the great flood in 1931. This flood also destroyed the oldest bridge in the district which was over the Gavenny in Lower Monk Street and which on very old maps was named Pont ar Wyn. An old bill in the museum collections has an engraved view of the Priory Mill as it appeared in 1866, with carts and wagons being loaded and unloaded, with the tall brick chimney smoking in the background.

Barley was also grown extensively, as inside the town there were several Malt houses, where malt was dressed for supplying every home as they all did their own brewing.

Timber felling and sawing was also a source of employment and at every local estate yard there were saw pits where trees were made into planks and boards. Cutting and hauling colliery pit props used to employ many, as also did charcoal burning in the vicinity of Abergavenny. When the oak trees were felled the bark was stripped off and used for leather making in the tanpits. Hurdle and gate makers worked in Lower Monk Street yards.

There were large tanpits beside Mill Street, and the large house (built in 1775) at the junction of Mill-street and Cross Street was once known as the Tan House. It has been extended and is now called Pegasus Court (a retirement housing complex). On the opposite side of Mill Street was The Tanners' Arms Inn. (now a furniture shop). The tan yard consisted of a tan house, tanpits, vaults, tankilns etc. The tan pits where hides were left to soak in oak bark tanning for 12 or 18 months were on a site opposite the present day bus station.

Tan House at the junction of Mill Street and Cross Street was built in 1775 on the site of a Master Tanner's house which was certainly there in 1691.

The making of boots remained a flourishing trade until the turn of the 19th century and a very old guide book to the town states that about forty men were employed as cobblers at Lion House in the High Street (opposite what later became the Woolworths shop). In Coxe's *Tours of Monmouthshire* we read: 'This place also supplied large quantities of shoes, which were conveyed to Bristol and exported from thence.'

Glovemaking was also an important industry at one time, and the workmen used to drink in the 'Glover's Arms' in Tudor Street which was the main street in those days and a hat making business was established there by a Mrs Lewis in 1808.

A thriving hatter's business was also run by a Mr Edward Restall in the early years of the twentieth century. He had a factory and shop next to the shop owned by Basil Jones in Cross Street. Apparently, it was a common sight in those days to see the old hatter walking down Cross Street with a huge quantity of old style felt hats to wash them separately in the mill stream near the Swan Hotel, to remove all the surplus matter after the hats had been dyed in his factory.

After shaping, dyeing and washing, the hats went into the trimming department to be dealt with by Mrs Restall. The materials for the linings were cut into suitable portions and stitched together. The bands and bindings came in rolls and the leathers in gross bundles. The leathers were pierced along the edge with a spiked wheel to admit the needle to complete the sewing of the hat bands by hand.

As well as making felt top hats, the firm also manufactured the beaver hats worn by the stage coach drivers, and Welsh hats for women were also produced. A custom in those days made it 'compulsory' for all workmen to wear box hats during their working hours.

There were cast iron foundries in Castle Street, Lewis Lane and Llanfoist. The railings which enclose Hyde Park in London were cast at Lewis' foundry. The order came to Abergavenny because the original contractors had failed to complete the order, and Sir Benjamin Hall, who was always singing the praises of Abergavenny, said he would find someone in the town to finish the work. Eventually the railings were completed by James Lewis of Abergavenny. Local examples of his work are the gates of Bailey Park and Linda Vista Gardens. He also made St Mary's Priory Church railings and the

Cemetery gates on the Old Hereford Road. Lewis's Lane is named after James Lewis, a journeyman craftsman from Merthyr Tydfil, who was the last proprietor. Like all respectable tradesmen of his time he was generally seen in a box hat.

Stone quarrying was another local industry which dated back to 1493, when Jasper Tudor, Lord of Abergavenny gave permission to the monks of St Mary's Priory to remove stones and fallen timber from the Sugar Loaf at a location then called, the Forest of Moyle. For this privilege they paid 6d a year. Scars of stone quarrying can be seen on the local hills and there also are remains of lime kilns in the vicinity. Much of the stone for buildings erected in Abergavenny in the 19th century came from old quarries on the side of the Deri. Clay bricks were manufactured by hand at four brickyards.

In 1870 a small general printing works and paper warehouse was established in Cross Street. From such beginnings grew the firm of **Sergeant Brothers Limited**. The founder was Henry Sergeant and at the start only a small staff was employed, among them a few girls who produced hand-made bags. The machinery at this time consisted of two or three hand-printing presses.

Within a very short time the business began to expand and provide more employment. In 1887 a spacious factory was erected in Queen Street. New machinery was installed, more outside representatives were appointed and additional staff employed.

Interior of Sergeant Brothers Printing Works

The firm started to win a high reputation for first-class work in printing, lithography and book binding. It continued to play a pioneering part in the Welsh bag-making trade. and every shop in the Principality knew of Sergeant's as the main bag-making house.

Henry Sergeant retired from active participation in 1909 and the firm became a limited liability company. Mr W. Percy was appointed Managing Director and under his leadership the business grew to such an extent that in 1913 the factory and offices had to be enlarged again.

In 1919 Percy Sergeant, son of the founder took over the running of the firm, but he had to retire shortly after because of ill health. Later, another son of the founder, Mr Stuart Campbell Sergeant was appointed to the board and also became secretary to the company.

A well remembered sound was the hooter which called employees to work each day and provided an accurate time check for residents of the town. The works closed in 1983 and the business was transferred to Pontypool. The printing works in Queen Street was demolished and is now the site of the Cibi Walk shopping precinct.

Sergeant Brothers Printing Works in Queen Street was demolished in 1990

Another printing business known as **Dover & Company** was founded in Frogmore Street by a Brynmawr couple, Mr and Mrs G. W. Dover in the early 1890s. Their first premises were at Nos 1 and 2 Chicken Street, a former road adjoining Flannel Street. The enterprise started in a small way and the work carried out included the printing of handbills, posters, ballot sheets and municipal election lists.

In 1912, a move was made to Lion Street, where the firm had the benefit of greatly increased floor space and were able to employ more staff. But in 1925 disaster struck when a fire destroyed much of their premises, forcing them to move again. They moved to their present site and the building they occupy is well over 450 years old.

Richards in Frogmore Street was initially opened as a hardware store by Mr Fenwick William Richards and it started as a saddlers business in a private house situated in Market Street. It was just after World War I that the business first moved into Frogmore Street, occupying premises on the eastern side of the Britannia Inn and in 1925 Mr Richards bought Nos 46 and 47 Frogmore Street, the site of the Old George Inn. He converted No 47 into a shop and rented out No 46 until he found need of it later as the business expanded. During the years between the wars he established an agricultural engineering department at Abergavenny Cattle Market.

Richards in Frogmore Street

Just after World War II No 46 was turned into a cycle department and in 1949 Mr Richards was joined in the business by his son Owen Richards. The business was then turned into a Limited Company and 5 years later Mr Richards Senior died and Owen found himself managing director. In 1955 the company acquired yet another property, No 48 Frogmore Street and over the years all three shops were adapted and improved to provide one big departmental store with retail departments on two floors and with a car park in Baker Street.

The *Abergavenny Chronicle* was founded in 1871 by Edwin Morgan and published from a premises at 21 Nevill Street with Mr W. M. J. Scanlan as editor. In due course the office was moved to 26 Frogmore Street where the paper was produced for the next one hundred years. During this period it remained a family concern and on the death of Edwin Morgan the ownership passed to his son-in-law Edgar Straker. who remained the company's director until his death in 1938. His four children, Stanley Morgan Straker, Miss Derrie Straker, Mrs J.A. Moxley and Mrs J.S. James then became directors.

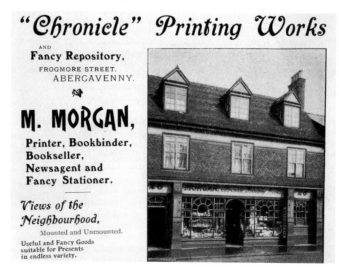

In 1960, Stanley Straker and his son John took over the running of the company, but sold it in 1965 to Berrows Newspapers Ltd, based in Worcester and the Chronicle Office moved to premises in 45 Cross Street. The *Abergavenny Chronicle* was then part of a 28 newspaper group covering an area from the industrial Midlands to the South Coast. In 1983 Berrows sold the paper to Tindle Newspapers Ltd., based in Farnham, Surrey. Then in 1996 the *Abergavenny Chronicle* moved to new offices in Tindle House, a listed building in Nevill Street. The new office was officially opened by HRH The Duke of Gloucester on the 125th anniversary of the founding of the paper.

Local newspapers that have disappeared are the *Abergavenny Gazette, Abergavenny and Monmouthshire Advertiser*, the *Abergavenny Echo*, the *Abergavenny Herald* and the *Abergavenny Free Press*.

The largest local employer used to be **Coopers Mechanical Joints**, a factory situated in Llanfoist, which was started during the Second World War, when the Lang Pen Company were induced to come to Abergavenny to undertake the manufacture of radiators for Spitfires and it certainly helped the local employment situation.

Visit by a Spitfire pilot to the Lang Pen Works in 1941

After the war the factory remained idle for some time and there were fears that it might become derelict although constructed on modern lines and well suited to light industry. Fortunately Coopers Mechanical Joints of Slough were persuaded to take over the factory and within twelve months the number of employees reached a total of 325. Of these, one third were males and of the females 25 per cent were married women.

The original buildings were extended and in 1961 a large extension was completed next to the main road. This was followed by a major development at the rear of the factory, which became known as the 'Top Factory' because of its elevated position.

All the filters for the London buses were made there and it was a proud boast that every vehicle on the road had something made at Coopers Mechanical Joints factories. Most of the components were for motor vehicles and stationary engines.

The Cooper King self cleaning air filter which was developed in the early 1960s was unique in design and concept. It was intended for off-highway application such as mines, quarries and major developments where high dust concentration makes the normal filters uneconomical. The self cleaning feature meant that the filter did not have to be changed as often as the conventional filter and this offered a considerable saving on service costs.

In 1966 the company was bought by Turner and Newall, a Manchester based firm with multi-national interests and five years later, the company name was changed to Coopers Filters. Turner and Newall sold the company in 1988 to Fiaam Spa, an Italian based filtration company and from that time the Abergavenny factory benefited from a major development programme with more than eight million pounds worth of new plant and equipment installed.

Machinery in the factory was of the most modern type for the tasks required, the largest being a 200 ton press and six of these were specially brought from America. There was a fully equipped tool room for making press tools of all types where thirty skilled men were employed and another fifty on sectional inspection. There was also an assembly section where all the parts were put together. (A filter was made up of fourteen different parts.)

Sadly, in January 2004, work began on the demolition of 'Coopers Factory' at Llanfoist. The site had been purchased by Newport based development firm Johnsey Estate Ltd and a planning application outlining the first phase of a large scale development of the site for new houses had been submitted to Monmouthshire County Council. In 2010 the first houses were built on the site which has inappropriately been named 'White Castle'.

In 2010 new Houses were built on the site of Cooper's Factory

Chapter Ten
HOTELS AND PUBLIC HOUSES

The population of the town of Abergavenny, according to the last census, is 7,640, and there are 51 alehouses and beerhouses on premises, and 4 beer off premises. Thus showing that there is one licensed house to each 121 inhabitants.

Police Superintendant J. Davies 1897

The **Angel Hotel** in Cross Street is a fine Georgian building, and the largest hotel in the town. In the early part of the eighteenth century the Angel Hotel belonged to William Dinwoody, whose family perhaps first came here as proprietors of this house. By his will dated 14 October 1736, he left it to his son Robert. It was later occupied by Samuel Saunders, and afterwards by his son Charles Hanbury Saunders.

The Angel Hotel was once an important coaching inn

During the coaching age, the Angel underwent extensive rebuilding, when the front entrance and the dining room (then the Assembly Room) acquired their present graceful character. It was a noted coaching inn on the road to Milford Haven, but in 1858 this service came to an end, while the Angel continued to be used as the terminus of a daily service from Ross-on-Wye. An 1835 Timetable provided the following information:-

To London, the Royal Mail (from Milford) calls at the Angel, every forenoon at 20 mins, past eleven. The 'Nimrod' (from Brecon) every morning (Sunday excepted) at half-past nine.

To Brecon, the 'Nimrod' (from London) calls at the Angel, every afternoon (Sunday excepted) at quarter past one.

To Hereford, a coach from the Angel every afternoon at four.

To Milford, the 'Royal Mail' (from London) calls at the Angel every afternoon at two; goes through Crickhowell, Brecon etc.

To Newport, the 'Royal Mail' (from London) calls at the Angel every morning at eight; goes through Pontypool and Caerleon.

The London coach which bore the name 'Champion' would leave Fleet Street in London at 3 pm and arrive at the Angel Hotel in Abergavenny the following morning at 11 am. This gives an average speed of 8 miles an hour, including numerous stops for changing horses. Another coach left the Angel Hotel every morning at 7am for Hereford, Worcester and Birmingham. There was also a coach travelling to Bristol via Chepstow, across the 'Old Passage' every other day.

The Brecon coach was described in 1875 as a very handsome one built by Messrs Holland of Oxford Street, London, and coloured dark blue and vermillion. The horses were well matched, good looking, short legged animals, suited to the hilly district. It would leave Abergavenny at 9.00 am and marked its departure with a twang of the post horn.

In June 1977 the Royal Mail Coach returned to Abergavenny and the Mayor and Mayoress celebrated the occasion by riding in style on the top of the horse drawn vehicle as it made its way along Cross Street to the Angel Hotel. This particular coach had once been a familiar sight on the London to Norfolk run.

Over the years many important functions and meetings have been held in this hotel, such as a fancy dress ball held in 1838. It took place in the 'Great Room' upstairs and was attended by two hundred ladies and gentlemen from most of the influential families of the neighbourhood. The ballroom was decorated with laurel and artificial flowers and banners painted with Welsh emblems and notices. Musicians came all the way from Cheltenham to play the dance music, but the quadrilles were danced to Welsh airs. There was an interlude when three local bards (one of whom was blind) who had won prizes for singing, sang a Welsh air beautifully harmonised. The guests included Sir Benjamin Hall and his wife and Crawshay Bailey the famous ironmaster. A detailed account of the event appeared in the *Hereford Times*:

> 'This novel assembly... was attended by upwards of two hundred ladies and gentlemen, comprising most of the influential families of the neighbourhood. The room was tastefully decorated with festoons of evergreens and flowers, and green and white flags bearing suitable Welsh inscriptions and the crest of the worthy President of the Cymreigyddion Society.'

The ladies were attired in 'Welsh" costumes of silk and satin and appear to have caused quite a sensation:

> 'The Beautiful Mrs Mountjoy dazzled all beholders in the costume of Gwent and Morgannwg, composed of satin, with a beaver hat and mop cap. The extraordinary beauty of this lady is too well known to need further eulogium; but it would be an incorrect report, if the buzz of admiration were not recorded, which attended her in whatever part of the room she appeared.'

Even the less-favoured townsfolk must have enjoyed themselves as they watched the coming and going of the nobility and gentry, the carriages bearing the crests of their owners and the servants and horses, both wearing large cockades of green and white. The outside of the hotel was decorated with flags, flowers and giant leeks, and the post-boys wore brightly coloured jackets of Welsh wool. Everyone wore leeks, either natural, or made of silver, satin or pearls.

The Morgan family once resided at the hotel and one of their sons was Walter Morgan who is worthy of a mention for he is the only Abergavenny man who ever became Mayor of London, and could thus be described as the local Dick Whittington! In 1846 when he was just 15 years old he left Abergavenny and went to work in London at the office of the National Provincial Cashier of England. He was appointed Sheriff in 1900, Lord Mayor of London in 1905 and was subsequently knighted.

A scene outside the Angel Hotel in 1904

Many famous people have stayed or dined at the Angel Hotel over the years. The first known visitor of significance was Sir Richard Colt Hoare in 1793, who was on his way from Wiltshire to study the antiquities of Wales. It was also at the Angel Hotel that Benjamin Pratt, one of the pioneer ironmasters at Blaenavon died in May 1794. He collapsed after a meal in the hotel and quickly expired, but I might add it was due to a heart condition rather than the quality of the food!

It is also of interest that the future Queen Victoria once passed through Abergavenny on her way to Haverfordwest. She was only a slip of a girl at the time and she stood patiently outside the Angel Hotel, while the horses were being changed on her coach.

In 1890 the new coach 'Comet', with seven passengers, performed its first journey from Ross to Abergavenny on Saturday 31st January, arriving at the Angel Hotel a minute or two before the advertised time. About a quarter of an hour before two o'clock a large crowd had assembled in Cross Street to witness its arrival. The coach came up the hill at a smart trot, drawn by four fine horses, the guard Bellamy, having signalled its approach by a cheerful flourish of the horn as they entered the town.

Resplendent in his scarlet coat, with gold brading and facings and a white beaver hat, the guard seemed to appreciate the importance and responsibility of his post and lost no opportunity of magnifying his already high and distinguished office. But for some onlookers, a little disappointment was no doubt experienced when it was observed that he had intentionally or in the hurry and excitement of the moment at starting, ommited to bring his blunderbus!

The coachman, Pennington, wore a more sombre coloured suit with a beaver hat. The coach was driven by Mr Hargreaves from Monmouth to Raglan, when, upon horses being changed, Mr McCalmont took the reins. In order to celebrate the arrival of this new coach a lunch had been thoughtfully prepared by Mr and Mrs Prichard at the Angel Hotel and a large party sat down to eat the meal.

In about 1937 alterations were carried out at the Angel which necessitated excavating part of the entrance hall, and about 18 inches below the existing floor level the old cobbled stone roadway was revealed. All vehicular traffic passed through this entrance into a courtyard at the rear, then through the building and flanked by stables etc., out into Upper Castle Street. From there they would proceed to the Westgate, into Tudor Street or down Nevill Street to the North Gate and Frogmore Street.

The old entrance passage through the front of the hotel, which now forms the vestibule or hall, was so low that persons sitting upon the coach had to stoop to avoid contact with the top of the arch.

Gregory Peck stopped at The Angel for a meal in 1945. He was accompanied by the well-known director, John Houston and they were en route to Fishguard in West Wales, to spend eight weeks filming 'Moby Dick'. Peck was then 38 years old and wore a heavy beard specially grown for the sea-faring role as Captain Ahab. This was his first visit to Wales.

On Wednesday 4th September 1963 a large American car purred to a halt outside the Angel Hotel and out stepped film stars Richard Burton and Elizabeth Taylor. Thirty-eight year old Burton and his attractive companion stayed at the hotel for two hours. They had a steak and kidney pie and a £2 10s bottle of Claret before driving on to Merthyr Tydfil.

Few people had seen them arrive, but a large crowd, most of them women, smiled and waved as they climbed into their cadillac. Richard Burton who had just finished filming 'Beckett' and Elizabeth Taylor, star of the much publicised 'Cleopatra' were said to be 'taking things easy.'

Present day view of the Angel Hotel

The Great George Hotel (now closed) stands on the site of Bellamy's Wine Vaults which flourished about 170 years ago. In the 1890s the proprietors were Charles Tucker & Son and one could buy a gallon of Scotch whisky for £1, 1s 6d and the same quantity of gin for 15s. Wood's town map of 1834 shows it as Bellamy's Wine Vaults and this is confirmed by the Poor Rate Book of 1839, in which is entered "John Bellamy, wine merchant. House, wine room and stabling." John Bellamy was a juror at the trial of John Frost, the Chartist leader in 1839.

The Abergavenny Mail directory of 1906 gives Alfred Jenkins, wine merchant, as the proprietor. The same year his manager, Walter Griffin commited suicide by taking cyanide of potassium.

The Great George Hotel in Cross Street

One side of the old sign used to show George Bernard Shaw, the great Irish dramatist who made such a mark with his wit and exposure of hypocrisy. On the other side was George Washington -the first President of the American Republic. But the name of the hotel really relates to the Great George Jewel - the badge of the Order of the Garter. It was first conferred upon the Duke of Wellington in 1813. Inlaid with diamonds, it was worn by Sir Winston Churchill at the Coronation of Her Majesty Queen Elizabeth II in 1953. It was stolen in 1965 and its whereabouts remain a mystery. In the cellars the vaulted low roofs of the series of chambers stretch under adjoining property and reputedly contain the entrance to an underground passage. Much of this has been filled in but a flight of steps can be seen to descend to a lower level.

The Swan Hotel in Cross Street

The Swan Hotel in Cross Street was built in the 19th century on the site of a previous building which was known as the New Swan and it became a posting house. Behind the building was a small yard where the stage wagons parked for the night when they brought shop goods two or three times a week from Caerleon, which was a place of importance in those days. There was building on the right- hand side of the hotel which was used as a ballroom, but it was destroyed in a fire.

The Abergavenny Hotel (now Closed), Monmouth Road was first known as the Cantreff Arms and subsequently the Bell Vue Hotel and the Rothesay Hotel.

The Great Western Hotel, Station Road was previously known as the Railway Hotel, the Railway Inn, the Railway and Commercial Inn and in 1877 it became the Great Western Railway Hotel.

The Kings Head Hotel , Cross Street, stands on the site of the old corn market and incorporates one of its original four stone arches. This medieval Gothic archway was built wide enough for carts to pass through and gives access to a cobbled courtyard, where the medieval corn market was held.

The Improvement Commissioners met here from 1797 to 1827 and then moved their meetings to a room over the Wheat Market and this was the first conception of a town hall in Abergavenny.

A one-time landlord of the King's Head was James Cole whose claim to fame was the fact that he sat on the jury at the Monmouth trial of John Frost the Chartist leader in 1839

Originally the hotel was much larger than it is now for part of it was sold to become a drapery business known as the Golden Fleece. At the rear of the hotel used to be large stables which were used by farmers from all around the district to stable their horses on market days.

The Railway Hotel, Brecon Road was first known as the White Hart, and then the London and North Western Railway Hotel. It became known as the Railway Hotel in about 1865, but by 1884 the name had changed back to the London and North Western Railway Hotel and then in 1914 it was again known as the Railway Hotel.

The **Kings Arms** in Neville Street stands just inside the old medieval town wall, adjacent to the site of the Tudor Gate.

The Kings Arms in Nevill Street

Experts have decided that the earliest part of the building appears to date back to about 1450 and it became an inn during the 17th century. It takes its name from the royal coat of arms displayed on the front wall. It was once believed to have commemorated Charles I who visited Abergavenny on 1st July 1645, after the Royalists' defeat at the battle of Naseby. Later opinion decided that it was the coat of arms of Charles II, but it is in fact that of Queen Victoria.

The first landlord known by name is Edward Blashfield who owned the pub in 1811 and had previously kept the Cow Inn. The Kings Arms remained in his family until at least 1860. During the 19th century the Kings Arms not only served as a post office, but was also a noted house of call for stage coaches. In 1858 a coach ran from here to Merthyr Tydfil on Tuesdays and to Tredegar on Fridays.

An inscription on an oak beam inside the pub was carved by soldiers who were briefly quartered there two years after the battle of Waterloo. They had been called to the district following serious rioting in Nantyglo and Tredegar in 1816.

'Good quarters for the 15th King's Hussars
October 14, 1817. To Arms for Ever.
Jas Hall F. Troop,24'

This was indeed a lasting tribute to the landlord and his hospitality for the troops stationed in Abergavenny nearly 200 years ago. It can now be seen inside the Barn bar.

During the ownership of Thomas Delafield, from 1873, the pub also served as a brewery and according to one advertisement the Kings Arms 'enjoyed a high reputation for pure ales and stouts obtainable in any quantities from a half pint bottle to a 54 gallon cask.' The pub remained in the ownership of the Delafield family until 1919.

Ben Jones, the present owner of the Kings Arms has set up a micro brewery on the premises to produce real ale. He had been fascinated by this building for a number of years and tried to buy it on two previous occasions, succeeding on his third attempt. His intention was to establish a business based around a gastro pub and decided that the brewing of real beer should prove of special interest to visitors. It was this pub's history of brewing which had really attracted him and he is keen to carry on the tradition. He commented, 'There is not any real beer being made in the town now, but about 100 years ago there may have been seven breweries here.'

The old barn at the rear of the pub has been converted into a venue with a stage that hosts live music events, two or three nights a week. One can sit down and enjoy an evening meal and listen to Jazz, Blues, Rock or Country music on a regular basis. The old fireplaces have been opened up and flagstones replaced on the ground floor, generally giving the interior a historic atmosphere. One of the bars still has some of the original oak partition wall of 1550.

The Hen & Chickens is an interesting buildings which fortunately survived the slum clearance in Flannel Street. It takes its name from the fact that a poultry market used to be held in nearby Chicken Street and St John's Street. Although altered and extended in recent years, it has retained a very special atmosphere, making it a favourite watering hole for many local people. It dates from the reign of William IV and in 1900 one could obtain dinner there for 1s 6d, tea for 6d and a bottle of Bass beer for 3d.

The Hen and Chickens Inn

W.H. Davies

Customers may also be interested to know that the famous tramp poet W.H. Davies once spent a rather inebriated night there in May 1911, during a walking tour of Wales.

He had set out to tramp the open road for a few weeks with no more luggage than a razor in one pocket and a spare shirt in another. On arriving in Abergavenny he found accommodation in the Hen and Chickens and before turning in for the night decided to wander around the town.

After exploring the streets for an hour or so, he entered one or two pubs and drank several pints of strong ale. Somewhat the worse for wear, he then returned to the Hen and Chickens and made his way up to his bedroom. Before getting into bed he took many fuddled precautions against the possibility of a robber visiting his room during the night. He first looked under the bed to make sure that no one was hiding there and then placed a chair against the door, which he had already locked.

Still, not satisfied he placed a china ornament on the extreme edge of the chair, so if the lock was picked, the least attempt to open the door would topple the ornament to the floor with a loud crash.

He then took off his hat and coat and lay down on the bed fully dressed. Beside him he placed his stout cane which concealed 'a strong, sharp toledo blade, about three feet long', at the ready to deal with any intruder. Very quickly he drifted off to sleep, no doubt very tired after his long walk that day, but also feeling the effects of six pints of strong ale.

He recounts how he suddenly woke up some time later and by the dim light of a street lamp saw a figure standing at the foot of the bed. For a few moments he could not remember where he was, but gradually his senses came back to him and he became very alarmed with the thought that someone had entered his room.

With his heart pounding, he sat up in bed with his weapon in his hand and said boldly, 'You have made a great mistake coming into my room.' He expected the man to run out of the room but, the 'intruder' did not move. So Davies then said in a threatening voice, 'Do you hear? If you do not leave this room at once, I'll run you through the heart!'

But still the figure did not move, so Davies then got off the bed with his weapon ready for action and as he drew nearer to the intruder, he realised his mistake. The figure was no other than the bedpost which, when he had first entered the room he had dressed in his coat and cap instead of hanging them behind the door.

He tells us how he then laughed at his mistake, then undressed properly, and got into bed, where he slept soundly until the morning. During his stay in this historic inn W.H. Davies is said to have penned the following lines:

'O what a merry world I see
Before me through a quart of ale.'

The Coach and Horses in Cross Street bears a plaque marking the 'Site of Medieval Town Gate', reminding us that this was the east gate to the town. This pub used to be called the Sun until 1974 and it was here the the Cymreigyddion Society was formed in 1832. The original Coach and Horses was in Castle Street and at one time the building had stabling for more than 50 horses.

The Coach and Horses in Cross Street

145

The Old Herefordshire House in Frogmore Street was formerly known as the Crown and Sceptre and also the Rose and Crown. It originally had a thatched roof and was named the Herefordshire House in 1822 and then the Old Herefordshire House in 1842. It was rebuilt in the 1960s and in 1997 it became known as the Colonial Inn and is now the Auberge.

The Britannia, in Frogmore Street was originally called the Cock and Horse in 1741, but by 1793 it was known as the Three Kings and then the Britannia in 1821. It was renamed the Welsh Guardsman in 1983 but in 1997 the name reverted back to the Britannia.

The Bailey Inn , on the Hereford Road was originally known as the Masons Arms and it became the Victoria Inn in about 1845. It was renamed the Bailey in 1992 and is best known for the day when Hitler's deputy, Rudolph Hess on one of his outings stopped for his daily bottle of lager and the landlord asked him to autograph a lager label which is now on exhibition in Abergavenny Museum.

The Bailey Inn on the Hereford Road was previously known as the Victoria Inn

The Black Lion in Lion Street is closed at the time of writing

The Grofield Inn, Baker Street

The Britannia Inn, Frogmore Street

The Grofield Inn, situated in Baker Street was built in 1839 and the first landlord was a Mr Prothero.

The Cantref Inn, Brecon Road was built in 1843 on a plot of land owned by the Duke of Beaufort. The first landlord was William Rowley.

The Station Hotel, Brecon Road was in existence in 1865 when the landlord was a Mr Frederick Phillips.

The Railway Hotel, Brecon Road was known in 1834 as the White Hart and renamed the North Western Railway Hotel in 1865. Since 1914 it has been known by the present name.

The Farmers Arms, Lion Street was built on the site of the original Bethany Chapel which was demolished in 1883 and rebuilt in Market Street. The name of the pub was changed to the Market Tavern in 1996.

The Black Lion (now closed) in Lion Street was previously known as the Lion Street Tavern and also for a short time, the Plough Inn.

Grasshoppers

The Belmont Inn, Monmouth Road was known as the Blorenge Inn around 1807 and the name was changed to the Belmont Inn in 1891.

The Greyhound Vaults in Market Street (now a restaurant) was previously the tap bar of the Greyhound Hotel built in 1872. It had 18 bedrooms, 4 reception rooms, a bar and a ballroom and was a popular meeting place for the rugby, tennis and bowling clubs.

The Vine Tree, St John's Square is now known as Grasshoppers. In 1835 the publican was Elizabeth Thomas and it was owned by Charles Edwards Brewery Ltd from 1914 - 1938. It was taken over by Whitbread in 1966.

The Lost Pubs of Abergavenny

In the first half of the nineteenth century Abergavenny could boast over fifty inns for during that period it became a particularly busy and thriving town. Pub names such as The Dog and Bull, the Blue Feathers, The Wellington, The Crown and The Parrot, which all used to stand in Cross Street are now nothing but a very distant memory. Taking the streets in alphabetical order, here is a list of some of the old pubs that have disappeared:

Baker Street: The Carpenters Arms, the Royal Victoria Brewery.

Brecon Road: The North Western Temperance Hotel, The Brecon Road Brewery.

Byfield Lane: The Bush Inn, later called the Tudor Arms.

Castle Street: The Coach and Horses Inn, the Clarence Inn, the Beehive Inn, and The White Swan. The New Duke Inn opened in November 1890 as a hospital. This was replaced by the Victoria Cottage Hospital in Hereford Road in 1902.

The Old Duke of York on the south side of Castle Street was destroyed by demolition. Records show that it was an inn as far back as the the commencement of Queen Victoria's reign.

Chapel Road: The Cider House.

Chicken Street: The Horse and Groom.

Cross Street: The Wheatsheaf, The White Swan Hotel, The Red Lion, The Borough Arms, The Cardiff Hotel, The Blue Feathers, The Crown Inn, The Duke of Wellington Inn, The Queen's Head, the Dog and Bull, the Blue Boar, and The Parrot.

Flannel Street: the Old Barley Mow.

Frogmore Street: the Golden Lion, the King William, the White Horse Inn, the Butchers Arms, the George Inn, the Three Salmons, The Crown and Sceptre, The Butchers Arms, the Old George Commercial Hotel, the Bell, the Griffin, the Welcome Temperance Hotel, and the Lamb Inn. The King David Inn (1822-1973) on the corner of Lewis's Lane - had a sign depicting David and his harp before King Saul, painted on canvas and fixed to the front of the building. This pub was noted for its home brewed beer and its stables could accommodate two horses. In the coaching era, the Golden Lion was one of the town's principal posting houses and sent coaches daily to meet the packet boats at Bristol near Newport. At one time it occupied a large area, and the rear yard was noted for its horse sales. When it was sold in 1897 it was stated as having stabling for fifty horses and was 'particularly celebrated for its Home Brewed Ale.' It was renamed Sugar Loaf in 1970 but that closed in the 1980s and the building is currently a shop.

High Street: The Greyhound Hotel, the Victoria Temperance Hotel, the Guildhall Inn.

Lion Street: the New Market Inn, the Royal Oak, the Green Dragon.

Market Street: the Market Tavern.

Merthyr Road: the Lamb Inn, the White Lion.

Mill Street: The Earl Grey Inn, the Boars Head, the Tanners Arms, the Black Horse, the Castle Stores Inn, the Two Reformers Inn, the Masons Arms, the Three Tuns and the Anglers Arms. The Unicorn Inn, in Lower Mill Street was one of the best public houses in the town, but it lost a large part of its custom when the new section of road from the Swan Hotel to Pen-y-Cawse was constructed.

Monk Street: The Gatehouse, The New Fountain, the Nags Head, the London Hotel, the Omar Pasha, the Globe.

Monmouth Road: The Bridge End Inn.

Nevill Street: The Raven Hotel, the King's Head, the Dragons Head and the Cow Inn.

Princes Street: the Carpenters Arms, the Albert Inn.

Ross Road: the Monmouthshire House.

St John's Square: the Bull Inn, the Six Bells, the Quarrymens Arms.

Tudor Street: The Albion Inn, the Tudor Arms, the Blue Bell Inn, the Tudor Inn, the Milkmans Arms, the Old Crosskeys Inn, the Coppers Arms, the Foresters Arms, the Beaufort Arms.

Victoria Street: the Beaufort Arms and the Mount Pleasant.

The Old Bull Inn, St John's Square has been replaced by the ugly Post Office

148

Chapter Eleven
ASSORTED CHURCHES AND CHAPELS

St John's was the parish church of Abergavenny until the dissolution of the priory, when the latter became the parish church and St John's was converted by Henry VIII into a grammar school.

Sir Joseph Bradney 1906

There is a dubious tradition that Ynyr, a sixth century king of Gwent built a simple church on the site of **St John's Church**, but there is more substantial evidence that the first church was erected here by Hamelin de Balon, the Norman knight who was responsible for building Abergavenny Castle. As he died in 1090 it is probable that the church was completed by his nephew Brian de Wallingford who inherited the castle. At that time the church stood almost in the centre of the walled town and in due course it consisted of two aisles, a cross aisle and a massive tower at the centre. Just beyond, at the western end of the church would have been the old cattle market. The burial grounds are believed to have extended to the area now occupied by the old Woolworths building in High Street, for human remains were discovered during the excavation of the foundations of this building.

St John's was once the parish church

St John's was the first parish church in Abergavenny, until the Dissolution of the Monasteries which resulted in St Mary's Priory becoming the Parish Church. In 1542, 'The Free Grammar School of King Henry VIII King of England' was founded in the old parish church of St John's utilising the revenues from the Priory. In addition the whole of the great tithes pertaining to the rectory of Bedgworth, in the county of Gloucester, alienated from the suppressed Monastery of Usk, were granted to the School. The king directed that a competent master should be appointed to the school at a yearly salary of £13 6s 8d and that he should be assisted by an Usher who would receive a yearly salary of £6 13s 4d. According to Henry VIII's Charter, the master was required to accept any boy into the school who possessed an acceptable level of intelligence.

The first headmaster was appointed by King Henry VIII himself and the man who obtained the job was Nicholas Oldsworth MA. At that time the school's primary aim was the teaching of Latin grammar. Boys started at the school at the age of seven. During summer the school day was from 6am to 11am followed by an afternoon session of 1pm-6pm. In winter the hours were from 7am to 11 am and 1pm to 5pm. Boys had to bring their own candles.

In the reign of Charles II a change was made in the funding arrangements for the school. A lease of the rectory of Bedgworth, 'to last ninety-nine years, was granted by the Corporation to Jesus College, in return for which a rent of £50 a year was to be paid by the College; the same body undertaking in addition to maintain out of the School, should any of its pupils be competent, a Scholar and a Fellow, to be called 'the scholar and Fellow of Bergavenny;' to divide £10 annually, in equal shares, among such scholars as should seem most hopeful and indigent; and to visit the School annually.'

When Abergavenny was deprived of its Charter during the reign of William III, the trust ceased. However, Jesus College, honourably continued to pay the rent of £50 a year to the master of the School, and to fulfil all other engagements.

In 1760, in answer to a joint petition from Jesus College and the town of Abergavenny - necessitated by the fact that the Rectory of Bedgworth, owing to the forfeiture of the Charter, would, at the termination of the lease, devolve upon the Crown - an Act was passed vesting the Rectory of Bedgworth in Jesus College, for ever, in trust, the College being expected to pay the Schoolmaster £40 a year; to place the Scholar and Fellow from the Abergavenny School on the same footing as the other Scholars and Fellows of the College; to pay yearly to two boys of the school the sum of £5 each; to visit the School once in three years, or oftener, if necessary; and to correct abuses.

It was also enacted that the tithes payable to the School should be vested in trustees; that the Usher should be paid a salary of £15 a year; and that the trustees were to apply whatever surplus there might be to the maintenance of the poor of Abergavenny.

There was also a requirement that 'the Master shall be a member of Jesus College, and shall be chosen by the College and the Vicar of Abergavenny, if resident. The Fellow and Scholar are to be natives of Abergavenny, or failing that, of the County of Monmouth, and must have been at least two years in the Grammar School. The Vicar is empowered to exercise inspection over the Master, and in case of negligence, in concert with the Bishop of Llandaff and the College, to remove him, and nominate another in his stead.'

By 1751 the building was in a very poor state and in June 1768 a minute of the Parish Records was passed 'that a rate of one shilling in the £ to be forthwith raised and collected towards the taking down and rebuilding the tower of St John's Church, commonly called the Old Church, the same being judged by several of the inhabitants to be in so ruinous a condition as to be impossible to be repaired.' Subsequently an agreement was made with a Mr Andrew Maud for pulling down and rebuilding the tower (using some of the stone from the old one) for £213 18s. It was also decided that the new building (a school room) adjoining the tower of St John's should be finished in a decent manner. In 1818 the tower was taken down and rebuilt, but the bells were sold and they are now in St Mary's Church, Radcliffe, Bristol.

It is recorded that in 1878 there were 73 pupils in three classes and they were taught: Classics, Mathematics, French, Writing and Divinity. A new board of school governors was formed in 1891 to appoint a new headmaster and arrange the sale of the school buildings at St Johns and build a new school at Pen-y-pound for 200 boys.

So after flourishing here for over 350 years the school in 1898 was moved to new buildings in Pen-y-pound which were erected at a cost of more than £6,000. It was opened on Thursday 29th September 1898 by the Marquess of Abergavenny. The first headmaster was Mr T. H. Sifton MA and in his first year there were just 56 pupils.

The Masonic Hall

In November 1899 a Masonic Hall was opened in the ancient parish church of St John and the occasion was marked with a gathering of brethren of the Craft lodges from various part of the country and by the holding of the Provincial Grand Mark Lodge under Brother John Owen Marsh R.W., provincial Grand Master. The formal opening of the new hall followed the meeting of the Mark Masons.

Freemasonry was first introduced into Abergavenny by the French officers, who were brought to the town as prisoners during the Peninsular War, and were released within the town boundary under parole. The collars used by the officers of that lodge were still in their possession and were until the the previous twelve months worn by the principal officers of the lodge. The French had their lodge in a mansion in Monk Street.

The first English Masonic Lodge was consecrated 'The Philanthropic,' No 658 in the year 1815, and the Worshipful Master was the vicar of the parish, the Rev William Powell, who took an active part in the government of the town, being the only resident magistrate. The lodge was first held in the King's Head Inn and the ceremony of consecration was performed by Brother Plummer, who held high office in the Grand Lodge of England, whose original certificate the Philanthropic Lodge held. It was printed in French and English, whereas certificates by this time were printed in Latin and English. A revival in Masonry took place in 1860 when the Abergavenny lodge, under the old name 'Philanthropic' was reconsecrated as No. 1120 and five years later it was changed to No. 818.

The church was converted by the architect Brother, A. E. Johnson and the builders were J. G. Thomas. The interior of the building was altered so much that it would have been difficult for any of the old grammar school boys to recognise it. Rooms were divided, the massive walls of the old tower pierced in places to give access to the newly arranged rooms. They also removed the weather cock and the clock on the tower which was declared beyond repair.

The Non Conformist Churches and Chapels

Nonconformity was established at an early date in Abergavenny and the Baptists appear to have been the first to make headway in 1652 when John Abbot was put in the living of St Mary's by the Puritans in the place of the vicar, Charles Herbert. Three years later this cause was removed to Llanwenarth Ultra (Govilon) where the oldest Baptist Church in Wales can still be seen.

In 1769 the Baptist cause was revived in the town and in 1791 a small chapel was built in Tudor Street, but the congregation appears to have fallen in strength towards the end of the 19th century, probably due to the decline in the number of Welsh worshippers. It was used until 1815, when the increasing size of the congregation resulted in a new chapel being built in Frogmore Street, on the site now occupied by the Tesco supermarket. It had a large burying ground at the rear and was considerably improved in 1849 , but it was superseded by the present day Baptist Church built on the other side of the road in 1878, to meet the needs of the growing congregation as Abergavenny developed as a railway town. The foundation stone was laid by Crawshay Bailey. Designed by the well known chapel architect George Morgan of Carmarthen and constructed in the Romanesque style with a central rose window it is a most impressive building with its twin towers and porch with carved decorations.

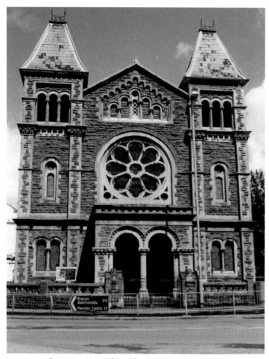

The Baptist Church, Frogmore Street

Completed in 1877, this impressive building provided traditional chapel accommodation with a large ground floor seating area and a gallery surrounding three sides and a pipe organ situated behind the pulpit.

William Pritchard became the first paid Baptist minister in Abergavenny, and his appointment caused a rumpus. This was before the days of chapels and people registered their houses for religious purposes.

There was one thing that worried the Abergavenny Baptists and that was whether they should sing Psalms. Another question which caused much discussion was which should be the Fast Day. They could not have it on a Friday, because the Roman Catholics had that day. They decided that the fast day should be the first Wednesday in every month, and added a rider 'for the manifestation of the favour of God.' Five years later when the question of fasting came up again it was decided that it should be discontinued.

The services are held upstairs

In January 1978 the Frogmore Street Baptist Memorial Hall (next to Tesco) was demolished to make way for a large extension to the supermarket. The sale of the site helped to finance alterations and improvements to the Baptist Church on the opposite corner. The work was completed by November and the church then re-opened.

Upstairs, on a new floor at balcony level is the church itself; while the ground floor has been converted into an attractive Church hall, with a large kitchen, cloakrooms and toilet facilities, plus ancillary rooms to cope with the congregation's day to day activities.

The rose window

In 1990 the members of both Bethany Baptist Church and Frogmore Street Baptist Church decided to unite once more. Bethany Church building in Market Street was closed and worship was continued in the Frogmore Street Church which was renamed Abergavenny Baptist Church.

By the year 2000 it was recognised that a major restoration of the building was needed to make it sound for the foreseeable future and its facilities also needed to be improved to meet the needs of the 21st century. Restoration work was commenced the following year. The four slate roofs were replaced with underfelt and new Welsh slate; some of the roof timbers were renewed and lightning conductors fitted. Since that work was carried out, the porch and several windows have been restored, the church heating system upgraded, a new sound system installed and a new kitchen fitted.

The Baptist Academy

In 1807 an Institution known as 'The Abergavenny Baptist Academy' was established at Aenon House in Pen-y-pound for the purpose of educating young men for the ministry. The first master of the Academy, the first in Wales, was the Reverend Micah Thomas, the minister of the Tudor Street Chapel and he was the sole tutor for 29 years and from a beginning of five students it quickly grew in size, with the total number educated here reaching 106. In 1836 after an existence of twenty-nine years the Academy was removed to Pen-y-garn, near Pontypool.

The Reverend Micah Thomas was born in 1778 and he was minister at Ross-on-Wye before he came to Abergavenny. In addition to his work at the Academy, he formed in 1809 the first Sunday School in Abergavenny and one of the first in Monmouthshire. In order to provide funds to build a new church to meet increased requirements, he made two separate journeys on horseback to London and Liverpool, covering over 1,000 miles to raise funds for the new meeting house at Abergavenny. Over £300 was collected and the building which became known as the Memorial Hall was opened in 1815.

The history of the Baptist cause is a very complicated one and goes back to the time of the Civil War. Christopher Price of Llanfoist was responsible for an Act for the Propagation of the Gospel, which sought to establish about fifty schools in Wales and there was one in Abergavenny, which was a rival to the Grammar School. The Act existed for only four years. During that time they gathered the tithes from the parishes to keep the schoolmasters. This was the first attempt to make a state system of Education in Great Britain.

The Catholic Church of Our Lady and St Michael

A fairly numerous and influential community of Catholics has long existed in Abergavenny as shown by the Recusant Roll of 1595, the Roll of Landed Estates in 1650 and other old documents. The community was for many years served by Franciscan priests in connection with their establishments at Perth-hir and Holywell.

In 1687 the Franciscans founded a house at the top of Frogmore Street near Lewis's Lane. Then in the middle of the 18th century a new chapel was built nearby which served as the church until 1860. The old house was then used as a school. The Franciscans handed over the parish to the English Benedictines (who had established St Mary's Priory) in 1857. One of their notable figure was the Venerable Father Augustine Baker, a native of Abergavenny.

Father Augustine Baker

The following year through the gifts of a number of generous donors, it was possible for them to undertake the building of a new church in Pen-y-pound which today is served by Benedictines from Belmont Abbey, Hereford. The foundation stone of this church in Pen-y-pound was laid on May19th1858, during the incumbency of Father Charles Wilfred Price, in whose memory the statue of St Joseph was erected.

Designed in the Decorated Gothic style by Benjamin Bucknell the Church of Our Lady and St Michael in Pen-y-pound is 100 ft long and 48 ft wide. It consists of chancel, nave and aisles and was opened by Bishop Brown on May 15th 1860. At the opening Mass, the chasuble used was one which formerly belonged to Richard Wharton, the last Catholic Bishop of Hereford in the reign of Queen Mary.

The elaborate reredos over the high altar was given by John Baker-Gabb of Abergavenny and was unveiled by Bishop Hedley on Rosary Sunday, October 7th 1883. The whole work is crowned by seven angels. They are, from left to right: Uriel, holding the scroll and book; Gabriel, holding the lily of the Annunciation; Samuel, holding the staff and cup. Michael is in the centre wearing armour, striking the dragon with one hand and holding the balance in the other. On the right hand side are Zadkiel, holding the sacrificial knife, Josephiel, holding the flaming sword, and Raphael,

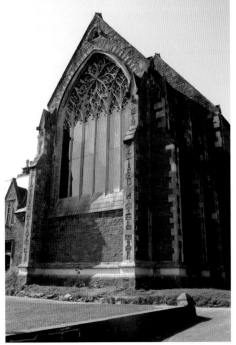

The Church of Our Lady and St Michael

pictured with the staff and fish that are mentioned in the story of Tobias and the Angel (Book of Tobit). Michael, Gabriel and Raphael are mentioned in the Bible, whilst the rest are found in contemporary Jewish writings.

In the Lady Chapel, on the north side of the Church, there are four stained glass lights. The two in the north wall depict St Martin of Tours and St Helen, whilst those behind the altar show Our Blessed Lady and St Joseph.

The impressive windows at the East End depict six well known saints. These are, from left to right, St Thomas of Canterbury who was martyred by Henry II, St Benedict, the Father of western monasticism, Our Lady and the Infant Jesus, St Joseph, St Scholastica, sister of St Benedict, and finally St Margaret, Queen of Scotland.

In the St Lewis Chapel the window shows two streams of religious life that have been prominent in the re-establishment of Catholic communities in the Counter-Reformation era. On the top left is depicted St Benedict, whilst on the top right is St Ignatius Loyola, the founder of the Jesuits. Below left is Dom Augustine Baker, a prominent Benedictine who was born in Abergavenny in 1575 and died in London in 1641. He was a famous Benedictine, and the author of several associated works. It was principally by his advice and efforts that the

The reredos over the high altar and impressive window at the east end of the church

congregation of English Benedictine, or Black Monks, after being driven out from their Monasteries and almost completely suppressed under Edward and Elizabeth was revived. He was brother to Richard Baker, Counsellor-at-law, whose tablet can be seen in St Mary's Priory Church.

Stained glass in the Lewis Chapel

The church also has a painting of St Michael slaying a Devil. This is the work of Kenhelm Digby, who was killed during the Civil War at the battle of Neots in 1648.

Preserved in the church is a rescript of Pope Clement X dated 1676 granting a plenary indulgence to those who visited the chapel of St Michael on the summit of Skirrid Fawr on the Feast of St Michael and All Angels on September 29th each year.

The altar rails are faced with Devon marble in memory of Father Augustine Wray, incumbent from 1894 to 1919. The rails round the baptistry used to form part of a screen across the chancel and the short rail near the Lady Altar is part of the old Communion rails.

In April 1920 the Roman Catholic community of Abergavenny decided on a unique and appropriate memorial to the members of their church who fell in the First World War. It is a Crucifix erected in memory of Captain Elidyr Herbert of Llanover and there are stone tablets bearing the names of those who had made the supreme sacrifice, to the number of twenty-nine.

The bronzed figure, just inside the church grounds is a life-size representation of Christ. It originally came from Rome and was a gift of the Baker Gabb family. It is mounted on a cross of oak, with a pitched roof and there is a rockery as a background, planted with flowering annuals.

The unveiling ceremony was performed on Good Friday and an impressive service was conducted by the Reverend Father E. Hilary Willson O.S.B., priest in charge of St Michael's assisted by the Reverend Father Exton, Llanarth. The reading of the roll call of the fallen was followed by the ceremonial blessing of the Cross. During the singing of the hymn, 'Soul of my Saviour,' wreaths and flowers were laid at the foot of the Cross in memory of the soldiers.

In 1960, the Centenary year, the St David Lewis Chapel, built by the Baker Gabb family was reconstructed with panelling belonging to the Chapel of Coldbrook House. Then in 1980, the sanctuary area was extended, the old altar rails were redeployed on either side, the nave altar erected and the pulpit moved forward.

On 3rd October 1970 about 1500 people attended a special service at the church to commemorate the forthcoming canonisation (on October 25th) by Pope Paul VI. The canonisation ceremony in Rome was attended by Father J.A. Cummingham of Our Lady and St Michael's Church and six of his parishioners.

During 1984 the whole of the interior of the Church was redecorated, and extensive work carried out on the interior stonework, particularly the reredos and the windows which had been damaged by vandalism. Also, a new screen was erected at the West End to create a separate Narthex.

The church posseses some priceless antiquities including pre-Reformation vestments handed down by the Franciscan Fathers. In an article 'Pre-Reformation Vestments in the Catholic Churches of Monmouthshire', R. H. D'Elboux puts forward the theory that they may have originally belonged to the old Parish Church of St John. The portrayal of St John certainly suggests the dedication of St John the Apostle, However, this Saint often appears in ecclesiastical embroidery of this time, and his appearance here may be quite accidental. Among the scraps left over from the mounting is the figure of St Edmund the Martyr, holding an arrow and an orb. This Saint belongs to the eastern counties and is rarely portrayed as late as the sixteenth century. The neighbouring Church of Crickhowell, however, is dedicated to St Edmund, so the presence of this figure at Abergavenny argues for a local origin of the vestments.

There is one chasuble which does not resemble the others, except in date of workmanship. This is known as the Wharton Chasuble, and it is thought that it may have been the property of Robert Wharton, the Marian Bishop of Hereford. On the back of the chasuble is the shield of Radcliffe impaling Stafford. Robert Radcliffe, Baron Fitzwalter, and afterwards Earl of Sussex, married Elizabeth Stafford in 1505, and was remarried after 1521, so the vestments may be dated accordingly.

A crimson velvet chasuble still remains unmounted, with orphries and ornaments superimposed, of linen embroidered with silver-gilt threads and coloured silks. The ground of the back is unusually closely powdered with fleur-de-lys and six-winged angels on wheels. On either side of the base of the back orphrey is an Annunciation lily in a pot, and having a worked support for the pot, an unusual decoration in such a position. The floral devices of the front suggest two stag's heads. On the front: a prophet mutilated; St Katherine with a book, a prophet with sceptre. On the back: Christ crucified, with two angels carrying chalices (one arm of the cross repaired out of line with the remainder), and the Dove above; St Peter with key; a prophet mutilated.

There also exists a green vestment, the orphries only of which are old. There is a modern white chasuble with old cross orphrey. The work is in good condition and some of the original silk work can be seen. There is a white cope with sixteenth century orphries, but a modern hood. There are two dalmatics with panels of old embroidery, much restored. Besides the chalice veil and stole and maniple there are about thirty pieces of embroidery left over from the nineteenth century remounting of the vestments.

There are also some objects which were dug up in the garden of the house in Cross Street where the Thomas Gunter lived in the days of the persecution of Catholics. These include a figure of Our Lord crucified and a portion of brass triptych of the crucifixion with the figure of St John.

On 15 September 2000, the Feast of Our Lady of Sorrows, this church of Our Lady and Saint Michael was solemnly consecrated by His Grace, the Metropolitan Archbishop of Cardiff, Most Reverend John Aloysius Ward.

Holy Trinity Church

This Victorian church stands in Baker Street, near the town Library. It was built in 1840 with finance from Miss Rachel Herbert of Little Hill House, a local benefactoress, who also built a parsonage, almshouses and school which closed in 1898 and is now the church hall. The nearby Carnegie Library was built on the old school playground.

Holy Trinity Church in Baker Street was built in 1840

The Alms Houses financed by Miss Rachel Herbert are still in use

Standing on each side of the church the almshouses were built to accommodate eight poor and aged women, who were each provided with a stipend of 2/- by the generous Miss Herbert. These little cottages are still in use under the original charity. On the south side is the Vicarage and on the north side a building erected as a small school where girls were once trained to be maid servants. It now serves as the church hall.

The church is a pleasing building of stone with a bell-turret and it was endowed for the free use of any who chose to worship there as an answer to the pew rents which were then charged on almost two-thirds of the 1606 sittings of the parish church. It was consecrated in 1842 by Dr Coplestone, the Bishop of Llandaff and Dean of St Pauls.

The Early English piscina, now in the sanctuary was found in the wall of the north transept of old St John's Church and presented by the Worshipful Master and Brethren of St John's Lodge of Freemasons to Holy Trinity Church.

The external pillar of the north arcade is different from the others, being octagonal. It is beautifully carved with cherubs round the capital and was the gift of the Sunday School children. In the south aisle can be seen a small altar which is the original altar consecrated by Bishop Capelstone in 1840.

In 1885 the church was enlarged, reseated and greatly improved at a cost of £1,250. The extension was carried out in accordance with plans prepared by Mr Nicholson (Hereford) and Mr J. G. Thomas (Abergavenny) and described in the *Abergavenny Chronicle* as follows:

> 'It is capable of holding a choir of from 30 to 40 voices for whom some handsome stall-like seats have been provided. The structure is in keeping with the character of the other portion of the building and has a modern lofty appearance, the roof being of pine wood with ornamental principles. On the north-east side an organ chamber has been built, and on the opposite side a large vestry with doors opening into the chancel and the body of the Church.
>
> The flooring of the chancel is paved with tiles worked in ornamental devices. The altar rails, presented by Mr Hampton, are of a very light and pretty design, while inside the rails the space has been increased so as to give more room than that which was formerly apportioned off for that part of the building. The whole of the appointments and fittings are modern in style, and the improvements they make in the appearance of the chancel is striking.
>
> A splendid pulpit, the work of Mr R. Price, sculptor, Lion Street, has been placed on the north-east side; and on the opposite side a reading desk of pine has been erected. The organ has been removed from the gallery to the new chamber where it has been reconstructed, and added to, by Mr King, Frogmore Street, in a very successful manner.
>
> A font worked in white stone has been given to the church by Mr Robert Price and has been placed at the west end of the church.
>
> The acoustic properties of the building have been much improved by the extension; this was particularly noticeable in the singing by the choir, which, from the gallery, was heard to great disadvantage, the choir being separated by the organ and in consequence of that fact, apt to get a little divided in their work.'

The official opening of the extended chancel was carried out by the Lord Bishop of Llandaff on May 20th 1886. The building was enlarged again in 1887 by the erection of a south aisle, relighted and beautified at a further cost of £1,500 and made to seat 650 persons.

On Sunday 20th May 1894, there was a celebration of Holy Communion at 8.00 am at a special service held for the re-dedication of the old altar slab from St John's Church which had been recently discovered by Iltyd Gardner and presented by him and his brother to the Vicar and Churchwardens of Holy Trinity Church.

Iltyd Gardner had been employing workmen to strip walls in a front room on the ground floor of the Cow Inn in Nevill Street. He happened to notice that the portion of the chimney breast, immediately over the fireplace was composed of one large slab of stone, 7 feet 6 inches long, 2 feet 8 inches wide and 5 inches thick. Near one corner of the slab he spotted a rudely formed cross cut into the stone. His archeological knowledge led him to look for four other crosses, which he found and at once recognised the stone as an ancient 'mensa,' or altar slab. The four crosses near the corners of the stone represent the wounds in the hands and feet of the crucified Christ and the fifth cross not far from the middle of the slab stands for the spear wound in the side.

The slab was duly taken to Holy Trinity Church and John Gearing was entrusted with the important work of placing it in position and it has been set on a massive panelled oaken table made by Mr J.G. Thomas. The front of the table is pierced with trifolate openings through which are visible the marks on the further side of the mensa.

No doubt the stone was dedicated to sacred uses in the early Norman days and from the eleventh century to the sixteenth it was the altar-stone of St John's which was then the parish church. Consequently it is the only communion table in the town, at which the good people of Abergavenny for nearly 500 years, 'ate of one bread and drank of one cup.' This was the altar to which they came to be married, and to which they brought their offerings, until the days of Cromwell, when altar stones, painted glass and other precious and sacred articles were torn from churches and often destroyed.

The altar and the east window which serves as a war memorial

In July 1905 the ceremony of the unveiling of what is called the Children's Window was performed by Iltyd Gardner, as treasurer to the fund while a second window was unveiled by his wife who was the donor. These two windows are in the south wall of the easternmost end of the south aisle, near the old altar. They were installed in memory of the Reverend Canon Williams who gave many years service to the church.

The east window serves as a war memorial and features the brightly coloured figures of Our Lord, St George, with the four saints, David, Illtyd, Dubritius and Teilo and below is a procession to Calvary. Two windows in the south aisle show dramatic scenes in the life of Elijah, and there is also a painting of St Francis by Carlo Dolci.

The easternmost of the two windows represents Elijah, as he is passing away in the chariot of fire, casting his mantle upon Elisha. The text is: 'They say the spirit of Elijah doth rest on Elisha.' It bears the inscription: 'In memory of Thomas Williams M.A. Canon of Llandaff, first incumbent of this church, this window is dedicated by the Sunday School which he founded, the divinity students whom he taught, and friends.' Also incorporated with the memorials are the Arms of the Province of Canterbury and the diocese of Llandaff.

The other window represents scenes from the history of Ahab and Elijah, the first showing Ahab and Jezebel in the vineyard of Naboth, confronted by Elijah; and the second showing Elijah resting under a juniper tree, and the Angel giving him food. The first bears the text 'Thou has sold thyself,' and the other 'Arise and eat.' The inscription is: 'To the glory of God, and in loving memory of Henry George Kemp and Susannah Kemp, formerly of Althorne, Essex, this window is dedicated by their daughter, Minnie Thornton, wife of Iltyd Gardner.' At the foot of this window are the arms of Kemp and of Gardner impaling Kemp. These fine windows are the work of the celebrated artist J. Jennings, who also made the stained glass work at Temple Church, London.

The church was again extended in 1909 by the addition of a north aisle and vestry at a cost of £1,300 to provide accommodation for a total of 700 worshippers.

Two windows in the south aisle showing scenes in the life of Elijah

Whitfield Presbyterian Church

A Presbyterian Chapel was first opened in Frogmore Street in November 1871. It was built on a site formerly occupied by some old cottages and the 350 seat chapel was completed in four months at a cost of about £650. This building is currently a shop.

George Whitfield the Calvinistic Methodist first came to Abergavenny in April 1739, at the age of 24 having graduated at Pembroke College, Oxford two years before. A platform was erected for him in a garden in Abergavenny and he preached to a gathering of 2,000 people.

Whitfield Presbyterian Church

In 1741 he married Elizabeth James a widow aged 36 of Hillcrest, Nevill Street, at St Martin's Chapel near Caerphilly. In August 1744 the Whitfields left Plymouth for New York where they landed on October 26th. They returned from America in June 1748. George Whitfield was to cross the Atlantic to America no less than thirteen times and his statue outside Princeton University testifies to his importance in the history of the American colonies.

George Whitfield died in America in September 1770 by which time he had become the most popular and influential preacher of his age. At his funeral, John Wesley said, 'Have we ever read or heard of any person who called so many thousands, so many myriads to repentenance?'

The Presbyterian church with its handsome tower crowned by a small spire was designed by Mr Johnson of Abergavenny & Merthyr and built in 1908 by Messrs J.G. Thomas & Sons of Abergavenny at a cost of £5,000. The builders experienced considerable difficulty when preparing the foundations for traces of an old watercourse were discovered under the choir arch and about 10 feet below this, indications of an ancient pond were found.

The style of architecture favoured was Perpendicular Gothic and the walls were built of Llangattock stone with dressings in Box Ground Bath stone. It was intended that the church should provide accommodation for 470 people and that there should be room for 270 scholars in the Sunday School. The church was opened on October 1st 1908.

Bethany Baptist Chapel

Some misunderstanding in 1827 led to a division in the English Baptist Church and the consequence was a separation of the disputing parties. The withdrawing group of English members of Mr Michah Thomas's congregation purchased a piece of land near the corner of Market street and Lion Street and built a chapel there and a separate congregation assembled for divine worship.

The first minister was the Reverend S. R. Young who was well known in the town and also throughout Wales being highly respected by all classes of opinion, both political and religious. He had come for just one year but ended up staying for fifty two years.

This chapel was used until 1882 and the building was subsequently demolished for the purpose of widening the entrance to Market Street from Lion Street. It was replaced in the same year by the Bethany Baptist Chapel on a new but adjoining site in Market Street. This fine structure could seat 380 persons.

The Reverend S.R. Young was followed by the Reverend R. J. Willoughby of Cardiff who stayed about three years. The next pastor was the Reverend T. J. Lewis who was there during the Great War and then moved to Manchester. The chapel was without a pastor for some years until the Reverend W. Neil came from Monmouth.

The building remained a chapel until March 1990, when it closed to amalgamate with Frogmore Street Baptist Church (opposite the war memorial) to become Abergavenny Baptist Church.

Bethany Chapel was then used as a Museum of Childhood until the new owner Bill Samuel sold the building to the Welsh Development Agency for possible inclusion in the regeneration scheme for Abergavenny town centre.

It was then leased to Homemakers, Monmouthshire community recycling project for two years before Suffolk businessman Giles DeLotdiniere bought it at auction for £220,000 in April 2005. It was later purchased by Alun Griffiths for possible use as an Art Gallery.

Bethany Baptist Chapel

Christchurch

In 1879 this building which consists of an iron framework clad in cedar wood was erected in North Street, Cantref as a chapel-of-ease in the parish of St Mary to serve the growing population of railway workers families in the Cantref and Grofield areas of the town. It meant that worshippers in this part of Abergavenny would not have to walk the muddy and unpaved roads to attend services at St Mary's.

It was built at a cost of about £950, by Messrs Francis Moreton & Co., well-known iron church builders and Government contractors of Liverpool, London and Glasgow. Built in the Gothic style of architecture, it consists of a nave with Clerestory side aisles and chancel, with organ chamber and vestry on each side of the chancel. It was designed to seat in comfort 350 persons.

The opening service at the 'New Iron Church' which took place on the evening of Thursday 22 January 1880 was conducted by the Vicar of Abergavenny, the Reverend Canon Bury Capel. The address was given by the Archdeacon of Llandaff, the Venerable John Griffiths. At that time Abergavenny was within the diocese of Llandaff and the present diocese of Monmouth was an archdeaconry. In 1897 a schoolroom was built behind the church and this was later enlarged to form a church hall.

Christchurch in North Street is a chapel-of-ease to St Mary's

The Chapels which followed in the wake of the reformers who came to Abergavenny, such as George Whitfield and John Wesley are very much a symbol of the town's fascinating history. There have been many changes over the years but the chapels now remaining and in use include the United Reformed, established as an Independent Church in 1690 and continuing as a Congregational Church in post-war years amd alongside it is the Methodist Church, originally Wesleyan, established in 1829.

Castle Street Methodist Chapel

John Wesley, the renowned founder of Methodism paid several visits to Abergavenny, in the footsteps of the celebrated George Whitfield. He wrote in his journal:

'Monday, Sept 15th, 1739 - I came to Abergavenny. I felt in myself a strong aversion to preaching there... About a thousand people stood patiently, while from the Acts XXVIII, 22 I simply described the plain old religion of the Church of England, which is now almost everywhere spoken against under the name of Methodism.'

Two years later he returned to Abergavenny:

'Saturday, October 3rd, 1741 - In the afternoon we came to Abergavenny - those who are bitter in spirit have been here also - yet Mrs James received us gladly, as she did aforetime; but we could not procure even two or three to join us in the evening, beside those of her own household.'

'Sunday, 4th October, 1741 - I had an unexpected opportunity of receiving the holy communion. In the afternoon we had a plain useful sermon on the Pharisee and the Publican praying in the temple, which I explained at large in the evening to the best dressed congregation I have yet seen in Wales.'

On these visits his hostess was usually Mrs James, who afterwards became Mrs Whitfield. Her house was situated in Nevill Street (then called Cow Street). It is likely that the first Methodist Society in Abergavenny was composed of the household of Mrs James and a few friends who gathered with them for worship.

In 1805 a house opposite the Welsh Baptist Chapel in Tudor Street was purchased and adapted for the purpose of a meeting house. The Methodists continued to assemble in this place until 1829, when the present Methodist Church, in Castle Street was commenced. Built in traditional Georgian style it cost £1,000 to build and it opened on November 12th 1829. The ceremony was performed by the Reverend Dr Robert Newton, a noted Methodist preacher of the day. From that period till 1851 Abergavenny was the head of a Methodist Circuit which included Pontypool. In 1851 Pontypool became

John Wesley

a separate circuit and this arrangement continued until 1900, in which year the two circuits again amalgamated. In 1903 for practical reasons, Abergavenny was disassociated from Pontypool and linked up with the Brynmawr Circuit.

165

The Methodist Church in Castle Street

The United Reform Church (centre) with the Sunday School on the right

The United Reform Church

The Independent Congregational Church in Abergavenny is one of the oldest Dissenting churches in the county. Monmouthshire was a stronghold of Independency in the time of Cromwell and it is of interest that Sir Trevor Williams and some other gentlemen of old Monmouthshire, who were taken prisoners by the Royalists a short time before the siege of Raglan Castle, and tried by Charles I in person, at Abergavenny, as adherents of the Commonwealth, were independents.

This cause had an existence in Abergavenny as far back as the early part of the seventeeth century and was certainly established by 1688 with some of the most wealthy and influential inhabitants of the town numbered among its members. The place of meeting at that period was in a spacious room in a building in Cross Street on the corner of Monk Street, and later it became the George Hotel.

In 1692 a Chapel was erected in Castle Street and the members of the Independent denomination worshipped there until 1792, by which time their numbers had so increased that it became necessary to erect a larger building. The old chapel was converted into a residence for the Minister. In 1839 the new Chapel was enlarged to provide accomodation for 800 people.

An academy for the education of students in the Independent ministry was established in 1692 in connection with the Castle Street Chapel, having been removed there from Bryn-llywarch in Glamorganshire. This academy was under the presidency of Roger Griffiths, who soon after, much to the consternation of his people, conformed to the Established Church and became Rector of New Radnor and Archdeacon of Brecon and died in 1708.

Soon after this the Academy was removed to Bridgend. Another Academy of Independents was founded here in 1755 by David Jardine, a native of Denbigh, who was minister of Castle Street Chapel. After his death in 1766, Benjamin Davies, also minister of the chapel, succeeded as president, and on his removal in 1782 to the college at Homerton the academy was transferred to Oswestry. After other removals the academy was finally settled at Brecon in 1839 and in 1869 a new building was opened there which became known as the Brecon Memorial College.

St David's Church

William, 5th Earl and 19th Lord of Abergavenny owned a large part of Llwyndu, the Deri and Llanwenarth Breast as part of the Nevill estates. When it was brought to his notice that there was no place of worship for the inhabitants of this portion of his estate, he altered two of the cottages on the Rholben, adjoining the road leading to St Mary's Vale and they became the small church of St David's.

It was dedicated by Bishop Lewis of Llandaff in 1897. The choristers of St Mary's were present having walked in their cassocks and surplices from St Mary's to receive the Bishop and the Marquess and his party who came in open carriages to the service of dedication. As there was a choir of over 20 boys and almost as many men present, it must have been quite an impressive service. The church closed after the death of the Marquess because the sum of £20 a year for its upkeep was no longer forthcoming.

The Primitive Methodist Church

This church in Victoria Street, on the Grofield was established in 1850 could sit 200 people. It now serves as a base for the Abergavenny Corps of the **Salvation Army**. This corps (No. 621) formed on 5th April 1885, by Captain Frances Hope, has its Citadel in the former Primitive Methodist Chapel in Victoria Street. There is also a Salvation Army Charity Shop on Frogmore Street which helps to provide income for the corps.

The Christadelphian Hall

In Sunnybank, off the Merthyr Road is a base for the Christadelphians who are a body of Bible believing people, who aim to live by faith in Jesus Christ, according to the teaching of his followers from the first century AD, finding their instruction in a wholly inspired Bible. Central to Chritadelphian belief is that Christ will one day return to the Earth to establish the Kingdom of God and grant eternal life to his people. The Christadelphian Church was founded by Dr John Thomas in about 1840, although the name was not given to his followers until 1864. There are Christadelphian congregations throughout the world. The Christadelphian Church in Lion Street has been demolished.

The Apostolic Church

An Apostolic Church meets in the chapel of the Old Town Cemetery in Old Hereford Road. The Apostolic Church originated in Great Britain by James E. Worsfield and it was developed in Wales largely by Evan Roberts of Loughor.

The Gateway Christian Centre

The old Pavillion Cinema in Monk Street was purchased in 1999 by the Abergavenny Family Church Group who previously were based at a premise in Castle Street which they named the Rheoboth Centre. With congregations growing to more than one hundred every Sunday it became necessary to seek a large building and the Pavilion Cinema which had been derelict for many years was purchased for £82,500. It was then refurbished at a cost of £165,000 and much of the work was undertaken by members of the church with professional guidance.

The old Pavillion Cinema has been converted into a church

Chapter Twelve
SOME LARGE HOUSES OF HISTORIC INTEREST

There are a number of country houses in the vicinity of Abergavenny, some of which have more than ordinary interest.

C.J.O Evans 1953

The Gunter House in Cross Street stands just outside the site of the medieval South Gate and it was a building of great pretensions in its day. It was once a good example of a 17th century mansion, with a large porch and massive doors, mullioned windows, and a large court in front enclosed with thick walls.

It is named after Thomas Gunter, second son of Robert Gunter, and grandson of James Gunter who was granted the Priory after the dissolution of the monasteries by Henry VIII. After the time of the Gunters it briefly served as a gaol and a prison for soldiers captured during the Franco-British War and at that time it had a thatched roof. The centre part of the building became the Parrot Inn in 1864 which was renamed the Cardiff Arms in 1898.

The Gunter House in Lower Cross Street is named after Thomas Gunter
and was originally a 17th century mansion but now consists of five separate shops

The building was purchased in January 1908 by Mr and Mrs Foster and during alteration work, Mrs Foster was called to see a highly decorated little room which the builders had revealed in the attic at the north end of the house. Originally the attic had a separate staircase at the west end and an entrance through a door which was still in existence, but had been blocked up since the adjoining cottages were built.

Mrs Foster made a careful inspection of the hidden room and found on the sloping ceiling some work painted in fresco, which appeared to have been beautifully executed. The subject of the painting on the plaster was the Magi bringing their offerings to the Babe of Bethlehem.

Dressed in a deep blue, the Virgin Mary, with a circlet halo above her head, nurses the Holy Child, whose halo is more ornate. The star in the east directs its rays towards the Child. On the left is a Wise Man with a hypnotic eye, while the kneeling figures of the two other Magi probably occupied the lost foreground of the painting. On the right is an ox, rendered with the poise and forthright style of a prehistoric cave-painting.

Mrs Foster decided that this painting was most certainly worth preserving. After having it photographed, she had the whole thing carefully removed, without any serious damage being done to it. It was then fixed behind glass in a handsome oak frame.

Painting representing the Adoration of the Magi
Copyright Monmouthshire County Council, Abergavenny Museum

Drawing by Fred Hando in 1954

Having secured the fresco, she further carefully examined the room in detail, and found above a little window overlooking Cross Street, the letters I.H.S. within rays, surmounted by a cross. Every part of the plaster and even the broken bits on the floor showed traces of ornamentation. Unfortunately, it was not possible to decipher all the objects painted on the wall apart from some cherubic figures.

At the east end of the room the partition was a simple construction, but when the men went to rip it out they found that it was a two-faced partition. Inside on a smooth face, just beneath the fresco, were discovered letters with a date in Roman figures and two grotesque human shapes, with a heart at the feet of a lady. The top line of writing read: 'T.G. his mark'.

It is significant that in the seventeenth century this building was the residence of Thomas Gunter. His grandfather, James Gunter was a Protestant and probably his grandson Walter, Thomas's elder brother, who entertained King Charles I at the Priory, was a Protestant, but Thomas was a Catholic. It was well known that he maintained a chapel, but where that chapel was had remained a mystery for 250 years.

During the days when the meeting of Roman Catholics was forbidden, Thomas Gunter allowed public services to be held in a secret chapel in his house. It is recorded that during the period of Cromwell's government more people attended Gunter's Chapel than the parish church! Two priests, Father David Lewis (son of the headmaster of King Henry VIII Grammar School) and Father Philip Evans officiated in this chapel but both were subsequently hanged, drawn, quartered and burnt in 1679.

In view of the discovery of the fresco representation of the scene at Bethlehem, and the marks of the Jesuits on the wall, this attic room was unquestionably used as a chapel. The fresco was obviously the altar piece, the altar standing beneath it. The letters on the plaster seem to have been the initials of personal names and probably memorials of marriages secretly celebrated in the chapel. The two grotesque figures may represent a man laying his heart at the feet of his lady love.

During the work of restoration several fragments of manuscript were found bearing Thomas Gunter's name - one fragment revealing the interesting information that he was a solicitor - the writing being: 'Thomas Gunter, Attorney-at-law'. Under the floor in the attic, a heap of manuscripts were found, all belonging to Thomas Gunter, ranging in dates from 1674 to 1697 and all just the kind of papers that one might expect to find in a solicitor's office.

In 1678 Parliament had appointed a committee to consider: '...the danger the nation is in by the Growth of Popery, and for providing Remedies to prevent the same.' Among the witnesses they called was Thomas Gunter who bravely declared...'I kept a priest in Oliver's time of severity, and I will keep one now.' Worship was certainly carried out in the attic where the walls bear faint traces of Jesuit markings.

The painting was then lost for some years but re-discovered in the 1950s half hidden behind an old dresser. Experts identified it as the long-lost 'Adoration of the Magi' and it was taken to Abergavenny Museum where it can now be seen. It was unveiled at the museum in May 1965 by Father G.R. Davies OSB in the presence of the Mayor and Mayoress of Abergavenny, Councillor and Mrs Martin Reeves.

St David Lewis (1617-1679)

David Lewis (also called Charles Baker) was born in 1617. His father was the Reverend Morgan Lewis, the first known Headmaster of King Henry VIII Grammar School. David was one of nine children and their mother was Margaret Pritchard, a Catholic and niece of Father Augustine Baker. Most of the children were brought up as Catholics, but not David. He converted to Catholicism in 1633 in Paris during his travels on the Continent after studying law in England.

At the age of 19 he went to London to study law, but soon afterwards gave up his studies and returned to Abergavenny to live with his parents who died of the plague in 1638.

St David Lewis
Painting in Catholic
Church at Usk

David Lewis then went to the English College in Rome and became a priest in 1642. Three years later, under the influence of his uncle, Father John Pritchard (alias Lewis), he entered the Society of Jesus. After serving his novitiate in Rome, and for a short time acting as Confessor to the English College, he was sent in 1648 to South Wales on mission where he ministered to the numerous recusant houses of the district.

Among his ports of call was the Gunter House in Abergavenny, where mass was regularly celebrated in a secret chapel contained in the attic.

For many years he lived with the Morgans of Llantarnam, to whom he was related, and became superior of the St Francis Xavier mission (with headquarters at Cwm, Hereford) from 1667-72 and 1674-9.

Although frequently denounced, he was not molested until the Popish Plot scare of 1678, when six armed men sent by John Arnold of Llanfihangel Court (Justice of the Peace and Member for the County of Monmouthshire from 1681 to 1698) arrested him at Llantarnam on 17th November, whilst on his way to mass. John Arnold was a most uncompromising persecutor of Roman Catholics and a fanatical hunter of priests. In his day he became notorious as the chief instrument who put in force the penal laws against the Papists.

David Lewis was conducted to the 'Golden Lion' Hotel in Abergavenny, where he was examined by John Arnold and committed. He was taken from there to Llanfihangel Court and the next day sent under an armed escort to Monmouth gaol.

On the 28th of March 1679 he was tried at the Monmouth Assizes before Sir Robert Atkins, the judge, and the charge against him was: 'Thou, being a national subject of the King of England, has passed beyond the seas, and hast taken orders from the Church and See of Rome and hast returned back into England and continued upwards of 40 days contrary to the Statute 27 Elizabeth in that case made and proved, which by statute is high treason.'

During this same year, an Anglican minister, Titus Oates, fabricated a story in which the King was supposed to be in danger of a scheme to put his brother James on the throne. It was known as the 'Popish Plot'. David Lewis was cleared of conspiracy in the plot, but was sentenced to death for simply being a Catholic priest.

On 27th August 1679 a scaffold was erected on a site in Porthycarne Street in Usk. It is said that the official hangman refused to carry out his task, so a convict was then offered his freedom in return for performing the hanging, but he was stoned by the crowd. Eventually a local blacksmith was persuaded to carry out the unenviable task.

Before his execution David Lewis spoke to the crowd in Welsh explaining his beliefs and why he had to suffer for them:

> 'I was condemned for reading Mass, hearing confessions, anointing sick, christening and preaching. As for reading the Mass, it was the old, and still is, the accustomed and laudable leturgy of the Holy Church, and all the other acts are acts of religion and worship of God. And for religion I die.'

After being hanged and disembowled, his body was burnt on the island in the River Usk. The remains were then buried outside the west door of St Mary's Priory Church in Usk. The original stone covering his grave bore the inscription: 'Here lies the body of Edward Lewis, who was condemned for a priest and was a Jesuit and executed the 27th August 1679.'

By the mid 19th century the words on the rough cracked stone could no longer be deciphered. A new stone has been inscribed and laid on the grave in recent years.

In 1888 David Lewis in company with 63 others were beatified, thus allowing public veneration of him to take place. Consequently the little Catholic church at Usk on the slope at the foot of the castle has become a place of pilgrimage for Catholics and inside are housed a number of relics relating to the martyred priest.

In 1970 David Lewis was canonised by Pope Paul VI as one of the forty martyrs of England and Wales. There is a chapel dedicated to him in the Church of Our Lady and St Michael, Pen-y-pound.

Old Court

Old Court used to be known as Beli Baker (Baker's Court or Yard) and for many generations it was the home of the Baker family. The building once adjoined the old Tudor Gate and with its extensive grounds lay for the most part outside the old town wall. Bounded by the castle on one side and Byfield Lane on the other, the grounds sloped down to Castle Meadows and the river Usk.

Old Court in Tudor Street fortunately escaped demolition in the early 1960's

The word 'Beli' is Welsh for 'Bailey' and is probably derived from the Norman-French word 'Baille' (Latin Ballium). It was used to indicate the outwork which protected the western gate (Tudor Gate), while 'Baker' records the name of the builder. Near the site of the Eastern Gate of the town occurred a similar name, 'Bailey Priordy,' which seems to indicate the site of the outwork protecting the gate which was near the Priory.

Being of the same stock as the Cecils, Marquises of Exeter and Salisbury the Bakers were a family of some importance. They were paternally descended from Robert Sitsyllt, who in the eleventh century assisted the Norman knight Robert Fitzhamon in his conquest of Glamorgan.

In the sixteenth century, for some unknown reason, a certain Thomas ap Roger obtained the surname of Baker. He married Joan, daughter of Tevan Preece of Elvel. His pedigree gives him three sons, Richard, John and Robert. Richard Baker, the eldest son of Thomas Baker, was born in 1496. He married Gwenllian, daughter of Thomas Rhys

Thomas ap Sir Robert Walys of Wern -y-cwm and is commemorated on a brass memorial tablet in the Herbert Chapel. The Latin inscription translated reads as follows:-

> 'To Richard Baker his father, and to his son of the same name, the father formerly a Burgess of this town, the son lately Recorder; who passed happily out of the troubles of this life, the former on 7th January A.S. 1551 at 54, the latter on 7th October A.S. 1598 at 41, each the father of a numerous family and having deserved well of his country. William Baker, with that reverence which a son owes to a father, and with that love which a father can give to a son, hoping to be partaker with each of them in the same happiness at the resurrection of the just among the eternal spirits in the Kingdom of Heaven.'

William Baker, the eldest son of Richard Baker, was born in 1584 and in 1606 married Joan, daughter of Henry Vaughan of Moccas in Herefordshire, a descendant of Sir Roger Vaughan, who fought with Henry V at Agincourt. In 1630 William was appointed High Sheriff of the county of Monmouth and nominated Deputy Chief Steward and Recorder of Abergavenny in the Charter granted by Charles I. On the outbreak of the Civil War he was ordered to raise one hundred men for the king's service.

William Baker died in October 1648 and was buried in the Herbert Chapel of St Mary's Priory Church. His tomb is surmounted by the 'arms' of Baker and Vaughan and supported on either side by carved bosses. In the arched recess are effigies of William and his wife, represented as kneeling on tasselled cushions.

Henry Baker (the younger son of Richard Baker, and younger brother of William Baker) was nominated Chief Bailiff of the Borough of Abergavenny in the charter granted by Charles I., and his name also appears on the Parliament Committee in 1648 for raising and calling out the Militia. He was also steward of the Barony of Abergavenny. He married Ann, daughter of Humphrey Baskerville of Pontrilas and niece of Joan, his brother's wife.

He presented to the town a bell which formerly hung in the old Market House, an inscription on the bell being 'Bayliff Baker -1640-Memento Mori.' When the old Market House was taken down prior to the erection of the present Town Hall, the bell was found to be cracked, whereupon it was recast at the expense of John Baker Gabb and re-presented to the town with the additional inscription: 'Joannes Baker Gabb, consang: rest: 1868 disce vivere.' The bell was then hung in the castle grounds.

Henry Baker died at an advanced age in 1861 and was buried in the Herbert Chapel of St Mary's Priory Church. He had a large family, seven sons and five daughters. Five of the sons died unmarried, a sixth, William, married but had no issue and the youngest, John, also married and had one child, a daughter named Francis.

Henry's nephew, David, born in 1575, became a lawyer and was appointed Recorder of Abergavenny. However, he later resigned his post and became a Catholic, taking orders as a Benedictine priest. Under the name of Father Augustine Baker, he was the author of several religious works.

The Baker family became extinct in the male line and the representatives were the Gabbs. James Gabb, the fifth son of Thomas Gabb was born in 1748 and died in 1806. He and his wife Charlotte (d.1807) were buried in a tomb in St Mary's Churchyard, Abergavenny. Their son James Ashe Gabb was the last of the family to live at 'Beli Baker', although the property remained in the family until about 1868, when the house was sold, together with the adjoining gardens and other land, by the descendants of James Gabb, in whom that portion of the property was vested under a partition of the family estate made in 1794. The purchaser changed the name to 'Old Court' by which it has since been known. During the Great War the house was used for a short time by the Army and before that as a nursing home for several years.

In 1966 the 18th century gateway to Old Court was demolished because it was considered unsafe after adjoining buildings had been pulled down some years previously.

Nevill Hall

At the beginning of the 18th century this grand building, was just a small tenement building belonging to Dr William Steel, who farmed the land known as 'The Brooks,' so named because several streams converged there. In 1860 it was purchased by James Charles Hill, one of the proprietors of the Blaenavon Ironworks. He demolished the old house and spent a considerable sum of money in constructing the present mansion and laying out the grounds. In 1890 it was purchased by the first Marquess of Abergavenny, who renamed it Nevill Court. The meadows between the house and the river already belonged to the Marquess, being part of the old demesne land of the castle and lordship. In the old days the castle was the residence of the Lords of Abergavenny, but after this fell into decay, the Nevill family, for many years, did not have an official residence in the town.

Nevill Hall with Sugar Loaf in the background

The following is a description of the interior of Nevill Hall as it was in the early years of the 20th century:

'The entrance hall at Nevill Hall is large and finely proportioned, though the arrangement of the staircase is distinctly unusual. The latter, which is to the right hand side on entry, slopes backward so that a half turn at the top of the first flight brings you to a landing over the top of the front entrance.

The walls of the hall are adorned with many hunting trophies, which at once bespeak the tastes of the Marquess of Abergavenny, who is a grand old sportsman, and who, though advancing years prevent him following the hounds across country or salmon fishing on his splendid water on the Usk, still takes a keen interest in sport of all kinds.

A nice set of Landseer prints bespeaks the love of animals which is another characteristic of the Marquess.

At the opposite end of the hall to the entrance is a cosy little smoking room, one wall of which is covered with shelves holding a wonderful collection of old jugs, many of which were procured by the Marquis in out of the way places. Some of them represent rural scenes of a festive nature, others go back to the days when cock-fighting was a fashionable sport, and there is one which bears a representation of the never-to-be-forgotten Sayers Heenan fight.

The dining room which occupies the northeastern corner of the house, is one of those apartments in which the light has been somewhat reduced. Formerly it had two large windows on the east side as well as on the north, but the former has been covered up and in the shallow recesses the Marquis keeps his collection of pewter.

There are some interesting pictures on the walls, including a painting of Henry, the second Earl of Abergavenny, who lived from 1755 to 1843 and who was the only member of the family to become a Knight of the Thistle. At the southern end of the room hangs a picture of Eridge Castle, the fine castellated Sussex seat of the Marquis, while in another part is a striking oil painting (by C. Jones) of Highland cattle in the snow.

The morning room which occupies the north-western corner of the mansion is a particularly charming apartment, and it is especially notable for the collection of old brass, in the acquisition of which the Marquis has taken a keen personal interest.

Behind the dining room is a cosy smoking room which, on winter evenings, is a favourite retreat of the Marquis. A feature of this is the fine series of Buck's prints of the castles of Monmouthshire, which hang on the walls opposite the fireplace, and which were a gift to the Marquis from that keen antiquarian, the late Judge Owen.

Crossing the hall to the drawing room one notes over the door, the Nevill coat of arms. This is in reality an ancient fire back, which formerly did duty in one of the cottages on the Sussex estate, and which has been cleaned and illuminated in colours, and which bears the date 1736.

The drawing room is in some ways the finest apartment in the house. It is at the southwestern corner of the house and is very tastefully decorated. There are big gilt mirrors at the eastern end to the right and left of the door. The pictures include one characteristic example of the late Mr Sidney Cooper - a rural scene with cows in a field.

Among the many interesting contents of the room is a large screen covered with very clever sketches of sporting scenes hand painted on silk. Quite a notable adjunct to the drawing room is a sort of covered-in verandah or lounge which was added by the present Marquis.'

Nevill Hall in about 1916

Nevill Hall in 2011

The Marquess died in 1915 and the estates were sold the following year. In 1917 the Board of Management of the Blaina & District Hospital bought Nevill Hall for uses as a convalescent annexe. However, the scheme was abandoned during the industrial depression that followed the 1914-18 War. The property was then leased to a local firm and during the Second World War was used by the military.

In January 1920 the Blaina & District Hospital Committee completed an agreement to purchase Nevill Hall, the residence of the late Marquess of Abergavenny., from Sir Herbert Cory MP., for the purpose of a convalescent home. The property included the hall, four cottages and a farm with about 30 acres of land and the sum agreed was £11,250. The hall consisted of '30 rooms of beautiful structure, carvings and mirrors have been left intact.' The committee estimated the cost of furnishing at £2,000.

When the National Health Service came into being, the newly appointed North Monmouthshire Management Committee immediately decided that Nevill Hall should be used as a hospital as soon as possible. With the support of the Welsh Regional Board, Nevill Hall became the group medical unit and it opened in January 1953.

A feature of the building is the large number of windows and from these the patients could enjoy excellent views from their beds. When the new hospital was built the old Hall was turned into an administrative office and today it is used as a conference centre and social club.

In July 1966 the foundation stone of the new district hospital was laid by Mr Eugene Cross, Chairman of the North Monmouthshire Hospital Management Committee. An act of dedication was then performed by the Archbishop of Wales, the Most Reverend A. E. Morris.

The Pentre is a house beautifully situated on the slope of the Rholben. In 1819 Frederick Fredericks, a Danish gentleman was living there and it was he who probably built the front to what was before just a small farmhouse and he also laid out the grounds. Afterwards, James Greenfield lived there as a tenant until 1845 when he moved to Brynderwen Court. The house was then sold to Robert Wheeley and it later became the home of his son, Lieutenant Colonel William Henry Wheeley.

A meeting of the Monmouthshire Hunt at The Pentre in 1906

The Chapel in 1906

The Chapel at the beginning of the fifteenth century, was the residence of David ap Gwilym Jenkin (Herbert), who held the property by lease from the prior and monks of St Mary's. At the dissolution of the monasteries the Chapel, with the Priory and other lands, was granted in 1546 to James Gunter and Henry Westcott. In later times the estate belonged to the Dukes of Beaufort, having been bought by the fifth Duke in about 1850.

Part of the house is very ancient for in its thick walls is contained the 15th century residence of David ap Gwilym. The place takes its name from a chapel dedicated to St David, which stood nearby, and it is possible that part of a barn may have been the chapel.

The Hill was built in about 1849

The Hill was owned by the Lloyd family in the early 18th century but it was purchased by William Morgan in 1776 and remained the property of his family until the middle of the 19th century. William Lloyd Powell bought the estate in 1849 and built the present house, which has remained largely unaltered since that time.

Edward Pritchard Martin, JP for Monmouthshire and Glamorgan purchased the estate in 1901, for £10,000. He came from a family involved with mining and engineering and was himself General Manager of the Blaenavon Ironworks for a time. He was appointed President of the Iron and Steel Institute in 1897 in recognition of his work with Sydney Gilchrist Thomas's experiments in the dephosphorisation of steel.

He carried out alterations and extension to The Hill during the period 1904-1908 and the crest over the main door of the Hill is that of the Martin familly. On his death the estate passed to his wife, who died eleven months later. Their son Charles inherited the property but was killed in 1915 whilst on active service in France during the First World War.

In 1916 the estate was auctioned at the Angel Hotel in Abergavenny and purchased by Herbert Clarke Lewis, the second Baron Lewis of Merthyr, for his three unmarried sisters Lillian, Anne and Gwendoline. When Lillian, the last remaining sister died on 15th June 1964 the estate was passed to the county council and then established as an educational centre. Hugh Strand Jones was appointed as its first Principal and under his direction the centre gained an excellent reputation. It was taken over by Coleg Gwent in 1995 and became part of Wales' largest educational establishment.

In May 2003, following extensive refurbishment at a total cost of £1.5m the Hill was re-launched as The Hill Education & Conference Centre and officially opened by Jamie Owen of BBC Wales. On 25 August 2009 the centre sadly closed and the future of the building at the time of writing is uncertain.

The historic Victorian walled gardens has been entered in the CADW / ICOMOS register of landscapes, parks and gardens of special historic interest in Wales. The register entry says, 'the gardens, grounds and related parkland of the Hill are a rare example of a type that is not often well preserved. Their principal character is that of an early 19th-century miniature country estate.' The statement also highlights the association with the distinguished horticulturist, John Wedgewood (of the famous potters' family), who rented The Hill from 1829 to 1836. He was one of the founders in 1804 of the Royal Horticultural Society. The gardens are now looked after by a team of volunteers known as the Friends of Gardd-y-Bryn

Linda Vista is Spanish for 'beautiful view' and the house of that name was built in the 1870's. In 1901 it became the home of James Straker, one-time Mayor of Abergavenny and a well known local auctioneer who formed a partnership with William Chadwick. His brother Edgar Straker was an early editor of the *Abergavenny Chronicle*.

Linda Vista was built in the 1870s

By the mid 1920s the property had been purchased by the Whiteheads who were wealthy industrialists, having interests in the steel industry at Ebbw Vale and Newport. It was Mrs Whitehead who established the beautiful gardens assisted by her gardening staff.

The beautiful gardens of Linda Vista are open to the public

The original garden begins at the circular rose bed and extends to the Byfield Lane boundary. In the years leading up to World War II, there were three gardeners employed here, but the number dropped to two after 1945.

On the death of Mrs Whitehead in 1957 the house and gardens came into the ownership of Abergavenny Borough Council and in the Spring of 1965 the grounds of Linda Vista were opened to the public. The park had been developed to include a viewpoint which looked towards Skirrid Fawr, the castle and the beautiful Vale of Usk.

Oriental and foreign shrubs and trees were obtained from various parts of the world. Among these rare trees, plants and shrubs were some Japanese Pagnuola trees, Chinese tortured willows (named for their odd branch formation), a foxglove tree and a corkscrew hazel.

In the new layout the ground level was raised some ten feet, making a new garden altogether without its familiar platform. Some ornamental gates were placed at the entrance to the park, in a surrounding stone wall.

The gardens were officially taken over by Monmouth District Council in 1974 and further land including the old fruit and vegetable gardens and part of the castle meadows were also bought in order to extend the grounds. Today Linda Vista and its gardens is owned and maintained by Monmouthshire County Council, with additional help from the 'Friends of Linda Vista Gardens'.

In April 2004 a wood sculpture depicting some of Abergavenny's history was unveiled by County Councillor Andre Arkell, chairman of the Bryn-y-Cwm Area Committee.

Sculpture by Neil Gow

It was the work of sculptor Neil Gow from Stroud who transformed a felled cedar tree into a fascinating work of art, illustrating various scenes from the town's history, including Owain Glyndwr's attack on the town in 1404 and the famous massacre at Abergavenny Castle in 1175.

Plas Derwen in 1906

Plas Derwen (the Oak tree mansion) was originally known as Dawkins after Nicholas ap Dawkin, who lived there in the fifteenth century. In later years it became the property of the Herberts of Coldbrook and was the residence of Mrs Margaret Powell, widow of Judge Andrew Powell and daughter of Matthew Herbert of Coldbrook. By her will, dated 7 January 1641, she left £4 per annum to the poor of Abergavenny, £1 per annum for the repair of the Herbert Chapel in St Mary's Church.

The house continued as part of the Coldbrook estate and was for many years the residence of Christopher Davies till his death in 1884, When Mr Ferdinand Hanbury Williams inherited it. On the sale of the Coldbrook estates in 188 it was sold to Mr Henry William Buddicom and later became the residence of Colonel Edward Bleiddian Herbert. Today it is a well appointed restaurant.

Nant-oer (so called as being the equivalent in Welsh for Coldbrook) was built by Mr Ferdinand Capel Hanbury Williams about 1860. Born in 1830, he was the son of Mr Hanbury Williams of Coldbrook Park, his mother being the only sister of Lord Hampton. In 1852 he joined the 16th Lancers and was for three years quartered in Ireland. He was a great sportsman, and from 1868 till 1886 master of the Monmouthshire hounds, having his kennels at the Spytty.

He married the eldest daughter of Robert Wheeley of the Pentre on 20th April 1870 and was entertained at a public dinner at the Angel Hotel, Abergavenny and presented with a silver horn and hunting whip as a mark of the esteem in which he was generally held. On his death he was buried in the family vault at Llanfoist Church. Nant-oer was afterwards the residence of his son who was also named Ferdinand.

Yspytty Farm is said to stand on the the site of an old hospice. Yspytty means a hospice from and comes from the Latin hospitium. It belonged to St Mary's Priory and sometime after the dissolution came into the hands of the Herberts of Coldbrook.

For many years the kennels of the Monmouthshire hounds were here during the mastership of Mr F. C. Hanbury Williams and until Mr Reginald Herbert became master when the hounds were removed to Clytha.

Pen y Pound House in 1906

Pen y Pound means 'the pond head' (pound being used in colloquial Welsh for a pond) and takes its name from a small reservoir fed by the Cybi brook, from which water for many years was taken in wooden pipes to supply the town. The house known as Pen y Pound belonged in the eighteenth century to Thomas Williams. By his will, dated 1 October 1784, he left to his son John the dwelling house with the reservoir of water, for which, and the passage of it through his yard, he was paid 11s per annum. The house was later occupied by Dr Samuel Hopkins Steel and re-named Dyne House.

Llwyndu Court in about 1907

Llwyndu Court (the black grove) stands on land which once belonged to St Mary's Priory, and after the dissolution of the monasteries it was taken over by William Lewis of Abergavenny. The court was erected in about 1830 by Mr Baker Gabb, who resided there till his death in 1896. It was then sold to Colonel Tomkinson and later became the residence of Robert William Kennard, Managing Director of Blaenavon Ironworks.

The lost house of Coldbrook

The story of Coldbrook House, which takes its name from a nearby brook covers a period of four and a half centuries. It was situated in the folds of a hill upon the left bank of the Usk, about a mile south of Abergavenny and first appears in history as the seat of Sir Richard Herbert in the reign of Henry VI, though how he acquired it is not evident.

Whether Sir Richard built the house which stood there in Tudor times we do not know, but some of the older parts of the reconstructed house were certainly of 15th century date or earlier.

Coldbrook House in about 1907

On Sir Richard Herbert's death the Coldbrook Estate went to his son Sir William and continued in the ownership of nine generations of his descendants. Among them was Henry Herbert, who in the Civil Wars, was almost the only member of his family who sided with Parliament. The eighth in descent from the old medieval warrior was Sir James Herbert, who sat in Parliament and died without male issue in 1719. The estate and seat were conveyed by Lady Judith, his only daughter to her husband Sir Thomas Powell, of Broadway, Carmarthen, one of the Justices of the Court of the King's Bench. Upon his death, without issue male, the fortune was divided between their three daughters and the landed property was sold.

The Coldbrook estate was then purchased by Major Hanbury of Pontypool and he settled it on his third son Charles (b.1709), who in accordance with the will of his Godfather, Charles Williams of Caerleon, assumed the name of Williams and became well known as Sir Charles Hanbury Williams.

Charles Hanbury Williams after being educated at Eton and doing the grand tour, settled down on his new estate at Coldbrook, marrying in 1732, the youngest daughter of the Earl of Conningsby. He was a very wealthy man and spent large sums on improving the mansion. A new front with a massive porch supported on Doric columns was erected and the interior underwent considerable attention.

Sir Charles Hanbury Williams

It may be assumed that up to this time the fifteenth century mansion, which would appear to have been irregular in shape had remained somewhat in its original state, though there was evidence of alteration in Tudor or early Stuart days. It is probable, however, that it had been allowed to fall into disrepair before it passed into the hands of the Hanbury family.

Originally it must have been an oblong building with two or three low-pitched storeys with a tower at each corner. The main entrance may have faced west and a plan drawn by Meredith Jones, dated 1753, shows avenues of trees radiating from each side of the house. A deer park was situated to the south and west of the house and probably extended to the fields on the north side as well.

Charles remodelled the northern side of the house in accordance with 18th century ideas and some of the fabric was removed to allow the construction of a spacious entrance hall, drawing room and dining room. It was once stated that 'As an example of 18th century decorative work at its best, there is no country house in either South Wales or Monmouthshire which is equal of Coldbrook.'

A building in the grounds was used for many years as a chapel and it was here that Lady Powell's daughter, Judith married Vedlters Cornewall in 1722. Sir Charles used the chapel as a summer house and no doubt wrote some of his poetry there. In later years it became a sort of rustic grotto and at one time even became a bathing pool.

On the death of his father in 1773 Charles entered Parliament, and supported Sir Robert Walpole with such loyalty that in 1739 he was appointed paymaster of marines. He is described as having been a man of affable manners, sprightly conversation and ready wit.

In 1746 he was knighted, and proceeded as British envoy to the Court of Dresden. He quickly displayed great adaptability for his new office and his dispatches were businesslike and spirited, but he will be best remembered for his verses. He wrote political satire, witty observations of his day, and privately circulated verses likely to cause trouble whenever they were brought to the notice of the people they concerned. He addressed poems to the fair sex and seemed to love all the ladies concerned. He eventually became insane and died in 1759 at the age of fifty.

Sir Charles left no male issue and Coldbrook passed to his brother George Hanbury, who assumed the name Williams and when he died in 1764 the estate was inherited by his eldest son, John Hanbury-Williams, who died in 1819 without male issue. He was succeeded by his nephew Ferdinand Hanbury Williams who died in 1888. His son Ferdinand Capel Hanbury-Williams subsequently sold the estate to Lady Llanover in 1891 and on her death it passed to her grandson Sir Arthur Herbert of Llanarth, and then to Robin Herbert, who decided to dispose of the mansion and live on his estate at Llanover.

Coldbrook House at that time was a square building with a tower at each corner. The drawing room occupied a position over the entrance hall and it contained some beautiful tapestry and a very fine mantlepiece said to have been brought there from Raglan Castle. Over the first floor a balustraded parapet extended from tower to tower and above this the roof sloped up at a sharp angle.

From each side of the house ran an avenue of trees. On its southern side was a large deer park and the Abergavenny and Raglan main road went much closer to the mansion than the present one.

The house used to contain a great deal of fine old furniture and large portraits of the Hanbury family. There were also valuable paintings by Vandyke and others of such famous people as Henrietta, Queen of Charles I, Oliver Cromwell, William and Mary, George II, the Duke of Cumberland, Sir Robert Walpole, Frederick II, Lord Hervey, Lord Catoret etc. There was a magnificent marble chimney-piece and some valuable china, collected by Sir Charles Hanbury Williams. There was also a curious oak mantle piece which formerly belonged to Raglan Castle.

There are many fascinating stories connected with Coldbrook House, including the inevitable claim of an underground passage leading to Abergavenny Castle and some floorboards stained with a pool of blood resulting from a sword fight on the stairs. Another story relating to the origin of the blood stain is a tale of unrequited love. A butler who lived in service in the house loved one of the maids, but she ignored his attentions and in jealous fury he murdered the unfortunate girl. According to Sir Joseph Bradney this is the true story of the bloodstain.

The Grand Sale of the Contents of Coldbrook House

In 1953 a large marquee was erected in front of the mansion and over a period of eleven days bidding took place for the 4,000 lots. These included a magnificent array of English and Continental silver, paintings by many well-known artists, including Van Dyke and Constable, Old English and Continental furniture.

On the first day of the sale it was estimated that the proceeds had reached more than £15,000. On the second day no fewer than 5,000 ounces of silver were bought by eager buyers. Twenty-one silver beakers realised £750, while Continental silver was sold for between £6 and £7 an ounce.

There was a keen demand for the furniture and £72 was paid for five Windsor chairs. The tapestries, Aubusson and Flemish, ranged from £60 to £160, and a Bokhara embroidered bedspread fetched £30. Books, too, were in demand, and Joseph Bradney's 'History of Skenfrith' was sold for £16 10s 0d.

On the seventh day a large painting attributed to Giovanni Pennini made £38. A painting of a Dutch interior by David Teniers, and bought originally by Sir Arthur Herbert in St Petersburg when he was in diplomatic service, was sold for £160. A portrait of Cardinal Richelieu by Phillip de Champaigne (1602-1674) was bought for £40, but a landscape by Constable fetched only £62. Coldbrook mansion was demolished in 1954.

The sale was probably the largest to be conducted in Wales for 100 years and the total realised was about £23,000. Dealers and collectors from Scandinavia, the Continent, South Africa and America and all parts of Britain were in attendance.

In 1963 Coldbrook was considered by Monmouthshire County Council as a possible site for a new County Hall. A report of that time stated that 'The land has a gentle slope and is more than sufficient in area. But it has disadvantages such as a lack of sewerage facilities, and piped water and gas are not available on the site. The bus services are more infrequent than in the more populated areas of the county, and the vast majority of people would have to travel to Abergavenny and then change to a bus passing the site.' Eventually a site was selected at Croesyceilog for the new County Hall to replace the one at Newport.

Chapter Thirteen
PUBLIC SERVICES AND FACILITIES

Abergavenny is a clean, well-lighted and healthy town, the water supply, obtained from St David's Well at Llwyndu, being of the purest quality.

Edward J. Burrow 1903

The first work taken in hand by the Commissioners under the 1793 Act was the repairing and extending of the lead pipes leading from the Pond Head to the town, which were in very bad order, and in 1794 a piece of land near the old Pond Head was purchased of John Hanbury Williams for a new Pond Head at a cost of £30. In the same year a contract was entered into for conveying the water to the town in pipes made of elm, but it was not carried out until 1805 when 44 tons of elm were purchased of Mrs Kinsey for that purpose.

In 1813 it was decided to lay 820 yards of iron mains and those pipes were in two yard lengths of 5 inches bore, weighing 1 cwt 2 qrs 14 lbs each and were ordered from Hill & Hopkins & Co of Blaenavon at £8 10s 0d per ton.

An Act from Parliament in 1860 gave the Commissioners further powers to construct a new waterworks and John White commented:

> 'By virtue of this Act... a bountiful supply of water of great purity [was] obtained from St Teilo's Well at Llwyndu. Within the past two years other springs have been discovered, yielding a larger additional supply of water, which has been diverted into the covered reservoir at St Teilo's Well. The height of this well above the general level of the town is about four hundred feet. The water is conveyed by pipes direct from the reservoir to the town, the supply being so abundant even in the driest seasons, that the pipes are nearly always full; and owing to the elevation from which the water proceeds, so great is the pressure, that in the case of fire, engines are not needed.'

A second larger covered reservoir was later constructed at this location in order to cope with the demands of an increased population in Abergavenny. In 1932 this reservoir was covered with concrete and the contractor for this project was Rees Edwards of Tredegar. Unfortunately an accident occurred when a scaffolding pole broke and three workmen fell 24 feet to the floor of the reservoir. William Henry Llewellyn of White House. Llwyndu sustained the most serious injuries and he died at the Cottage Hospital later in the day. The other two men, David Jones and George Hill of Tredegar suffered only bruising and shock.

On April 15th, 1932 the Abergavenny Chronicle commented:

> 'It is hoped that the scheme for covering will for ever solve Abergavenny's water troubles. There is no purer water in the country than that which comes from the Llwyndu and Sugar Loaf springs, but it is well known ... that underground spring water must not be exposed to the sun's rays before it reaches the consumer. It is in open storage that diatoms develop

which while not really harmful, are unpalatable and unpleasant.

Experiments with chlorinating plant were partly successful in that the fearsome-sounding amphipleura pelldica was eliminated, but still the growth of diatoms continued and affected the pristine purity of the water.

There were two alternatives, a filtration plant, or covering the reservoir. Financial considerations decided the council in favour of covering the reservoir, for a filtration scheme would not only involve a large capital expenditure but future expense of maintenance.'

When the work was completed there was a small civic event occasion to mark the event. In the presence of about fifty people the Mayor of Abergavenny, Councillor A.E. Tillman was presented with a lever which he used to turn on the supply to fill the newly covered reservoir. Alderman Bishop then proposed a vote of thanks to the Mayor. He suggested that the Mayor should keep the gilded lever and hang it on his watchchain for it might be useful at council meetings!

Today, Abergavenny receives its water from the Talybont Reservoir while Llwyndu is used as a service reservoir with a capacity of 7 million gallons. The yield of the springs averages some 500,000 gallons per day and this can be supplemented by water from a borehole with a vertical shaft electric pump which could provide up to 100,000 gallons per day.

Local Wells

At one time Abergavenny was supplied with water from a number of wells. The people who lived in Frogmore Street took their water from St Lawrence's Well, which was a spring of excellent water in a nearby field. Ireland Street (now Ross Road) was supplied from Sarah's Well, which was situated by the side of the Ross Road, on the other side of Priory Mill.

This ancient well in Holywell Road was the water supply for the Benedictine Priory

Mill Street was chiefly supplied from Ffynon y Cwm ('The well in the dingle'), behind Pen-y-Cawse. This well was originally called Ffynnon-y-garreg (the well by the stone) and at one time was noted for its medicinal properties. There was also the Priory Well, in Bailey Prody, used as a timber yard at one time and down Byfield Lane there was a spout near the Old Channel. Pant's Well in Tudor Street supplied the residents there with water.

Priory Well in Beili Prody, near the old Tythe Barn was supplied from a stream which ran in an open gully through fields now covered by the Hereford Road.

Holy Well can be found on the east side of Abergavenny in the aptly named Holywell Road. On the side of this road you will find a stone trough set into a low wall. This part of the town was once known as Holy Well, which was sometimes corrupted to Hole-in-the Wall. The stone trough is fed by springs and long ago it was the water supply for the Benedictine Priory and said to have healing powers. In those times it would have been situated in a field, which was part of the land owned by the priory.

In 1825 the Rev John Thomas who had been an Usher at King Henry VIII Grammar School died suddenly after drinking water from this well but it may have just been a coincidence! The horse trough that you see here today was constructed by a Mr Foster, who was an Abergavenny builder. Nearby Fosterville Crescent is named after him.

Street Lighting

Prior to 1796 there were no public lamps but in that year 20 lamps were ordered to be put up in certain places in the town. The number was later increased to forty and they were lit by oil. The contract for lighting these lamps for 6 months from 29th September 1799 to 25th March 1800 was £6 per month.

In 1823, Thomas Davies erected a gas works on a small scale on a portion of the site of the later works and power was granted to him to lay pipes through the streets in consideration of him supplying gas for 20 lamps free of charge and supplying any further gas at £2 per lamp per annum.

Electricity came to Abergavenny on April 12th 1932.
The supply was switched on at the sub station in Park Crescent.

It was in the early 1930s that an electricity supply was first made available in Abergavenny by means of 11,000 volt lines from Hereford power station, under the control, of the Shropshire, Worcestershire and Staffordshire Power Company Ltd. This company also owned generating stations at Stourport and Upper Boat and in 1931 issued a contract for the construction of a double-circuit 66,000 volt line via Abergavenny to interconnect these two stations. This was an enterprising and far sighted decision at the time.

In July 1953 the Town Council approved a scheme prepared by Mr D. J. Meredith, the town's lighting superintendent, whereby the whole town would be lit by electricity and all gas lighting would be done away with.

> 'The scheme suggested would effect a great improvement over the present standard of lighting by gas,' said Mr Meredith. 'It would also effect a considerable saving per annum in the present cost of street lighting. At present there are about 160 gas lamps in the side streets of Abergavenny and these will be replaced with about 200 electric ones. The capital cost of the scheme would be about £6,338.'

In October 1981 the gas tanks in Merthyr Road were removed after nearly 100 years. The two great gas storage tanks known as number one and number two were built in 1894 and 1939 respectively. The principle of the gas holders is that storage was needed to cope with the fluctuation in daily demand. There were two peak consumption times such as the morning, when the normal pipes could not cope, so these tanks were filled overnight and when the rush came they supplemented the piped gas. Various improvements made to the pipeline system in the Abergavenny area meant that peak demand could be met without the tanks, thus making them redundant.

This picture taken in Frogmore Street shows some of the old gas lamps that used to be in the town. Abergavenny was not lit by electricity until 1953.

Town Drains

Prior to 1866, the sanitary system of the town was in a very unsatisfactory condition; in fact there were no town drains worthy of the name, but about that time powers were obtained enabling the Commissioners to construct a through system of drain age and the work was done as soon as was possible. When the town boundaries were extended in 1880, powers were also obtained for extending the Sewerage Works.

The Old Cemetery

Just outside the town, bordering the Old Hereford Road is the Public Cemetery which was formed in 1855 at a cost of £2000 and opened in 1859 under the control of a joint committee and covers three acres.

It is divided into three parts. The long, narrow strip, running alongside the road, is the Roman Catholic ground; next to it but divided from it by a path, is the Nonconformists' ground. The space at the eastern extremity of the latter was apportioned between the Episcopalians and the Roman Catholics; while the upper portion of the Cemetery, divided from the latter by the central drive is the portion appropriated by the Episcopalians. There are two mortuary Chapels - one used by the Nonconformists and situated near the gate; the other used by the Church of England and situated in the upper portion of the ground.

This stone which displays a hand holding a bell commemorates Henry Preece, who for many years was a grave digger at St Mary's churchyard and also this cemetery. In addition he was the Town Crier, which office he held until his death at the age of 68 on 21st January 1881

Another interesting stone in the Old Cemetery commemorates Tom Williams of Monk Street who died at the age of 70 in February 1925. A native of Abergavenny, for 42 years he was the sexton of St Mary's Church and the last man to ring the curfew bell at St John's Church. He had been in business in the town as a carpenter and joiner for 45 years.

The New Cemetery

In 1894, a new cemetery, covering about 13 acres, was opened in the parish of Llanfoist, to serve the parishes of Abergavenny Urban and Abergavenny Rural. The gates and piers at the entrance are Listed Grade II and as is the Victorian Chapel at the top of the cemetery. Unfortunately the chapel is no longer in use (closed in 1989), apart from providing storage for tools and machinery. Inside is a beautiful stained glass window.

Of literary interest is a memorial stone commemorating the well known Author Alexander Cordell who died on 13th November 1997 at the age of 83. He wrote 30 books in total but is best remembered for his novel 'Rape of the Fair Country' which was published in 1959 and sold millions of copies.

Memorial to the famous author, Alexander Cordell in Llanfoist Cemetery

The Workhouse

The provision of a Workhouse in Abergavenny was first mooted in 1761 and on November 6th it was agreed that 'John Stiff and Thomas Gamage of the said town, shall be appointed governor and master of the intended hospital and workhouse in the said town for the reception, maintenance, education and clothing of the poor, to commence from the 1st January next for the term of three years.' A sum of £200 a year was to be paid to these two gentlemen. Subsequently this was increased by 40 shillings. They were also to be paid £50 towards providing household goods, bedding, furniture and other materials for the Workhouse.

In September 1764 on the expiry of the agreement, James Powell of Llanover and his wife were appointed to the care and management of the Workhouse, but on a different basis. They were to be paid a salary of £20 a year, and evidently did not have to find all that was necessary for the inmates at a fixed sum.

The first purpose-built workhouse in Abergavenny was established in Mill Street. It was built as a result of the 1824 Poor Law Amendment Act and in 1838 this was where you had to go if you had no money or job, or someone to take you in. Later on, soon after the passing of the Poor Law Act in 1834, a workhouse, with accommodation for 100 persons was built by George Wilkinson of Oxford, in Union Road (originally called Brook's Lane), outside the town but over the years Abergavenny increased substantially in size and the building was absorbed into the town. It used to have a bell tower in the centre of the complex which was rung to wake up the residents in the morning, summon them to meals and send them to bed. The bell is now in Abergavenny Museum.

A hundred years ago Brook's Lane would have been a peaceful country lane with just a couple of buildings along its sides. The name was changed to Union Road because Abergavenny was in 'union' with twenty five parishes in the area to maintain the new workhouse.

Records show that in 1905 the workhouse held twenty-eight persons from 60 to 70 years of age, thirteen from 70 to 80 years, three from 80 to 90 and one above 90. This longevity was attributed to 'abstemious and regular habits, plain and wholesome food, hygienic conditions, and to freedom from worry and anxiety of providing the daily subsistence.'

In August 1920 some eighty inmates of the Abergavenny Workhouse enjoyed their annual picnic in a field at Grove Farm, Llanfoist. They were conveyed from the Workhouse by brake and charabanc. Tea was served in the open, and the races and other competitions, including singing and recitations kept everyone interested and amused. During the afternoon, tobacco was distributed to the men, tea and sugar to the women and sweets to the children.

This Grade II listed building In Union Road was built during 1837-38
as the Abergavenny Union Workhouse and was in use until about 1945.

Christmas Day in the Workhouse in 1923

'The inmates of the Abergavenny Union celebrated Christmas in their usual joyous manner. The Institution presented a very festive appearance as a result of the many weeks' preparation on the part of the inmates and staff in decorating the wards, nursery, dining-hall and corridors. The Male Infirmary was very tastefully decorated in brick and black with garlands of flowers, and the Female Infirmary with its mauve and white had a very pleasing effect to the eye. The dining-room was decorated in evergreens and snow, one corner representing a bush with birds twittering on it.

The breakfast consisted of bread and butter, tea, bacon and sausage, after which tobacco, snuff, tea and sugar, oranges, apples and sweets were distributed. An excellent dinner comprising roast pork, apple sauce, vegetables, Christmas pudding and beer was served in the presence of His Worship the Mayor (Councillor J.R. Jacob).'

Abergavenny Chronicle December 28th 1923

Law and Order in Abergavenny

A set of stocks once stood by the main gates of St Mary's Churchyard and these were erected as an instrument of punishment as the result of an Act in 1405 which required that stocks should be provided in every town in England and Wales. Sometimes a whipping post was installed as well.

In 1531 a law passed by Henry VIII directed justices to assign to the poor a limit in which they were to beg and anyone begging outside that limit was to be imprisoned for two days and two nights in the stocks and fed just bread and water. An able bodied beggar was to be whipped and sworn to return to the place where he was born, or last dwelt for the space of three years and there put to labour.

Stocks were usually made of wood, although they were sometimes constructed of iron. They consisted of two boards, or pieces of iron, with holes through which the legs of the culprit were placed. The two sections were then padlocked together. A seat was provided for the offender and sometimes the stocks were designed so that two people could be accommodated at the same time. Stocks were used as a punishment for such offences as forgery, perjury, cornering the market and putting up the prices of goods. The general aim was to make the prisoner look ridiculous in the eyes of his or her friends and local people would throw rotten vegetables and shout disparaging remarks.

In the Abergavenny Improvement Act of 1794 it was stated that watchmen were to be appointed and by 1810 a prison had been established in one of the town gate houses. Soon after 1827 four watchmen were appointed to patrol the town in the winter and they received 12/- a week. During the summer months their number was reduced by half and the two men were paid 7/6d a week. They had to start their beat at 11 o'clock at night and finish hat half past three in the morning. The town was divided into two beats; one comprised Mill Street, Monk Street, Cross Street, High Street and Butcher's Row (Flannel Street), and the other beat included Frogmore Street, Nevill Street, Tudor Street and Castle Street.

The Commissioners in 1843 appointed a Day Policeman who was to take over the duties of Inspector of Nuisances. The man appointed was Patrick Cusack and he was to walk around the town from eight o' clock in the morning until ten at night in the winter and eleven in the summer. He had to make monthly reports on the watchmen, check that they were on their beats and attend meetings of the Commissioners.

In 1847 the Commissioners decided to appoint a superintendent of police (who should not be a native of Abergavenny), at a salary of 25s a week. Patrick Cusack was appointed second day policeman at 17s per week and three night police were appointed at 15s per week each. Out of twenty two applicants, David Mereweather of Blaenavon was appointed superintendent and George Pritchard was elected night watchman. In the following year an application was made by the superintendent of Police for three staves, three rattles, three dark-lanterns and three pairs of handcuffs.

From 1854 there was a full time police force consisting of four men. When the Monmouthshire Constabulary was formed in 1857, it was based in Usk and the Abergavenny police force became part of it. The headquarters was moved to Baker Street, Abergavenny in 1871. The Petty Sessions were held weekly in a spacious upper room and the County Court monthly. The Turnpike Trust also met in the building once a month.

Headquarters of the old Monmouthshire Constabulary in Baker Street

In 1880 the County Constabulary took over a building in Lower Monk Street and occupied it until 1940. Then they moved into the corner house which had previously been used as a gentlemens' Club. This late Georgian house is listed as a building of special architectural interest.

A new headquarters was established at Croesyceiliog in 1971, but for some years a small traffic unit was continued to be run from the old premises in Lower Monk Street, with retained garages and workshops behind the building. A few years later the building on the corner of Monk Street became an information centre and warden's office for the National Park section of the Monmouthshire County Planning Department.

Abergavenny still needed a police station and a new one was built in Tudor Street in 1972 at a cost of £17,000. It opened on April 1, 1973 and the old station in Baker Street (opened in 1888) ceased to function.

On the first floor of the new station is a reception area, a communications room, interview rooms and a cell block divided into two so that both male and female detainees can be accommodated. Previously all female prisoners in Abergavenny had to be taken to Pontypool Police Station as the old station in Baker Street had no facilities for them. Facilities on the first floor included a parade room, locker rooms, a specially equipped drying room for uniforms, CID offices and a photographic studio complete with dark room. Situated on the second floor is a spacious canteen with a large kitchen, administrative offices, conference room and a lecture theatre. Other facilities include a prisoners' exercise yard and garages.

Soon afterwards a new magistrate court was built beside the police station in Tudor Street. It was officially opened on May 8, 1974 when Colonel Roderick Hill, Lord Lieutenant of Gwent, unveiled a commemorative bronze plaque.

The First Fire Service

It was recorded at a parish meeting on 5th April 1736: 'It is agreed that a fire engine of the second or third size, with the appliances, and also a hand engine of the first size, and also two dozen and a half of leathern buckets be forthwith, or as soon as convenience permits, be purchased with the money already collected and to be collected for the purpose.'

The first reliable steam powered appliances were adopted by brigades in the 1850s and replacing the manual engines they allowed a much greater quantity of water to be directed onto a fire. It was another 50 years before they were replaced by the introduction of the internal combustion engine.

In 1938 the Abergavenny Fire Brigade (formed in 1863) honoured four of its members who had each given many years service. They were the Powell family: Mr Henry Powell, one of the founders who was with the Brigade for 56 years, and his sons Mr W.H. Powell (54 years) and Captain H.C. Powell (52 years).

Abergavenny Fire Service showing off its new fire engine in 1938

The first fire station was at the bottom of Market Street within the perimeter of the cattle market. Today, the Fire Station in Hereford Road is one of the larger retained stations in the South Wales Fire and Rescue Service.

Abergavenny Fire Service in the 1930s

Present day Fire Station on the Hereford Road

Post Offices in Abergavenny

The first postal box in Abergavenny was at a little building opposite the present Town Hall. Anyone requiring letters and stamps would have to knock on a small window. In due course trade increased and the business was moved further down Cross Street to a building known as the Stamp Office (later the shop of Fred Sadler, stationer and bookseller).

On May 27th, 1857, a Mr Bigglestone who occupied the premises was, on the recommendation of Lord Llanover, appointed Postmaster by the Postmaster General at that time, the Duke of Argyll. In 1866 Mr Bigglestone applied for permission to place a letter box, near a lamp post at the junction of Brecon and Merthyr roads. The Commissioners, ready to encourage progressive ideas, granted the application.

He was succeeded by his two daughters when the business was moved from the Stamp Office to a premises on the opposite side of the street, which was eventually demolished to make room for an extension to Lloyd's Bank. Miss Bigglestone was in the service of the Post Office for 43 years. She retired with the imperial decoration in 1914. The Post Office remained in Cross Street until 1915 when a new one was built in Frogmore Street.

A new Post Office (now Nicholls) was opened in Frogmore Street in 1915 by the Mayor, Alderman Z. Wheatley. The Post Office moved to its present site in St John's Square in December 1968.

At that time there were no post office motor vehicles employed at Abergavenny and most rural areas received their correspondence on only three or four days a week. By 1934, when extensive structural alterations were carried out to the Post Office, all rural areas enjoyed the privilege of a daily delivery of letters.

The National Telephone Company was formed in 1889 and by 1894 it controlled over 73,000 lines while its competitor, the Post Office, had only between 5,000 and 6,000 lines. This was because the Government of the day favoured private enterprise. The trunk service passed to the control of the Post Office in March 1896.

In October, 1900 the National Telephone Company secured a shop and premises in Monk Street, previously occupied by Watkins and Co., painters, as a public telephone call office and subsequently an exchange was opened there. Before that there had been a call office in the shop of Mr. W. Howells, stationer, High Street. A Post Office directory of 1907 shows that there were 115 Post Office subscribers in Abergavenny (all but three in the t0wn area) and 31 in Crickhowell.

The Carnegie Library

The Abergavenny Reading Association was formed in 1846 and tits members had use of a reading room in the Town Hall. A Free Library Committee was formed in 1901 with Mr E. H. Restall appointed as Librarian and Secretary. Their stated aim was to set up a free lending library and this was initially run from the Reading Room in the Town Hall.

In January 1905, Major William Williams led the Town Council in the adoption of the Public Libraries Act. A little later a Reading Room was opened in the Corn Exchange and Mr E.H. Restall became the first Borough Librarian.

Then in 1905, the Town Council made an approach to that great friend of public libraries, Andrew Carnegie of Skibo Castle, Scotland, and it was rewarded by a grant of £2,000 towards the building of the library premises. The site was purchased by public subscription from the trustees of Miss Rachel Herbert's Charity. The building was designed by Mr J.B. Francis of Abergavenny and its foundation stone was laid by the Mayor, Major W. Williams, who was Chairman of the Library Committee.

A procession from the Town Hall, headed by the mace bearer (Mr Manuel) and the Borough Silver Band, passed along High Street, Frogmore Street and Baker Street to the site of the Free Library at the corner of Victoria Street and Baker Street, opposite to the Police Station. Here a large crowd had assembled to witness the ceremony.

The Reverend J.R. Phillips opened the proceedings with a prayer. Mr. B.J. Francis, the architect, then handed a silver trowel, suitably inscribed, to the Mayor, with a short conglatulatory speech. The Mayor responded appropriately and the stone was lowered into its place. The Mayor used the trowel and declared the stone duly and properly laid. It is of interest that 'Abergavenny' on the stone was accidently spelt with three 'N's.

The low cost of the earlier Reading Room had enabled a book fund to accumulate and numerous valuable gifts of books enabled the Library to start with a reasonable book stock.

It had been estimated that the library would have about 400 borrowers a week so a large supply of books would be needed. At that time the Council only had about 1,500 volumes and would need at least 3,000 before the library was opened. As readers increased about 6,000 books would be needed to keep the supply going.

There were also plans to start a reference library which would be of great use to technical students. The committee hoped to have the new reading room and library opened by September. They were also keen to start a museum in connection with the new library and requested that local people who had items of interest relating to the town and neighbourhood could either give or lend them so that a collection could be started.

The Library was officially opened by the Marquess of Abergavenny on Saturday, 8th September 1906 in the presence of the Mayor of London, Sir Walter Vaughan. It contained a library of 10,000 volumes, including a bequest of over 2,200 valuable books belonging to the late Mrs Attwood Matthews, of Llanfihangel Court.

This picture was taken in 1905 on the occasion of the laying of the foundation stone of the town library in Baker Street. The stone was laid by the Mayor, Major W. Williams, who was chairrman of the Library Committee.

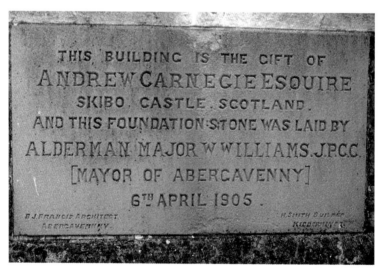

The inscription on the foundation stone has an unfortunate spelling mistake for the stone mason has spelt Abergavenny with three 'N's (bottom left of stone). In 1907, Andrew Carnegie was made a Freeman of Abergavenny.

The Carnegie Library in Baker Street was opened in September 1906

High on the front gable is the sculptured figure of Minerva holding a book and on each side of the entrance are the carved heads of the marquess of Abergavenny and Andrew Carnegie. This fine little library serves as a reminder that Abergavenny has long been a centre of culture. Lady Llanover, wife of Lord Llanover, formerly Sir Benjamin Hall, fostered a society established here in 1832 for the study of literature, music and learning.

The carved head on the left depicts Andrew Carnegie and the one on the right represents the Marquess of Abergavenny

The Library income in the early years was found to be inadequate, although the position was relieved a little in 1923 when the lending rate of 1d was raised to 1 ½d. But it was not possible to provide an adequate fund for the purchase of new books and the library was stagnating as a result. There were however, many gifts, the most notable being the Attwood-Matthews bequest of 1924, which enriched the Library in quality as well as quantity.

In 1933 a sub Committee was appointed to study the situation and it was decided to apply to the Carnegie Trustees for a book grant. The Carnegie Trustees arranged a conference between the Monmouthshire Education Committee and the Abergavenny Town Council. The idea of unifying the service was discussed and a scheme subsequently prepared for the Trustees to submit to the two authorities, a grant of £200 to be given for the benefit of the Abergavenny Library when the amalgamation took place. The suggestion was made that the building and stock should be taken over by the County Library and that the place should be adapted for the free access system.

It was not until March 1938, that the formal agreement was signed. Miss Horseman was appointed Branch Librarian and she took up her position with great enthusiasm. It was not long before the number of borrowers was increased from a few hundred to 3,000.

In 1948 under the supervision of the County Architect the County Branch Library at Abergavenny (formerly known as the Carnegie Free Library) underwent redecoration and alterations. The changes provided for the open access system, by which the borrowers could select their own books from the shelves. There was also new heating and lighting installed. The upstairs room was made into an office and the whole interior redecorated at a cost of about £500.

Lord Raglan performed the reopening ceremony, in his capacity as chairman of the local committee. He formally opened the door and then speeches were made inside the building.

This County Branch Library in Abergavenny was the first scheme of its kind in Old Monmouthshire and by association with the County Library there would be access to their standard works and the latest literature. It was hoped that the example of the Abergavenny Library would stimulate every town in Monmouthshire to demand a Public Library and that the experience gained at this one would make it much easier to meet the demand when it arose.

The Centenary Garden was established as a storytelling area to celebrate the centenary of the opening of the Abergavenny Carnegie Free Library in September 1906. It was designed by the Friends of Abergavenny Library, led by Alison Newsam, Tony Lewis and Marion Pearse garden designer. The site was cleared by C&C Binley and the bardic chair carved by the sculptor Neil Gow. His carving incorporates a reproduction of the statue of Minerva which stands above the front porch. The garden provides an open space for groups of children to take part in activities involving art, music, storytelling, reading and writing.

The Centenary Garden at the Carnegie Free Library

Chapter Fourteen
HOSPITALS AND SCHOOLS

A hospital is no place to be sick.

Samuel Goldwyn

In the mid 14th century (1349-52) Abergavenny fell victim to the Black Death which had been ravaging Europe. It was initially carried by fleas living on black rats travelling on ships, but later it spread from one infected person to another. Few who caught the disease survived and about one fifth of the town's population died.

By contrast, between 1750 and 1760 Abergavenny gained a reputation for being a healthy place to visit. Several eminent physicians prescribed whey from goats' milk to people with consumption and as large flocks of these animals roamed the surrounding hills, the town had a plentiful supply. Physicians began to send their wealthy patients to Abergavenny to drink the whey. Thus the town became a sort of spa. You went to Bala to take the waters and to Abergavenny to take the milk. It became fashionable for the English to visit Abergavenny to enjoy the fresh air and partake of the goats' milk. William Coxe wrote in 1801 that: '... numerous invalids still come to Abergavenny every summer for the mildness and salubrity of the air and to enjoy the scenery...'

Abergavenny was certainly an attractive place for the wealthy to visit and improve their health but for some of the less fortunate residents there were public health problems that led to early deaths for many.

In 1847 a 'Report on Sanitary Conditions in Abergavenny' was compiled by Dr Samuel H. Steel:

'In the upper room of a house in Traitor's Lane (Market Street), with a window of one foot square, I found a father and mother and six children sleeping. In Price's yard, in a house of exactly similar descriptions, I also found an Irish family of eight persons. This yard, inhabited by a number of Irish was the chief seat of the epidemic fever of last summer.

As a general rule the worse the house the higher the proportional rent. Two shillings a week is paid for the miserable tenement of two rooms 12ft square in Traitor's Lane. The houses in Price's yard are let by the mortgagees of the property at one shilling per week each, and the owner charges one shilling more for a miserable bedstead and table, scarcely worth the week's rent.

The Gate or Lock-up, is a small stone building in Monk Street; the Kibby runs directly beneath the pavement. It is close and liable to damp and the separate cells are much too small and would exercise a very pernicious effect upon the health of prisoners being confined in them; but as they are seldom tenanted for more than a few days at a time no ill consequences have hitherto been observed.

Houses for the reception of tramps and poor travellers are numerous in Abergavenny, and their sanitary condition forms no exception to what is generally observed in these rest places in all other towns, though some of them are much better than others.

The rooms are low, small and ill-ventilated. I have seen in one of the best, seven beds contained in two small rooms with only one window, two feet by one foot, that would open, while the fire-place was boarded up. They are subject to no restrictions as to the number of persons received, which is only limited by the area of the floor.

The head policeman informs me that he has seen more than twenty persons in a small house of two rooms, the lower room so close as to be scarcely endurable, while the breath of the inmates might be seen issuing in steam from the open door. All ages and sexes lie together indiscriminately. Fever and illness of all kinds are very prevalent in these places. The charge per night is generally 3d per person. Sometimes a family is taken for a stay of some nights at a smaller sum.

There are two tan-yards in Mill Street which impregnate the air with odours incidental to the manufacture of leather. The smell of tan is not, perhaps, in itself injurious to health, and to many persons it is not disagreeable, but the earlier processes in the preparation of leather are often offensive. The smell from the skin-yards in Mill Street, especially from heaps of the horns and hoofs left till they putrefy can be innocuous.

A stable in Castle-Street used as a slaughter-house is a great public offence. A revered gentleman whose house is close to this place has been subject to most serious annoyance from maggots crawling from under the door into the street, and thence into his house in such numbers that his servants have removed them with a shovel. The smell was so intolerable that he and his family were often unable to take their meals from disgust.'

In 1871 small pox was raging in Mill Street and the Board of Commissioners were considering spreading chloride of lime. The local clergy were criticised by the press for not using the special prayer for times of plague. In an outbreak of scarlet fever 12 of the 16 deaths were in Mill Street.

Pen-y-fal Hospital

Standing on rising ground on the Old Monmouth Road and overlooking the town, a large public building known as the Joint Counties Lunatic Asylum was erected in 1851 at a cost of £37,083 on a farm of about seventy acres. The architects were Messrs Full, James and Waller of Gloucester and this fine ornamental building was well designed for the comfort and accommodation of its unfortunate inmates, but it had long narrow windows and high prison-like walls.

Originally it was known as the Joint Counties Lunatic Asylum, because in 1847 an agreement was entered into by the Counties of Monmouth, Hereford, Brecon and Radnor and the city of Hereford to form a union for the purpose of building a joint asylum, but within a few years it proved too small to contain the patients sent from these counties. Not wishing to contribute further money, Herefordshire decided to withdraw from the union and build an Asylum for itself.

The three storeyed frontage is over 600 feet long (183 metres) and is Tudor Gothic in style. Initially there were twelve wards and 210 patients, who were all described as pauper lunatics. In those days depression was classed as melancholia, schizophrenia as dementia and manic depression as mania.

Abergavenny Lunatic Asylum was built between 1847 and 1851 for joint use by the counties of Monmouth, Brecon and Radnor and the city of Hereford. This fine building was well designed for the comfort and accommodation of its unfortunate inmates.

When the Joint Counties Lunatic Asylum was found to be too small it was extended in 1891 - 1892, 1909, 1903 and 1925, by which time it could accommodate 1,170 patients. The additional buildings included a stone chapel erected at a cost of £3,500 which stands apart in the grounds. The name was subsequently changed to Monmouthshire Mental Hospital and in 1948 following the establishment of the National Health Service it became Pen-y-fal Hospital.

A report written by the Medical superintendent in 1855 states that:

'129 patients were admitted since the last visit of the Commissioners on the 23rd June 1854. Within the same period 63 have been discharged and 45 have died. There are at the present time 266 patients in the establishment, namely 115 men and 151 women. The men patients are generally tranquil, but several of the women were disorderly and noisy... The dinner provided for the patients was abundant, of good quality and well cooked. It consisted of boiled beef, potatoes and cabbage... '

'One case of sudden death took place during the year, on which a coroner's inquest was held, and a verdict of 'Died by the visitation of God' returned; it occurred in an epileptic patient...

A considerable proportion of the cases admitted during the year had previously to admission, either attempted suicide, or displayed strong suicidal propensities. In the majority of such cases, the quiet and regularity of an asylum, the moderately nutritious diet and the absence of all cares and annoyances had had in a short time a surprisingly beneficial effect, both on the mental and bodily health: such cases are, however, very liable to relapse when they go out into the world, and have to undergo the cares and anxieties inseparable from their condition in life.

The hereditary taint and congenital deficiency of intellect combined, form a large proportion of the admissions during the year; it is however gratifying to state, that but one case of 'idiocy' now remains in the asylum.'

Supposed Causes of Insanity in Patients Admitted in 1855

Desertion	3
Disease of brain	9
Disappointed love	5
Drink	5
Epilepsy	19
Fright	3
Grief and over anxiety of mind	9
Hereditary and Congenital causes	14
Injuries to head from falls and other violence	7
Jealousy	1
Pride	1
Religious Subjects	1
Causes Unknown	23
Total	100

In 1867 there were a total of 464 patients resident there despite the fact that it had only been intended for a maximum of 210. In due course the building was enlarged to provide accommodation for 844 inmates. Further enlargements were made in 1891-2, 1909, 1913 and 1925, making the hospital available for 1,170 inmates. The cost of additional land and the subsequent additions and alterations involved an expenditure of £120,375.

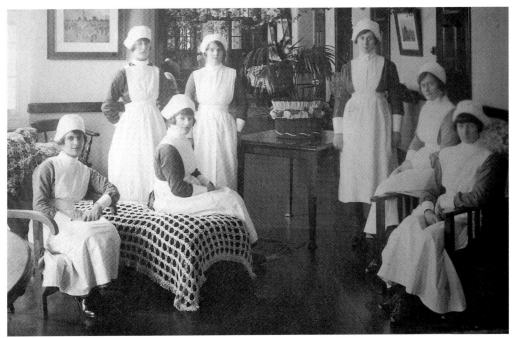

Nursing staff at Pen-y-fal Hospital in 1916

The additional buildings included a chapel of stone erected at a cost of £3,500, which stands apart in the grounds and consists of chancel, nave, transepts, north porch and a central turret containing one bell. A stained window was presented by the architects, Messrs Giles and Gough, of London, and a fine organ, donated by superintendent Dr McCullogh.

The name was subsequently changed to Monmouthshire Mental Hospital and in 1948 following the establishment of the National Health Service the name was altered to Pen-y-fal Hospital. Between 1851 and 1950, over 3,000 patients died there and a commemorative plaque for the deceased has been placed at the site.

In its heyday the hospital employed about 184 male and female nurses, four doctors, six chief nursing officers, two night superintendants, four gardeners, five administration staff, two telephonists and a host of direct labour staff including painters, carpenters shoe makers, bakers, waggonmen, cowmen, stokers and engineers.

Four attendants at Pen-y-fal Hospital in 1919

The hospital closed in 1996 and two years later the 146 year old building and 24 acres of grounds and parkland were bought by Redrow Homes for housing development. A local firm of conservation architects, Graham Frecknall Associates of Monmouth were appointed to create a sensitive scheme based on a well researched conservation plan. While many of the listed buildings had to be demolished, the original hospital building dating back to 1851 (Listed Grade II) was refurbished to create luxury apartments. New houses were also built in the hospital grounds

The Cottage Hospital

The Victoria Cottage Hospital had its origins in the town's Dispensary, established to provide medicines for the poor. The first Dispensary was funded by donations and subscriptions from the richer families of the area and from 1828 it was held in the front room of a house at 45, Castle Street, between 11 and 12 o' clock on Mondays, Wednesdays, Thursdays and Fridays.

During the first year, 402 people were treated at the Dispensary and, by 1854, this number had risen to 910. Doctors who worked at the Dispensary gave their services freely, while the local chemist who supplied and dispensed the medicines was paid for his time and trouble.

The old Dispensary in Castle Street

In 1890 the first Cottage Hospital and Dispensary was established in a rented house at 56 Castle Street, opposite the top of Flannel Street and was initially quite independent of the Dispensary. It was maintained by subscriptions supplemented by income from fetes, balls, gymkhanas etc. Patients were admitted to the hospital on receipt of their letters of recommendation and were charged 3/6d per week for their stay.

This facility gave a useful service to the sick and needy folk of Abergavenny by providing hospital accommodation adequate to the requirements of the town and its surrounding area. Much was done however to raise the necessary funds for a larger establishment.

In 1897, the year of Queen Victoria's Diamond Jubilee, it was decided that efforts should be made to provide a combined Hospital and Dispensary for the town. Land beside the Hereford Road was made available by the Abergavenny Urban District Council on a lease of 999 years at a rental of £1 per annum for the erection of a combined Cottage Hospital and Dispensary. A contract for the building of this new hospital at £1,925 was entered into by the trustees with the council who made a free gift of the site and work commenced.

At last the day came on Friday 28th June 1901 when the foundation stone of the new hospital was to be laid. After a civic luncheon in Bailey Park, the Marquess of Abergavenny proceeded to the site to perform the historic ceremony.

In a recess under the stone was deposited a glass jar containing copies of newspapers including the *Abergavenny Chronicle, The Times, Standard, Daily Telegraph, Western Mail, South Wales Daily News* and a document stating that the foundation stone was laid by the Marquess of Abergavenny on 28th June 1901. This document bore the signatures of the members of the Corporation, the Joint Committee, Hospital Committee, doctors, secretary and treasurer. There were also specimens of silver currency: 5s., 4s., 2s. 6d., 2s., 1s. 6d., and 3d. pieces placed in the jar.

The Mayor then asked the Marquess to lay the foundation stone. His lordship duly complied using a silver trowel and then dramatically struck the stone with a mallet declaring, 'Mr Mayor, ladies and gentlemen, I declare this stone to be well and truly laid.'

The Marquis then placed a cheque for £200 on the stone as a donation towards the cost of building the new hospital. His generous example was followed by many of those present.

The building was designed by Mr E.A. Johnson, architect and built by Messrs J.G. Thomas & Sons and it was officially opened by Lord Tredegar, the Lord Lieutenant of the County in October 1902. as a memorial to Queen Victoria. Accordingly it was named the Victoria Cottage Hospital & Dispensary. The fact that on the day it opened it was completely 'free of all debt' was received with acclamation.

The Abergavenny Cottage Hospital which opened in October 1902
now provides residential accommodation for the elderly

It was intended for the reception of non-infectious diseases, of curable diseases and accidents, which could not be efficiently treated at the homes of the poor residing in the town and neighbourhood of Abergavenny. Originally there were just nine beds, two of which were presented in memory of the men who fell in the Great War of 1914-18. There were also six cots.

Further additions were made over the years including a War Memorial ward in 1922 and a children's' ward in 1924. The maternity ward and further extensions were then planned and the foundation stone for these was laid by Lady Mary Herbert in November 1929.

In August 1973 a petition was launched and signed by more than 9,000 people in an attempt to stop the closure of the Victoria Cottage Hospital. It had been stated in a Welsh Hospital Board report that this 37 bed hospital had given good service to the town in the past, but the opening of the £1,650,000 second stage at Nevill Hall Hospital would leave 'no use for it.'

In 1982 the former cottage hospital now renamed Victoria Court was altered to provide sheltered accommodation for elderly people by the Corlan Housing Association. The original building was remodelled and several extensions added to create space for 22 single flats, 22 doubles and a specially designed room for the disabled. The centre was opened by Sir Harry Llewellyn who unveiled a commemorative plaque.

Maindiff Court Hospital

Maindiff Court before demolition

In 1924 Maindiff Court, was presented to the Monmouthshire Asylum Committee by Sir John W. Beynon Bart CBE DL JL. The buildings of this mental hospital were erected in the early 1930s. They are situated beside the Ross Road about 2 miles from Abergavenny town centre.

The original building, which was once the home of Crawshay Bailey Junior and his family has been demolished and today the hospital consists of four wards, one day hospital and an ECT (Electro-Convulsive Therapy) Department. It was built as a subsidiary to Pen-y-fal Hospital and is famous for housing Rudolph Hess, Adolf Hitler's second in command during World War II.

Ty Skirrid with 12 beds, caters for men and women who have a mental disorder and have offended or are at risk of offending. **Lindisfarne** is a 3 bedded unit which provides unsupervised semi-independent living for clients prior to discharge. **Ty Bryn** is a 18 bedded ward which provides services for Monmouthshire, Torfaen and Blaenau Gwent for patients over the age of 65 years who have been diagnosed with mental health disorders such as Alzheimer's Disease. **Tregaron** is an 18 bedded ward for the treatment and assessment for patients suffering with a functional illness. The **Hiraeth** Day Hospital provides 12 places a day for 5 days a week for those suffering with dementia or a functional illness and offers social, psychological and physical therapies.

Nevill Hall Hospital

In 1920 Nevill Hall and its estate was sold by the owner at that time, Sir James Cory MP to the trustees of the Blaina & District hospital for £11,250. In 1948 it was transferred to the Ministry of Health, and then in April 1950 it was moved from the Endowment Fund to the Hospital Fund.

The Welsh Regional Hospital Board in September 1951 approved the adaptation of premises at Nevill Hall mansion to accommodate 17 patients on the ground floor and 19 patients on the first floor. Ancillary rooms, residential accommodation for Matron and bedrooms on the second floor for sisters was also to be provided.

In January 1953, Nevill Hall was opened as the North Monmouthshire Group of Hospitals first Medical Unit by Sir Frederick Alban, Chairman of the Welsh Hospital Board and the first patients were admitted. The seven wards were occupied by 42 patients and there was a staff of 28 nurses. Each ward was named after one of the areas served by the hospital and the largest ward as a tribute to the early pioneers of the scheme was called the Blaina Ward.

The consulting physician in charge was Dr Aneurin Hughes, formerly a tutor in medicine at the University of St Andrews, Dundee. The Matron was Miss Gwyneth Morgan who trained at the Cardiff Royal Infirmary.

In 1960 it was decided to build a new general hospital for the whole of North Monmouthshire on the site. A ceremony was held to mark the laying of the foundation stone which was performed on 29th June by Mr Eugene Cross. The first phase of the new Nevill Hall Hospital was officially opened by the Secretary of State for Wales, the Right Honourable George Thomas on Friday 10th April, 1970.

In September 1975 a suggestion that Nevill Hall Hospital should be renamed the Aneurin Bevan Hospital was made by the Secretary of State for Wales, Mr John Morris, when he opened phase two of the hospital. He paid tribute to the Gwent men who pioneered the National Heath Service, with special reference to the late Aneurin Bevan MP for Tredegar and Ebbw Vale, who established the service in 1948.

The total cost of the new hospital had been £4.6 million which brought the total number of beds available to more than 500, making Nevill Hall one of the largest and most up to date general hospitals in Wales.

Nevill Hall Hospital in July 2011

Abergavenny Schools

Education is what remains after one has forgotten what one has learned in school.

Albert Einstein

King Henry VIII Grammar School which was founded in 1542 is one of the oldest schools in Britain. It was then under the control of Jesus College Oxford. A Headmaster was appointed at a yearly salary of £13 6s 8d, and an undermaster at a yearly salary of £6 13s 8d. The first Headmaster was Nicholas Oldsworthy, Master of Arts, who was appointed for the duration of his life.

Henry VIII

When it opened, the school had 26 pupils, all boys aged between 7 and 14. Their day was long with two sessions: the morning from 6.00am (7am in winter) to 11.00am and the afternoon from 1.00pm to 6,00pm (5.00pm in winter). Besides Latin grammar they may have studied what were then the literal arts: logic, rhetoric, arithmetic, music, poetry and astronomy.

In the original grant made 'on the 24th July in the 34th year of King Henry VIII', certain prayers were ordered to be said daily, and these included the following in the morning:

> 'O Lord save the King and hear us in the day when we shall call upon thee, we pray O Lord God Supreme, King of Kings preserve, we beseech thee our King Henry the Eighth, chief and only founder of this school, very long unto this society safe and flourishing, and grant that after the course of his life happily run, he may by Thy mercy be advanced to the reward of Eternal Life and grant we beseech Thee furthermore that Edward, the most deserving prince, may succeed his fathers in the Throne fortunate and long lived. Amen.'

In the evening there was a similar prayer, and also the following one:

> 'O Lord God who hast given the most bright light of the day unto them to perform their undertakings and hast mercifully given the grateful silence of the night to refresh the strength of their bodies with sleep, and to wash away the cares of their minds, we pray Thee that if we have committed anything this day through human carelessness which may displease the eye of Thy Majesty, Thou wouldst forgive accordingly to thy wanted clemency and also grant that this night approaching may be happy to us the prospering may be pure thou being our Guardian and safe from the nocturnal wiles of the Devil thou being our protector that this sleep may tender our bodies and minds more carefully to serve thee the day following unto whom with the Son and the Holy Ghost be eternal glory. Amen.'

For the foundation of the school the King granted certain tithes subject to a rent of 40 shillings to the king and the payment to the master and usher of the school of the salaries - £13 8d to the master per annum and the usher £6 13s 4d. These tithes, belonging to the suppressed priory of Abergavenny were the rectorial tithes of Llanfihangel Crucorney, Llandewi Rhydderch, Llanelly, Llandewi Skirrid and Bryngwyn, a portion of the rectorial tithes of Llanwenarth, together with the tithes of the Rectory of Bedgworth in Gloucestershire, belonging to the suppressed priory at Usk.

In 1685 the Trustees lost their power to collect tithes and as a result most tenants kept their money rather than give it to the school. In 1717 the King was petitioned to resolve the situation but nothing happened until the passage of an Act of Parliament in 1760.

The 1760 Act reorganised the school's government. Henceforth Jesus College, which had gained control of the Gloucestershire tithes, was to be responsible for paying the headmaster £40 a year, while locally named trustees paid his assistant, £15 a year. It was at this time that the old school building was pulled down and replaced with the religious tower and fine Georgian master's house which still stands today. The increased salary led to a better quality of head but still combined the post with that of vicar. By 1765 the school was flourishing with some 70 to 80 boys under the headmastership of the Reverend William Morgan.

By 1818 the number of pupils had declined to 18 boys, most of whom were on scholarships while the rest paid 5 guineas a year. The situation did not improve throughout much of the 19th century with the number of pupils not exceeding 37 and as low as 14 in 1868.

Henry Peake, the Headmaster who had been responsible for much of the school's decline retired in the early 1870s after 42 years. He was replaced by James Webber who brought the school back to life. He reorganised the curriculum, teaching classics, maths, drawing, French, writing, divinity and arithmetic. He built two new classrooms within the confines of St John's and by 1878 there were 73 pupils being taught by three masters

In 1880 a former pupil of St John's Free School as it was then called, wrote the following account of his school day memories:

'Generally speaking we were a self-willed, mischievous lot. There were some special methods of punishment, one of which was to place the offender in a large basket, and by means of a pulley in the roof, pull him up to a height of 20 to 30 feet and leave him suspended, mid heaven and earth, like Mohammed's coffin.

I can speak with experience of the sensation attending the elevation and suspension of the culprit. The process to me was rather agreeable than otherwise, except for the loss of a meal or two, which it usually entailed.

One of the crimes for which this special punishment was reserved was that of being late for church. The scholars met in the Free School every Sunday morning to march to St Mary's Church and woe to the luckless lad who happened to be a few minutes late. But Parson Williams, as we called him (the Reverend Thomas Williams) who was kind and benevolent to a fault, always insisted upon our immediate release when he discovered any of us sitting aloft like 'a sweet little cherub.'

Then I remember another special mode of punishment, reserved exclusively for fighters, and it reminds me of the Turkish bastinado or the Russian knout.

Each belligerent was deprived of his boots, placed stomach downwards across a table or desk, or on the floor, and beaten by his opponent upon the soles of his feet with a stick or cane. When a sufficient chastisement had been inflicted, places were changed and the other delinquent received his share.

When a boy had acquired sufficient knowledge he was passed on to Parson Williams, who had a school in a contiguous building, to learn Latin. I believe I was passed on because the school methods were all lost upon me, and I doubt very much whether I made any considerable progress in the study of Latin.

We paid nothing for our schooling, as it was a Free School, and I think there were 70 to 80 scholars in those days. There was no other public school in the town, and the National and British schools were not thought of. There were, however, a few small private schools, in Cow Street (Nevill Street), Monk Street, Frogmore Street, and one in Mill Street, near the Unicorn Inn.'

In June 1887 the foundation stone of a new Grammar School was laid at a site in Pen-y-pound. The inscription on the stone reads: 'This Grammar School was erected by the trustees of the Bedgworth Charity, assisted by inhabitants of Abergavenny and the district, to commemorate the 50th year of the reign of Her Most Gracious Majesty the Queen, and this foundation stone was laid on 21st June, 1887, by Mrs Bury Capel, wife of the chairman of Bedgworth Charity Trustees.'

In a cavity underneath the stone was placed a bottle containing copies of the following newspapers: *The Times, Standard, Daily News, Western Mail, South Wales Daily News, Abergavenny Chronicle, Hereford Times, Monmouthshire Beacon* and coins of the Realm, comprising all the new coinage from a three-penny piece up to a £2 piece.

After a speech by Mr Bishop, the Mayor, who expressed his hope that he 'might be spared to see the school erected and thriving for years to come,' Mrs Capel took the mallet and striking the stone in several places, said, 'I lay this foundation stone of the Abergavenny Grammar School to the honour and glory of God, in the name of the most blessed Trinity, the Father, Son and Holy Ghost - Amen.'

In March 1889 the Worshipful Company of Haberdashers agreed to grant a sum not exceeding £3,000 to the Trustees of the Grammar School on the understanding that a similar amount would be raised by local subscription. The remainder of the cost was to come from the sale of old school buildings, the accumulated income of the Foundation, and the Queen's Jubilee Building Fund.

These new premises for the King Henry VIII Grammar School were built at a cost of £6,945 and opened on Thursday, 29th September 1898 by the Marquess of Abergavenny. A description of the occasion is contained in the School Annual for 1899:

'It is much to be regretted that the unfavourable weather spoiled what otherwise would have been a brilliant ceremonial at the School's doors... His Lordship... made his way, through drenching rain, to the Grammar School, where in spite of the wet, a large company was assembled to await his arrival... The meeting then broke up, with cheers for the Marquess, Mr Webber and the School...'

In 1898 new premises for the King Henry VIII Grammar School were built at Pen-y-pound

The first headmaster was Mr T. Headland Sifton MA, who was paid £100 per annum, the second master and science teacher was A.A. Hilton, and Mr A.H. Platt was a Maths graduate. There was also a visiting teacher, Mr W.R. Carr who came to give music lessons. The school was initially attended by 56 boys aged 8-16 at fees of £6-£12 per year. They had to sit an admission test which required the ability to read, write from dictation, and do sums in the first four simple rules of arithmetic.

In order to overcome the school's financial problems a new Governing Body was created in August 1910 and this gave the County Council control for the first time. Admission was now open to boys between the age of 10 and 18 with tuition fees between £3 3s od (£3 15p) and £10 and £35 boarders' fees. Its first inspection in 1912 saw it with 51 pupils and 4 staff with a curriculum of Maths, English, Geography, Scripture, Latin, French, Science, Drawing, Manual work, Singing and Drill.

In 1919 Mr Sifton who had been headmaster since 1898 retired to be replaced by Mr Newcombe who was to be head for 35 years. He soon appointed new teaching staff and men such as E. O. Jones, J. B. H. Mawer, Harold Sharpe and Leonard Porter were to spend their working lives enhancing the school.

The school was extended in 1926 with the addition of a gymnasium and handicrafts room, three new classrooms and a library. By 1930 the school had 150 pupils and this peaked at 174 in 1935 before dropping back at the end of the decade.

In 1944 Butler's Education Act gave greater control to Monmouthshire County Council to reorganise secondary education and after the war the council began to plan changes. But King Henry VIII remained an independent Boys' Grammar School until 1963 when it was amalgamated with the Girls' Grammar School.

On June 10th 1963 the new King Henry VIII Secondary School, which cost £181,038 to build, on a 10 acre site beside the old Hereford Road, was officially opened by James Griffiths MP for Llanelly. It was the first stage of the new school - the first in Monmouthshire to be erected with the ultimate aim of becoming a multilateral school. It was to be made up of pupils from King Henry VIII Grammar School, the Girls intermediate High School and some pupils from St John's Private School and the Convent School. There were 216 boys and 232 girls in its first year.

In 1971 King Henry VIII School merged with Grofield Secondary School to form the Abergavenny Comprehensive School. Since 1972 it has been a mixed Comprehensive School with about 1200 pupils. It is situated on an elevated site of about 36 acres, which includes its own playing fields and also houses the Abergavenny Leisure Centre. The facilities include a heated indoor pool, a large sports hall and squash courts. The school motto is 'Ut Prosim' - 'In order that I may be of service.'

Other Schools in the Town

In addition to King Henry VIII Grammar School there were several educational establishments. There was the **Westgate School**, Westgate buildings, the Principal of which was Thomas Kilner and where the course of instruction embraced 'every branch of a sound English education, including Latin, French mathematics, bookkeeping, drawing, music etc.' Then there was **Milford House**, the Principal of which was Mrs Yates, assisted by resident governesses; Hillcrest House, Nevill Street, the Principals of which were Misses Saville and Malcolm, 'an establishment adapted to meet the requirements of Christian parents who wish to secure for their daughters a thorough education and careful training.

The Boys' National School was built in 1848 on the Hereford New Road with funds obtained from three different sources, these being, a grant from the Committee of Council on Education, a donation from the Trustees of the Penbiddle Charity, properly belonging to the Grammar School, and from public subscriptions. Originally it was built to contain one hundred and ninety boys and consisted of a school room, a class room, over which was another room of the same dimensions, intended primarily as as dormitory; and a dwelling house for the master. Management of the school was in the hands of a committee which was chaired by the Vicar and members included the incumbent of Trinity Church, the churchwardens of the Parish Church and others chosen chiefly from the Trustees of the Penbiddle Society.

The Girls' and Infants' National School was built in 1865 in Castle Street, on the ground formerly occupied as the Sheep Market. The buildings were designed to accommodate one hundred and forty girls, and two hundred infants. Initially there were two large rooms and a house for the Mistress and in 1898 the school was enlarged to cater for 200 girls.

Victoria Street School (also known as the British School) was built in 1872 in Victoria Street, on the Grofield, by the Nonconformist bodies of the town. The building comprised school rooms and class rooms for mixed and infants and could accommodate three hundred children. The building was demolished in 1977.

Trinity Girls' School was attached to Trinity Church and was financed by Miss Herbert. It could accommodate about eighty girls. The nearby Carnegie Library was built on the old school playground.

Victoria Street School which was built in 1872
and known locally as 'the British School' has been demolished

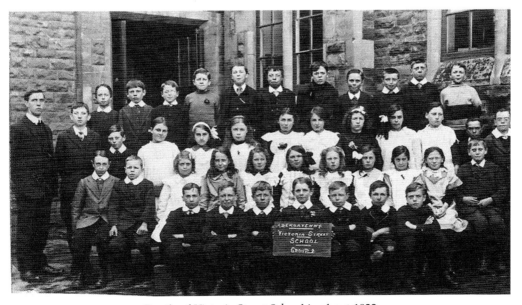

Pupils of Victoria Street School in about 1922

St John's School was founded in 1881 at Finsbury Park, London, where it was carried on until it was evacuated to Abergavenny in 1939, the original premises having been destroyed by enemy action. The Head master, Mr J.S. Bousfield MA decided to establish the school permanently in Abergavenny. On his sudden death in 1953 it was taken over by Mr D.C. Johnstone MA, a First Class Honours Graduate of the University of St Andrew's, Scotland.

Old St John's School in Chapel Road

The school aimed at providing a sound general education with a broadly based curriculum for boys between the ages of 11 and 15. Those showing special aptitude were prepared for Public School Scholarships. The school games (football and cricket) were played on the ground of the Abergavenny Cricket Club, close to the school.

About 50 per cent of the boys were resident in Abergavenny, the remainder being principally drawn from the counties of Monmouthshire, Herefordshire, Brecon, and Glamorganshire.

The Abergavenny County Intermediate School for Girls was founded after the Welsh Intermediate Education Act of 1889 and funded under the Welsh Intermediate Education Act. It was built in Stanhope Park, which was given for the purpose by William Jenkins. The official opening was performed by the Marquess of Abergavenny on the 29th September 1898 which was the same day that he also opened the new King Henry VIII Grammar School at Pen-y-pound.

It was originally intended to provide for 60 pupils, but it opened at once with this number and before long considerable additions to the building became necessary when the number of pupils rose to 80. Miss Houliston of Newnham College was the first headmistress and her salary was £120 per annum with and additional £1 10s 0d for each child attending the school..

In 1937 The name was changed to the Abergavenny County High School for Girls and in later years it became the Grofield Girls' School. This amalgamated with King Henry VIII Comprehensive School in 1963 and the old building which became **Harold Road Junior School** is now **Cantref Primary School**.

Park Street Infants School was founded in September 1894 along with Grofield and Hereford Road schools as 'church schools' by the then bishop of Llandaff. It was originally called Christchurch Infant School and the wooden school room behind Christchurch was the first building used for the purpose. There were initially 34 pupils and Mary Graham Telford was the first mistress. She was assisted by Miss Augusta Chivers. Being a church school, the Reverend W. Felix visited weekly. Park Street Infants School closed in 2005 and the pupils were moved to Deri View School. A group of residents have since formed Abergavenny Community Centre Ltd and have campaigned to obtain money to turn the old Park Street School building into a community centre.

Grofield School in Victoria Street closed in 1972 after the introduction of the comprehensive school system. The site is now a housing complex.

Our Lady and St Michael's Roman Catholic School in Pen -y-poundwas founded in in 1857 in what is now Dover and Company Printers in Frogmore Street. The school moved to its present site in Pen-y-pound in 1873 and, situated next to Our Lady and St Michael's Church, it has extensive grounds. In 1995, following the introduction of Grant Maintained status the school was enlarged to improve facilities and provide new accommodation for its 200 plus pupils. In July 1998 the school celebrated its 125th anniversary. Today, it continues under the auspices of Monmouthshire County Council.

Ty'r Morwydd Environmental Study Centre provides environmental education and is housed in a listed building which in 1906 became a convent for the Order of St Michael's and the Sisters of the Holy Spirit. When the Order of St Michael's left Abergavenny in 1976 the building was purchased by the Inner London Education Authority for use as a fileld studies centre. The aim was to help students increase their knowledge of subjects such as geography and biology and give them an experience of a different environment. Small groups would work on projects which would take them out and about in the area and give them an opportunity to get a taste of life in Wales. Ty'r Morwydd (house of the Mulberry Trees) Field Studies Centre was opened in January 1977 and the first Warden of the centre was Harry Foster, a former lecturer in environmental studies, from Northumberland.

In 1992, when the Inner London Education Authority was disbanded by the government, ownership of Mulberry House was passed to the Royal Borough of Kensington and Chelsea. It has since become a registered charity and continues to provide residential environmental education to school groups across Britain. The Mulberry House Residential Conference Centre is a trading subsidiary of the charity Ty'r Morwydd andthe name of the building was inspired by the Mulberry trees which were planted in the private gardens of the Old Convent about 150 years ago.

Ty'r Morwydd Environmental Study Centre in Pen-y-pound

St David's Junior School in the Mardy, was partly demolished in 2007 to provide a site for the town's **Ysgol Cymraeg y Fenni**, a Welsh medium school, which was started in 1995 at the Bryn and it moved to a former youth centre on the Old Hereford Road in 2002. The new building, which is of a timber frame construction, utilizes part of the old St David's School in its design, having been built onto the foundations of and around the kitchen block.

Deri View Primary School was officially opened on Tuesday October 11th 2005. It stands on the site of the former Llwynu Infants School and provides accommodation for pupils from Llwynu Infant Schools, Croesonnen Infants School and St David's Junior School. Built at a cost of £6.8 million, this was the first new community school to be built in Monmouthshire since Local Government reorganisation and it is of a modern spacious design.

Deri View Primary School stands on the site of the former Llwynu Infants School

'No one can look back on his schooldays and say with truth that they were alltogether unhappy.'

George Orwell

Chapter Fifteen
SPORT AND RECREATION

Every prospect pleases, the hunting is good and sufficiently exciting, the Usk is famed for its salmon and trout fishing, and for those who feel inclined there are excellent golf links and opportunities for cricket, hockey and other sports.

Edward J. Burrow 1903

The riverside meadow known as Castle Meadows was once part of the Lordship lands and passed to the Nevill family in 1445. A map in William Coxe's *Tours of Monmouthshire* (1801) shows the meadows divided into smaller fields by hedges, while today it is of course one large field. At one time these water-meadows were used by the Welsh drovers as a pound for the cattle that they had driven to Abergavenny from the mountains of Mid Wales. In the 1870s the meadows began to have a recreational use, for the Abergavenny Cricket Club played here. The Nevill family owned this land until 1916, when William Nevill the 1st Marquess of Abergavenny passed away and the Monmouthshire estates were sold.

The Abergavenny Bathing and Swimming Society was formed in July 1879 with the object of providing a suitable place for bathing in the river Usk. The bathing season was identified as commencing on Monday 28th July and the place selected was in the second field from Llanfoist Bridge.

Along the side of the river a strip of land between the path and the river was fenced off for about 90 yards. Admission to the bathing area was by ticket only. No bathers were permitted on Sundays after 9.30 am and bathers trespassing off the footpath would be liable to prosecution by the Society. For trespassing and for offending against the byelaws, bathers were also liable to forfeit their tickets. Tickets could be obtained from the honorary secretary in the General Market Place on Saturday evening at 6.00 pm.

Opening of a new Swimming Pool in 1940

The official opening of the town's new riverside swimming pool took place in the presence of a large crowd. Messrs J. G. Thomas & Sons were the contractors and the pool was designed by the Borough Surveyor, Mr F. J. Mansfield. The work had been supervised by Mr Jack Thomas.

The main contract was about £4,500, but with filtration plant and other equipment the whole scheme had cost about £6,000. Funding by a grant of 75% was obtained under the Physical Fitness Act.

The pool was 130 ft long and 40 ft wide, the shallow end being 2 ft 9 ins and the deep end 8 ft to 8 ft 6 ins. It held 160,000 gallons of water, which were turned over every six hours. Constructed in concrete, it was finished in waterproof cement of blue colour. The pavements of the wide promenades were of red and brown concrete slabs.

The external dimensions of the buildings were 200 ft by 82 ft. They were built of brick and cemented with a finish of yellow Cullami. There were 55 cubicles and dressing rooms for both sexes, fitted with the latest clothes hangers and there were four shower baths. Chutes and diving boards were provided and there was a cafe where refreshments could be obtained. The filtration plant of the latest type was installed by the Candy Filtration Company of Hanwell, London.

Changing rooms beside the river Usk for the first swimming pool were built in 1879

Mayor W. Rosser performed the opening ceremony on behalf of the contractors and he was presented by Mr Jim Thomas with a golden key to open the door.

The idea of a swimming pool had started many years previously and it had been built mainly for the benefit of the children of the town and district but it was hoped that everyone would take advantage of it and not abuse it.

The Mayor, after receiving the key from Mr Jim Thomas, explained how the scheme had been partially funded:

> 'On the passing of the Keep Fit Act it was found that Abergavenny was eligible for a grant and those who paid their rates with such pleasure (laughter from the crowd) - would be pleased to know that 70 per cent of the cost had been defrayed by the Government. We were fortunate to receive the maximum grant and I thank the Government for what they have done.
>
> The remaining 30 per cent will have to be found, but it is not going to be a burden on the rates, for it is anticipated that the revenue will balance the cost.'

He then paid tribute to Messrs J. G. Thomas & Sons, for the work done in constructing the pool. It was good to have a firm in the town which was capable of carrying through any job entrusted to them in the building line. Unfortunately, Mr Jack Thomas, the junior partner, who had supervised the work was unable to be there to participate in the ceremony, having set a noble example by going away that day to join the Forces.

The Reverend Canon Davies (Vicar of St Mary's) then offered an appropriate prayer of dedication, after which the Mayor opened the door and the spectators poured in to inspect Abergavenny's fine new acquisition. It was later announced that the admission takings, which were to be given to the Mayor's War Fund totalled £14 18s 9d.

Castle Meadows with the Blorenge mountain in the background

Today, Castle Meadows is a popular area for dog walking or enjoying a pleasant riverside stroll. There is also a surfaced cycle path and the soft grass provides an ideal landing for hang gliders and paragliders descending from the Blorenge escarpment.

Of interest to conservationists is the wetland area established with assistance from the Gwent Wildlife Trust, the Environment Agency, Monmouthshire County Council and the Abergavenny Tourist Association. The entire length of the river Usk has been designated a Special Area of Conservation of European importance.

Bailey Park

Before being established as a park, an area of land, adjoining the Hereford Road, was known as the Priory Meadow and in 1871 the Abergavenny Bicycle Club secured part of it for use as a cycle racing track. It was a quarter of a mile long and cyclists wishing to make use of the circuit had to pay a few pence which went towards the rental charge for the land.

On December 25th, 1883, Crawshay Bailey Junior of Maindiff Court became the lessee of the Priory Meadow, and the adjoining lands. The term of the lease was for 21 years and during that period an annual sum of £100 was to be paid to the owner, the Reverend William Walter Roberts of Brackley Erith, Kent.

In 1884 Crawshay Bailey, accompanied by Edwin Tucker met with the Abergavenny Board of Commissioners and explained that there was a parcel of land on the Hereford Road which he was desirous of making into a park; but it would be necessary for the Commissioners to divert certain footpaths which ran through the meadows from Lion Street across the fields in the direction of the National Schools.

Edwin Tucker read the draft rules for the management of the Park which would be under the control of a keeper to be appointed by Mr Bailey. The right to let the Park for any special occasion, such as an agricultural show or anything which he might consider beneficial to the town and neighbourhood, would be reserved by Crawshay Bailey.

223

The principal entrance would be sited beside the Hereford Road and would include two ornamental gates hanging from massive piers and two side gates for the entrance of pedestrians. The central entrance would be wide enough to accommodate a four-in-hand with ease.

On the left hand side a lodge would be erected in the Gothic style. Shrubs would be planted inside the fence and a half-mile course would encircle the ground. Inside this would be a bicycle track, football, cricket and other grounds; an ornamental pond, a grandstand and pavilion, a bandstand and the necessary offices to make the Park as complete as possible.

A resolution expressing appreciation of Crawshay Bailey's generous intention to provide a place of recreation for the town was proposed, seconded and approved. In due course the Board entered into arrangements with Crawshay Bailey, whereby the public were to use and enjoy the park, subject to certain conditions. After the proper formalities the paths were diverted and Crawshay spent between £2,000 and £3,000 in enclosing the park with handsome iron railings, putting up entrance gates and planting a belt of shrubs. He opened the ground for public recreation, appointed and paid a park keeper, fixed a schedule of charges for clubs using the land and appointed a committee of management.

The iron entrance gates to Bailey Park were financed by Crawshay Bailey Junior

No doubt, had Crawshay Bailey Junior lived a few years longer, it would have been his intention to purchase the freehold and to have presented the park to the town. Unfortunately he died rather suddenly in April 1887 and his affairs were left in the hands of his trustees to deal with. The Park was being well used by the public and had most certainly fulfiled the purpose for which it was intended. However, the land had been taken on a 21 year lease and would on expiry revert to the owner.

The Board of Commissioners ascertained that the 21 acres of land, including some cottage property, could be purchased by the town for £5,000. Mrs Crawshay Bailey promised to give £500 towards the purchase money; Mrs Gordon-Canning also promised £500 and Mrs Curre another £500. The Trustees who were desirous of carrying out the wishes of Crawshay Bailey agreed to contribute another £1,000.

Dr S.H. Steel moved a resolution that an application be made to the Local Government Board to raise £4,000 for the purchase of the freehold. The Park was an attraction and a source of wealth to the town, affording space for various exhibitions, volunteer camps etc. The proposal was that the purchase money should be raised as a loan. He did not think that anything more important to the town than the purchase of this site was likely to arise within the next half century. The sum of £4,000 would cost them about £160 a year and the revenue might be enough to maintain the Park. This resolution was put to the meeting and carried.

In 1894 the land was purchased from Reverend W.W. Roberts for £5,000 and of this amount £2,500 was paid out of the rates. The other half was contributed by the trustees of the Bailey estate, who surrendered the lease to the Improvement Commissioners the very next day (the £4,000 loan was repaid by 1936).

By Deed of Poll signed on December 24, 1894, the park became known as Bailey Park and was 'henceforth to be known by no other name or designation whatsoever.' It was also stated that the land had been purchased 'for the purpose of being used as a public park or pleasure ground or place of public recreation in the manner authorised by the Public Health Acts relevant at that time.'

On August 6th 1883, there were crowds of people from all parts when Bailey Park was officially opened by Mr Edwin Tucker. Crawshay Bailey Junior was in Brighton at the time and he died a few years later at the age of 46.

Every Whitsun the annual Abergavenny Steam Rally, currently organised by the Abergavenny Rotary Club is held in Bailey Park and it ranks as the eighth largest steam rally in Britain, attracting participants from some considerable distance away.

Annual Steam Rally in Bailey Park

Bailey Park Swimming Pool

In 1938 the Town Council decided that it was time that the town had a proper swimming pool and initially Swan Meadow (adjoining the present day bus station) was considered as a possible site, but in due course the members chose a site in Bailey Park next to the tennis courts.

The contract went to J. G. Thomas & Sons and the total cost of the project was £6,500 which was grant aided by the sum of £4,750 from the National Advisory Grants Committee under the Physical Training and Recreation Act 1937. By April 1940 the pool was completed and a reception clerk and attendant were appointed. The Mayor, Alderman W. Rosser performed the opening ceremony on 30th May 1940 using a key which is now in the museum. The pool was 44 yards long by 14 yards wide and 2ft 9ins to 8ft 6ins deep and held 162,000 gallons of water. There was also an adjoining pool for youngsters and learners.

Sadly, the Bailey Park swimming Pool, which gave much pleasure to local people during the summer months has been demolished.

Staff of Bailey Park Swimming Pool in 1946

The Race Course at Llanfoist

Initially the Abergavenny races were held on the Ynys-y-bwa, the fields on the opposite side of the river to the later course at Llanfoist. In due course they were held in the Chapel Meadows, adjoining Chapel Road for one year and then in the meadows on the Company Farm on the other side of the river opposite the castle, until the Squire of Coldbrook gave the final site for the racecourse at Lower Llanfoist Farm. This is a site of historic interest for the manor of Lower Llanfoist was retained by descendants of Ynyr, King of Gwent after the arrival of the Normans, and it was here that Garwyn ap Caradog the uncle of Sitsyllt ap Dwynfal lived. From those distant times right up until the middle of the 18th century, his descendants, who latterly adopted the surname of Price, remained at Llanfoist, occupying a leading position among the gentry of the county.

A ferry boat was engaged on the river just below the grandstand to convey people across the Usk and one day some hooligans pelted the occupants with sods. In the confusion the boat capsized and two men and a girl were drowned. The body of the girl was picked up below the racecourse; the body of one of the men was several days afterwards discovered below Llanelen bridge and that of the other man at Hardwick Wood. The two men were in the employ of Dr W. Steel at 'The Brooks'.

A man by the name of Cook was once a patron of the Abergavenny Races. One of his mares was a magnificent animal called 'Fanny'. She stumbled at the water jump and before she could recover herself a horse named 'Bold David' jumped upon her and broke her back and she had to be destroyed on the spot.

By 1864 the Abergavenny meeting was considered one of the best in Monmouthshire and South Wales. There were no restrictions then to composite race meetings and five furlong races were sandwiched in between steeplechases and hurdle races."

Old painting depicting the Abergavenny Racecourse

The Grand National Hunt Club decided in December 1871 to hold the Grand National at the Abergavenny racecourse. It was reported at the time that the proposal had the backing of the Duke of Beaufort, Lord Coventry, Lord Abergavenny and many other sportsmen of the district, 'both in voice and purse.' In addition to the bonus of 300 sovereigns for the hunt race, 750 sovereigns were put up as stakes for the Grand National Steeplechase. It was held in April 1872 at Abergavenny racecourse with seventeen races held over a period of three days. There were nine runners in the National itself, which was won by Red Nobb, owned by a local sportsman, Reginald Herbert of Clytha and ridden by Captain Hollyoak.

The Abergavenny Steeple chase was one of the most important gatherings in the racing world. At one time these races were the chief event in the locality, in which the town took a lively interest. But one by one the organisers and patrons nearly all passed away and their places were not filled, the interest of the townspeople gradually diminished and by 1900 ceased altogether. Although spasmodic efforts from time to timewere made to resuscitate the sport, the promoters had to eventually yield to the inevitable and the races at Abergavenny came to an end.

In February 1904, Reginald Herbert of Clytha Park wrote to the Mayor of Abergavenny to say that he was being pressed by his agent to have the old stands on the race grounds at Lower Llanfoist Farm pulled down and removed.

'Before consequenting to such a course, I should like to know if the inhabitants of Abergavenny have given up all hope of resuscitating their old established races. The abandonment of this very old meeting has been a matter of sincere regret to me, and I am sure equally to yourself, especially when we see other towns in the county supporting their race gatherings.

If you could ascertain the feeling of the town on the subject and let me know I should be under an obligation. Nothing would annoy me more than to do anything that might spoil the chance of sport in the future, or interfere in any way with the interests or wishes of the inhabitants of Abergavenny.'

In 1906 the racecourse and clubhouse became the site of the Monmouthshire Golf Club, and initially they established a nine hole course. Today, the 18 hole course is recognised as one of the most beautiful in Britain.

The Monmouthshire Golf Club was established in October 1892,
under the presidency of Lord Llangattock, with the Marquess of Abergavenny as patron

Flying Displays at Llanfoist

In April 1918 a flying exhibition took place at Llanfoist Farm on Easter Tuesday, with the permission of the Air Ministry and four 'modern' aeroplanes were flown by officers of the Royal Air Force, giving a display of all the latest aerial evolutions.

The four machines were 275 h.p. Rolls Royce Bristol fighters, a type of fighting reconnaissance machine which was used with great success during World War One. The formation was led by Captain S. B. Collett, with Captain A. S. Glynn as observer.

The flying ground was an 18 acre field on the Llanfoist farm which Percy Denner kindly allowed to be used for the occasion. The exhibition was timed for 12 noon and on time to the minute, the four machines gracefully soared into view flying at a height of

5,000 feet. The airmen quickly spotted the crowd lined up at the side of the field and circled the ground several times before landing to off load some petrol. They had come from the airfield at Filton, Bristol, having flown there overnight from Salisbury.

Ascending again, the machines which were capable of flying 120 miles per hour and climbing 1,000 feet per minute, were soon circling through the air, and a wandering cow, frightened at the sudden appearance of these monsters of the air, made off as fast as she could go. Then commenced the real business of the day, and in unison all the latest aerial evolutions were performed in a manner which showed the perfect mastery which the airmen had over their machines. The stunts included formation flying, nose diving, climbing almost perpendicularly, looping the loop, rolling and spinning etc., together with the dropping of signal lights. All the spectators were entranced with the performance.

Fresh air and exercise

In June 1881 a number of carriage drives were opened up on the slopes of the Sugar Loaf and it was announced in the *Abergavenny Chronicle*:

'Up to within the last twelve months it was considered quite a feat for a lady to ascend the Sugar Loaf. But now it is possible for a lady to walk up - no climbing as of old - right to the very top of the great Pen-y-fal. Not only is this the case but roads have been constructed by means of which visitors can drive up to within a few minutes walk of the top.'

'The official opening of these drives took place on Whit-Monday 6th June 1881. At 11.00 am a procession was formed on the Monmouth Road, close to the Bellevue Hotel, consisting of the Road Committee (on horseback), the Commissioners and officers in two breaks, the Abergavenny Band in a break, visitors in a break and Press Reporters in a break.

The cavalcade moved off to the strains of the band through the town, which wore a very holiday appearance, the shops being closed and the pavements filled with spectators. From every available point flags were fluttering in the breeze - flags of every description, and a few nondescripts as well. Then there were banners bearing inscriptions, such as 'May our paths be prosperous,' others again having expressions of 'Welcome' etc.

Amongst those on horseback were many of the leading tradesmen and professional men of the town. As the cavalcade passed on by way of Triley Court, the people from the farms and neighbouring houses came flocking to the roadside and were loud in their expressions of delight at seeing such a show.

On arriving at about 1,500 or 1,600 feet above the level of the town, it was found that the Chairman of the Commissioners had provided refreshments for all comers, free of charge, sundries, biscuits, bread, cheese, wines, bottled beers etc.

The top and sides of the peak itself were covered with people, some going by way of the new paths, and others going along the old climbing way, up the face of the mountain.'

Sugar Loaf carriage drive constructed in 1883

In June 1883 the Abergavenny Public Footpaths and Neighbourhood Improvement Society reported:

'The following works have been carried out: The sugar Loaf carriage drive, with stable erected for housing horses during the climb to the summit of the mountain; the Sugar Loaf footpath making the ascent to the peak easy for old and young, and such as are not accustomed to climbing over rocky crags; the Rholben footpath by which the early stages to the Sugar Loaf are accomplished without fatigue. In fact, so nicely laid out are the paths that a safe ascent may now be made by families with ponies or donkeys to carry the children, with provisions etc. We would here observe that it is a matter of surprise that enterprising individuals do not keep ponies or donkeys, properly equipped for hire during the summer months. Many are the enquiries from time to time, and many the families deprived of one of the most healthy and pleasant trips we know of, and that at a price within the reach of all - because 'Neddy' is not available.'

Proposal for a Sanatorium and a Sugar Loaf Railway

In the late 19th century a serious suggestion was made that a Sanatorium should be constructed near the summit of the Sugar Loaf as a memorial to the recently deceased Lord Tredegar. Writing to the *Abergavenny Chronicle* the man who came up with this idea commented:

> 'There are near the summit of the Sugar Loaf several never failing springs, and what I propose is, that water from one of these be conveyed by pipes on the summit of the Deri to be used for working a similar railway to the Clifton Rocks Railway, and the one connecting Lynton and Lynmouth, this railway to extend to the summit from a point in the meadow at the back of Mr E.P. Martin's house (the Hill) adjoining the Llwynddu Lane leading to Pentanlace.
>
> There are no engineering difficulties whatever (the matter has been reported on by an expert), the cost of construction depends upon how near to the spot where the lanes crossing the railway would come, but in any case it would not be large over and above the cost of the land, and once built the cost of working would be very low. (the whole staff consisting of two men). The wear and tear would be small and the water would be returned to the stream from which it would be taken.
>
> The railway would not deface the side of the hill to any extent worth considering, and when made it would be possible to drive from the Great Western Station or the North Western to its foot, ascend to the top of the Deri, and from there (with a small expenditure on the track leading into the road made some years since) drive, with magnificent scenery on every side, over two miles to the site of the shed on the side of the Sugar Loaf without any exertion whatever in about twenty minutes.
>
> The railway would hardly be a goldmine, but I am under the impression that without reckoning upon the traffic which a sanatorium would create, it would make the Sugar Loaf so easy of access that it would be used to such an extent as to make it just pay a little interest on the cost; and others may think with me that a scheme which would make it easy for residents in the county and visitors to reach the top of the highest mountain we have worth considering is worth attempting even though it might not be a profitable one; for how few even of those living in Monmouthshire and Glamorganshire have ever viewed the beautiful scenery from its summit, and how few there are who in our own town get to the top in the course of a year.'

In 1919 the Sugar Loaf was purchased from the Marquess of Abergavenny by Lord Rhondda and after he passed away his widow, Viscountess Rhondda and the Dowager Vicountess Rhondda donated to the National Trust some 2,130 acres of the Sugar Loaf together with covenants over Park Lodge, the farm in the hollow below. A large part of it was subject to grazing rights and at that time the farm did not become the Trust's property. The vesting of this land in the National Trust assures it of protection for all time from any developments that might spoil its beauty or restrict the access of the general public.

The Seven Hills of Abergavenny

Overlooking Abergavenny are the four dominant peaks of Sugar Loaf, Skirrid Fawr, Skirrid Fach and Blorenge; and three distinctive rounded humps of Llanwenarth Breast, Rholben and Deri, which are really part of the Sugar Loaf. Collectively they are known as the Seven Hills of Abergavenny.

A record was set up, just after the Second World War, for completing a circular route connecting these seven summits, by Percy Fraser (Junior) and Paddy Sherman who completed the route in 6 hours 6 minutes. However, they both felt that they could improve on this time and on 27th March 1949 they had another go and reduced it dramatically to 4 hours 54 minutes.

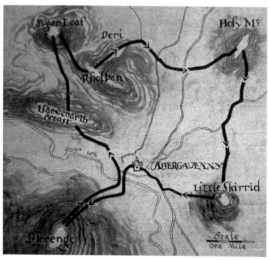

On April 10th, 1954 an open Mountain Marathon Race was held at Abergavenny over the Seven Hills route. It was organised by Les Williams a local long distance runner. There were eleven competitors and the race was started from the Town Hall by the Mayor of Abergavenny, Councillor J.A. Morgan who also presented the prizes at the end.

Only five of the field of eleven managed to finish the course and as they began the ascent of Skirrid Fach, F.C. Bailey of Preston looked like being the winner, but Les Williams a 48 year old Newport Harriers runner from Gilwern managed to overhaul him and reached the Town Hall in an excellent time of 4 hours 10 minutes and 22 seconds.

Five years later, Ken Flowers and Ray Hardee, two Abergavenny cross country runners decided to attempt to establish a new record for the route on April 17th, 1959. Choosing April was probably a mistake for it is traditionally a rather wet month. In fact heavy overnight rain and early morning rain made the route a sea of mud. Ray unfortunately developed cramp halfway round the course and Ken had to massage his legs to get him going again. They were then chased by barking dogs as they passed through a farmyard and the wet conditions certainly slowed them down in several places. However, by the time they reached the summit of Skirrid Fawr they were well ahead of the previous time. After a brief pause for some coffee and a tot of rum they set off on the last section.

In due course they arrived back at the Town Hall, mud spattered, tired but triumphant, for they had brought the record down to an impressive 4 hours 4 minutes and 5 seconds, beating the previous best time by 6 minutes and 17 seconds.

Ken Flowers, winner of the Seven Hills Race in 1955 being congratulated by the Mayor

Ken Flowers and Ray Hardee setting out from the Town Hall in 1959

Eleven years later, Ken Flowers and Peter Maloney decided to have a go at reducing the record even further. For six months before their attempt they were in strict training and carried out several practice runs over the route. Councillor John Lewis set them off and by the time they had reached the fifth summit they were 19 minutes ahead of Ken's previous time. They then slowed up for a while and their advantage dropped to eight minuts, but they made it up on the homeward stretch. They triumphantly arrived back at the Town Hall having successfully reduced the record to 3 hours 39 minutes 19 seconds.

The Three Peaks Trial

In March 1963, Chris Barber (the author of this book) organised an event which he called The Three Peaks Trial and it was designed as an annual challenge walk involving the ascent of the Blorenge, Sugar Loaf and Skirrid Fawr.

In the early years of the event it was started from Crickhowell Youth Hostel (now defunct) and the majority of the entrants came for the weekend. The route was 22 miles in length and entrants were offered the choice of walking it in a clockwise or anti-clockwise direction. Certificates were presented to everyone who completed the route successfully.

Twenty four people took part in the first event, held on Saturday 9th March, in wet and windy conditions. Heavy rain and very strong wind on the Blorenge caused fourteen of the entrants to call it a day and return to Crickhowell. The remaining ten walkers persevered and fortunately enjoyed better weather in the afternoon and all completed the routee. Alistair Mackinnon was the first man home and he finished the 22 mile course in about 8 hours.

In 1975 the starting point for the event was transferred to the Fairfield car park in Abergavenny and this shortened the route by about 4 miles and the amount of road walking was thankfuly reduced.

The Three Peaks Trial has been held without a break since 1963 and as a firmly established event on the challenge walkers' calendar it now attracts as many as three hundred starters. Since 1977 it has been organised by the Cardiff Outdoor Group and the money raised from entry fees is donated to good causes. Further information may be obtained by visiting their website: www.threepeakstrial.co.uk/

Abergavenny Cricket Club, established in 1834, is one of the oldest in Wales. Originally the club played on Castle Meadows beside the river Usk and then moved to a site which later became the Cattle Market. In 1884 matches were played in Bailey Park and the club in 1895 acquired a field at Avenue Road from the Marquess of Abergavenny and this has been their base ever since.

Pen-y-fal Hospital Cricket team in 1892

Abergavenny Bowling Club was formed in 1860 and is one of the oldest in Wales. They initially had a green at the Great Western Hotel near the Monmouth Road Railway Station. The club moved to a new green in Avenue Road in 1910.

Abergavenny Bowling Club Ladies Team with Mayor Richard Smith

Abergavenny Hockey Club was started in October 1897 and was originally a men's hockey club only. It was one of the first hockey clubs to be formed in Wales. Today, the club has two mens teams, a ladies team and Junior teams for various ages. There is also a mixed team that enjoys hockey tours all over Britain.

Abergavenny Hockey Club in about 1970

Abergavenny Thursdays Football Club was founded in 1900 by local traders in the days when Thursday was early closing day in Abergavenny which enabled them to have time to play matches. The club used to be known as Abergavenny United before becoming the Thursdays but they were also nicknamed 'The Pennies' because their ground is situated in Pen-y-pound. The team's song is Marty Wilde's 1968 hit 'Abergavenny'.

Abergavenny Thursdays AFC, Champions of South Monmouthshire League, 1912-13

Abergavenny RFC team, season 1945-46

Abergavenny RFC was formed in 1875 and at first the club played on Castle Meadows and then at Ysguborwen Fields near Pen-y-pound. After a few seasons in the Fairfield the club started playing on the council pitch in Bailey Park in the 1890s and have been there ever since. The grandstand in Bailey Park was built in 1999 using seating from the old Cardiff Arms Park. It was officially opened by Sir Tasker Watkins, President of the Welsh Rugby Union.

Abergavenny Road Club was founded in 1979 and one of their most famous riders is Julian Winn who represented Wales at the Commonwealth Games in Kuala Lumpur in 1998 and in Manchester in 2002. He was also the British Road Race Champion in 2002 and in 2004 he was in the British team at the Athens Olympics. The following year he was appointed Welsh Cycling Coach.

One of the club's current star riders is Becky James who won a silver medal in the women's sprint at the Commonwealth Games 2010. She also won a bronze medal in the 500m time trial. She was nominated for the 2010 BBC Cymru Wales Sports Personality of the year but lost out to footballer Gareth Beale.

The annual Abergavenny Festival of Cycling is held in July and racing takes place in the heart of the town with competitors sprinting around a circuit at speeds of up to 40mph. The streets are packed with spectators and this is one of the biggest cycling festivals to be held in Wales. The weekend also includes public rides, the 'Iron Mountain' race and the 'Tour of the Black Mountains'.

Elite riders participating in the Welsh Open Criterium held in July 2011 on the opening night of the Abergavenny Festival of Cycling.

'Road cycling is fast and furious and as riders hurtle around the town centre it is an exhilarating spectator sport.'

Bill Owen - Organiser

A fascinating sight for visitors to Abergavenny is to see paragliders and hang gliders soaring above as they fly from the top of the Blorenge escarpment, to land on Castle Meadows beside the river Usk. This occurs when the wind conditions are just right, not too windy, and of course blowing in the right direction.

Members of the South East Wales Hang Gliding and Paragliding club purchased the summit of the Blorenge in 1998 after two years of fund raising and negotiations and became the first UK club to own a major flying site.

Chapter Sixteen
ENTERTAINMENT

Not only do I intend bringing some of the best bands to Abergavenny, but I hope to offer the local public some really outstanding attractions from time to time.

Eddie Tattershal 1960

On July 3rd, 1903, William Frederick Cody, better known as 'Buffalo Bill' brought his Wild West Show to Bailey Park and this is one of the most remarkable open air events to have been held in Abergavenny. His Wild West Show travelled the world leaving a lasting impression of the American West.

Born in Iowa in 1846, William Cody became one of the riders of the Pony Express which was set up in 1860 and then a scout and guide for the Union Army at the start of the American Civil War. The nick name 'Buffalo Bill' was given to him when he provided buffalo meat for workers constructing the Kansas Pacific Railroad. He claimed to have slaughtered more than 4,000 buffalo between 1867 and 1868.

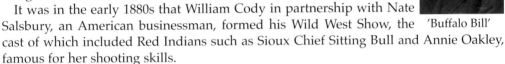

'Buffalo Bill'

It was in the early 1880s that William Cody in partnership with Nate Salsbury, an American businessman, formed his Wild West Show, the cast of which included Red Indians such as Sioux Chief Sitting Bull and Annie Oakley, famous for her shooting skills.

A European tour for the Wild West Show was arranged by James Bailey of Barnum and Bailey Circus and it involved the use of four trains to transport 800 people and 500 horses to the locations where it was held.

Bailey Park was an ideal venue, with its mountain background and space for many thousands of spectators. Seat prices ranged from 1 shilling (5p) to 7s 6d (35p) and the two hour programme included an Indian attack on a waggon train, rodeo, lassoing, and displays by 'mounted warriors' which included Bedouin Arabs, Russian Cossacks and the US Cavalry. The *Abergavenny Chronicle* commented: 'This long awaited visit has left many thousands of people highly gratified not only by the spectacle but by having seen so celebrated a hero as Colonel Cody.'

The Borough Theatre

It was during the First World War that the Town Hall was first named the Borough Theatre by Mrs Vivyan Thomas who was then responsible for its management and she did her utmost to 'put Abergavenny on the theatrical map.'

During the 1930s the theatre was regularly visited by shows from London and famous names appearing included Dame Clara Novello Davies, mother of Ivor Novello, Clive Dunn and operatic star Stella Carroll.

Several well known pop bands appeared at the theatre in the 1960s but the best remembered of all was of course The Beatles who appeared in Abergavenny on June 22nd 1963 and this was the only time that they played at a dance in Wales.

Paul, Ringo and George travelled by road and John Lennon was flown from London in a helicopter, having been delayed by taking part in the BBC TV programme 'Juke Box Jury'. He didn't finish filming until 9.15pm and was immediately taken to Battersea Helipad, from where a yellow helicopter, at a cost of £100, took him to Pen-y-pound football ground in Abergavenny. John and the Beatles' manager, Brian Epstein were then driven to the Town Hall just in time for the start of the show at 9.50pm. Paul McCartney had celebrated his 21st birthday a few days before the dance and he was presented with a huge birthday card signed by hundreds of those present. More than five hundred of the fans had travelled from as far afield as Cheltenham, Newport, Pontypool and neighbouring districts in special coaches. Tickets for the performance, which included a support act by The Fortunes (a local group) cost 12/6d.

Civic reception for the Beatles in the Mayor's Parlour

The Beatles had recently enjoyed success with their single 'Please Please Me', with the album still holding the top position in the UK charts at the time of the performance. Brian Epstein had signed a contract with Abergavenny promoter Eddie Tattersal in April for a payment of £250. By the time the event took place they were commanding fees of twice that amount, but agreed to honour the booking.

Backstage before the show George Harrison observed, 'Things are hotting up', but the noise was a mild fortaste of what was to follow, for the Beatles were greeted by a mighty roar of applause, with screaming, stamping and general hysteria. As the music began the very building seemed to vibrate with excitement.

Following their first twenty minutes set the Beatles were due to appear at the town hall for a civic reception with the mayor and mayoress, Councillor and Mrs J. Thurston. Before leaving the Mayor's parlour the boys were invited to sign the visitor's book. On noting that a recent previous visitor had signed 'Elizabeth R' one of the group with typical Beatle humour commented 'I wonder if that's her stage name?'

Leaving the hall after the show was an ordeal lasting fifteen minutes, as the group ran the gauntlet of autograph hunters and wildly excited, clothes clutching teenagers, eventually to reach the haven of the Angel Hotel, where they spent the remainder of what had been a memorable night for Abergavenny.

The Beatles performing on stage in Abergavenny 1963

Albert Lyons who took some pictures of the Beatles recalled in his book of old photographs of Abergavenny, published in 1983:

> 'I had the pleasure of meeting the Beatles, individually, finding Paul McCartney to be a very intelligent person, able to speak three languages, while Ringo Starr explained that his nickname was the result of his fondness for wearing large numbers of rings.'

Eddie Tattersal was the man responsible for bringing the Beatles to the town. Born in Manchester he first came to Abergavenny in 1941 during his army service. He married a local girl at Holy Trinity Church on October 4th 1943 and after leaving the army in 1946, Eddie got a job in the engineer's office with Great Western Railways. After Dr Beeching wielded his infamous axe, Eddie took a job as technical assistant in the public health department of Abergavenny Council.

In 1947 he had become a member of the Arthur Davies Ambassadors dance band who played `at the Town Hall on Saturday nights for seven years. When his playing days came to an end he carried on at the Town Hall as an MC and then until 1968 as the

Eddie Tattersal

borough's entertainments officer; when he was responsible for bringing many big-name groups and bands to Abergavenny.

He brought more than twenty famous pop groups and singers to the town, including the Beatles, Lulu, Status Quo, The Hollies, Pink Floyd, Billy Fury, Marty Wilde, Gene Vincent, the John Barry Seven, the Bachelors, and Dave, Dee, Dozey, Beaky, Mick and Tich.

In the eleven years that he was in charge of entertainments he paid into the borough's coffers the sum of £16,000 after all the expenses apart from the hall hiring fee had been paid. When the 'Fab Four' came to Abergavenny, Eddie even asked them to make a 3d charge for each autograph they signed and the group agreed to do this, when told that the money would be used to support the Freedom from Hunger Campaign.

Just two years later the 'Fab Four' were performing before 55,000 fans in New York's Shea Stadium, but their performance to Abergavenny has never been forgotten.

Eddie in 2005, at the age of 86, was given a community award for his service to Abergavenny, an annual award given by the town council after nominations from members of the public.

In June 2003, forty years to the day of the Beatles' appearance in Abergavenny's Borough Theatre, the tribute band The Cavern Beatles filled the theatre for a special anniversary concert. It was appropriate that the group was introduced by Eddie Tattershall, who once again took to the stage.

An extensive programme of refurbishment of the Borough Theatre was started by Monmouth Borough Council in 1989 and improvements have been continued by Monmouthshire County Council.

The pop singer 'Marty Wilde' (born Reginald Leonard Smith) certainly helped to put Abergavenny on the map when in May 1968, he released his song 'Abergavenny'. Its opening line 'Taking a trip up to Abergavenny' and the catchy tune certainly did much to encourage visitors to the town. The song proved a big hit in Europe, Australia and Sweden, but sadly failed to get into the charts in the UK. In the Netherlands the song peaked at number 5 and in America it became a top 50 hit under Marty Wilde's pseudonym 'Shannon'. For those looking for the song 'Abergavenny', it appears on the album 'Born to Rock and Roll' - the Greatest hits of Marty Wilde. It can also be heard on the internet with old film of Marty Wilde performing it on stage.

The Melville Theatre

Named after Melville Thomas, who formed the Young Peoples' Theatre in 1956, this small intimate theatre is at the Drama Centre in the old King Henry VIII School building at Pen-y-pound. Since 1976 it was been the home of the Gwent Theatre Company which presented an average of four productions a year. These have been performed at schools and village halls throughout Gwent. The company closed down following the Arts Council of Wales decision in 2011 to axe its £250,000 a year funding. The last performance was 'A Pocketful of Magic' at the Pen-y-pound Drama Centre on February 11th 2011.

Abergavenny Cinemas

In 1912 a Victorian corrugated iron hall in Park Road, behind where Tesco now stands, became the first cinema in the town and it was known variously as 'The Picture Palace', 'The Park Hall' and 'The Tin Hut'.

The following year on 21st July, the 'Abergavenny Coliseum Company' was registered with £3,600 in £1 shares. Land was acquired in Lion Street and within three months a purpose built cinema capable of seating 600 people had been built by J.G. Thomas and sons. It opened on Monday 3rd November 1913 and with the Mayor and Corporation in attendance, the first film to be shown was 'Quo-Vadis'. It was of course a silent film and such productions were often given a verbal explanation by a lecturer, such as the manager Walter Glover, who pointed things out with a long stick. At other times a pianist might provide a musical accompaniment to a film and some were even backed by an orchestra of three or more instrumentalists.

In about 1928 the Abergavenny Coliseum Company Limited began work on building a second cinema in Monk Street and this was christened The Pavillion. Storm damage to the roof caused it to close in 1930. Five years later, on Monday 6th May, The Pavillion was re-opened by the Mayor of Abergavenny, Councillor M.L. Beveridge and the first film to be shown was 'Forsaking all Others', starring Joan Crawford and Clark Gable.

The Coliseum closed for a short time in 1930 during which the seats were increased to a total of 700 and a sound system installed so that 'Talkies' could be shown and the first one was seen and heard at the Coliseum on Monday 6th October 1930. It was 'Rogue Song' featuring Lawrence Tibbett, the famous operatic baritone. Everyone was delighted with the Western Electric Sound System which had been installed. It meant that here at the Coliseum Abergavenny folk could see and hear the very best of the modern productions of the movie world.

The old Coliseum Cinema
is now a Wetherspoons pub

Coliseum staff
on opening day in 1913

The old Pavillion Cinema is now the Gateway Christian Centre

Both cinemas continued to be well supported during the next three decades and then in January 1967 it was announced that The Pavillion was to close as a cinema and re-open as a Bingo Hall, for registered members only, who had to be over 18 years of age. Putting on the last reel of film, the chief projectionist, Brian Webb said, 'It is the only job that I have had since I left school.'

In 1987 the Coliseum was also under threat of closure and there were proposals to demolish the building in 1988. By May 1989 the stalls had been converted into shops and there was a much reduced cinema upstairs. Three years later this closed and the Bingo sessions held at the Pavillion were transferred to the Coliseum. Today, the Coliseum is a Wetherspoons pub.

In 1999 the old Pavillion cinema which had been empty for a number of years was purchased by the Abergavenny Family Church for £82,500. It had to be completely renovated and refurbished which cost a further £165,000 and in March 2003 it was officially opened as the Gateway Christian Centre.

Baker Street Cinema in the old Drill Hall

The Baker Street Cinema, a new two screen cinema, with Dolby Surround sound and luxury seating, was opened in the Spring of 2010 in the former Drill Hall. The Victorian building was purchased by Peter and Irene Davies, owners of the successful Coliseum Cinema in Brecon and the Palace Cinema in Haverfordwest. They had previously considered a number of possible sites in Abergavenny including the former Baptist Chapel in Market Street but had been unable to make any progress on such a project. The official opening took place on Monday May 17th with the screening of 'Sherlock Holmes' in front of an invited audience. Such a film seemed most appropriate with the building being situated in Baker Street.

Abergavenny Pantomime Society can proudly claim to be the oldest Pantomime Company in Wales, for it was founded in 1932 and was initilly known as 'Trinity Sunday School' (Holy Trinity Church in Abergavenny). Its main aim is to perform a traditional pantomime in February every year in order to raise money for local charities.

Abergavenny Amateur Operatic and Dramatic Society was founded at the beginning of the twentieth century and was first known as the 'Abergavenny Operatic Society'. The patron at that time was the Marquess of Abergavenny and the first production in 1911 was 'A Nautical Knot' with a cast which included many prominent people in the town. The society became the 'Abergavenny Operatic and Dramatic Society' in 1961 and this meant that plays would also be staged. On its 60th anniversary the society produced 'The Student Prince' with a total of 63 performers; the 70th anniversary production in 1981 was 'Camelot' and the 80th birthday of the society was marked with 'Annie Get Your Gun'. In 2000, to mark the Millenium the company commissioned a new musical, 'Can't Sing, Can't Dance' which was written by Timepiece author Liz Davies.

The Abergavenny Light Opera Company is a breakaway company formed by a group of Abergavenny Amateur Operatic and Dramatic Society members. In July 2011 the name was changed to the Abergavenny Musical Theatre Company.

Abergavenny Symphony Orchestra was originally known as the Abergavenny Orchestral Society, and founded in the mid nineteenth century it is now over 150 years old. Rehearsals take place in the Angel Hotel on Sunday evenings and concerts (usually three times a year) are performed in such venues as King Henry VIII School and Our Lady and St Michael's Church, Abergavenny.

Abergavenny Orchestral Society rehearsing in the ballroom of the Angel Hotel

Abergavenny Borough Band was originally known as the Abergavenny Silver Band when it was formed during the nineteenth century. It is recorded that in 1884 a Mr Thomas Hardy, formerly of the Hussars took over directing the Abergavenny Town

Band. It was given the title Borough Band in 1906, the year that Earl Roberts, commander in chief of the British forces during the Boer War visited Aergavenny. Members of the band proudly headed the parade through the town.

Abergavenny Borough Band in 1925

The Gwent Bach Society had its inaugural meeting in October 1951 which was the year following the bi-centenary of the death of Johann Sebastian Bach. A group of Abergavenny musicians had been inspired to come together to play and sing Bach's music. The main instigator of the society was Dr Lloyd Davies and he was enthusiastically supported by his brother, Dr Trevor Davies.

In 1956 the choir was successful in winning the Second Choral competition at the National Eisteddfod, held that year at Aberdare. The First J.S. Bach Festival was held in July 1985 and further festivals followed at two year intervals until 1995.

Roger Langford was appointed conductor in 2001 and under his leadership the choir has performed a wide range of choral works including Bach's B Minor Mass, Haydn's Creation and Monteverdi's Vespers of Our Lady of 1610.

Elvis Presley impersonator Keith Davies, an Abergavenny electrician, helped by some of his friends (the 'Memphis Mafia') began in 2004 to raise large sums of money for various charities. The following year Keith did a show at Abergavenny Castle, arriving by helicopter and performing 48 songs in 3 hours.

He was later joined by The Sweets, Lisa-Marie and Emma-Jane Williams and at the time of writing the band have raised more than £160,000 for charity. It is to their credit that they have never accepted any fees whatsoever.

Two of the floats in the 1985 Abergavenny Carnival

Medieval Market in Nevill Street 1993

Talented musicians and singers are regularly seen busking in the town centre providing enjoyable entertainment for shoppers.

The Abergavenny Food Festival

The Food Festival at Abergavenny first started in 1999 and has gradually become so popular that it takes over the whole of the town centre for two days in September each year. The venues include the Victorian market hall, the Priory Centre, the castle grounds, hotels, pubs and many of the streets in the centre of the town.

Cookery demonstrations, tastings, lectures and guided walks all feature as well as over 200 stalls selling all kinds of food produce. The castle grounds have a huge tent in which the best musicians play, over the two days and this culminates in an evening party on the second day, followed by a firework display which is an exciting way to end the carnival atmosphere of the festival.

Abergavenny Food Festival 2010 - pictures by Malcolm Lewis

Chapter Seventeen
EISTEDDFODAU IN ABERGAVENNY

Among the institutions of Wales the Abergavenny Cymreigyddion was formerly very prominent. It was formed by a body of patriotic tradesmen in the town and its vicinity.

Edward J. Burrow 1903

Eisteddfodau were first held in the neighbourhood of Abergavenny in the reign of Edward III, in the 15th century, under the patronage of the Earl of Warwick. Lewis Glyn Cothi, the chief bard of the 15th century, spent much of his time in the neighbourhood, sang odes to Gwladys Gam, to Sir William Herbert, the first Earl of Pembroke, and to his brother Sir Richard Herbert of Coldbrook. Other patrons of Welsh literature and bards of repute also lived in the neighbourhood during the 16th and subsequent centuries.

In the 19th century Abergavenny became a centre of Welsh cultural revival when the Cymdeithas Cymreigyddion Society (The Society of Welsh Scholars of Abergavenny), promoted by Lady Llanover was formed at the Sun Inn (now called the Coach and Horses), Cross Street on Nov 22nd 1833. This society was established in the town for the purpose of encouraging Welsh literature, harp playing and the local industries of making woollens and hats.

Lady Llanover

There were 25 founder members with the Reverend John Evans, Vicar of Llanover, appointed president; Thomas Bevan, known as Caradawg, of Llanwenarth, secretary; Thomas Evan Watkins, known as Eiddil Ifor, of Blaenavon, bard; and the Reverend Thomas Price, the scholarly vicar of Cwmdu, correspondent.

Within three months, seventy-five members had been enrolled and the Society had the patronage of Sir Charles Morgan of Tredegar, Benjamin Hall of Llanover (who was subsequently knighted and later became Lord Llanover), and by the gentry of the county generally.

The word 'Cymreigyddion' signifies 'A Society of Welshmen' and the original aims of the society were to set up a Welsh medium school and a Welsh library in the town. It held an Eisteddfod in November 1834 which was the first of a series, known as Eisteddfodau y Fenni, held annually for the next five years. Not only did the literary masters of Wales come to Abergavenny, but poets and scholars were also attracted from places as far afield as India, Germany, Denmark and Brittany. The Cymreigyddion y Fenni were a society of national importance centred on Abergavenny and it was only in this area that the gentry took an interest in Welsh traditions.

Besides the prizes ranging from £100 to £1, for prose, poetry and playing the harp, they were also given for the best specimens of Welsh woollens and of hats made within the district. In a few years, no less than twenty harps were given as prizes at these events, several of them being won by blind competitors.

The second anniversary of the Society was publicly celebrated by a meeting at the Free Grammar School, then in the Old St John's Church, on Wednesday and Thursday,

Benjamin Hall

25th and 26th November, 1835, when the president was Sir John Guest of Dowlais. In the next year, on 23rd and 24th November, the third anniversary of the Society was again held at the Free Grammar School under the chairmanship of Mr W. Williams of Llangybi, and was notable for the establishment of the Welsh Manuscript Society.

Benjamin Hall presided over the Eisteddfod held in October 1837, and among those present was Ioan Tegid who had just transcribed the *Red Book of Hergest* for Lady Charlotte Guest and also helped her in her translation of the *Mabinogion*.

The 1838 Eisteddfod was again held in the Grammar School and was presided over by Sir Charles Morgan, Bart., of Tredegar and was attended by a deputation from Brittany, consisting of the Comte de la Villemargue, and four other noblemen of that province. The Comte was presented by Sir Charles Morgan, on behalf of the Cymreigyddion y Fenni, with a Hirlas Horn. This was a fine mottled horn with bands of silver around the top, middle and bottom. It was edged with trefoil leaves, wrought in silver and lined throughout in the same metal. Inside, at the bottom of the horn, was set a fine Snowdon crystal, and upon the upper band was engraved in Welsh: 'From the Cymreigyddion y Fenni to the Breton deputy of the King of the French, 10th October, 1838.'

The president of the Eisteddfod attended by the neighbouring gentry entered the town, forming a procession which was often a mile in length. The horses and servants of the president and the principal families had large cockades of green and white ribbon said to be the colour of the banner of Wales carried at Bosworth field.

The Procession
through Abergavenny
London Illustrated News 1845

The ladies wore the national costume and every person who could afford it wore a silver, satin or pearl leek. It was generally worn in the hats of the ladies, and the button-hole of the gentlemen.

The president was met outside the town by all the inhabitants who were members of the society, marching two by two, preceded by flags and banners. They were attended by a pyramidal cart filled with harpers and drawn by four fine horses, accompanied by the Society of Druids in full costume. The address having been spoken and replied to by the President, the whole procession slowly filed through the town, and the taking of the chair by the president was announced by a flourish of trumpets, followed by a band of harps playing an ancient Welsh march. The proceedings of the day then commenced and lasted two days.

A Gorsedd ceremony was held in an enclosure behind the George Hotel with the bards standing in a circle which had been constructed of pebbles and small stones. Later, to celebrate the Eisteddfod, a spectacular 'fancy dress ball' was held in the 'Great Room' of the Angel Hotel. A detailed account of this event appeared in the Hereford Times:

'This novel assembly was attended by upwards of two hundred ladies and gentlemen, comprising most of the influential families of the neighbourhood.' (These included Sir Benjamin Hall. his wife, Lady Llanover and Crawshay Bailey, the ironmaster). 'The room was tastefully decorated with festoons of evergreens and flowers, and green and white flags bearing suitable Welsh inscriptions and the crest of the worthy President of the Society.

The beautiful Mrs Mountjoy Martin dazzled all beholders in the costume of Gwent and Morganwg, composed of satin, with a beaver hat and mob cap. The extraordinary beauty of this lady is too well known to need further eulogium; but it would be an incorrect report, if the buzz of admiration were not recorded, which attended her in whatever part of the room she appeared.'

The 1840 Eisteddfodd was opened by a procession led by a troop of mounted cavalry and, in addition to the bards and members of Cymreigyddion y Fenni, there were representatives of the Ancient Order of Druids and of the Independent Order of Odd Fellows in full regalia and with banners flying. The President, John Etherington Welch Rolls, of the Hendre brought up the rear in his horse-drawn carriage. The Gorsedd ceremony was presided over by Taliesin ab Iolo and he admitted seven new members, including John Evans (Ieuan ap Gruffydd), vicar of Llanover and chairman of Cymreigyddion y Fenni. This was the last Gorsedd ceremony held at Eisteddfod y Fenni.

The 1842 Eisteddfod was presided over by Sir Benjamin Hall and was attended by a great number of high ranking and celebrated persons, amongst whom were Prince Lucien Bonaparte, Prince Dwarkanouth Tagore of Calcutta (whose magnificent native costume was the centre of attraction in the great procession), distinguished visitors from Germany, Denmark, the Williamses of Aberpergwm and the learned Rev Thomas Price (Carnhuanawc) from Cwmdu. Published on 25th October 1845, *The Illustrated London News* contains two full pages describing the 12th eisteddfod of the Abergavenny Cymreigyddion.

Chorus singers

Post boys on these occasions wore jackets of Welsh wool, and the gentlemen's servants wore cockades of green and white ribbon as an emblem of their nationality. Ladies of eminence condescended to don a Welsh steeple hat and the native dress of chequered flannel.

By the late 1840's the Abergavenny Eisteddfod was almost the largest in Wales and it attracted poets and scholars, not only from Wales, but from as far afield as India, Germany, Denmark and Brittany. The event had grown so popular under the joint planning of the Reverend Thomas Price (Carnhuanawc) and Lady Hall (Gwenynen Gwent), that a special Cymreigyddion Hall, capable of seating 2,000 people was built in Tudor Street. It was opened with great ceremony in 1845, under the presidency of Sir Benjamin Hall.

Opening of the Cymreigyddion Hall in Tudor Street - *Illustrated London News* 1845

An Eistedfodd was held in the town on October 11th and 12th, 1848 in the purpose-built hall under the patronage of the Prince of Wales. No less than four hundred carriages were in the procession on the opening day. Colonel Kemeys Tyme was President of the meeting and among the people present were Lady Hall of Llanover, the Marquis of Northampton, Lady Charlotte Guest, Miss Angharad Llwyd, Chavalier Bunsen of Germany, Madam Bunsen and her sister, Calimaki of Turkey, Lady Charles Somerset and Lady Llanover.

A prize of 25 guineas was given by the Prince of Wales for the best critical essay on the history of the language and literature of Wales from the time of Gruffydd ab Cynon and Meilyr to that of Sir Gruffydd Llwyd and Gwilym Ddu. It was won by Thomas Stephens of Merthyr and the essay was subsequently published under the title, *The Literature of the Cymry*.

Reverend Thomas Price

The chief organiser of these events, which used to last two days was the Reverend Thomas Price, known by his bardic name of Carnhuanawc. He was an expert player on the Welsh or triple-stringed harp. He wrote a history of Wales *Hanes Cymru* in Welsh which was printed at Crickhowell by a local printer named Thomas Williams. Thomas Price died on 7 November 1848 aged 61.

As the town became more English in speech and sentiment, these meetings came to an end in about 1853 when the procession was two miles long. The Society was dissolved on January 14th 1854. In its twenty-one years' existence it had revived interest in the Welsh language and culture to such an extent that other societies sprang up all over the country, bards were encouraged, and books published, the woollen industry revived and numerous other good results achieved. As a result, wherever an Eisteddfod is held today, Gwenynen Gwent (Lady Llanover), Carnhuanawc (Reerendv Thomas Price) and the Cymreigyddion y Fenni are remembered with considerable gratitude.

On 14th January 1854, the Cymreigyddion Society Committee met for the last time, resolving 'that the undersigned forming the committee of the said Cymreigyddion Society now give instructions to the Treasurer to discharge forthwith all liabilities and the Abergavenny Cymreigyddion Society be this day dissolved', the Resolution being signed by two of the founders, John Evans and John Michael.

The Society had achieved its aim in reviving interest in Welsh literature, music and history, it had been instrumental in the foundation of the Welsh Manuscript Society, and its work led to the establishment of the National Eisteddfod as we know it today. This was first held in 1860 and it grew into a very large festival held alternately in North and South Wales, and lasting a week.

It was largely through the Society that Lady Charlotte Guest was inspired to cause *The Mabinogion* to be translated and that the connection with Brittany was established.

The Cymreigyddion Hall afterwards became 'The Cymreigyddion Inn' and by 1873 was known as the Volunteers' Inn for it was then being used by the Abergavenny Volunteer Rifle Company as a drill hall.

Proclamation of the National Eisteddfod of 1913

On Wednesday 3rd July 1912, a Gorsedd meeting took place in Abergavenny for the proclamation of the National Eisteddfod of Wales to be held in the town the following year. The Abergavenny Gorsedd Committee couldn't have chosen a more appropriate site for the formation of the Gorsedd Circle than that portion of Coldbrook Park which became known as The Grove. It is about a mile from the Town Hall on the Monmouth Road at the bottom of what was locally known as Cae Kenfy pitch, just past Plas Derwen, the one-time residence of Alderman James Straker and opposite Yspyty Farm. The site was on rising ground, several feet above the level of the road with a beautiful panoramic view of the Usk Valley and the Blorenge Mountain.

Coldbrook was closely associated with the historic houses of Pembroke, Powys, Llanarth and Raglan and Sir Arthur Herbert had kindly allowed the erection of the Gorsedd Circle on his land.

The seventeen stones forming the inner and outer circles, and which stand over 6ft high by 2ft square and average something over 2 tons each in weight, were placed in position by Messrs Robert Price & Sons. They were rough from the quarries, of a grey colour and had not suffered any chiselling or fashioning by human hand, which is in strict accordance with the Gorsedd rules.

On the day of the opening ceremony held on Easter Monday, March 28th 1913, there were festoons of oak and ivy leaves from stone to stone and trails of ivy over and about the 'maenllog' or 'stone of the covenant' in the centre of the circle, upon which stood the Archdruid and others when offering up a prayer and delivering addresses.

The formal opening of the picturesque ceremony took place in the morning when the sun was very near the meridian, in due accordance with ancient Bardic rules - 'Yn Nghwynel Haul a llgad Golenni.' ('In the face of the sun and in the eye of light.')

Afterwards an adjournment was made for lunch at the Angel Hotel which was presided over by Colonel J. A. Bradney in the absence of General Sir Ivor Herbert MP, President of the local Eisteddfod Committee, and was supported by the vice president, Alderman James Straker, the Gorsedd officials, the Mayor, Aldermen and Councillors of the Borough.

No fewer than 170 guests enjoyed an excellent luncheon provided by Mr H. B. Stoken and speeches were made by the Chairman, the High Sheriff of Monmouthshire and the Mayor. A move was then made to Bailey Park where a large procession assembled to march through the town, led by Mayor, James Straker.

Eisteddfod procession through the town in 1913

The Welsh National Eisteddfod was launched on Easter Monday, March 28th 1913 with a procession through the town, led by the Town Band, playing 'The March of the Men of Harlech,' followed by the Mayor, James Straker, the Mace-bearer (Mr Manuel) and members of the Corporation and officials. Then came members of the Honourable Society of Cymmrodorion, ladies and gentlemen and some distance behind these came vehicles carrying members in their bardic robes. A striking figure in the procession was the Reverend Ceitho Davies, attired as an ancient Welsh minstrel with top hat, shooting jacket, with brass buttons, knee breeches and stockings of a dark colour.

The Abergavenny Gorsedd Stones

The Gorsedd Stones which can be seen on Swan Meadow were originally erected by Horsingtons, a local building firm, in a field beside the Monmouth road in 1912, the year before Abergavenny hosted the Royal National Eisteddfod. It is customary for all Gorsedd stones to be erected a year before the National Eisteddfod visits any town.

A year and a day before the event opens, a Proclamation ceremony is held at the circle with all the Bards in attendance. A list of all the competitors is presented to the Archdruid, to give all competitors a year's notice to prepare their work.

There are seventeen stones in the circle and the central stone inside the circle is called the Logan Stone. The circle is supposed to measure 21 to 28 yards in diameter, these being a multiple of seven. Facing directly east of the Logan stone is the Covenant stone which is in line with the sun rising in the east during the month of August when the Eisteddfodd ceremonies take place. Either side of this stone are the largest stones - the Portal stones, which are in line with the sun rising of June 21 and December 21.

If you draw a line following these rays of light between these stones it forms the mystic sign of the Gorsedd of the Bards. The other nine stones making up the circle are of little significance for these ceremonies.

The Gorsedd stones on the Swan Meadows Park

In 2000 the Gorsedd stones were moved from the private ground beside the Monmouth Road to a more visible public place on the Swan Meadows public park, which runs alongside the Abergavenny bus station. Before being removed the positions of the seventeen stones were accurately measured in order to erect them in exactly the same layout at the new location.

The work was carried out by local contractors Alun Griffths Ltd., who provided heavy lifting gear and transport free of charge. Abergavenny town council gave a donation towards the cost of the works and the project also received money from the community grant scheme administered by Monmouthshire County Council.

The stones were officially unveiled on Thursday, March 21, 2002, the bi-centenary of the birth of Lady Llanover, one of the prime movers in promoting the original Abergavenny Eisteddfod. This date also coincided with the opening of an exhibition at the museum on the life and work of Lady Llanover.

In recognition of his invaluable help in moving the stones, local contractor Alun Griffiths was asked to perform the opening ceremony. Also in attendance was the mayor, Anthony O'Donovan and members of the town council.

In 2002 the Abergavenny Eisteddfod was revived by a local group led by town councillor Douglas Edwards and his wife Edna and Mrs Bronwen Green, head teacher of Abergavenny's Welsh primary school. Competitiors were initially invited from local schools with events taking place at King Henry VIII Comprehensive School. Adult competitors were attracted from 2003 onwards and the evening competitions are now held in the Borough Theatre.

These twin standing stones have been erected to highlight Abergavenny's importance in the history of eisteddfod tradition and the work of Lord and Lady Llanover in promoting Welsh language and culture in this area. The images and symbols on the stones were designed by pupils at Llanfair Kilgeddin Church in Wales Primary School and Ysgol Gymraeg y Fenni.

Chapter Eighteen
ROYAL VISITORS AND COMMEMORATIONS

King Charles I, stayed at the Priory, as the guest of Mr Gunter, on the 1st of July 1645 on his way from Hereford to Raglan, having had lunch that afternoon with Mr Prichard at Campston.

Sir Joseph Bradney 1906

In 1094, seven years after the death of William the Conqueror his son William Rufus, paid a visit to Abergavenny on his way to subdue a rebellion of the men of Gwent, Brecknock and the Gower peninsula.

William II

The next monarch to visit the town was King John who made a hurried visit to Abergavenny in 1211. He scarcely ever slept more than a night or two in the same place and must have ridden 50 miles a day for many weeks. He arrived on Saturday the 12th of March, having been at Hereford on the 9th and Kilpeck Castle on the 10th. On the 16th he was back in Hereford. Why he came to Abergavenny, the records do not state. Perhaps it was to see the fair domain which he now possessed. William de Braose had fled to France and his wife Maud had been starved to death in Windsor Castle the year before.

King John

Henry III paid a brief visit in 1234 and the next monarch to come here was Edward I who stayed in Abergavenny for a week in 1291 and held a council lasting three weeks. His visit came about as the result of a quarrel between the Earls of Gloucester and Hereford, whose followers were carrying on a private war on the Brecknock borders, belonging to Earl Hereford, and on the Glamorgan estates of the Earl of Gloucester. Edward issued a decree that all private wars must cease, but neither of the earls took any notice of him. The King then decreed that both earls be tried for contempt of his honour

Edward I

and ordered the trial to take place at Abergavenny Castle on 25th September 1291. The whole of the Grand Council were to be the judges, and the Council consisted of the Archbishops of Canterbury and York, together with numerous earls, barons and other bishops, each with their retinues, their standards, and full pageantry of armorial bearings. It is not recorded how long the trial lasted, but both earls were deprived of their estates in Brecknock and Glamorgan and sentenced to imprisonment, but through the influence of their friends both were later liberated.

During the Civil War Charles I paid a visit to Abergavenny on his journey from Hereford after the Royalists' big defeat at the battle of Naseby. He left Hereford on Tuesday July 1st 1645 with Lord Bernard Stuart's troop of Life Guards, the Queen's Guards, and Prince Rupert's troop of Guards, as well as his regiment of horse. The Governor of Hereford, Colonel Scudamore, and the chief gentry of the County accompanied the King to 'Mr Pritchard's House, near Grosmont, where the King dined.' In those days the road to Abergavenny, was through Grosmont and Mr Pritchard lived at Camston or Campstone as it is known today. The Herefordshire gentlemen then returned and King Charles continued to Abergavenny.

He stayed at the Priory that night as the guest of Mr James Gunter, whilst on his way to Raglan. Whilst he was there he gave orders for Abergavenny Castle to be made untenable. He then went on to Raglan Castle and returned to Abergavenny on September 8th to see the results and 'to try five chief hinderers, who were slow in going to the relief of Hereford.' The King let them go free and the Marquis of Worcester chided him for his

Charles I

leniency, saying, 'You may join the kingdom of Heaven by such means, but if you keep the kingdom of England, I will be your bondsman.'

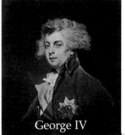

George IV

At this time, the people of this part of Monmouthshire were becoming somewhat backward in their support of Charles I and he was the last monarch to visit Abergavenny Castle.

George IV once passed through Abergavenny on his way from Haverfordwest to Monmouth. The townsfolk who watched him pass through were bitterly disappointed that he did not stop and some of his escort of yeomanry were apparently exhausted by his rapid pace, almost to the point of collapse.

Two years before his death, Prince Albert Victor, Duke of Clarence, eldest son of Edward VII, visited Abergavenny on his way to Crickhowell to open the Clarence Hall on 18th September 1890. This was then the first time within living memory that a royal personage had passed through the town (excepting the somewhat insignificant visit of the Prince of Orange some thirty years earlier).

The royal express arrived from York at 7.30 am. As the Prince stepped on to the platform, Superintendant Kynch gave a signal to Sergeant Capper who was standing, with a white flag, on the bridge crossing the line. The sergeant then signalled to the mountain

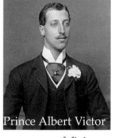

Prince Albert Victor

artillery who were stationed on the side of the Little Skirrid for the purpose of firing a salute.

Sir Arthur Herbert, KCB, and Colonel Herbert, CB, Grenadier Guards, having obtained the necessary permission from the War Office, had arranged with Major Radcliff, commanding officer of the X Mountain Battery, Royal Artillery, who were quartered at Newport, for the services of the battery. A special train chartered by Lady Llanover had conveyed the battery to Penpergwm. The mules were detrained and the men were marshalled to enjoy a meal provided in an adjacent tent, while the officers were entertained at lunch by Colonel Herbert. At a quarter to five the mules were loaded and soon after a start was made for the Little Skirrid which formed part of Lady Llanover's Coldbrook Estate. Just before sunset the battery arrived on the summit of the hill where a flag pole had been erected, from which St George's Royal Standard was gaily flying.

The guns were dismantled, refreshment in the form of gingerbeer was provided for the men, while Mrs Ivor Herbert invited Major Radcliff and the other officers to a picnic tea which had been provided for them. When the Royal train arrived a salute of twenty-one guns was fired amid the distant clamour of bells. Soon afterwards, the battery made its way down to Penpergwm, where their special train was waiting.

Prince Albert shook hands with the Duke of Beaufort and was then, with due ceremony, made acquainted with the other men on the platform, whom he did not know He greeted them with a cordial 'How do you do, sir,' as he shook hands. Then he went up to the ladies, Mrs Herbert and Mrs Fitzmaurice, with whom he shook hands, the ladies acknowledging the honour conferred upon them with a graceful and courtly obeisance.

An address was then read by Mr Rutherford, clerk to the Improvement Commissioners. The address, which had been beautifully illuminated by Messrs Sergeant Brothers, on vellum, with filligree border, on ground of pure gold, was contained in a case of blue Russian leather and bore the inscription; 'To HRH, the Duke of Clarence and Avondale, KG, KP, from the Abergavenny Town Commissioners, 15th September, 1890.'

The address read as follows:

'To HRH the Duke of Clarence and Avondale, KG, KP.

We, the Abergavenny Improvement Commissioners, on behalf of our townsmen, humbly desire to express our sincere gratitude at the opportunity afforded us of most cordially welcoming your Royal Highness on visiting the neighbourhood of the ancient border town of Abergavenny and of testifying to the loyalty and devotion of the community amongst whom we dwell, to the throne and person of Her Most Gracious Majesty, our beloved Queen.

We trust your Royal Highness will derive pleasure from your visit to the Principality, from which your august sire, His Royal Highness the Prince of Wales derives his title; and that your Royal Highness will carry away a pleasing remembrance of the good wishes of the Welsh people.

Our earnest prayer is that long life, happiness and every blessing may attend your Royal Highness.

Given under our common seal this 15th day of September, 1890.

Joseph Bishop, Chairman'

The Prince then read the following reply:

'Improvement Commissioners and Townsmen of Abergavenny, Gentlemen - I thank you most heartily for the cordial welcome accorded me in the address which has just been presented and read; and also for the reception you have given me on this, my first visit to the ancient town of Abergavenny. I can assure you that I am looking forward with the greatest of pleasure to the next few days, during which I hope to become more closely acquainted with the Principality of Wales and its loyal people. It will be my agreeable duty to inform Her Majesty the Queen of your sentiments of loyalty and devotion. Gentlemen, allow me to again thank you for your kind wishes for my own welfare.'

Prince Albert stayed the night at Glanusk Park and on the following day again passed through Abergavenny, on his way to Cardiff. The people gave a hearty cheer as the Prince passed on the box seat of Sir Joseph Bailey's coach. Mr Russell Bailey was driving and apparently made some remark to the Prince, who turned in his seat and acknowledged the salute with a genial smile.

Following the coach in an open barouche, driven by four horses with two postillions, were Sir Joseph Bailey, Viscount Cross and Viscount Emlyn.

The streets and roads to the station were lined with people who cheered lustily as the royal cortege drove along to the station, where the special train was waiting.

At 11.40 am the train left the station amid cheers from the assembled crowd. The Prince was expected on his return from Cardiff to arrive back at Abergavenny at 5.30 pm, but his train did not leave Cardiff until 5.25 pm, instead of as arranged. Furthermore the Prince accepted the invitation of Mr Herbert to tea on the platform of Nantyderry Station. The train bearing the Royal party eventually arrived at Abergavenny at 6.46 pm. A thick mantle of mist shrouded the beautiful mountain scenery from view and a light rain was falling. Accordingly, the Prince, instead of riding on the coach. took his seat in his own barouche, the hood of which was partially raised and followed by his suite, went at walking pace through the town, which was brilliantly illuminated and, despite the falling rain was thronged with cheering people.

Four months later on Thursday 14th January 1892 news was received in Abergavenny that His Royal Highness the Duke of Clarence, eldest son of the Prince of Wales had died at Sandringham of pneumonia following a bout of inflenza. He was buried in St George's Chapel at Windsor Castle.

The Death of Queen Victoria

On Monday January 22, 1901 groups of townspeople assembled near the Post Office in Cross Street, anxiously awaiting the telegrams which from time to time appeared in the Post Office window bearing the latest bulletin as to the condition of the Queen.

When news of her death finally arrived at 7.15 pm the following day, the passing bell of St Mary's was tolled and tradesmen around the town put up their shutters. By Wednesday, the town presented an appearance of deep mourning, drawn blinds and closed shutters being the rule in all the principal streets. Abergavenny's Mayor wired a telegram which read as follows:

Queen Victoria

> 'To the King's Most Excellent Majesty, Osborne. The inhabitants of the ancient borough of Abergavenny deeply sympathise with Your Majesty and the rest of the Royal Family.
>
> William Williams, Mayor'.

A special meeting of the Town Council was held that evening and the Mayor commented that the meeting had been convened in consequence of the death of their Sovereign Lady, Queen Victoria, 'who had been endowed by Almighty God with wisdom, purity, love and courage, and, during whose reign there had been an immense amount of good done in the country.' He wanted the Council to be the mouthpiece of the town in expressing the regret that was felt throughout the country at the loss of their glorious Queen.

Queen Victoria had ruled the British Empire for more than 60 years. Surrounded by her children and grand-children, including Germany's Emperor Wilhelm, the Queen's strength had 'diminished' during the day (Tuesday January 22) and she died, peacefully in her sleep at 6.30 pm.

Albert Edward, the eldest son and second child of Queen Victoria at the age of 59 now became King Edward VII. He had been born at Buckingham Palace on November 9th 1841 and on the 4th of the following month Queen Victoria issued letters patent creating him Prince of Wales and Earl of Chester.

When he succeeded to the throne he decided to assume the title of King Edward VII in accordance with the wish of his mother. He respectfully left the memory of his father's name Albert 'the exclusive treasure of his dear mother.'

Proclamation of Edward VII

On January 26th 1901 a crowd of about 3,000 people assembled outside the Town Hall to hear the proclamation of King Edward VII which was read out by the Mayor, with the usual accompaniment of fanfares. At the conclusion of the reading the crowd shouted 'God save the King' and then dispersed.

The Death of Edward VII

Abergavenny went into mourning on the death of Edward VII in 1910. All tradesmen displayed black boards in their shop windows, and the mayor (Mr J.O. Marsh) ordered a muffled peal from the bells of St Mary's Priory Church. Local events which had been organised were cancelled.

The Coronation of King George V and Queen Mary

In June 1911, Abergavenny celebrated the coronation of George V and Queen Mary. The Mayor and Corporation attended Divine Service at St Mary's Church, accompanied by various public bodies, the Abergavenny troop of the Royal Gloucester Hussars, and the members of Friendly Societies in the town.

The Reverend J. R. Phillips, R.D., Vicar of Holy Trinity and chaplain to the Mayor of Abergavenny, delivered an appropriate address from the First Book of Samuel. He then commented how King George had 'won the hearts of many peoples,' while the 'sweet woman at his side - Queen Mary shared his responsibility. '

George V and Queen Mary

The *Abergavenny Chronicle* commented:

> 'King George, who, came here by hereditary succession, had had his training on the best spot in the world to make a man and a gentleman - the quarter-deck of a British man-o'-war. A great deal depended upon the training of a man for kingship.
>
> King George had inherited the noble qualities of his father, King Edward VII, the peace-maker, well loved by all who knew him. George the Fifth inherited from his father and his mother the highest qualities of manhood and his training had been the best possible.

The townspeople of Abergavenny gave outward expression to their loyalty by decorating their homes and their places of business. It was pleasing to see the effort made at decoration by many of those who could ill afford to part with the few pence which represented the trade value of the little group of flags proudly displayed over a front door or a window.

Alderman James Straker addressed the multitude gathered outside the Town Hall in terms complimentary of the Mayor and Mayoress for the energy they had put into the festivities, and asked all present to express their appreciation of the programme that had been prepared for them and they responded by cheering.

That night there was a fine view of the blazing bonfire on the Sugar Loaf from Frogmore Street, and hundreds who, had the weather been fine, would have climbed the mountain or the neighbouring hills, as on former occasions, were content with this distant view from the town.'

In 1925 Edward, Prince of Wales (later Duke of Windsor), paid a private visit to Glanusk Park, and he took part in a pheasant shoot. He also visited Abergavenny informally on two occasions, when in his typical unaffected way, he walked along the main street.

The Duke and Duchess of York (later King George VI and Queen Elizabeth)came to Abergavenny in March 1932 to pay a brief visit to the Cottage Hospital. Hundreds of adults and school children stood on the road outside the hospital and cheered the couple as they alighted from their car to be received by Lady Herbert. As they entered the hospital grounds, a pleasant sight awaited them, for Scouts, Guides and St John Ambulance Cadets formed a Guard of Honour.

Visit of the Duke and Duchess of York in 1932

After they had inspected the Hospital and had spoken to the patients, more rousing cheers greeted the Royal couple as they left the grounds and proceeded to Llanarth Court, where Lord Treowen entertained them to luncheon before they travelled to Severn Tunnel Junction to catch an express to London.

The Royal Silver Jubilee of George V

In May 1935, patriotic fervour broke out in the Abergavenny area during the week's celebration of the Royal Jubilee of the accession of George V. Local people young and old, in common with the rest of the country demonstrated their loyalty in no uncertain manner. Abergavenny had never been so gaily decorated with flags, streamers, bunting and other decorations and the main streets were a blaze of red, white and blue, which created quite a carnival atmosphere. Many wore red, white and blue ribbons, rosettes, or other designs to show that they were all participants in this momentous occasion.

The celebrations in Abergavenny really started on Saturday 4 May, for on that day at the Market Hall the Mayor (Councillor Max Beveridge) handed out to about 370 unemployed and about the same number of old people bright new half-crowns.

King George V

Monday's proceedings started at 10 am with bellringing at St Mary's Church and two sets of bellringers did duty in the morning and afternoon. In the morning there was an imposing motor cycle and cycle rally, which assembled in the Cattle Market, was led by the Abergavenny Borough Band in a motor-coach, through the main streets. A large number of pedal cyclists were in front, followed by motor cyclists, motor cars and commercial vehicles. The procession was about a mile in length. From the tower of St Mary's Church it could be seen that it stretched from the County Club in Hereford Road up to Prangley's corner and all the way down Park Crescent to Pen-y-pound. Though there were no prizes for decoration, some of the vehicles had been tastefully decorated and the decoration of Mr Basil Evans's car was much admired.

Athletic sports for children, in Bailey Park, followed in the afternoon. There were about 700 entries and as many as 22 races in one section. The winners each received a prize value 2s 6d. After the sports the children accompanied by the Borough Band, marched in procession to the General Market, where they were provided with tea. The tiny tots marched hand in hand with a look of pleasant expectation in their faces. The children sang lustily as they marched and gave themselves an added appetite for the good things that were to follow.

Afterwards the children were marched to the Castle, where an entertainment was provided and a further entertainment followed at the Town Hall, which was packed with eager youngsters.

Everyone waited for the signal rocket to be fired from the Deri, where a huge bonfire had been erected. This was lit at 10 o'clock by the Brigadier General J. G. B. Tulloch, C.B., C.M.G., D.L., and the combustibles immediately fired up and lit up the whole countryside. Clouds of smoke from the tyres and sleepers somewhat obscured the blaze from the view of those people who were watching it from the town, but the hundreds of people who made the ascent of the mountain saw the bonfire at its best from the north side. It was one of the biggest bonfires in South Wales and easily eclipsed anything for miles around. Another good bonfire which could be seen well from the town was that erected on the Holy Mountain by the Llanvapley Scouts.

For many people the day was fittingly concluded at the Jubilee ball which was held at the Angel Hotel. Here some 450 dancers entered into the carnival spirit of the Jubilee and the proceedings were kept up until 3.30 in the morning. Decorations in the ballroom were most artistic and created the right atmosphere. The walls were draped with crepe paper in the national colours of red, white and blue. There were large photographs of the King and Queen on each side of the centre panel, over which was draped a Union Jack. On the balcony was the inscription 'Long Live Their Majesties,' and on the opposite wall 'Long Live The King.'

Enthusiasm reached its highest at midnight, when dancing was suspended so that the whole company could honour Their Majesties. Dr P. Lornie O.B.E., presented the Mayor with a suitably inscribed pewter tankard in which he gave the toast of 'Long life to Their Majesties'. This was heartily honoured and all joined in the singing with great feeling, 'Here's a Health to Their Majesties' followed by the National Anthem.

Acknowledging the gift of the tankard, the Mayor said:

'We are at the end of one of the most memorable days in the history of the British Empire. Today we celebrate the 25th anniversary of the accession of our beloved King to the Throne. I have been to the villages around Abergavenny and I have visited all sorts of people and everybody with one accord, no matter what their political opinions, are today, with smiling and happy faces, combining with one another to make this a great day. I feel that we ought to thank God that we are living under the jurisdiction of such a King and under the happy conditions of the Union Jack.

Right throughout the British Empire today the accession of King George V has been celebrated. I remember one particular day, August 4th, 1914, when I was 8,000 miles from Abergavenny. What a thrill it gave me to see the Union Jack flying from the flagstaff of a Town Hall in a town which was hostile to the British Empire. That Union Jack was put there and it stayed there. Today I feel that Almighty God has expressed His opinion of the life of our Royal Family by giving us such a beautiful day. I feel very proud of Abergavenny and its people. I never felt so proud of it because of the loyal way they have shown their appreciation of living under the reign of King George the Fifth. I give you his health. Long may he reign.'

Though the hour was late (or rather early) it was with general regret when the proceedings concluded at 3.30 am and everyone went home tired and happy. So ended one of the most memorable days in the history of Abergavenny.

At the time of the First World War George V changed the name of the royal house to Windsor (from the Germanic Saxe-Coburg-Gotha). During his reign of 25 years the British Empire started to move towards independence and he welcomed the concept of the Commonwealth.

The King is Dead, Long Live the King !

On January 24, 1936 the *Abergavenny Chronicle* commented:

'Following the death of King George V who had reigned for twenty five years, Edward VIII was proclaimed King with colourful pageantry in London and more simple ceremonies throughout the country.

The Proclamation ceremony in Abergavenny was simple, but impressive. A large crowd of townspeople and pupils from various schools in the town assembled outside the Town Hall. As the last stroke of twelve by the Town Hall clock died away a bugler sounded a fanfare. Then the Mayor (Lt. Col. J. G. Bishop OBE), in a clear voice, read the Proclamation. All eyes were upturned to the window from which he spoke, and all the crowd, without exception listened intently in profound silence but for the sound of the Mayor's voice.

After he had finished reading the Proclamation, there followed the sounding of the Royal Salute by the bugler and the flag on the Town Hall, which hung at half mast as a mark of mourning for the late King, was hoisted to full mast in honour of the new King.

The Mayor's Chaplain (the Rev M. E. Edwards MA, Vicar of St Mary's) then pronounced the Benediction and the short proceedings concluded with the singing of one verse of the National Anthem.

No King has ever come to the throne of England with so great a degree of affection and popularity than King Edward VIII. The nation knows him as a man of wisdom and human understanding who is determined to carry on the great tradition for the goal of his people and to maintain and strengthen the British constitution, which is the envy of the world.'

Abdication of Edward VIII

On 11th December 1936, King Edward VIII abdicated and immediately left the country for exile in France. The *Abergavenny Chronicle* commented:

Edward VIII

'It seems a dream - at the time it seemed a nightmare - that the most popular King in British history, Edward VIII, renounced his Throne as recently as Thursday of last week, and is now an exile in a foreign land.

In spite of what was regarded at the time as a dire calamity, Great Britain and the Empire goes about its business with as much equanimity as before, and it is difficult to believe that we are living under a new reign.

We enter upon a new era, and because of the challenge to our capacity to meet an unprecedented situation, we enter upon it with more determination and more unanimity than ever. We are filled with sympathy for King George VI, who has stepped into the breach to carry out the traditions of the British monarchy which were enhanced by his father George V.

King George VI may not have the qualities which have been admired in his elder brother King Edward VIII, and may not easily attain to such popularity, but he has other qualities which are necessary to kingship.

It is in the ordinary course of events that any king must be tested by time, and there is every reason to believe that King George will add lustre to the British Throne. It is fully evident that he has a real interest in the well-being of his people, and with as much humility and zeal as his revered father he has dedicated himself to the service of his country and Empire. He has the advantage of a popular and gracious Queen who will play her part.

With the people behind an enlightened and democratic monarchy, Great Britain and the Empire can look forward to the future with courage and optimism and remain a bulwark of sanity and right thinking in a world of turmoil and conflicting interests. The era of George VI will leave its beneficent mark not only on Empire history but on world history. That is a consummation devoutly to be wished and towards which we can all work.'

The Proclamation of George VI

Driving rain which persisted at Abergavenny on Monday 13, December 1936, marred the ceremony of the Proclamation of King George VI. An outdoor ceremony was out of the question and the formal proceedings were staged in the Town Hall. Owing to the bad weather and the fact that the arrangements were not generally known, there were only a few people present.

After the sounding of a fanfare by two buglers the Mayor at once proceeded to read the Proclamation which had been issued from St James Palace on 12th December. When he had finished, another fanfare by the buglers was followed by three hearty cheers for the King and the singing of a verse of the National Anthem, after which those present dispersed.

Subsequently a peal was rung on the bells of St Marys. Forty-one clashes were sounded in honour of the King's 41st birthday.'

Coronation of King George VI

On May 12th, 1937 the *Abergavenny Chronicle* commented:

'There had never been a greater display of royal fervour in Abergavenny and district than on the occasion of the crowning of King George VI and Queen Elizabeth. In town, village and hamlet it was a day of great rejoicing and young and old participated in a memorable celebration.

For a week previously, Abergavenny had started preparing for the great day and business people and private residents had given to much pains and expense to ensure that the town presented a festive appearance. From Frogmore Street to the bottom of Cross Street was a fluttering of colour. Flags of all sizes, streamers, pennants and festoons floated in the breeze and shop premises displayed a variety of decorative schemes and designs. From the Town Hall to the bottom of Cross Street it was particularly impressive with its profusion of streamers across the street. The front of the Town Hall looked very effective with half-a-dozen tubs painted red, white and blue, holding up similarly painted poles, which suspended festoons of the Coronation colours.

There was probably not a private house throughout the town which did not display some evidence of the Coronation spirit and some were lavish in their decorations. Streets vied with one another, and Mill Street and Stanhope Street were fine examples of combined effort. Not only were the houses well decorated, but even the lampposts and downpipes. The judges of decorations were the Mayor (Lt. Col. J. G. Bishop), Mrs Beverley Burton and Mr Max Beveridge. They gave the first prize for streets to Mill Street, the second to Stanhope Street and the third to Tudor Street and a special prize of 10s given by Mrs Beverley Burton was awarded to St John's Square.

The bells of St Mary's were rung at an early hour and throughout the day. A motor cycle and cycle rally paraded the thronged streets of the town. There were about twenty children on fairy cycles, tricycles etc and they were headed by the Salvation Army Band while the Borough Band headed the general procession, which was led by the Mayor and Mayoress in a car.

In addition to the cycles and cars, there were vans, lorries and buses, and many of them were decorated. The Fire Brigade, under Capt. H. C. Powell, turned out in full force, with the fire engine. The Ambulance van was also in the procession and the Police car with P. C. Parsons and P.C. J. Allen heading the adult procession.

There was a comedy element, too, which tickled the crowd. A man rode a hobby horse and was led by a small cowboy. A horse drew what purported to be a motor-car. This strange vehicle bore the inscription '1,000 miles non-stop, fuel two trusses of hay.'

The entertainments committee organised a non-stop dance at the Town Hall in the evening and music was provided by the Paramount Dance Band and the Rhythm Aces.

The *Abergavenny Chronicle* marked the occasion as a 'New Era' - which may have a beneficent influence on the future of the world. In these days of international strife and complexities, a steadying influence for sanity and peace, is required. It is at this moment that King George VI comes to the throne of England, called not by his own personal inclinations but by the will of the people, from the lowest to the highest, and he has accepted that call in a spirit of service. To carry on the monarchical principle surrendered by his elder brother, who might have been a great king if fate had not dealt unkindly with him is no easy task. Shy and retiring and with no pretence at oratory, King George VI has not had the opportunity of the late King of touching the hearts of the masses of the people. Most people had not even heard his voice, but now his qualities have been brought into the limelight and he is regarded at his true worth.

It is a pity that there could be no composite pictorial record of the whole country, to show Their Majesties the whole-hearted support and sympathy of the people on entering upon their onerous task. Abergavenny, from the highest to the lowest, has done itself proud, but Abergavenny is only typical of the country as a whole. Merthyr, Brynmawr and other places in the hills, which have suffered severely from the blight of industrial depression, have risen to the occasion and shown that in the sombreness of the slough of despond the fires of British Loyalty still burn bright.'

Princess Margaret visits Abergavenny

In November 1950 Princes Margaret came to Abergavenny in the course of her tour of South Wales. The gaily decorated streets were thronged with schoolchildren lined up in front of the crowds so that they could have a good view. The procession proceeded along the main streets to the Monmouth Road and then along Holywell Road en route to Coed Glas where the Princess paid a visit of inspection to the County Council nursery.

On arrival at the nursery Princess Margaret was presented with a bouquet by little Margaret Wood (daughter of the Matron) and was then introduced by Lord Raglan (Lord Lieutenant of Monmouthshire) to the Mayor and Mayoress of Abergavenny (Alderman and Mrs S.D.S James) and other dignitaries.

Princess Margaret was impressed with the condition of the twenty three infants and inquired as to their background before they entered the institution. She was told that some were there because they came from neglected homes and others because of housing difficulties.

Before leaving, the Princess signed the visitor's book and the proceeded to Cefn Tilla Court where she had dinner as the guest of Lord Raglan.

Death of King George VI

On 6th February 1952, like all towns throughout the country, Abergavenny was profoundly shocked on learning that the King who was suffering from lung cancer had peacefully passed away in his sleep.

At Abergavenny Petty Sessions the Bench adjourned for several minutes on hearing the tragic news. Members of the local Licensed Victuallers Association at their annual meeting stood with heads bowed as a mark of respect to a much loved monarch.

The news of the King's death spread through the town like wildfire. In one large store the girl assistants had tears in their eyes as they were told, "The King has passed away." The flags at the Town Hall, Constitutional Club and other

King George VI

buildings in the town were flown at half-mast, and in common with other towns, it was announced that Abergavenny's two cinemas would not be open that night.

Soon after the news became known a telegram was sent from the Town Hall to the Queen. It read as follows:

'To Her Majesty, The Queen, Buckingham Palace, London S.W. The Mayor, Aldermen and burgesses of the borough of Abergavenny learn with the deepest regret of the death of their beloved King, and hasten to convey their heartfelt sympathy with you and all members of the Royal Family in their tragic bereavement.

John Bousfield Mayor'

Proclamation of Queen Elizabeth II

The Mayor, Councillor J. S. Bousfield, accompanied by robed members of the Town Council and a number of local magistrates emerged from the Town Hall to the front of the building. The Mayor stood on a special dais in his scarlet robes. Beside him were the bewigged Town Clerk, M. T. G. Hardwick and Canon M. E. Davies, M.A. (Vicar of St Mary's) wearing a black gown and the Mace bearer (Mr E. Walkley) in uniform shouldering the mace.

A fanfare arranged by Mr G. R. Silverthorne, rang out from the Town Hall and then the Mayor unrolled the proclamation and read it impassively and in a clear voice to the assembled throng, his voice carrying to the extreme limits of the crowd. After the reading, Canon Davies pronounced the Benediction and another fanfare and the playing of 'God Save the Queen' ended the simple ceremony and the crowd slowly dispersed.

Proclamation of Queen Elizabeth II in Abergavenny, February 1952

Memorial Service to King George VI

To the ancient parish church of St Mary came people from all walks of life to honour the memory of his late Majesty King George VI, who a few hours earlier had been laid to rest in St George's Chapel, Windsor, that hallowed shrine of English chivalry.

The Mayor, aldermen and council leaving the town hall for a memorial service to King George VI at St Mary's Priory Church in 1952

Present at the service was the Mayor (Councillor J.S. Bousfield) and members of the Town Council whose robes, as they approached the Church door, rustled in the slight afternoon breeze. Members of the Rural Council, Justices of the Peace and local police officers were there too, among the sorrowing congregation, which included many old age pensioners and some children, very quiet and seemingly a little overawed.

There was scarcely a vacant seat and the congregation sat motionless as the strains of Handel's moving 'Largo' rose from the organ and echoed round the church. The white surpliced choir of men and boys, together with the clergy, made their way to the chancel where they were to lead the congregation, which was still assembling.

The service began and the congregation, young and old alike, were in the words of the minister 'remembering with thankfulness, George, our late sovereign Lord, of Blessed Memory.'

In his address, the Vicar, Canon M.E. Davies reminded his listeners that the passing of the king had made the nation pause and consider. He emphasised that the king was called Defender of the Faith, and he defended the faith by living it. The fact that so many people had paid their tributes to King George emphasised the fact that he had been a very good man.

After the sermon had ended, for the first time in St Mary's since the days of Queen Victoria, those present feelingly sang 'God Save the Queen' which the Vicar had asked them to sing 'as a prayer'. Then the congregation knelt for the blessing, and the service was over. Slowly, led by the Mayor and his Councillors, with the mace-bearer at their head, reverently and thoughtfully they filed out of the church into the fading February sunlight.

Coronation Day 2nd June 1953

The Coronation of Elizabeth II in Westminster Abbey was a day in which the true communal spirit was shown for those who were the fortunate owners of television sets displayed a readiness to throw open their homes for the day and share their privilege with friends and neighbours. In the Town Hall a television set was installed for the occasion by Mr G. R. Silverthorne. At the Frogmore Street Memorial Hall, Curry's provided similar facilities for members of the Baptist Church.

The occasion was ushered in at Abergavenny by merry peals on the bells of St Mary's which were repeated throughout the day. Then at 12.30 a reverberating salute was fired from the Fairfield by the 637 H.A.A. Regiment Royal Artillery T.A.

The spectacular event of the evening was the bonfires on top of the Sugar Loaf and Deri arranged by the Boy Scouts in connection with a chain of similar bonfires throughout the country.

At a fancy dress dance at the Town Hall, the Mayor, Councillor J. A. Morgan lit a torch which was carried by relays of scouts who had a motor cycle escort through the town provided by the Auto Club.

As darkness fell, people in the town could see the progress of the Scouts up the mountainside by the gleam of their flaming torches. As they reached the summit rockets were fired to give a signal to Scouts on the Sugar Loaf to light their beacon. When fully ablaze the beacons lit up the whole countryside. Other beacons which could be seen from these eminences on the horizon recalled the old-time means of communicating throughout the land the approach of danger. The beacon lights of 1953, however, were symbols of peace and joy.

Coronation decorations in Mill Street

The decoration of the Town Hall was an outstanding feature of Cross Street. Its long facade lent itself to effective treatment. Apart from the street window display the profusion of geraniums and hydrangeas which adorned upper windows was artistically pleasing.

Mill Street in particular was a beautiful sight. The wealth of flags, banners and pennants was enhanced by a row of decorated tubs of rhododendrons which flanked the road and the variety of individual initiatives which marked the window displays. Mill Street truly lived up to its reputation for doing things on a grand scale.

Tudor Street was a blaze of colour from end to end and one had the impression of walking under a continuous canopy. It took one's breath away to gaze up at the street from the bottom end and the effect was overwhelming.

Stanhope Street, too, made a brave show and the community spirit was shown to the full. The profusion of overhead streamers in the whole length of the street was a fine sight. Artistry had been displayed in the arrangement of window box flowers and evergreens and downposts were also decorated.

Stanhope Street Coronation party

Union Road Coronation party

There were several other streets which were given a picturesque effect by the residents and a number of houses had taken elaborate pains to make their contribution to the general picture. A few showed individuality by introducing fairy lights and flood lighting.

Queen Elizabeth II Visits Abergavenny

Queen Elizabeth II and the Duke of Edinburgh paid the town a visit on Friday, May 10th 1963. They arrived in driving rain at Abergavenny Road Station, where they were welcomed by Lord Raglan, the Lord Lieutenant of Monmouthshire. From there they were driven up gaily decorated Cross Street to the Town Hall, where they were received by the Mayor. It was the first time in the history of the town that the royal standard was flown from a flagpole on the Town Hall tower.

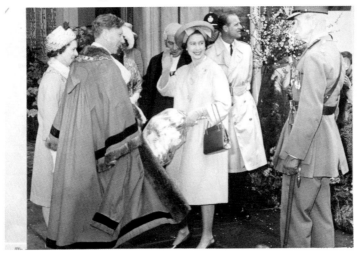

Queen Elizabeth arriving at the Town Hall on 10 May 1963. Also present are the Duke of Edinburgh, Lord Raglan and the Mayor and Mayoress, Councillor and Mrs G.R. Silverthorne

As they climbed the flower-lined steps to enter the freshly decorated Council Chamber, the Mayor apologised to the Queen for the lack of a traditional red carpet. When she was told of the Council decision to paint the steps with red liquid linoleum she remarked with a smile, 'I think it's a wonderful idea.'

An Abergavenny man who was temporarily living in Malaya wrote to the local paper a few weeks later to say that he was disgusted to read that Abergavenny Town Council were unable to afford a red carpet for the Queen's visit. He thought that after the large amount of money recently spent on a new recreation ground, surely the Town Council could have 'scraped together sufficient money to obtain some sort of a carpet.' As a loyal townsman he enclosed £1 to start a public collection to help the 'overt stricken' Town Council to be prepared for the next Royal visit.

Queen Elizabeth leaving the Town Hall on 10 May 1963

Queen Elizabeth was on her way to officially open the new £500,000 Headquarters of the Welsh Brigade at Cwrt y Gollen. The bells of St Mary's Church had been pealing out a welcome since the arrival of the royal train but they were silent as the Queen and the Duke inspected the interior of the ancient church. As they left the bells began a stirring quarter-peal in honour of Her Majesty.

They both showed considerable interest in the remarkable effigy of the Jesse tree and the monuments in the Herbert Chapel and the Queen expressed her hope that one day they would be restored to their former splendour. Next, they were shown the ancient choir stalls, which were occupied by the monks in pre-Reformation days and before returning to their car they spoke to several of the choir boys and the organist. They spent nearly 20 minutes in the church.

It was then a fifteen minute drive to Cwrt y Gollen where they were received by the Lord Lieutenant of Breconshire, Sir William Pinker. Five trumpeters standing on the roof of the brigade's new museum sounded a fanfare as the royal car drove to a dais where the Queen and Duke were welcomed by the colonels of the three regiments which make up the Welsh Brigade.

Queen Elizabeth II's Silver Jubilee

In 1977 the Queen's Silver Jubilee was celebrated in Abergavenny with street parties, church services and other festivities. The *Abergavenny Chronicle* printed a four page souvenir supplement which covered the Queen's 25 year reign and recalled her visit to the town in 1963.

A service was held at St Mary's Church, led by Canon Henry Sproule Jones and an address was given by the Assistant Bishop of Monmouth, the Right Reverend Edward Gresford Jones, who was High Almoner to the Queen for seventeen years.

Prince Charles Visits Abergavenny

On 24th July 2000 HRH Prince Charles, Patron of the St Mary's Priory Development Trust visited Abergavenny to open the new Priory Centre and the service of dedication in St Mary's was attended by more than 150 invited members of the congregation. During his two hour visit the Prince met representatives of various groups within the Church and people who had been involved with the work of the Development Trust.

After the service the Prince was given a conducted tour of the restored Herbert Chapel. He was then invited to open the new St Mary's Priory Centre which stands on the south side of the church on the site of the old Priory House and the refectory of the original Benedictine Priory.

The Prince commented: 'As proud patron of this project, I could not be more delighted to come here this afternoon, albeit briefly. I have been so impressed with what I have seen. I hope and pray that the next stage of the development will be equally successful and look forward to coming back to see the Abbot's Garden and the Tithe Barn.' He then unveiled a slate plaque commemorating his visit and the opening of the Priory Centre.

In October 2008, Prince Charles kept his promise and returned to Abergavenny to officially open the nearby Tithe Barn which had been restored and converted into a Heritage Centre.

HRH Prince Charles with Simon Boyle, Lord Lieutenant of Gwent, Canon Jeremy Winston, Vicar of St Mary's and Sir Trefor Morris, Chairman of the Development Trust
Picture by Malcolm Lewis

Chapter Nineteen
WAR AND PEACE

With grave and anxious feelings we have entered upon the grim encounter which has been forced upon us. There are dark days in front of us. We expect disasters as well as victories, but calm and determined we shall win through the crisis by united efforts.

Pontypool Free Press 1914

The Zulu War

One of the most famous of the local heroes who fought in the Zulu War of 1879 was Private John Williams who was born in Merthyr Road, Abergavenny on May 24th, 1858 and baptised two days later in the old Franciscan Mission which was the original church of Our Lady and St Michael. When he was about 5 years of age the family moved to 3, Penywain Cottages, near St Dials, in the parish of Llantarnam, near Cwmbran, his father having obtained work locally as a labourer.

John William Fielding VC
(alias John Williams)

John Williams is famous as the last survivor of the heroic band who were awarded the Victoria Cross for their bravery in the epic battle at Rorke's Drift when 85 British held at bay 3,000 Zulus.

His real name was John Fielding and he took the name Williams when he enlisted on January 22, 1877, two years to the day before the fight at Rorke's Drift. He used a false name because he had run away from home anddid not want his family to know that he had joined the army. Three months later he enlisted in the old 24th Foot (which in 1881 became known as the South Wales Borderers and many years later was absorbed into the Royal Regiment of Wales)

In 1929 at the age of 71 and then living in Cwmbran, he described the events at Rorke's Drift as follows:

> 'My company was stationed at Rorke's Drift, a mission station which consisted of a few low buildings. We were in charge of the hospital as well as the commissariat. There were 95 of us at that post and we knew that 3000 Zulus, flushed with their victory at Isandhlwana, and mad for further slaughter, would soon be upon us.
>
> It was 3.30 in the afternoon when we saw them begin to round the hill, and never did an enemy seem to have an easier prey. We had time only to improvise barricades with biscuit tins and mealie bags, when they were upon us.
>
> We realised the seriousness of the affair, but we had no time to sit down and think about it. There was one watchword for all of us: "we must keep the enemy at bay." I heard that many times during the night that followed.
>
> When the attack started we had precious little time for thinking and for the next eighteen hours we knew all about it.'

He was reluctant to say much more, just adding: 'It was a terrible time. All we were concerned with was to keep the enemy at bay and to save the patients if we could. When the fight ended, I had just two rounds of ammunition left.'

John Williams was one of eleven men who won the Victoria Cross in this famous battle which took place on 22nd January 1879. Seven went to the men of the 24th, and this was the greatest number of VCs ever awarded to one regiment in one action. The VC is the highest military award for gallantry and these men were awarded the honour in view of their stubborn resistance to the force of between 3,000 and 4,000 Zulu warriors who attacked Rorke's Drift with such bravery.

The Boer War

The 20th century began with Britain at war against the Boers in South Africa which rumbled on until 1902. Many volunteers were moved out of Abergavenny by train to fight in South Africa while at home two funds were launched to provide for the wives and families of servicemen.

Lord Roberts

On August 30th 1905, Field Marshall Lord Roberts, who had commanded British troops in the Second Boer War from 1900, arrived in Abergavenny, having spent the previous night at Nevill Court, the residence of the Marquess of Abergavenny. A mounted escort ushered Lord Roberts to St Mary's Church, where he was to unveil a War Memorial tablet in memory of the Abergavenny Volunteers who fell in the Boer War (1899-1902).

Field Marshall Lord Roberts arriving at St Mary's Priory Church

The *Abergavenny Chronicle* reported that:

'Such a gathering had seldom been seen in that church, the elite of the county were assembled. The difference of creed as well as of rank were put aside for once to do honour to the gallant soldier who had come to show his sympathy with them in their desire to perpetuate the memory of the dear fellows who had gone forth to fight the enemy of their country and their sovereign.

Councillor Z. Wheatley, addressing Lord Roberts said:

'My Lord, it gives me very great pleasure, as the chairman of the local war fund, to have the honour of asking your Lordship to unveil this tablet. Our thoughts run back to the early stages of the war in South Africa, when our army was suffering reverses, and an appeal was made for volunteers to go out and fight for the honour of the Empire. We know how readily our own volunteers and those of the colonies responded to the appeal. Amongst the units which formed part of that large army, was that from Abergavenny; and we felt proud to watch their various actions, and we know how they merited the high opinion we had formed of them...'

Lord Roberts was then presented with the Freedom of the Borough 'for the eminent military services which he had rendered to the Empire'. This ceremony was followed by a public luncheon at the Town Hall where the Marquess toasted Lord Roberts and said that it was not his intention to detail all the great services that the Field Marshall had rendered to the country; they knew all about them, the world knew all about them. He would only say that they were all proud to see that distinguished man amongst them in their small but very ancient town.

The Great War

The Declaration that 'Great Britain is at war with Germany' was made at 7pm on Tuesday 4th August 1914, following the summary rejection by Germany of a British ultimatum to which an answer was demanded by midnight.

Germany in alliance with Austria and Hungary was now at war with Great Britain, France, Russia and Belgium, while Austria was at war with Serbia. The following announcement was issued from the Foreign Office:-

'Owing to the summary rejection by the German Government of the request made by His Majesty's Government for assurances that the neutrality of Belgium would be respected, his Majesty's Ambassader in Berlin has received his passports, and his Majesty's Government has declared to the German Government that a state of war exists between Great Britain and Germany as from 11 pm on August 4th.'

Three days later the *Abergavenny Chronicle* commented:

'Great Britain is at war with Germany. The declaration was made by Great Britain at seven o' clock on Tuesday night, following the summary rejection of a British ultimatum to which an answer was demanded by midnight. Proclamations of war were signed at Buckingham Palace at a meeting of the Privy Council on Tuesday night.'

'Abergavenny, as was only to be expected of such a patriotic and loyal town, has been stirred to its very depths of feeling by the momentous conflict of rival nations. The shadow of 'Armogeddon' has blotted out every subject but war and rumours of wars.

Troops leaving for France at the GWR Station during the Great War

Soldiers marching through Abergavenny in 1914

Our town has responded nobly to its country's call, and her sons have gone forth with a fixed and grim determination to do their duty with credit to themselves and to their nation. When the order for mobilising the Territorials was put into effect, and the 3rd Monmouthshire Battalion was assembled at Abergavenny from the outlying districts, ready for departure to Pembroke Dock, there were scenes of enthusiasm such as have not been witnessed for many a long day in either the peaceful or tumultuous history of the ancient borough.

Abergavenny is in what is probably a unique position in being without a Mayor or Deputy Mayor, for both have been called out in service with the Territorial Force. The Mayor (Lieut Col J. H. G. Harris), commands the 1st Herefords and the Deputy Mayor (Major J. G. Bishop) is on the field staff of the 3rd Monmouthshire Battalion.

Two advance parties had left early in the morning, but it was nearly 10 am before the main body took their departure for the Great Western Railway Station, where special trains were in readiness and they were entrained in half battalions. The main streets had long before this been packed with a singing mass of humanity, for thousands of people had congregated to witness the final scenes. The men were in cheerful spirits and as they swung along at a rapid pace, sang and joked and shouted "goodbye" to all and sundry, they might, to judge by their demeanour, have been going on a holiday. The women folk, who looked with glistening eyes at the retreating forms of their husbands, sons or brothers, were sad.

Suddenly, there came a shout from the ranks, "Are we downhearted?" and in a reverberating roar the response was "No!" And so the tramp of feet died away and this band of brave men passed from the sight of their friends and relatives.

The deputy Territorials numbered about 700 and about 50 National Reservists had also answered the call to arms. They and the new recruits would be drilled in Bailey Park, the tents and equipment which had been used by the cadets having been placed at their disposal. Abergavenny was also to provide its quota to the Welsh Horse, local horsemen in the district having responded readily to the appeal of Owen Rhoscomyl (Captain Vaughan of Cardiff). Local ambulance men, too, had shown themselves ready to respond to an appeal from their headquarters at Shrewsbury to offer their services with the expeditionary force.'

Alderman Z. Wheatley, the recently elected Mayor of Abergavenny said in his ceremonial address in September, 1914:

'We are living in very critical times at present and there are various duties devolving upon the Council. Our principal duty is to do all we can to encourage men to enlist in the Army. It is a matter of life and death to us, and we must each one and all do all within our power to secure the fulfilment of Lord Kitchener's requirements, so that he can go forward in the work of bringing success to our arms. It may not be out of place if I state what Abergavenny has done on behalf of Lord Kitchener's Army.

Since the 3rd of August, acting as the recruiting officer for this district, I have issued cerificates for no fewer than 405 recruits from Abergavenny (applause). Then we have to think of the care and consideration of the wives and dependants of our brave men who have gone forth to fight our battles and if need be to give up their lives, and it behoves us to do all we can on behalf of their wives and families and other dependants.

When we have done all these things we can surely say we have heard the call of Lord Nelson and have answered it by doing our duty.'

In October 1914, Maindiff Court became known as the 1st Monmouthshire Convalescent Home under the Red Cross Society who that month took in 40 Belgian soldiers who had received injuries whilst gallantly defending their country.

They arrived from Ramsgate and Sandgate, travelling by the L&NWR line via Shrewsbury and alighting at Junction Station. They were all in a convalescent state. One man had a leg missing and another was minus an arm; such injuries bearing silent testimony to what they had gone through. All the men were able to walk though and even the unfortunate man who had lost his leg was able to get about on crutches.

Cars were in readiness at the station to convey them to Maindiff Court and it was not long before they were comfortably quartered for the night and receiving every attention from the staff.

On December 27, 1915, Edward H. Pearce sent a letter from the Front to his parents in Abergavenny:

'I enjoyed Christmas Day all right. I was lucky to be at headquarters and not with the battalion, as they were in the trenches on that day and lost a few more members. I am in the pink and feel fit for anything that comes along. I expect I shall have to join the battalion next time they go in the trenches, but I am not sure.'

On December 30th, 1915 he wrote:

'Just a line to let you know I am in the pink and in the trenches. We got here about 6 pm last night. I passed out of my class all right. There were six of us and I was 2nd on the list, so it was not so bad. I am on the wire at the trenches now.

Just fancy us in a dug-out in the trenches with a buzzer stuck in the ground between us, one with a receiver fixed on his head and the other having a snooze. We take it in turns, night and day. We are in for four days. This is not so bad, as the dug-out we have is dry and warm inside, but outside the door it is up to your waist in mud and water.'

The Marquess of Abergavenny took a keen interest in the Royal Engineers based at Abergavenny and in March 1915, accompanied by the Hon Mrs Duberly, he was a constant visitor to the bridges which had been erected on his land and to other engineering work. On one occasion he visited the trial trenches and despite his 88 years, went into one of the dug-outs. He also showed his thoughtfulness for the men by bringing them a number of packets of tobacco and boxes of matches.

Private W. B. Barry of B Company of the 3rd Monmouthshire Regiment wrote to his parents in Abergavenny on March 12. 1915:

'I have had my baptism of fire, as I was in the support trenches for 24 hours. I can assure you that it was fine sport, crossing the fields with the bullets flying around, although I had one narrow escape, one bullet passing within half an inch of my head. It is remarkable how little notice one takes of things when in the trenches because all one has to do is keep down and you will be all right. On our way back we passed through a rather large village and every house in it had been smashed to nothing; also the church. I sat all day in the trenches and watched the shells from the German guns falling in this same village.

We must have travelled about 500 miles from where we landed, so you see I have moved about a bit since I landed here. I expect by the time you get this letter I shall be in the trenches again, but don't you worry, because I shall be all right.'

Private A. E. James of the Machine Gun Section, 3rd Monmouthshire Regiment wrote home on 26 March, 1915:

'I expect that you will think I have forgotten you, but this is the first time since we have come out of the trenches that I have had a chance to write as we have been moving about so much. The Gun Section has been in the trenches. We went in last Friday week and came out Wednesday night, so we had five days and five nights without coming out; so I think we had our share for the first time in, but I am glad to say we came out safely.

We had two killed and eight wounded out of our battalion, so you can gues we had it a bit rough. I did not think we should come out alive on the Tuesday, as the Germans bombarded our trenches with their big guns. The trench I was in had it the worst I think, as they knew we had the machine gun there. I thought our number was up, as they shelled us for an hour and ten minutes. One good thing was we had fine weather during the time we were there, only it was very cold at night. I had your parcel the day after we came out of the trenches; what a treat the cake was; we didn't half enjoy it!'

Sergeant A. F. Davies of A Company 3rd Monmouthshire Regiment wrote on April 9 1915:

'We have had about six killed and a dozen wounded, so far, in our battalion, but none of the Abergavenny boys yet. The trenches are not so bad and are fairly safe if you don't want to be too inquisitive and want to see what is going on all round. The most danger is from the shells, and when they do start shelling, all we have to do is to lie still and take our chance. It is nice to watch what damage the shells are going to do - that is when they fly over us; we watch where they drop, then the mud flies.

It is the aeroplanes that worry the Germans. Our airmen are very daring and it is a treat to see how they take things when they are being shelled.'

Private E. T. Bowen of the Signalling Section of the 3rd Monmouthshire Regiment wrote home to Yew Tree Cottage, Mardy, Abergavenny on April 25 1915:-

'The trenches we have been in were made under fire. They are not dug out much, but built up with sand bags. Every battalion when they go in try to improve their trench as much as possible. When a shell explodes on the parapets you see the sandbags go up, some about 10 feet; it is a sight. We say to ourselves, "How many have copped it," and wonder where the next will explode. It is possible for a shell to explode at say three yards in front and do you no damage, save plaster you with mud; but if it comes the other way, well it's all up - you go "west," as we call it. The weather is clearing up, although it rained yesterday.'

By the middle of May 1915, serious losses among the 3rd Battalion brought into greater prominence the urgent need for recruiting. An impromptu meeting was called by the Mayor at the Town Hall to help recruitment and to express sympathy with the bereaved.

It was hoped that all eligible young men who did not have greater responsibilities at home would realise their duty to their country and that all employers would remove any obstacle in the way of young men enlisting and would as far as possible substitute female labour. No fewer than 1,500 recruits were needed to enable the necessary draft to be sent out from the Reserve Battalion and to bring both Reserve Battalions up to the required strength.

On June 18th 1915, Abergavenny Town Council expressed their confidence in Lord Kitchener for the admirable way in which he had conducted the war as far as lay in his power. A man of that personality who could raise an Army of three million men in a few months deserved the support of the community instead of the censure to which he had been subjected in certain quarters.

The Drill Hall in Baker Street was used by the 3rd Battalion Territorial Force, Monmouthshire Regiment and it was a purpose built military building, large enough for soldiers to practice marching and drilling. Underneath the ground floor was a shooting range. The building has now been converted into a cinema.

After several months of basking in the splendid hospitality of the townspeople of Abergavenny and in the enjoyment of the beautiful scenery around the town, the three companies of the Royal Engineers left Abergavenny for encampment at Winchester.

Cheshire Brigade camp at Abergavenny

On the anniversary of the start of World War I, the Mayor of Abergavenny reviewed the work which has been done in the town towards raising money for the war effort. Over £2,800 had been raised for various war funds and the local Red Cross working party had distributed about 4,000 garments to the troops. If one took the population of Abergavenny at 10,000 it worked out at £2,800 per 1,000 contributed by the inhabitants of the town.

German prisoners being escorted from work on a farm during 1914-18 War

In February 1916 a captured German gun arrived in Abergavenny by the 2.38 pm train. It was loaded to the town for exhibition purposes. The gun was collected from the GWR station by Captain J. R. Jacob and several non-commissioned officers and a num,ber of the invalided men of the 3rd Monmouthshire Battalion. They fastened ropes to the carriage and pulled it into town with their progress marked by a bombardment of snowballs from youngsters.

It had been intended to take the gun to the castle but owing to the weather it was taken to the Market Hall instead. A large number of people gathered there to witness its arrival.

The gun, a 15 pounder with a 3 ⅛ inch bore was dated 1907. On it was inscribed the Latin motto 'Pro gloria et patria.' The breech had been removed, so that it was not in working condition.

The Mayor, Alderman Z. Wheatley, made a speech and said that on behalf of the town he had much pleasure in accepting the gun for a few weeks. They had tried to get one sited in Abergavenny previously, but had been told to wait intil the war was over, when it could be established how many guns had been captured. They would then be divided out as far as possible. Every town wanted a gun and at the present time there were not sufficient to go round, so Abergavenny could only have the loan of this gun for a short time.

In November 1918 news reached Abergavenny that the Great War had at last come to an end at 11 o'clock on the morning of Monday 11th November, following the signing of the armistice six hours earlier .

Mayor Z. Wheatley received the official telegram announcing the news at about 10.50 am, and in accordance with a previous decision by the Town Council, the town clock was allowed to run down so that the bells were continuously striking, as an intimation to townspeople of the receipt of the news. Before long there was a crowd outside the Town Hall and the Mayor read the telegram to them. The announcement was received with cheers. Then John Owen started the singing of the National Anthem and the crowd fervently responded. Cheers were then given for the King and the Mayor.

In a very short space of time the whole town was decorated with flags and bunting. Everywhere, people seemed to have found flags from various sources and it was said that there had not been such a display in Abergavenny since the somewhat riotous days of Mafeking. Hooters were sounded and fog signals were discharged on the railway line during the day.

There was a general feeling that on such a great day work was out of the question and tradespeople readily responded to the Mayor's suggestion that they should close their premises for the afternoon. Meanwhile the bells of St Mary's had been rung, although the Chief Constable had intimated to the Mayor that according to his instructions from the competent military authority this must not be done until their permission had come through.

A thanksgiving service held at St Mary's Church was said to be the most memorable event of the kind that had ever been held in Abergavenny. The Mayor and members and officials of the Town Council proceeded to the church in procession, but before they arrived the interior was crowded to capacity. With one common assent the whole town seemed to make its way to St Mary's and very quickly the building became packed with people.

There had never been such a congregation in St Mary's in the whole of its long history. Members of all denominations were there, and many no doubt of no professed religion at all who had been driven out of their customary apathy by the spirit of thankful news.

The Vicar, Reverend M. E. Davies, conducted the service and in his short address or sermon he said that peace had not been signed, but the armistice had been signed and they had reason to believe that the signing of the armistice meant the end of the war altogether. They had gladly come together to thank God that the armistice had been signed and that there was no fighting at the present moment. When the terms of peace were signed, that was the time for citizenship, the time to fight as citizens for the good of everyone of this nation, which had been bled for and died for in every class of the community.

In the afternoon the Mayor sent the following telegram to the Prime Minister:-

'Mayor, aldermen and burgesses of Abergavenny rejoice with you at the signing of the armistice, and place absolute confidence in your leadership in the settlement of peace.'

Peace Day Celebrations

On July 19, 1919, celebrations were held to mark the end of the Great War. Every city, every town, every parish and every hamlet had its own programme of celebrations to mark the end of the Great War. Everywhere there was a spirit of rejoicing, especially among the children. It was and rightly so, the Children's Day.

The main object of the programme at Abergavenny was to give the youngsters a good time and they evidently enjoyed themselves, in spite of the downpour of rain in the evening. The streets of the town were well decorated with flags, bunting, streamers and other decorations.

A souvenir programme had been prepared for the occasion and this included not only the day's programme but photographs of the King and Queen and Prince of Wales, the Mayor and Mayoress and officials, a record of war work performed by Abergavenny organisations, a list of distinctions gained by local men and women in the war and the names of 210 men who made the supreme sacrifice. The latter were remembered by the hanging of laurel wreaths on the war shrine outside the Town Hall, while underneath was a table on which relatives and friends placed flowers in memory of the fallen.

The programme commenced with bell ringing at St Mary's Parish Church by the Abergavenny Bell ringers who rang merry peals throughout the day. Athletic sports took place in Bailey Park from 10.00 am to 1.00 pm.

In the afternoon the schoolchildren met at the various day schools and marched to the cabstand in Frogmore Street where they were joined by the Mayor, members and officials of the Town Council, Fire Brigade and Borough Silver Band, who had assembled at the General Market. The procession headed by the Borough Silver Band, proceeded along Frogmore Street, High Street, Cross Street, Monk Street and Hereford Road to Bailey Park. The children assembled round the platform in the centre of the park, on which members of the Council and officials of the day occupied seats. To the accompaniment of the Borough Silver Band, the children sang two verses of the National Anthem and a short address by the Mayor followed:-

'Ladies and Gentlemen, Boys and Girls - Today we have come to the last page of the book, wherein has been written the history of the most terrible warfare that the world has ever known between civilised people. Nearly five years ago Germany plunged this world into a murderous war and we have by the energy and levation of our people and that of the Allies, defeated them and robbed them of the great victory that they anticipated.

The British Empire had to put forth all her vast strength and to send 8,654,000 soldiers, 450,000 sailors and 300,000 mercantile seamen into the struggle. It is estimated that the Allies had to sacrifice 5,000,000 of their noblest lives and spend no less than 25,000,000,000 millions in this effort to secure the freedom that we all so much love.

Abergavenny has played her part and responded nobly to every call that has been made. Out of a population of about 8,000 no fewer than 1,600 of her bravest sons and daughters went forth in response to the nation's call. Ninety-one of them have brought honours to the Borough and while we admired these, our hearts go out specially on this day of peace to the relatives of the 210 men who have made the supreme sacrifice.

We shall close the festivities tonight by joining with others in forming a ring or chain of bonfires or beacon lights throughout this Empire of ours. It may be a coincidence, but it is remarkably strange, that on the 19th July in the year 1588, or 331 years ago, another chain of Beacon fires was lit, and that was to celebrate our victory over the Spanish Armada.'

The 3rd Mons Memorial

On March 25th 1920 it was announced that a War Memorial of the 3rd Battalion, Monmouthshire Regiment was to be erected at the bottom of Frogmore Street near the Baptist Church, on a site given by the borough of Abergavenny.

Abergavenny is synonymous with the 3rd Battalion. First formed around 1860, the regiment went through changes of name and status until, in 1908, Colonel W. D. Steel VD (then lieutenant) was given the task of raising two new companies from Blaina and Cwm. The companies conbined to form the Abergavenny Company, popularly nicknamed 'The Bulldogs' after a breed of dog peculiar to the town. Their first ever camp was in Abergavenny, beginning the association which still exists. The Abergavenny Company eventually spawned the 3rd Batallion.

Essentially a border regiment, it nevertheless drew recruits from across the valley and border areas. The regiment built on a tradition which had seen Monmouthshire men fight in the 1346 battle of Crécy; under Harry of Monmouth at Agincourt in 1415 and at the Peninsular, Crimea and South African Wars.

In 1797 the Loyal Abergavenny Corps of Volunteer Infantry was founded and commissioned by King George III in 1803. The Corps was incorporated in the 24th Regiment of the South Wales Borderers in 1834 and given the title 4th Volunteer Battalion of the Regiment. In the wars which followed right up to and including the South African (Boer) War many volunteers of the Battalion served as volunteers with the regular battalions.

When Lord Haldane created the Territorial Army in 1907 the title of the Regiment became the 3rd Monmouthshire Regiment. The area covered by this regiment included Abertillery, Ebbw Vale, Tredegar and the borough of Abergavenny and the rural district.

On February 4, 1915, the Battalion embarked for France. After bitter front-line service, on May 8th, obeying the order to stand to the last man in the Second Battle of Ypres, the Regiment was practically annihilated. Without giving an inch of ground to the enemy the Regiment lost 703 in killed and wounded. By August 24, 1916 the loss was so great that only 50 riflemen and a few officers remained.

In the Second World War the Regiment again distinguished itself at the Battle of Caen and although sustaining heavy losses in killed and wounded was chosen as the spearhead of the 2nd army in facing the bridgehead. The remains of the Regiment fought in the great advance through France, Belgium and up to the Rhine.

In the reorganisation of 1947 the role of the 3rd Mon Regiment was necessarily changed and its title became the 637 Heavy Anti-aircraft Regiment of the Royal Artillery and in recognition of the gallant and distinguished services, His Majesty King George VI specially authorised the inclusion of '3rd Mons' in the full title. They thus became possessed of the 3rd Mon King's and Regimental Colours which were the work and gift of Lady Llanover and had been presented to the 3rd Monmouthshire Regiment by His

Majesty King Edward VII on June 19th 1904. The first Colonel of the Regiment was Major-General the Lord Treowen, who was succeeded on his death in 1933 by the Colonel - the Lord Glanusk.

This realistic figure of an infantryman stands at the junction of Frogmore Street and Pen-y-pound. It was erected by public subscriptions from the people of Abertillery, Ebbw Vale, Cwm, Tredegar, Rhymney and Abergavenny as a memorial to the officers and men of the 3rd Battalion Monmouthshire Regiment who fell in the Great War. The statue weighs 25cwt and depicts a soldier in full fighting kit being realistic even down to the mud on his boots. He stands on a plinth of Cornish grey granite and leaning wearily on his rifle gazes at the passing shoppers. It was sculpted in bronze by the London based artist Gilbert Ledward RGA, who was a young man at the time, but later became one of the leading sculptors in the country.

The memorial was unveiled on 29th October 1921 by Lord Treowen C.B., C.M.G., Hon Colonel of the 3rd Mons and Lord Lieutenant of the county. He commented that the statue depicted 'one of those typical citizen soldiers who, giving up their ordinary vocations, performed such deeds of valour on the fields of Flanders and elsewhere. He possesses a wonderfully expressive face representing the whole gamut of human emotions. It speaks of love of home and country and comrades and sorrowful memories of pals no more.'

Almost 5,000 people were gathered in Frogmore Street and Brecon Road to watch the unveiling and the moving ceremony ended with the playing of the Last Post and Reveille and the singing of the Welsh and English national anthems.

After the unveiling Lord Treowen handed over the Memorial to the care of the Corporation and burgesses of Abergavenny. Colonel J. G. Bishop OBE, the Mayor, received the charge on behalf of the borough and said that it would be handed down to their successors as a sacred trust.

An old soldier commented in November 1926:

'Ever since its erection, I have been impressed by its facial expression. It is the outstanding work of the artist and an honest expression of the civilian soldier who served in the Great War. It suggests, to me, a soldier artist's impression of soldier life on active service. Its features are food for thought. Perhaps if I express my interpretation of it, it may have new meaning to all who look upon it, not merely as a work of art, but also as a message to the age.

It is a Memorial to remind us of duty well done. I see the face of a soldier returning home from the line after perhaps a week or so of active service in the trenches, to his company's billets a few miles behind the firing-line. He reaches a front where the lorries meet them to convey them down. He is waiting to load up. The strain and tension are relaxed; he has time for thought and meditation about other things after the strain of line work.

Leaning upon his rifle, relieving the weight of his kit, his thoughts turn to Blighty - to Home, to wife and children or parents. There he reviews the situation. Then Tommy says, "Is it worth it all?" Fortified by the patience and pluck of those at home he carries on until victory is assured to his country, the country he loves.'

Mons Day is held on the nearest Saturday to May 8 each year, and the veterans assemble at the Royal British Legion Headquarters (sold in 2011) in Nevill Street to march to the memorial and pay homage, at a service, commemorating those who died to ensure freedom for future generations.

Following the 1939-45 war an inscription was added to those serving in the Second World War. Another plaque added to the memorial in 1995 reads as follows:

'This plaque commemorates on the 8th May 1995 the 80th anniversaryof the 3rd Mons Memorial Day in the 1914-18 War. On that day in 1915 the battalion suffered heavy casualties in the second battle of Ypres. This monument is the work of Gilbert Ledward, O.B.E, R.A., F.R.B.S. Sculptor.'

In September 2005 the memorial was cleaned and layered in a micro-crystallised wax which would help to preserve the statue. The work was funded by Monmouthshire County Council's Local Agenda 21 Grant Scheme and the Bryn-y-Cwm Area capital fund to a total of £1,600.

Roll of Honour

Abergavenny's Roll of Honour in the Great War contains nearly 1400 names. For a population of just under 9,000 this was a fine record. There is a memorial in the north aisle of St Mary's Priory Church to the parishioners of St Mary's and Christchurch who lost their lives in the 1914-18 war; the 79 officers and 946 men of the South Wales Borderers 24th Regiment and Monmouthshire Regiment who died in in 1939-45 and all those who lost their lives at sea. There is also a brass memorial to the men of the staff of Pen-y-fal Hospital who died in the Great War.

War memorial in St Mary's Priory Church

The Second World War

When Hitler invaded Poland on the 1st of September 1939, Britain required him to withdraw or face war with this country. He did not and Prime Minister Neville Chamberlain announced from Downing Street at 11.15am on Sunday, September 3rd that the country was now at war with Germany.

The outbreak of World War II caused the Abergavenny Town Council to abandon its normal agenda of business in order to discuss 'emergency matters'. Alderman W. Rosser, the town's mayor was chairing the meeting and he spoke of his hopes that the conflict would be short and he expressed his confidence that the people of Abergavenny would 'maintain the high traditions of the Borough during the period of conflict'.

Within a short time, Abergavenny received about 700 evacuees from the city of Birmingham which was regarded as a likely target for bombing raids. A total of 1,500 children were originally expected and the townfolk prepared to find homes for the children, their teachers and adult helpers. However, less than half that number arrived at Abergavenny Station and they were all soon found accommodation in local homes. Large numbers of troops also began arriving in Abergavenny.

At Christmas 1939, 350 parcels were despatched to members of His Majesty's forces at home and overseas. These parcels contained a woollen comfort, chocolate, cigarettes, sweets, book, playing cards and writing paper and envelopes. The cost of this parcel was approximately 6s.

In May 1940, Anthony Eden announced the formation of the Local Defence Volunteers. Men aged 17 to 65 were invited to join and within hours 250,000 had volunteered. In July of that year the force was renamed the Home Guard.

The 3rd Battalion of the Monmouthshire Regiment

Soon after World War One, the Battalion amalgamated with the Brecknock Battalion, later reverting to 3rd Mons, 53rd Welsh Division. In mid-1942, together with the 4th KLSI and 1st Herefords it became the 3rd Mons, 159 Armoured Division - fighting its way from Normandy into Belgium and Holland through to the ancient forest Teutburgerwald in North-west Germany.

There, overlooking the Dortmund-Emms Canal, outnumbered by a force of elite German officer cadets, the casualties sustained weakened the Battalion to such an extent it was withdrawn from the Division. All within one month of victory on May 8, 1945.

Following the last ever battle fought by the battalion, a Victoria Cross was awarded to Corporal Edward Chapman for his outstanding bravery. During that last battle despite all odds, the battalion did not give an inch. Veterans believe a fitting epitaph is contained in a quote from General 'Pip' Roberts CB DSO MC - 'They never flinched or faltered.'

War Weapons Week 1941

The following telegram was received by the Mayor from the Chancellor of the Exchequer, Sir Kingsley Wood:

> 'I send you my warmest good wishes for the success of Abergavenny's War Weapons Week. A fine result of the first year's War Savings Campaign is the best encouragement we can possibly have to redouble our efforts. To meet the mounting costs of the War, it is becoming increasingly clear that all of us are in duty bound to spend as little and lend as much to the Nation as we possibly can. Selfish spending to-day is weakening our War effort. Civic effort is of outstanding value in this vital campaign, and I am sure that the Citizens of Abergavenny will do their utmost during War Weapons Week to reach a total of which they may be justly proud..'

The Second War Weapons Week

Abergavenny had the proud distinction of being the first borough in Great Britain to hold a second War Weapons Week. People were not asked to give anything but to lend as much as they could. The aim was to raise £60,000.

The residents were told that they should regard the lending of the money as a privilege and not something which should be looked upon with disfavour. The country needed still more and more voluntary savings. The Chancellor of the Exchequer made that quite clear when he said that he expected at least 3 million pounds of voluntary savings that year. The national income would be increased by 500 million pounds during the next year.

Servicemen gave their services and risked their lives, and the least the public could do was to give their money. Servicemen depended on personal courage and equipment, and it was the duty of the nation to see that they did not go short of anything they required.

Brigadier Mascall, DSO, OBE, said that he felt greatly honoured that he had been invited to inaugurate Abergavenny's second War Weapons Week. In the past eighteen months he had come to know that the citizens of Abergavenny were a patriotic and generous people and it was no surprise to him to find that led by their determined and resolute Mayor, they shared with Leeds the honour of being the first towns in England and Wales to hold a War Weapons Week. He had no shadow of doubt that the second week would be worthy of the first effort.

He was confident that once again the patriotic and generous citizens of Abergavenny would produce a sum which would put their previous record in the shade, be an honour to their ancient town, a compliment to their Mayor, an encouragement to the Chancellor of the Exchequer, and an example to every other town in the British Isles.

The Arrival of More Evacuees

In 1941 over 7,000 children and teachers evacuated from the South East of England arrived in Monmouthshire. They were from Chatham, Gillingham, Dover, Rochester and Folkestone. Of these 403 children and 33 adults came to Abergavenny to be billeted in the rural district.

Crowds of people assembled to await their arrival at the GWR station, along the streets and at the Market Hall. At the station were Mr S.B. Davies, representing the Chairman of the Rural Council, the Reverend C. Bews and the Clerk (Mr T.G. Hardwick), who had the duty of organising the allocation in the various parishes. Also present were the Mayor (Alderman W. Rosser) and Councillor Max Beveridge.

The long train drew in at the platform about three-quarters of an hour late. The children had endured a seven hours' journey but in spite of the tiring experience they were full of curious excitement as they reached the end of their journey as to what kind of a place they were coming to. They hung out of the windows and received a cheery wave from those who were waiting to receive them.

With their small personal belongings, they were quickly disembarked and sorted in groups to be transported by bus to the Market Hall. There, a host of energetic workers were waiting to give them a good feed with plenty of bread and butter and a variety of cakes. The appetites of the children did full justice to this welcome provision.

Afterwards, the children were allocated to their various buses and taken to various parishes where voluntary workers were working to direct them to their new temporary homes.

One of the children from the East Coast, later recalled her impressions of Abergavenny:

'So this is Abergavenny! That is what we murmured with a sigh of relief as we climbed down - stiff limbed and weary - from our long journey from the East Coast. Monmouthshire and its hills was unknown to us, for we were evacuees from East Anglia, from the county of dumplings and fresh sea breezes. We wondered a little fearfully how we would be received. But we need have had no fears, however, for we found the citizens of this pleasant little borough most friendly disposed and our reception on the first night was so kind that never for a moment did we feel we were unwanted strangers.

We quickly settled down to work in the school with which we had joined forces, and our lessons proved most interesting as we viewed the subjects from a new standpoint. No longer were we in a county which had been overrun by successive waves of Danes and Saxons, for the castle by the Usk reminded us of wild Welsh border raids and of the stormy lives of Llywelyns and Glendowers. That grand old Priory Church, too had its silent story to tell in stone of the Reformation and of the foundation of Grammar School education.

But it was in geography, perhaps that we appreciated most our change of surroundings. Rivers became real to us and we tracked from its source the trickling Cibby and the comparatively dashing Gavenny along their tree-lines banks to where they mingled with the Usk on its way to the mighty ocean. How we loved the hills that greeted us every way we turned! They were not, as we found, the grim grey hills of North Wales, but friendly accessible hills - hills you could climb up and in places, roll down: in fact, hills you need not fear, but ones which became good companions.

So we climbed them, had meals on them, studied them from the Castle wall and then drew contour maps of them to send home, to show how clever we had become.

Yes, we felt that we had been fortunate indeed in our evacuation areas, and though at times we longed for the level stretches of our home county - Abergavenny and all that it offers, quickly made us love this snug little valley that had so kindly taken us to its heart.'

Air Raid Shelters

It was generally felt that there was not the same need for public air-raid shelters in Abergavenny as there were in more important areas. Many people made their own shelter arrangements and the tenants of one street by communal effort succeeded in constructing a very fine shelter, well equipped and capable of accomodating quite a number of people. Other people had more simple arrangements which they expected to be adequate. It was felt that in Abergavenny there was no need to rush to a shelter some distance away. One would be better off at home by selecting the safest part of the house, because the odds against a direct hit on a particular house by a stray bomb were very great. The important thing was to keep away from windows because the concussion of a bomb can shatter glass for a considerable distance and cause injury.

How to distinguish enemy parachutists

In view of the possibility of landings by enemy parachutists the following advice was given in the *Abergavenny Chronicle*:

'The parachutists, apart from those dropped in disguise, are not likely to be seen singly or in twos and threes. Those in uniform will usually appear in groups. They drop from aeroplanes at very low altitudes, generally from 300 feet, thus securing accuracy. A plane carries anything up to 30 parachutists, and 12 of these can be dropped in 10 seconds. The men, therefore arrive in groups and at once split into action units of six or eight to carry out the work assigned to them.

Parachutists do not, as far as is known, carry bicycles, which are brought only by air-bourne troops. They try to secure bicycles or cars from civilians.

The parachutists' uniform can readily be distinguished from that of any British soldier or airman. Over tunic and trousers are always worn gre-green gabardine overalls, loose in the body, with short legs and full long sleeves, fastened down the front with a zip fastener. The steel helmet differs from the British type in having no flat rim in front or behind, and is secured by two straps.

Weapons are dropped separately in containers. Three or four of these are carried in each 'plane, and are dropped singly, attached to parachutes. From the containers the parachutists may obtain rifles, stick grenades, anti-tank rifles and machine guns. The parachutists carries a revolver at his belt and one man in five has a machine pistol.'

Rudolf Hess, the 'Kaiser of Abergavenny'

Rudolph Hess

On May 10, 1941, Rudolph Hess the Deputy Feuhrer of Nazi Germany took off from Augsburg in an unarmed Messerschmitt BF-110, a twin-engined fighter and was escorted for part of the way by four ME109s led by Reinhard Heydrich, head of SS intelligence. His destination was probably RAF Acklington in Northumberland but Hess made a navigational error and decided to head for Dungavel Castle in South Lanarkshire, home of the Duke of Hamilton. But the castle only had a short landing strip and Hess realised that an ME110 could not land there. So he baled out by parachute and broke his ankle when landing in a field in East Renffrewshire near Eaglesham Moor in southern Scotland. He was captured by ploughman David Maclean.

Hess was a tall, broad-shouldered man and wearing the uniform of an officer of the Luftwaffe had hoped to contact the Duke of Hamilton with the aim of persuading the British government to cease its 'senseless war' against the might of the Third Reich. He believed that the duke was a man sympathetic to the 'British Peace Movement' and that he would have personal contact with King George VI.

He had come to Britain in order to convince responsible persons that, singly England could not win the war and her wisest course was to make peace at once. The proposals could be considered only on the understanding that they were negotiated with an English Government 'other than the present one.' The Fuhrer would not be prepared to negotiate with Churchill and his colleagues.

Hess said, 'I am on a mission of humanity. The Fuhrer does not want to defeat England and wants to stop fighting.' He added that he had come without the knowledge of Hitler. Hess affirmed the certainty of England's defeat by blockade, if not very quickly, in the course of two or three years. He gave his word of honour that the Fuhrer had never entertained any designs against the British Empire, nor had he ever aspired to world domination. In fact the Fuhrer would sincerely regret the collapse of the British Empire.

Hess emphasised that his flight was intended to give Great Britain a chance of opening conversations without loss of prestige. If this chance was rejected it would be the Fuhrer's duty to destroy Great Britain utterly and to keep the country after the war in a permanent state of subjection. The main points of the solution that Hess put forward were as follows:

1. That Germany should be given a free hand in Europe.
2. That England should have a free hand in the British Empire, except that ex-German colonies should be returned to Germany.
3. That Russia should be included in Asia, but that Germany had certain demands to make of Russia which would have to be satisfied either by negotiation or as a result of war. There was, however, no truth in the rumours that the Fuehrer contemplated an early attack on Russia.
4. That the British should evacuate Iraq.

The 'terms were' re-stated by Hess in a signed document dated June 10, 1941.

On being taken prisoner, he was first held for four days in the Queen's House at the Tower of London, then in a Kent country house. Then after spending 13 months at Camp 2 (Mytchett Place in Aldershot) he was taken in June 1941 to a POW reception centre at Maindiff Court Military Hospital where he remained until October 8th, 1945, when he was flown to Nuremburg then being sent for trial as a war criminal. He was sentenced to life imprisonment and after the trial, Hess commented:

'It is just incomprehensible how these things (atrocities) came about... Every genius has the demon in him... You can't blame him (Hitler) - it is just in him. It is all very tragic. But at least I have the satisfaction of knowing that I tried to do something to end the war.'

It is of interest that the Hess family had a previous connection with Monmouthshire towards the end of the nineteenth century. Carl Hess, a brilliant linguist, met and married Elizabeth Mackie, who was in the domestic service of the Bishop of Gloucester, She was born at Michaelstone-y-Fedw, between Newport and Cardiff.

Just twelve months later, she died of pneumonia and her body was brought back to her home parish for burial. The bereaved husband paid for her tombstone which can be seen beside the path leading to Michaelstone-y-Fedw Church. The inscription reads:

'Erected by Carl Hess of Schleswig
in loving memory of his wife Elizabeth Mackie
who died at Bystock, Exmouth, Devon
June 13th 1891, aged 35 years.
In life beloved, in death never forgotten.'

Carl Hess subsequently entered the service of an American and, during his travels in Egypt, remarried at Alexandria. He then returned with his second wife to Germany where he bought the Hotel Cecil in Hamburg. Rudolph Hess was a son of this second marriage.

One cannot help wondering whether Rudolph Hess was aware during his imprisonment at Maindiff Court that just over 20 miles away, his father had once stood in sorrow beside a grave in which his first wife was buried.

During his time at Maindiff Court Hospital, Hess wrote numerous letters to his wife Frau Ilse Hess. In one of them he describes 'the peculiar beauty' of the Abergavenny district 'especially the astounding play of colour on the hills and mountains and the ever-changing effects of light.'

He was allowed to visit places of interest in the area such as Whitecastle and even permitted to enjoy a drink in local pubs. Referring to local walks that he enjoyed he said:

'In the villages through which I passed, the inhabitants would run to their doors to gaze at the German who had come down to them from the sky. They were often quite friendly and one of the officers who had been assigned to me informed me that large numbers of the population hoped that my mission would be successful and the war brought to an end.'

Dr Ellis Jones was the psychiatrist who attended Hess when he was Maindiff Court Hospital and he described the German as 'a psychopathic personality, definitely a deviate from the normal. And it is likely that he will continue to live in the borderlands of insanity for the rest of his life.'

Towards the end of September 1942, his condition worsened and he began complaining about noises. For example he complained about the noise of passing trains, alleging that Maindiff Court Hospital had been chosen because it was well-known that the sound of engines would annoy him. A statement that he wrote at this hospital was translated at Nuremburg: 'The whistles and screeches sounded constantly when the trucks hit each other. There was no thought of sleep; if I tried to catch up during the day, this would be presented by the slamming of doors.'

Another delusion from which he suffered, was that he was being poisoned, and often he would ask those entrusted with guarding him to act as 'tasters'. He would not face realities and refused to recognise the defeat of Germany. He had followed the war very closely until the Battle of Alamein. Then he shut up his atlases and did not want to hear any more about the war.

On February 4th, 1945, he attempted to commit suicide by stabbing himself with a bread knife after he had changed into his Air Force uniform. He maintained that the knife entered his body to a depth of eight inches, but in fact, the wound was very superficial.

In October 1945, Dr Jones and the prisoner Rudolph Hess travelled to Madley, near Hereford and from there they were flown to Brussels and then on to Nuremburg. Hess was adjudged insane and incarcerated until his death at the age of 93, in Spandau Prison, Berlin, where he had been held for 45 years. The prison had been built for 600 prisoners, but Hess was the only prisoner held there at that time.

On August 17th, 1987, at the age of 93, he committed suicide by hanging himself because he had been given a black orderly who guarded him along with the British, French and Russian prison staff. As an anti-semite Hess was so outraged that he decided to kill himself. Shortly afterwards the prison was demolished. A shopping centre and car park now stands on the site.

In August 1942, Abergavenny was represented in the historic and daring raid on Dieppe by commando Len Fraser, son of Mr and Mrs Len Fraser of Deri road. He was with Lord Lovatt in the 4th Commandos who achieved the important task of putting the battery of six-inch naval guns out of action.

Mr Fraser was very modest about his part in the encounter, but he said to his friends, 'I enjoyed every minute of it.'

He brought back as a momento, a 20-franc note which was part of a sum of money which an officer was preparing to pay out to German soldiers. The officer was shot in a raid on his office.

There were several local men in Commandos, but only one other took part in this raid. He was Captain R. J. Pettiward, who lost his life.

Mr Fraser was invited to attend the concert at the Town Hall one Friday night in August and was introduced with his father and mother, by the Mayor (Alderman W. Rosser) to the large audience. He received a tremendous ovation on his appearance. The Mayor expressed the honour felt by the town and his particular pride at the fact that Commando Fraser was one of his old schoolboys at Hereford Road.

Mr Fraser, with natural shyness, spoke a few words of thanks for the reception given him and said he would rather go through three such raids or face another battery of naval guns than stand up there and make a speech.

On the fourth anniversary of the War the Mayor, Alderman Wheatley, read a message received from the Prime Minister to a crowd gathered in the castle grounds.

'The message which I send to the people of the British Empire on the fourth anniversary of their entry into the war is 'Hold Fast!' We are in this war for no selfish ends. We are in it to recover freedom for the nations which have been brutally attacked and despoiled, and to prove that no people, however powerful can surrender itself to the lawless ambitions of militarism, without meeting retribution, swift, certain and disastrous, at the hands of the free nations of the world. To stop short of victory for this cause would be to compromise the future of mankind.

I say "Hold Fast," because our prospects of victory have never been so bright as they are today. Six months ago the rulers of Germany, deliberately rejected the just and reasonable settlement proposed by the Allies. Throwing aside the last mask of moderation, they partitioned Russia, enslaved Roumania, and attempted to seize supreme power by overwhelming the Allies in a final and desperate attack. Thanks to the invincible bravery of all the Allied armies, it is now evident to all that this dream of universal conquest, for the sake of which they wantonly prolonged the war can never be fulfilled.

But the battle is not yet won. The great autocracy of Prussia will still endeavour by violence or guile to avoid defeat, and so give militarism a new lease of life. We cannot seek to escape the horrors of war for ourselves by laying them up for our children. Having set our hands to the task, we must see it through till a just and lasting settlement is achieved.

In no other way can we ensure a world set free from war. "Hold Fast!"'

Toward the end of 1944, the end of the war appeared to be not too far away and compulsory drills and training of the Home Guards were ended. The black-out was replaced by half-lighting and the obligation to carry out fire-watching drills was also suspended.

Abergavenny Wardens' Service: Post A.4, October, 1944

In February 1945, 'Gobannium' writing in the *Abergavenny Chronicle* commented:

'There are small indications that we are gradually changing over from a full war effort to peace-time activities, though we must not relax until Germany is well and truly beaten. There is a call, however, for a relaxation of some of the controls which were perhaps necessary in war time, but even so some of them seemed to be overdone. In spite of grumbles, food control has been a great success and has to a large extent prevented unfair distribution, but we are looking forward to the time when the supply will more than equal the demand, and that control can be dispensed with. It is time some other controls went by the board. The bugbear of wartime is that there is so much unnecessary form filling which delights the official mind. Production is the basis of well being, and form filling has too often tended to hinder rather than help production. It will probably take longer to demobolize some of our war-time officials than to demobolize our fighting men, though many of the latter will feel that they are not demobbed quickly enough.'

A few weeks later 'Gobannium' reminded every one that:

'Even though a few months may see the end of the war in Europe, there is still no need for complacency. Japan has still to be utterly and completely defeated. The Japs are just as fanatical as the Nazis and their Emperor is just as much a god to them as Hitler was to the Germans. It must be remembered that the Japanese population is about as large as that of Germany and they can put a formidable army of millions in the field. In

In spite of spectacular successes in the Pacific, that army is still largely intact. There may be surprises in store, but a mere recital of these bold facts should be sufficient to convince anyone that the successful conclusion of the war against Japan will be no light task.'

In April, 1945, several of Abergavenny men who had been prisoners of war began arriving home. Some of them had been captive for five years and they all had varying experiences. They received a hearty welcome from the neighbours in their own particular streets, and Cantref Road, Mill Street and Junction Cottages were especially well decorated with flags and bunting.

On May 7th, 1945, the Germans announced their surrender and the British Government declared that the following day (Tuesday) would be celebrated as 'VE Day' (Victory in Europe) to mark the unconditional surrender of Germany to the three Allied Nations of Great Britain, Russia and the USA. For the British people, the war had lasted 2,094 days (just over five years and eight months). This was 526 days more than the war of 1914-18.

In Abergavenny VE Day was celebrated with great rejoicing. Flags and bunting appeared in profusion in every street and there was much dancing and music. However the merrymaking was tempered by the thought that victory over Japan still had to be achieved before the war was really won.

VJ Day Celebrations

Though there was no set organisation for celebrating Victory in Japan Day there were many spontaneous events which ensured that VJ Day in Abergavenny was remembered for many years afterwards.

In Brecon Road a bonfire was lit in the middle of the A40 by a military unit and people brought all sorts of things to add to the flames. Some people even took off their footwear and warmed their feet by the fire.

When a man started ringing the Christchurch bell he pulled the rope with so much enthusiasm that it broke. Another fellow started the hooter at Seargeant Brothers Printing Works and used it to sound the V sign in Morse code. On the Fairfield a large bonfire of timber and tyres was lit and bandsmen from a military unit, seated on a lorry parked in the adjoining road, played music for dancing.

There were plenty of fireworks going off and the succession of bangs and flashes alternated with laughter and singing. Many premises and houses had special illumination and the Town Hall was floodlit.

The Falklands War

During the Falklands War in 1982 the Conservative Member of Parliament who served under Margaret Thatcher was Francis Leslie Pym and it is of local interest that he was born near Abergavenny in 1922. He was the son of Leslie Ruthen Pym and Iris Rosalind Orde and his father was the Conservative MP for Monmouth from 1939 until his death in 1945.

Francis Pym served as a captain with the 9th Lancers during the Second World War and after fighting at Alamein he was awarded the MC (Military Cross). He entered politics in 1961 having been elected as Conservative Member of Parliament for Cambridgeshire.

As a member of Margaret Thatcher's cabinet, Francis Pym served as Foreign Secretary throughout the time of the Falklands War and his appointment was as a result of the resignation of Lord Carrington from this position. He was not reappointed after Margaret Thatcher's next election victory because he was on the left of the party and he left the House of Commons in 1987 when he was given a life peerage as Lord Pym of Sandy. He died in 2008.

The Iraq War

This military campaign began on March 20th, 2003 with the invasion of Iraq by a multinational force led by troops from the United States under the administration of George W. Bush and the United Kingdom under Prime Minister Tony Blair.

It is of local interest that on 31st March 2003, Lieutenant Helena Bevan (26) from Abergavenny was one of four women officers directing big guns of the British Army on the Basra front and she was caught in the middle of fierce exchanges between American and Iraqi tanks close to the southern city of Basra.

Manning a 7.62 calibre machine gun on an armoured vehicle she guided huge As 90 self propelled guns to the front line and led more than sixty British soldiers into the thick of the tank battle. When later interviewed, she commented:

> 'Some people find it hard to understand why a woman would want to do a job like this but I wouldn't change it for anything. It's exciting, honourable and better than being stuck behind a desk from nine to five. We've had some close calls, particularly when we went forward near Basra.'

The War in Afghanistan

A local man Private Richard Hunt (21) became the 200th British soldier to die after being severely wounded in Afghanistan when his Warrior vehicle hit an Improvised Explosive Device near Musaqala. He was on a vehicle patrol with A Company the 2nd Battalion Royal Welsh when the incident occurred.

His company commander, Major Huw Jones subsequently paid the following tribute to him:

> 'Richard was a fine soldier; fit, professional and extremely brave. He had huge potential and was at the peak of his game, having just completed an arduous and demanding sniper course. It was typical of him to volunteer to drive a Warrior when the need arose. Despite the danger, he threw himself at the task with the boundless enthusiasm and selfless commitment which was his hallmark - he set an example for us all. We have lost a man of great courage and skill and it has wounded us deeply. Our thoughts and prayers are with his family.'

On 24th August 2009 up to 2,000 people attended a parade to the war memorial in Frogmore Street, Abergavenny. Richard's family and friends, members of his regiment, the 2nd Battalion The Royal Welsh, and local councillors were among the mourners. The Act of Remembrance was read by Sergeant Major David Davies and this was followed by a trumpet sounding to mark the start of a minute's silence at 2.15pm which was the time at which Richard Hunt had died eight days earlier in a military hospital in Birmingham. Private Hunt's funeral later took place at St Mary's Priory Church where he received full military honours.

His mother Hazel Hunt (a retired vet from Abergavenny), with family and friends set up The Richard Hunt Foundation and within ten weeks an excess of £10,000 had been raised and passed on to 'Help the Heroes', the Poppy Appeal and other charitable organisations.

It was also as a Result of Richard Hunt's death that the 'Big Lottery Fund' set up 'The Forces in Mind Trust' to provide long term support and advocacy for former forces personnel to make a successful transition to civilian life, including those who served in Iraq, Afghanistan and the Gulf War.

World War I Memorial Tablet

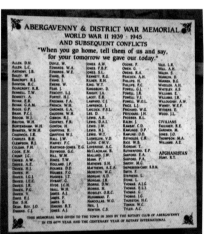

World War II Memorial Tablet

On the 60th anniversary of the ending of World War II a memorial to the men and women of the area who had died in the conflict was unveiled during a cermony held in St Mary's Priory Church. The service of dedication was conducted by the vicar of Abergavenny, the Reverend Jeremy Winston, assisted by the Reverend Stephen Bywater and the Reverend Derek Lee.

The list of 162 names who had died had been compiled by Mrs Iris Coldrey and the project was organised by David Yendell with funds provided by Abergavenny Rotary Club. Mr Yendell commented that it was the most rewarding task that he had ever undertaken. The tablet was initially installed at the top of the first flight of stairs in Abergavenny Town Hall.

In March 2011 the tablet was moved to the entrance to the Market Hall, where it could be seen by a greater number of people. The 1914-18 memorial tablet restored by Simon Morgan the managing director of Mossfords of Cardiff was also installed in the same location.

A service of dedication was performed by the Reverend Derek Lee, chaplain to the British Legion and the World War One memorial was unveiled by the Mayor, Councillor Norma Watkins. Mrs Hazel Hunt unveiled the new memorial for the 1939-45 War which also bears her son's name as a casualty in a later conflict. His commanding officer, Lieutenant Colonel Mark Wheeler, CO of the 2nd Battalion the Welsh Regiment was present to watch the ceremony and the Last Post was played by Diane Mogford of the Abergavenny Borough Band.

Chapter Twenty
RAILWAY NOSTALGIA

*Abergavenny was a railway town, with the railways of the area employing over a thousand
people during its heyday.*

W. W. Tasker 1986

The first railroad through Abergavenny was constructed in 1811 for the purpose of
conveying coal and lime from the canal at Govilon Wharf towards Hereford. An
Act was passed 'for making a railroad from the Brecknock & Abergavenny Canal
in the parish of Llanwenarth to or near Llanfihangel Crucorney,' and by this Act the
proprietors were enabled to form 'The Llanfihangel Railway Company.'

The engineer was John Hodgkinson of Cheltenham and the first section to be
constructed ran from Govilon Wharf on the Brecknock & Abergavenny Canal to
Llanfoist and then across the River Usk on a stone bridge which was built alongside the
old highway bridge on its western side. The tramroad then continued round to the north
of the town, passing close to the New Inn at Mardy, and the churches of Llantilio-
Pertholey and Llanfihangel Crucorney to end in a field just east of the latter church. The
total distance was just under 8 miles. Private sidings ran from the tramroad to the lime
works at Llanfoist, to the gas works at Abergavenny (for the conveyance of coal) and to
Triley Mill, near Llantilio Pertholey.

The old stone bridge built to carry the tramroad over the river Usk had eight spans, corresponding
with the spans of the ancient highway bridge and it was built about six to eight feet higher

In 1812 the second section, 5.5 miles in length and known as the Grosmont Tramroad
was constructed. It ran from Llanfihangel Crucorney, following the natural contour of
the ground in a westerly direction for about one mile. Its route then followed the line of
the present day A465 and finished at Monmouth Cap, near Pontrilas. The final section
called the Hereford Tramroad which ran from Monmouth Cap to Hereford was not built
until November 1825, due to organised opposition from barge owners and other vested
interests.

On Monday 21 September, 1829 at 10.00 a.m. the final section of the tramroad connecting Govilon Wharf with Hereford was opened for traffic and the first consignment of coal from Abergavenny arrived at the Wyebridge Wharf. During that day a total of thirty-four trams arrived at the wharf and Thomas Hill, the Blaenavon Ironmaster, who was a generous man, gave orders for ten tons of coal to be distributed amongst the poor of Hereford.

The Llanfihangel Tramroad ran successfully for the best part of twenty years but in 1845 a new company was formed to construct a steam railway from Pontypool to Hereford and negotiations began with the purpose of aquiring the three tramroads operating between Abergavenny and Hereford. These continued to be operated by the Newport, Abergavenny & Hereford Railway Company whilst its new railway to Hereford of standard gauge was being erected alongside the existing route, with diversions of a few hundred yards on certain sections.

The Act passed in 1846 for a Newport, Abergavenny and Hereford Railway included six branch lines to Panteg, Llangeview, Llanbadoc, Raglan, Abergavenny Gas Works and Portfields in Hereford, but none of these were made.

The Company had a capital of £733,000 in £25 shares and the contract was given to James Rennie of Newport. The new line, from its junction with the Monmouthshire Railway at Coedygric to Barton Station, Hereford was opened on the 2nd January, 1854 and on that day Abergavenny received its first train which clanked its way down 'the bank' from Llanfihangel and came to a squeaky stop at the new station. The railway should have opened on 6th December 1853, but a landslip at Llanvihangel Crucorney caused a delay.

Abergavenny GWR Station opened in 1854 and was renamed Monmouth Road in 1950

In 1860 on 1 July, the Abergavenny & Hereford Railway Company was taken over by the West Midland Co., who in turn were swallowed up by the Great Western Railway on 1 August 1865.

With industry growing in the Monmouthshire Valleys it was essential to provide a a link with the Midlands and in 1859, Parliament was presented with a Bill to build the Merthyr, Tredegar & Abergavenny Railway to join these places through Hereford to the North.

The Merthyr, Tredegar & Abergavenny Railway

The Act for building the Merthyr, Tredegar & Abergavenny Railway was passed on 1st August 1859 and the specified completion date was to be within five years. The Company's capital was given as £150,000, consisting of 7,500 shares of £20 each.

Crawshay Bailey, the well known ironmaster was the first chairman of the Company and he put considerable energy into the enterprise. Strong doubts had been expressed concerning the possibility of building a railway on so severe a gradient between Llanfoist and Brynmawr. However, Crawshay insisted that in his opinion the severest gradient likely to occur on the proposed line would be 1 in 40 and this would be perfectly workable within the estimated cost of £10,000 per mile.

Crawshay Bailey

Prior to the building of this railway, the mail coach took two hours to travel the nine miles on the turnpike road between Abergavenny and Beaufort. Other road carriers in the 19th century were William Thomas, who went to Brynmawr after starting from the Old Duke at Abergavenny on Tuesdays and Fridays, and George Watkins and Hannah Hughes, who left from the Kings Arms on Tuesdays.

On Monday 18th June 1860, the ceremony of turning the first sod was performed in pouring rain by Mrs Crawshay Bailey at Abergavenny. Mr John Gardner, the Engineer presented Mrs Crawshay Bailey with the ceremonial spade and she raised the turf with considerable difficulty, depositing it in a wheelbarrow. This was to be the site of the Brecon Road Station.

In June 1861, Gardner reported on the first year's progress which was certainly impressive: 'The works on this line are progressing very rapidly; the bridges in the neighbourhood of Abergavenny are nearly all completed, and the progress of making cuttings and embankments is being carried out with vigour between Gilwern and Brynmawr. A considerable length of permanent rail has been laid and a locomotive is shortly to be put on to facilitate the construction of the long embankment between the canal and the River Usk.'

 The Company's account became overdrawn in the latter part of 1861 and the London & North Western Railway Company then took control of the project with a 1,000 year lease. In just two years this first section of the line from Abergavenny to Brynmawr was completed and it was opened on 29th September 1862. A new iron bridge had been built over the river Usk and a long embankment constructed between the canal and the river. Seven more bridges had to be built between Llanfoist and Brynmawr, two tunnels, each about a quarter of a mile in length and long stretches of stone retaining walls. This was one of the most severely graded railways in the British Isles with a 3 mile section of 1 in 34. When the trains reached Brynmawr it was necessary for them to take on additional water, having climbed no less than 1,000 feet over a distance of eight miles to the highest town in Wales.

This railway bridge (now demolished) carried the LNWR line over the river Usk

LMS Staff serving the Abergavenny to Merthyr branch line in 1923

During this period branches were added to Nantyglo, Ebbw Vale, New Tredegar, Rhymney and Blaenavon.

In 1877 the increase in traffic resulted in a need for the line to be doubled, the Engineer John Gardner had to make all the viaducts wider and to bore two additional tunnels as well as to lay extra track and this was all completed in a surprisingly short time.

When the Engineer John Gardner died on 15th January 1894, his obituary notice carried the citation: 'He was an engineer of ability, upright in all business transactions and much esteemed for the conscientious manner in which he carried out the works entrusted to his care.'

This was one of the most spectacular railways in Britain, but it was also one of the most expensive to operate for the long and steep gradients caused coal to be consumed at the rate of 90lbs per mile.

> 'Travelling the line when the autumn mists were about was magic. We would leave Brecon Road Station with a shrill little whistle, go down past the loco sheds and give another whistle, across the bridge over the Usk, through the cutting at Llanfoist, round by the old Llanfoist brewery and on to the steepest part of the line between Llanfoist and Gilwern, gaining height on the easier countryside ready for the haul through Clydach Gorge itself.'
>
> Philip Lovell

Old postcard showing the road and railway bridges spanning the river Usk

Shrieking Railway Whistles

In 1885 the Reverend W. Vigors, Rector of Llanwenarth wrote a letter to the *Abergavenny Chronicle* complaining of the noisy engine whistles on the L&NWR Railway:

'I have resided in many parts of England, yet never have I lived in any place where the dangers to life and limb from horse and carriage accidents caused by horses taking fright at the railway whistle was anything like so great as it is in the immediate neighbourhood of Abergavenny.

In driving or riding to or from the town the public have constantly to run the gauntlet not only with the trains (which is bad enough, but cannot be helped) but what is infinitely worse and a greater danger in frightening a horse, namely the railway whistle. At Brecon Road railway bridge as well as the road to Llanfoist and also to Abergavenny Junction the public are constantly subjected to the great and absolutely unnecessary danger of a sudden outburst of the whistle, that unearthly, frightful, alarming whistle; the shriek of which is more terrifying to a spirited horse than a dozen trains passing by. Moreover, I have reason to believe that this frightful whistle is sometimes sprung in fun by the engine driver in order to make approaching horses dance and jump about that they might see the fun. I have seen a man on the engine, his engine standing still, wait until a horse approached near the bridge and then suddenly and without the slightest warning send forth a most fearsome and unearthly shriek.'

An engine driver, E. Wilkinson of Blorenge View replied to this letter:

'Clearly, he thinks that the enginemen in general are as ignorant of the nature of horses as he is of an engine. Further, he seems to consider that they are a set of children just let loose from school knowing no responsibility and regardless of anything but their own fun. If he will take the trouble to walk down to the sheds he will see notices posted up directing drivers to use their whistles according to certain rules. The said drivers are men specially selected by examination as to their qualification for their most important duty as men of discretion, steadiness and general knowledge. As one of the drivers on the line named, and in the name of every driver on it, I deny that the occurrence named by Mr Vigors as having taken place at Brecon Road bridge in the manner he seems to wish it to be understood ever took place. No engine driver in his senses would dream of doing the act he declares was done, and particularly at such a point, knowing as he must, the penalty for such an infringement of the rule.'

The Proposed Railway to Monmouth

In 1884 a Bill was presented to Parliament for the Abergavenny & Monmouth Railway, but it was never passed. The object of the Bill was to incorporate a company to make and maintain a railway to commence with a junction with the London & North Western Railway at Pen-y-pound, then passing through Hardwick, Llantilio Pertholey, Llandewi Rhydderch, Llanvapley, Llantilio Crossenny, Penrhos, Llanvihangel Ystern Llewern,

Llangattock-vibon-Avel, Parke Grace Dieu, Rockfield and ending at Monmouth by a junction with the Wye Valley Railway.

The company required powers to purchase and take by compulsion land and houses for the purposes of the railway and workers and the right to levy tolls, rates and duties. It also required powers to run over the work and use with their engines carriages and waggons, parts of the London & North Western Railway, the Wye Valley Railway between Monmouth and Coleford, the Severn & Wye Railway and the Severn Bridge Railway.

The Proposed Usk Valley Railway

Another railway scheme which failed to get off the ground was a proposal to build the Usk Valley Railway which came before the Select Committee of the House of Commons on May 13, 1898. The object of the Bill was to authorise the construction of a railway along the Usk Valley from a junction with the Great Western Railway near Abergavenny to a junction with the Brecon & Merthyr line and the Cambrian Railway at Tal-y-llyn, near Brecon.

The Bill was opposed by Mr Gabb of Abergavenny who complained that the new line would go through his property; by the Cambrian Railway Company who objected to running powers over their line; and by the Brecon & Merthyr Company, who also objected to the granting of running powers to a competitive company.

Mr Littler, QC opened the case for the promoters and pointed out the necessity for a railway in the Usk Valley, not only for the convenience of the population of the valley, but also for the accommodation of the large picnic parties from the mining districts of South Wales, which visit the beautiful Usk Valley.

Sir Joseph Bailey, Lord Lieutenant of the County of Brecon, and Chairman of the Rural District Council, and a large landowner in the valley, gave evidence in favour of the Bill.

Mr Richard Henry Davies, solicitor in Crickhowell and steward to the Marquess of Worcester, also supported it. The existing methods of conveyance between Crickhowell and Abergavenny, he said consisted of a small mail cart, which made two journeys each way daily, with accommodation for about five passengers, two carriers, and a number of carriages kept by individuals.

Sir James Slumper said that he was the engineer of the proposed railway. He had an intimate knowledge of Wales and its railway system, and had so laid out the route of this line as to avoid interfering with property in a manner 'to excite the hostility of the landowners,' many of whom were opposing the scheme.

The gradients of the proposed line were favourable. The worst being 1 in 50 for a length of a little over two miles. The total cost of the line, would, according to his estimates, be £122,330. He calculated that its earning capacity after a few years would be £18 per mile per week, which, after allowing 60 per cent working expenses and paying the interest on debentures, would leave sufficient to pay a dividend of 4 per cent to ordinary shareholders.

This proposed line would effect a saving of seven miles between South Wales and Aberystwyth. It would be worked independently. Authorisation to take running powers over the Great Western line had been withdrawn, because the promoters were satisfied with the attitude of the Great Western Company. With regard to the running powers over the Cambrian to Three Cocks Junction, if an exchange station was erected at Llangorse, and the Cambrian Company would undertake to forward and deliver the traffic, they might do without running powers. He would not, however, advise the promoters to give up the running powers to Brecon, because to have a change on a short line between two important places was a very bad thing.

The Committee decided that the preamble of the Bill was proved. Compulsory running powers were to be given to the Usk Company for passenger trains to Brecon, but not to Three Cocks. The promoters were to bring up a clause providing that the Cambrian Company should give proper facilities for interchanging traffic at Llangorse Junction and that a station should be erected at that Junction at the expense of the Usk Company.

The Bill passed through the Committee stage and was ordered to be reported for the third reading. But unfortunately the scheme was dropped. A map of this proposed railway used to be on a wall in the King's Head Hotel and is now in the Town Hall.

From Peak to Decline

During World War I railway activity in Abergavenny reached its peak with over 1,000 men employed in jobs associated with this form of transport. There were 450 engine-men of all grades who worked the 100 or so engines held in the loco sheds which consisted of four roads 290 feet long, seven roads 162 feet long and one road that was 133 feet long and nearby was a large turntable.

The goods yard at Brecon Road Station was provided with additional sidings and the Junction Station carriage sheds were erected together with additional sidings accommodation. Adjacent to the Brecon Road goods yard the District Engineer's Depot was established together with a new barrack building, used as sleeping quarters for train crews. There were also stables, a weighing machine and a pumphouse opposite the gasworks on the 'down' side of the line. The pump was steam driven until about 1928, when electricity took over. Water was raised from the river Usk, to supply Brecon Road and the Junction.

The large locomotive shed which adjoined the town gas works

Abergavenny Junction Station was unique in that it was a purely LNWR station though situated on a GWR main line.

Brecon Road Station of the LNWR on the Abergavenny - Merthyr line

The Great Western Railway bus service ran from Abergavenny to Brecon and was one of the first bus services in the county introduced in about 1906. A Milne Daimler petrol engined double decker bus with a stairway leading from the lower to the upper deck.

A railwaymen's trip on a Great Western Railway chrabanc in 1910

The introduction of the Abergavenny, Crickhowell and Brecon Great Western Omninbuses began on 1st July 1905, when the first omnibus arrived at the Great Western railway station early that morning. It was a powerfully built vehicle, capable of carrying fourteen passengers and had a compartment for luggage. A second omnibus capable of carrying twenty passengers arrived the following day.

One of these vehicles would convey mail to and from Brecon, leaving Abergavenny at 3.40am, arriving at Crickhowell at 4.20am and at Brecon at 5.30am; returning from Brecon at 6.30pm, arriving at Crickhowell at 8.10pm and at Abergavenny GWR Station at 9.10pm. The second omnibus would leave Abergavenny at 8.20am, reach Crickhowell at 9.10am. A third omnibus would leave Abergavenny at 11.15am and arrive at Brecon at 1.30pm.

Parcels and packages must not exceed 1cwt. The single fare from the GWR station at Abergavenny to Crickhowell was 9d and to Brecon 2s 6d. A passenger leaving London by train at 5.30am could reach Brecon at 1.30pm. If leaving London at 11.35 the arrival time at Brecon was 6.30pm.

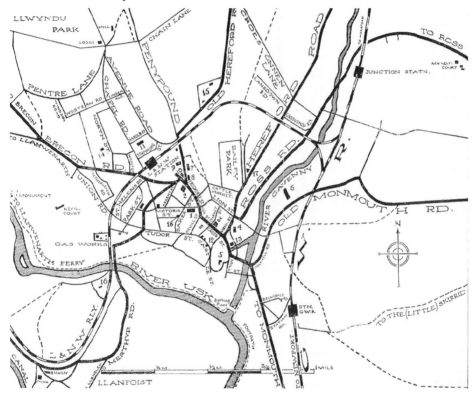

Map showing the three railway stations serving Abergavenny

The district was known as the South Wales Division of the London and North Western Railway, and being semi-independent was self contained with its equipment and facilities to maintain its rolling stock and permanent way.

To make sure the railwaymen of the day could live near their jobs, the authorities built houses for them in the nearby streets. The Cantref Inn was the first building to spring up in the area, even before the Brecon Road Station. But afterwards came the houses in Stanhope Street, North Street and St Helen's Road, followed by the influx of railway men and their families to occupy them.

The workers lived so close to the station and rail-yard that a bell was erected nearby which was tolled to bring the men running to their jobs on time. And, of course to signal finishing time. This bell is now an exhibit in the Abergavenny Museum.

In those exciting times, now remembered with much nostalgia, the town was alive with a symphony of railway sounds - the clang of hammers, the hiss of steam, whistles hooting and wheels clattering over joints and points.

There were magnificent locos to be seen in the old LNWR livery of black and red with gold bands, ranging from the sturdy tanks which worked the Merthyr and the Valleys line to the giants to whom such names as Crewe and Carlisle and Glasgow were everyday words. They came into the sheds for service and left gleaming.

Picture taken at Brecon Road signal box in about 1920 showing the engine and single coach used as a mobile inspection office by the district engineer of the LNWR

The decline began in 1941 when some 40 firemen were made redundant in one day and once started the general decline continued, to be halted only by World War II. After that the depression was even worse. Then came nationalisation and the South Wales division lost its independence and with it went the railway centre at Abergavenny which became part of the Western Region of British Railways, the London and North Western completely withdrawing from Abergavenny.

In 1957 it was announced that British Rail wished to close the Abergavenny to Merthyr line and a meeting was held in the town by local people to prepare a case to fight this decision. Unfortunately passenger and freight traffic on the line at that time was so small that closure was inevitable. It was duly announced in the *Merthyr Express* and the *Abergavenny Chronicle* on the 29th November, 1957 that the line would close, thereby saving British Rail about £60,000 a year.

In January 1958 a special train arranged by the Stephenson Locomotive Society (Midland Area) completed the journey from Abergavenny to Merthyr to commemorate the sad closure of this line. It was driven by George Lewis, who had first started work in the sheds at Brecon Road in November, 1911. He was assisted by fireman Derek Hinton, and the train guard was Hubert James of Abergavenny.

The Stephenson Locomotive Society organised this special train in January 1958 to commemorate the end of an era. The leading engine, 0-6-2 Webb coal tank No. 58926 and the second engine 0-8-0 No. 49121, can be seen hauling the last passenger train on the Abergavenny to Merthyr line under the Hereford Road bridge.

The engine was boosted by engine No. 49121, a super-heated 'D', driven by Mr F. Brown whose grandfather was one of the first drivers to make the trip after the line opened in 1879. The Fireman was Mr. A.E. Baker.

At Monmouth Road station, copies of a 12 page souvenir programme edged in black were handed out to the travellers before the start of the five hour trip to Merthyr and back again. On board the train were 250 members of the Stephenson Locomotive Society, besides railway employees, who were travelling for the last time on the line.

Leaving at 12.45 pm it took 30 minutes to complete the climb up through the Clydach Gorge to Brynmawr where huge crowds had gathered to pay their respects. In fact large numbers of people gathered at all the stations along the route, with everyone cheering and waving.

When the train returned from Merthyr, there was a 'whistle up' at every station and on the approach to Abergavenny there was a tremendous eruption of steam, with showers of sparks illuminating the night sky. Householders adjoining the line even switched their lights on and off in reply.

Engines and carriages were then moved away to be scrapped and the men retired or were transferred to other depots at Pontypool or Hereford. The Brecon Road yard remained as a feeder for coal merchants until April 1971. In 1977 the Brecon Road, Chapel Road and Pen-y-pound railway bridges were demolished and a large area of former railway land was reclaimed in a Welsh Development Agency scheme to tidy up Abergavenny.

Strangers to the town are often surprised to learn that Abergavenny used to be a very important railway centre with three stations: the Great Western on the north to west main line; Brecon Road, on the former L & NWR Abergavenny to Merthyr line, and Abergavenny Junction at the point where the two lines met, north east of the town. Only the old Great Western Railway station has survived.

The old M. T. & A railway line has now become a cycle track between Llanfoist and Brynmawr and whilst riding or walking the route one can appreciate the impressive feats of engineering that were achieved in such a short time by skilled Victorian engineers and large numbers of manual workers.

A Memorial to the Railway People of Abergavenny

In November 2000 a bronze plaque was unveiled at Hatherleigh Place, just yards from the site of the local engine sheds at Brecon Road which once housed a large number of steam engines. It was unveiled by John Harvey, the Mayor of Abergavenny who said:

> 'Abergavenny had an unrivalled part in the industrial revolution with its ironworks, canals and railways. Our Principality can claim to be the first to have a steam locomotive run on rails and to have the first passenger carrying railway in the world.
>
> Our town's part in railway history is unchallenged, the LMS and the Great Western were both established here and the building of the Abergavenny to Merthyr Railway made Abergavenny the ideal venue for a day out.'

The plaque was based on a drawing by local artist Michael Blackmore, whose two grandfathers spent a lifetime working on the railways. The engine portrayed is an 0-6-2 Webb coal tank bearing the name of the LMS company, but which originally belonged to the LNWR. The project cost about £1,400 and money was raised by selling limited editions of Michael Blackmore's original drawing of the steam engine adorning the plaque.

The inscription reads:

> 'This plaque is to commemorate the railway people of Abergavenny 1860-1960 and is near the local engine sheds which once housed nearly 100 steam engines.'

CHRONOLOGY OF SIGNIFICANT EVENTS

4000 BC Neolithic man first settles in the locality

57- 400 A garrison town grows up around the Roman fort of Gobannium

1071 Death of William FitzOsbern, Earl of Hereford

1087 Hamelin de Ballon begins work on a motte and bailey castle

1089 Hamelin de Balun builds St Mary's Priory as a cell of the Abbey of St Vincent, near Le Mans

1090 Hamelin de Ballon dies and is buried in St Mary's Priory Church

1093c The town wall is constructed

1094 William Rufus, the son of William the Conqueror pays a visit to Abergavenny whilst on his way to subdue a rebellion of the men of Gwent, Brecknock and Gower

1135 Richard de Clare is murdered by the Welsh

1165 Walter, Earl of Hereford and 3rd Lord of Abergavenny, is appointed Constable of England and the Lordship of Abergavenny is transferred to his brother Henry

1172 Abergavenny Castle is attacked and captured by the Welsh. Henry is killed and the castle is now in the possession of Sitsyllt ap Dynwal

1174 Abergavenny Castle is restored to William de Braose, the fifth Lord of Abergavenny

1175 Christmas Day massacre of Sityslt ap Dynwal and 70 Welshmen at Abergavenny Castle

1182 The castle is attacked and partly destroyed by the Welsh

1188 Archbishop Baldwin and Giraldus Cambrensis visit Abergavenny to preach the third Crusade

1191 William de Braose gives King Richard 1,000 marks for the wardship of Gilbert, Lord of Monmouth

1206 William de Braose petitions King John for the possession of Grosmont, Skenfrith and Whitecastle. He pays the king 800 marks, 3 horses, 5 hunters and 25 greyhounds

1209 The estates of William de Braose are confiscated by King John

1211 Maud de Braose and her son William are imprisoned and starved to death in Windsor Castle

1213 William de Braose dies in France. Giles de Braose becomes 6th Lord of Abergavenny

1215 Giles dies at Gloucester and is buried in the choir of Hereford Cathedral. His title is taken by his son Reginald who becomes the 7th Lord of Abergavenny

1222 Reginald dies and his son William becomes the 8th Lord of Abergavenny

1230 William de Braose the Second has an intrigue with Prince Llywellyn's wife Joan, but is discovered and hanged

1233 King Henry III visits Abergavenny

1256 William de Cantelupe dies. His two year old son George becomes the 10th Lord.

1262 Llywellyn ap Gruffyd attacks Abergavenny Castle

1273 George de Cantelupe, 10th Lord of Abergavenny dies

1291 Edward I holds a council at Abergavenny Castle

1319 John de Hastings, Lord of Abergavenny, petitions Pope John XXII to reform the Priory

1324 Death of John de Hastings whose effigy can be seen in St Mary's Priory Church

1348 The Black Death strikes Abergavenny and claims more than a fifth of the population

1389 Lawrence de Hastings is killed whilst jousting

1404 The town is sacked by Owain Glyndwr

1415 William ap Thomas takes a band of Gwent bowmen to the battle of Agincourt

1417 Richard Beauchamp 18th Lord of Abergavenny is killed in France

1450 Sir Edward Nevill becomes the first baron of Abergavenny to enter Parliament

1464 Death of Gwladys, the daughter of Sir Dafydd Gam and wife of Sir William ap Thomas. 3,000 knights, nobles and peasants attended her funeral

1495 Jasper Tudor, Earl of Pembroke holds the Lordship of Abergavenny for 12 years

1536 Following the Dissolution of the Monasteries Act, St Mary's becomes an Anglican parish church. The Priory House and grounds are bought by the Gunter family.

1542	King Henry VIII Grammar School is founded at St John's Church
1586	Thomas Churchyard visits Abergavenny
1602	A new Market Hall is erected in the town
1638	Charles I grants a Royal Charter to Abergavenny
1645	Abergavenny Castle is made untenable by Colonel Proger on the orders of Charles I
1657	Oliver Cromwell grants Abergavenny a Royal Charter
1669	Jesuit priest David Lewis is executed at Usk Prison for saying Mass at the home of Thomas Gunter
1690	Abergavenny's Charter is revoked when the inhabitants refuse to take the oath of allegiance to William of Orange and his wife Mary
1739	John Wesley preaches in Abergavenny
1784	George Nevill, the 15th Lord is created Viscount Nevill and Earl of Abergavenny
1790	The first Abergavenny Bank is started in 5 Nevill Street by the Hill family
1794	A new Market Hall is designed by John Nash and built at a cost of £810
1795	The South Gate is demolished
1796	Street lighting comes to Abergavenny. Twenty oil lamps are installed in the town
1799	William Coxe visits Abergavenny during his tour of Monmouthshire
1801	The population of Abergavenny is 2,573
1815	Cannons are hauled onto the castle keep mound and fired to celebrate Napoleon's defeat at Waterloo
1819	The Nevill family build a hunting lodge in the grounds of Abergavenny Castle
1823	Abergavenny Gas Works is constructed by Thomas Davies, who is allowed to lay gas pipes through the town in return for supplying 20 gas lamps free of charge
1828	The Old Town Dispensary opens in 45 Castle Street
1831	The population of Abergavenny rises to 4,230 and the property is assesed at £11,075
1833	Formation of Cymreigyddion y Fenni
1834	Abergavenny Cricket Club is formed
1838	The Workhouse in Union Road is opened
1840	Holy Trinity Church is built
1844	First Abergavenny Horse Show is held
1848	Eisteddfod held in Abergavenny under the patronage of the Prince of Wales
1851	Joint Counties Lunatic Asylum is opened at Pen-y-fal
	The population of Abergavenny is 5,506
1854	Abergavenny & Hereford Railway is opened and the first train arrives at the new station
1860	The Abergavenny Bowling Club is formed
1863	Abergavenny Livestock Market is built
	Abergavenny Fire Brigade is formed
1864	Edwin Morgan launched the *Abergavenny Gazette* weekly paper but it only survives for a few issues
1865	Castle Street Girls School is opened
1866	Sewers are laid in the town for the first time
1871	The *Abergavenny Chronicle* is first published on 12 August by Edwin Morgan
	Abergavenny Town Hall is completed.
	The County Police Headquarters opens in Baker Street
1872	Victoria Street School, known locally as 'the British School' is built.
1873	George William Shackleton opens his first chemist's shop in Frogmore Street
1875	Abergavenny Rugby Football Club is formed
	Maindiff Court is built by Crawshay Bailey Junior
1877	Frogmore Street's new Baptist Chapel opens
1878	The Town Hall narrowly escaped being burnt to the ground, when an escape of gas from a Magic Lantern caught fire.
1879	The Abergavenny Improvement Commissioners decide to extend the limits of the town
	Christchurch was built of iron and wood in North Street

1880	Brecon & Abergavenny Canal is taken over by the GWR
	The County Police Headquarters is moved to Lower Monk Street
1881	The Marquis of Abergavenny leases the Castle grounds to the Abergavenny Improvements Commission
1882	The west front of St Mary's Church is rebuilt
	Abergavenny auctioneer, James Straker begins holding weekly auction sales of stock at the Cattle Market.
1883	A vegetarian banquet at Abergavenny Castle included 'grand dishes of fruit and vegetables' and was followed by a lecture on the benefits of Vegetarianism.
1884	Creation of Bailey Park as a recreational area on land leased to the town by Crawshay Bailey Jnr.
1887	Death of Crawshay Bailey Jnr
1890	A strong earthquake 'rattled the windows' in buildings throughout the town
1891	Coldbrook Estate is purchased by Lady Llanover
1892	Abergavenny Golf Club is Established
1894	Abergavenny becomes an Urban District
	A new Cemetery is opened in Llanfoist
1897	Work begins on the Victoria Cottage Hospital, marking Queen Victoria's Golden Jubilee. The Abergavenny Municipal Borough and Rural District Sanitorium was erected at a cost of £850 to hold 22 patients.
	Abergavenny Hockey Club is formed
1898	Formal opening of Abergavenny Grammar School and Girls Intermediate School in Pen-y-Pound
1899	Queen Victoria grants a Charter of Incorporation, making the town a municipal borough governed by a mayor, four aldermen and eleven councillors. The first Mayor to be appointed is Joseph Bishop
1900	Abergavenny Thursdays Football Club is founded, attracting its players from local shop assistants
1901	The town is plunged into mourning when Queen Victoria dies after a reign of 63 years
	The town celebrates the return of its soldiers from the Boer War
	The College of Heralds grants a coat of arms to Abergavenny
1902	Victoria Cottage Hospital opens and is named as a memorial to Queen Victoria
1903	The dangerous condition of the Town Hall is discussed and concerns about safety of forthcoming productions involving amateurs and children is voiced
1904	Borough Surveyor, Mr Haigh produces plans for the proposed improvements at the Town Hall including new dressing rooms and exits to Market Street
1905	Foundation stone of the Abergavenny Carnegie Library is laid
	Visit by Earl Roberts who had commanded British tropps in the Second Boer War
1906	Discovery of 17th century mural painting is discovered in the Gunter Mansion
1908	Abergavenny councillor, Zachariah Wheatley is invited to hold an official position on the Olympic Committee
	The Whitfield Presbyterian Church in Pen-y-pound is opened
1911	Abergavenny Operatic Society holds its first production - 'The Nautical Knot'
1912	The GWR starts a passenger bus service from Abergavenny to Crickhowell and Brecon each day
1913	Welsh National Eisteddfod held in Bailey Park
	A group of Suffragettes burn down the town's cricket pavillion
	Buffalo Bill's Wild West Show visits the town
	The Coliseum cinema opens
1914	Public meeting held in the Market Hall to encourage recruits for what is known as Lord Kitchener's Army
	Maindiff Court is offered to the British Red Cross Society as a Convalescent Home

1915	The Marquis of Abergavenny dies and the estates are sold off with the exception of the castle grounds
1916	Hundreds of people packed Brecon Road to witness the arrival of 110 German prisoners of war heading for an internment camp in the Black Mountains
1917	Nevill Hall, home of the late Marquess of Abergavenny is sold to a syndicate of 'a few prominent country gentlemen' for conversion into a private asylum
1918	The bells of St Mary's are rung to celebrate the end of the War
1919	Nevill Hall is sold to the Board of Management of the Blaina & District Hospital
1920	A crucifix is erected in the grounds of the Catholic Church in Pen-y-pound as a war memorial to the fallen members of that church
1921	Alderman J. R. Beckwith is elected Mayor of Abergavenny. He is able to claim the distinction of being the first working-man in the town to be awarded this honour, following ten years continuous service on the Town Council. Lord Treowen unveils the War Memorial in Frogmore Street
1922	The War Memorial at the Town Hall is unveiled by the Lord Lieutenant of Monmouthshire
1923	A new fire engine is purchased by Abergavenny Rural District Council
1924	Bailey Park Bowling Club is formed
1925	Tom Williams of Monk Street dies. His claim to fame was that he was the last man to ring the curfew bell in St John's Church
1926	A war Memorial tablet is unveiled at St Mary's Church and dedicated to the men of that church who gave their lives in the Great War
1929	The Town Council propose to introduce electric lighting to the streets of Abergavenny
1931	Llwyn Du Reservoir is covered A fierce storm hits Abergavenny and Monmouth Road is flooded to a depth of 8 feet
1932	The Duke and Duchess of York visit Abergavenny to open a new maternity wing at the Victoria Cottage Hospital
1933	Last commercial traffic to pay a toll on the Brecon & Abergavenny Canal A diptheria epidemic hits Abergavenny.
1934	Abergavenny Cricket Club celebrates its centenary Empire Day is celebrated An Air Display at Llanfoist Farm raises funds for the Victoria Cottage Hospital
1935	The Sugar Loaf is given to the National Trust by Viscountess Rhondda The Pavilion cinema opens
1938	A new hospital is opened at Maindiff Court
1939	An open air swimming pool is opened in Bailey Park Skirrid Fawr is presented to the National Trust by Major J. Herbert War is declared and Abergavenny once again responds bravely to her country's call
1941	A proposal to relieve traffic congestion in Abergavenny is considered by Town Council
1942	Rudolph Hess is taken from the Tower of London (last man to be held there) and brought to Abergavenny where he is interred in Maindiff Court Hospital
1943	A 'Wings for Victory Week' is staged in Abergavenny with the aim of raising £100,000 towards the purchase of two Sunderland Flying Boats The local Home Guard hold a mock 'battle of Abergavenny'
1944	Abergavenny Chamber of Trade welcomes its first lady member, Miss Brown
1945	V.E. Day is celebrated in Abergavenny
1946	The peal of bells in St Mary's is replaced in thanksgiving for the end of World War II
1947	The worst snow storm on record hits Abergavenny Field Marshall Montgomery visits Abergavenny
1950	Princess Margaret visits Abergavenny during a tour of South Wales
1951	Abergavenny Town Council approves a recommendation that £1,200 be spent on ornamental gates for the Swan Meadow as part of the town's contribution to the Festival of Britain

1951	A new telephone exchange is opened in Frogmore Street
1952	Priory House is demolished
1953	Nevill Hall Hospital opens to serve North Monmouthshire
	Coldbrook House is demolished
	The Cattle Market is improved with the construction of a covered sale ring
	Abergavenny celebrates the Coronation of Queen Elizabeth II
1954	Alexander George Graber, 39 year old ex-Army officer has his first novel, *A Thought of Honour* published. He later adopts the pseudonym, Alexander Cordell
1956	Tabernacle Methodist Church, Victoria Street closes
1957	Slum clearance of Flannel Street, Castle Street and Tudor Street commences. The Elizabethan buildings are described as being 'of little historical importance'
1958	Last Train from Abergavenny to Merthyr
1959	Abergavenny Museum is opened by Lord Raglan in the house adjoining the castle keep
	Publication of Alexander Cordell's best selling novel *Rape of the Fair Country*
1960	The grave yard on north side of St Mary's Priory Church is converted into a Garden of Remembrance
	The running of the *Abergavenny Chronicle* is taken over by Edwin Morgan's grandson Stanley Straker, his son John and their wives
1961	An Abergavenny Round Table is formed with the inaugural dinner at the Angel Hotel attended by 163 members from branches in South Wales, Gloucestershire and Herefordshire. Mr G. Colin Clarke, a solicitor is chosen as the first chairman
	Mrs E. A. James is elected as the first woman councillor on Abergavenny Town Council
1962	First stage of the Heads of the Valleys Road from Hardwick Roundabout is opened at a cost of £700,000
	Demolition of slums in Castle Street, Tudor Street St John's Square, Chicken Street and Flannel Street commences
1963	Chris Barber organises the first Three Peaks Trial on Saturday 9th March
	Queen Elizabeth II and the Duke of Edinburgh visit Abergavenny on 10th May
	The Beatles play at Abergavenny Town Hall on 22nd June
	King Henry Grammar School is amalgamated with the town's Grammar School for Girls in new premises built on the Old Hereford Road
1964	During excavation of foundations for the new Post Office, evidence of the Roman fort of Gobannium comes to light
	700 people attend St Mary's Priory Church to take part in BBC 'Songs of Praise' television programme
1965	Abergavenny Borough Council open Linda Vista Gardens to the public for the first time
	After almost 100 years in the same family, the *Abergavenny Chronicle* is sold to Worcester-based Berrows Newspapers Ltd and becomes part of its 28 newspaper group with editorial and advertising staff moving to new premises at 45 Cross Street
1966	The 18th century gateway to Old Court is demolished being considered unsafe
	Horace Davies, the first Abergavenny traffic warden is appointed
	Abergavenny Civic Society is formed
1967	Official opening of the Hill Residential College by the Minister of State, Welsh Office, Mrs Eirene White
	Work is completed on the new Abergavenny telephone exchange in St John's Square
1968	Abergavenny & District Civic Society is formed
	Abergavenny is twinned with Oestringen in Germany
	The first Welsh Motor Show is held in the Town Hall
	Much of Mill Street is demolished
1969	The new Nevill Hall Hospital is opened
1970	Saint David Lewis of Abergavenny is canonised
1971	Abergavenny Town Hall and Market Hall are listed as a historic building
	The *Abergavenny Chronicle* celebrates its centenary

1972	Abergavenny Borough Council approves a £100,000 scheme for the improvement of the Cattle Market
1973	The north side of Lower Monk Street is demolished
	A new Police Station is opened in Tudor Street at a cost of £170,000
1974	Local Government reorganisation brings the end of Abergavenny Borough. Together with Monmouth, Usk, Chepstow, Caldicot and the surrounding rural parishes, Abergavenny is absorbed into the new Monmouth District Council administrative area. In August the town has a mayor and town council once again. The new mayor is Councillor Pugsley who was an alderman on the former borough council
1975	The Monmouthshire & Brecon Canal bursts its banks at Llanfoist
	Abergavenny northern by-pass opens at a cost of £2 million
	The demolition of buildings at the junction of Pen-y-pound and Frogmore Street were part of a £150,000 Park Road Improvement Scheme which included widening and re-alignment of the road.
	The old Castle Street School which had closed in 1973 is knocked down to extend the existing car park.
	An extension to the Hill Residential College is completed, providing 50 study bedrooms, lecture seminar halls and a new dining room.
1976	Abergavenny experiences the longest spell of dry weather since records began. There is a spate of fires on the tinder-dry hillsides
	First Annual Steam Rally is held in Bailey Park
1977	Repair of the Monmouthshire & Brecon Canal commences at an estimated cost of £483,000
1978	Abergavenny History Society is formed
	Abergavenny & District Tourist Association is formed to promote the town and local area as a tourist destination
	Demolition of former shop premises on the corner of Cross Street and Flannel Street.
1979	The ancient Tithe Barn becomes a saleroom for fine art and antiques. In recent years the building had served as a theatre, a corn merchant's store, a discotheque and a computer work-shop.
	The old entrance to the Old Bank in High Street is uncovered as part of a street improvement scheme.
	The Tudor Day Centre opened at the corner of Tudor Street and Merhyr Road
1980	Abergavenny suffers the worst floods in living memory
1981	A 250 year old barn in Castle Street is demolished
	Work begins on the restoration of the keep at Abergavenny Castle
1982	Scaffolding is removed from 'Red Square' when a new building is completed at the end of Flannel Street
	An ambitious plan to provide an arcade of shops in the centre of Abergavenny is considered by Monmouth District Council's Planning Committee
	Seargeant Brothers printing firm ceases trading in Abergavenny and moves to Pontypool
1983	The *Abergavenny Chronicle* is sold by the Berrows Newspaper Group to Tindle Newspapers Ltd. An article on Abergavenny appears in the New York Times.
1984	Buildings in King Street demolished to make way for Cybi Walk shopping development
1985	Work begins to create an arcade of shops in Abergavenny town centre
1986	Floodlighting is installed at Abergavenny Castle at a cost of £1,200 raised by Abergavenny Local History Society
1987	An archaeological dig in Cross Street reveals Roman artefacts dating back to 50AD
	The Coliseum Cinema closes
1988	Six telephone boxes in Abergavenny are declared Historic Monuments to prevent them from being removed
	Abergavenny is twinned with Beaupréau in France

1988	An Abergavenny time capsule, in stainless steel is buried in a wall at Tan House while it is being converted into retirement houses. It contains a copy of the *Abergavenny Chronicle*, a magistrate's court list, a King Henry VIII School magazine, credit cards, a set of minted coins, a set of stamps, a letter explaining the contents and a short history of the Tan House, with a map of 1804. These items were chosen to represent everyday life in Abergavenny
	Proposals to 'pedestrianise' Nevill Street and part of Frogmore Street are approved by Monmouth Borough Council
1989	The Cybi Walk shopping precinct is officially opened
1990	Abergavenny celebrates the 900th anniversary of the building of the Castle and St Mary's Priory. An Abergavenny 900 committee is set up to co-ordinate the celebrations.
1991	The population of Abergavenny is 13,688
1992	Safeway plan to develop an out of town store at Llanfoist
1996	Local Government reorganisation brings an end to Monmouth Borough Council and Gwent County Council
	The *Abergavenny Chronicle* celebrates 125 years with a move to new premises in Nevill Street
	Pen y Fal Hospital closes and in due course the site is developed by Redrow Homes and converted into luxury apartments and houses.
1997	Safeway open their new out of town shopping store at Llanfoist, despite strong opposition
	Monmouthshire County Council introduce car parking charges in the town
1998	Welsh Transport Minister Peter Hain makes the dualling of the A465 top priority
1999	The debate over the future of Abergavenny Cattle Market begins
	The first Abergavenny Food Festival is held
2000	The Prince of Wales visits Abergavenny to officially open St Mary's Priory Centre
	Unveiling of the Millennium Mural painted by Frances Baines
2001	The *Abergavenny Chronicle* and the Town Council celebrate their 130th anniversaries
	The population of Abergavenny is 13,594
2002	The Reverend Canon Jeremy Winston blessed the first stitch of the Abergavenny Tapestry, a millenium project celebrating 1,000 years of the town's history.
	A Post Graduate Medical Centre is opened at Nevill Hall Hospital
2003	Discovery of the Roman Leopard cup at Llantilio Pertholey. It is one of the finest Roman artefacts to be found in Wales.
2004	Work on the demolition of Coopers Factory site at Llanfoist began shortly before Christmas, the site having been purchased by Newport based development firm Johnsey Estates Ltd.
2005	Raymond Hill (71) is chosen to be mayor of Abergavenny for the fifth time
	Abergavenny celebrates the 60th anniversary of VE Day
	Park Street Infants School closes
2006	The Library Garden in Victoria Street is opened
	The proposals for the Brewery Yard scheme are revealed
2009	Closure of The Hill Education and Conference Centre
	A presentation of medals is made by the Town Council to Abergavenny former mayors in recognition of their hard work and dedication.
2010	A new cinema opens in the old Drill Hall, Baker Street.
	After a 17 month construction period the £3.2m new-look Brewery Yard is officially opened.

ACKNOWLEDGEMENTS

This book is the result of many years of research and in particular I am grateful to Liz Davies, Editor of the Abergavenny Chronicle for permission to include extracts from this excellent weekly newspaper which was first published in 1872. It has certainly proved a mine of fascinating information. Many of the old photographs that I have used have come from those produced and collected by Alfred Lyons. I am also grateful to Ken Flowers, Malcom Lewis, David Bowen and Keith Davies for the use of their pictures and also Rachael Rogers, Curator of Abergavenny Museum for permission to include certain photographs. Michael Blackmore is also thanked for permission to use some of his pen and ink drawings and the paintings of Abergavenny Castle.

I am also most grateful to my wife Anne Marie for all her help, encouragement and enthusiastic support for this very time consuming project. Finally, I give warm thanks to Alan Breeze for casting his eye over the manuscript and making some very helpful comments as well as writing a much appreciated Foreword.

A Tribute to Albert Lyons

Albert Lyons, one of a family of nine children, was born on November 5th 1918, in Princes Street, Abergavenny. His father was a locomotive shed man and both his father and his grandfather became keepers for the Herbert family on the Coldbrook Estate.

As a boy Alfred attended the former 'British School' in Victoria Street before joining the former LMS railway company at Brecon Road, where he first worked in the locomotive sheds and later became a locomotive fireman. He worked on the railways from 1935 and served in the Second World War, returning to the railways until the loco sheds closed in 1958. He then spent 22 years as a porter and a ward orderly at Pen-y-fal Hospital before taking early retirement because of his wife's ill health.

He was a founder member of Abergavenny Camera Club and a well respected local historian, who recorded much of the life in his beloved town with his camera. He was regularly asked by local people to capture memorable family occasions like weddings and christenings, and took a keen interest in photographing any event with a historic connection.

He was responsible for recording most of the pictures which remain of the old Tudor Street and Byfield Lane areas of the town, which were completely demolished in the late 1950s. He even attended the Beatles memorable concert in Abergaveny on Saturday June 22, 1963, and took several pictures of the 'fab four'.

Albert published many of his photographs in two volumes which came out in 1983 and 1990. The second volume was published to coincide with the Abergavenny 900 celebrations. Albert died in Nevill Hall Hospital in 1993 at the age of 75, following a short illness.

BIBLIOGRAPHY

Abergavenny Local History Society, *Abergavenny Street Survey* 1979-1984

Ashmore, P.J. and Ashmore, F.M. 1972-3 *Excavations at Abergavenny Orchard Site 1972*

Back numbers of the *Abergavenny Chronicle*

Back numbers of the *Abergavenny Gazette*

Bannon, Louis *Remember Abergavenny* Vol I

Barber, Chris, *The Seven Hills of Abergavenny* (Blorenge Books 1992)

Barber, Chris, *Abergavenny in Old Picture Postcards*, (1995)

Barber, Chris & Michael Blackmore, *Portraits of the Past* (Blorenge Books 1996)

Blackwell, Kay, *The Tithe Barn of St Mary's Priory Church*, Abergavenny (2008)

Bradney, J.A., Sir *A History of Monmouthshire*, Part II The Hundred of Abergavenny (London 1906)

Burrow E.D. *The Gate of Wales* - the official handbook to Abergavenny 1903

Churchyard, T. 1587, *The Worthiness of Wales* (reprinted 1776)

Coxe, W. 1801 *An Historical Tour Through Monmouthshire*, 2 vols (facsimile repr., 1995)

Davies, Richard (Editor), *A Town Remembers: Memories of Wartime Abergavenny 1939-45* (2002)

Davies, Richard, *Around Abergavenny, Photographoc Memories* (Francis Frith 2004)

Davies, Richard, *Abergavenny - A History and Celebration of the Town* (Ottakars 2005)

Davies, M.E. Reverend Canon *The History of St Mary's (Priory) Church* (1956)

Gilbert, Reverend Morgan, *A Guide to The Priory Church of St Mary The Virgin* (Oxford 1910)

Jackson, Alfred *Historic Abergavenny* (M. Morgan & Co Ltd 1964)

Jones, Gwyn, *A Walk around Abergavenny* 1990

Jones, Gwyn, *Prehistoric Abergavenny*

Jones, Gwyn, *Roman Abergavenny* 1982

Jones, Gwyn, *Medieval Town and Market of Abergavenny*

Jones, Gwyn, *Medieval Abergavenny* 1984

Morgan, I.M. *Abergavenny Past and Present* (Sutton Publishing 2003)

Olding, Frank, *Vanished Abergavenny - Y Fenni Ddiflanedig* (Tempus Publishing 1994)

Olding, Frank, *Abergavenny, The Urban Archaeology* (Abergavenny History Society 2004)_

Olding, Frank *Abergavenny Castle, A History* (Monmouthshire Museums Service 1998)

Olding, Frank, *Abergavenny Pubs* (Tempus 2005)

Olding Frank, *Gobannium: The Romans in Abergavenny* (Abergavenny History Society 2009)

Soulsby, I. 1983, *The Towns of Medieval Wales* (Chichester 1983)

Sproule- Jones, Reverend Canon H.R., *St Mary's Priory Church*, Abergavenny (1968)

Thorpe, L. 1978, *Gerald of Wales - The Journey through Wales / The Description of Wales* (repr. 1986)

Tucker, Anna, *Abergavenny in Old Photographs* (Abergavenny Museum)

White, J.G. *Guide to Abergavenny* (1877)

Winston, Reverend Jeremy, *St Mary's Priory Church, Abergavenny* (RJL Smith & Associates 2000)

OTHER TITLES BY CHRIS BARBER

Walks in the Brecon Beacons (1976)
Exploring the Waterfall Country (1976)
Ghosts of Wales (1979)
Mysterious Wales (1982/2000)
Exploring the Brecon Beacons National Park (1980/85)
Exploring Gwent (1984)
Cordell Country (1985)
More Mysterious Wales (1986)
The Romance of the Welsh Mountains (1986)
Hando's Gwent (*Volume I* - 1987/2000)
Hando's Gwent (*Volume 2* - 1989)
The Ancient Stones of Wales with John Williams (1989)
The Seven Hills of Abergavenny (1992)
Journey to Avalon with David Pykitt (1993)
Abergavenny in Old Picture Postcards (1995)
Walks in Cordell Country (1996)
Portraits of the Past with Michael Blackmore (1996)
Classic Walks in the Brecon Beacons National Park (1997)
In Search of Owain Glyndwr (1998)
Eastern Valley - The Story of Torfaen (1999)
Exploring Blaenavon Industrial Landscape World Heritage Site (2002)
Exploring Kilvert Country (2003)
History of Llanfoist Church (2003)
Llanover Country (2004)
The Legacy of King Arthur with David Pykitt (2005)
In the Footsteps of Alexander Cordell (2007)
40 Classic Walks in the Brecon Beacons National Park (2009)
Arthurian Caerleon (2010)